ADVANCED PROFESSIONAL WEB DESIGN

TECHNIQUES & TEMPLATES (CSS & XHTML)

ADVANCED PROFESSIONAL WEB DESIGN
TECHNIQUES & TEMPLATES (CSS & XHTML)

CLINT ECCHER

CHARLES RIVER MEDIA
Boston, Massachusetts

Cover Design: Tyler Creative
Cover Image: (Painting): Clint Eccher

CHARLES RIVER MEDIA
25 Thomson Place
Boston, Massachusetts 02210
617-757-7900
617-757-7969 (FAX)
crm.info@thomson.com
www.charlesriver.com

This book is printed on acid-free paper.

Clint Eccher. *Advanced Professional Web Design: Techniques & Templates.*
ISBN: 1-58450-494-3

All brand names and product names mentioned in this book are trademarks or service marks of their respective companies. Any omission or misuse (of any kind) of service marks or trademarks should not be regarded as intent to infringe on the property of others. The publisher recognizes and respects all marks used by companies, manufacturers, and developers as a means to distinguish their products.

Library of Congress Cataloging-in-Publication Data
Eccher, Clint.
  Advanced professional Web design : techniques & templates (CSS &
XHTML) / Clint Eccher.
     p. cm.
  Includes index.
  ISBN 1-58450-494-3 (pbk. with cd-rom : alk. paper)
  1. Web site development. 2. Cascading style sheets. 3. XHTML
(Document markup language) I. Title.

  TK5105.888.E365 2006
  006.7--dc22
2006024423

Printed in the United States of America
06 7 6 5 4 3 2

CHARLES RIVER MEDIA titles are available for site license or bulk purchase by institutions, user groups, corporations, etc. For additional information, please contact the Special Sales Department at 800-347-7707.

Requests for replacement of a defective CD-ROM must be accompanied by the original disc, your mailing address, telephone number, date of purchase and purchase price. Please state the nature of the problem, and send the information to CHARLES RIVER MEDIA, 25 Thomson Place, Boston, Massachusetts 02210. CRM's sole obligation to the purchaser is to replace the disc, based on defective materials or faulty workmanship, but not on the operation or functionality of the product.

Mom and Dad—Without your love, support, and encouragement,
I would never be where or who I am today.
I thank you, Mom, for teaching how to use the right side of my brain, and,
Dad, I thank you for teaching me the left.
I thank you, Mom, for editing both my books, and you, Dad,
for giving me the *Art of War* book, which motivated me
to give childbirth through my frontal lobe yet again.

Contents

Preface

Table-based HTML (HyperText Markup Language), now XHTML (Extensible HyperText Markup Language), designs have been the staple for laying out Web sites for more than a decade. The Web design industry, however, continually evolves, requiring designers and developers to update their skill sets. Not only is cascading stylesheet (CSS)-based design quickly becoming the standard, but designers and developers are being pushed past what used to be the standard knowledge base for Web-development skills.

The purpose of this book is to educate both designers and developers on skills that are becoming increasingly required by Web site clients. Some of these skills include designing Web sites with CSS, rather than just XHTML, building database-driven Web sites, and developing e-commerce solutions. The book also offers 140 templates that can be easily customized and/or deconstructed to drastically decrease the learning curve of creating CSS- and XHTML-based designs if the designer chooses to still use this technology.

The philosophy of this book is to educate the reader about concepts and techniques, using as little terminology-heavy content as possible. Once the major concepts are understood, learning the finer details becomes much easier because how everything fits together makes sense. The database-driven and e-commerce examples in the book are written using CFML (ColdFusion Markup Language). Because the purpose of this book is to give a high-level explanation of such techniques, the techniques can be easily translated to other languages, such as ASP/ASP.Net, JSP, and PHP.

The various components of this book are applicable to both designers and developers, depending on their backgrounds. Everyone has different knowledge levels on design and development. The particular techniques and templates included in this book have been proven effective by A5design staff.

Acknowledgments

Beanie—For always asking me about the book and giving me the unconditional love I truly cherish every day. I love you "infinity."

Lori, Justin, Charlie, and Kata Discoe—For always being there whenever I need anything. Everyone needs people like you in their lives. You also take incredibly unique photos.

Matt Idler—For all the great photographs you contributed to this book. You're truly a hard-working, talented photographer in the wings just waiting to be discovered by the masses.

Dennis "Big Mac" Anderson—One of the best things that came from my first book was meeting you. Despite the fact you use an Etch A Sketch, you're one of the most creative people I know. Keep the minority going strong.

Meredith "Quit Your Whining" Lawton—For forcing, encouraging, and, of course, forcing me to keep the body as healthy as the mind during this endeavor. Personal training is definitely your calling.

Michele McCreath—For giving me the encouragement to jump off the cliffs of insanity to begin Chapter 1.

Mark Celano—For shoving me off the cliffs of insanity to begin programming.

Daniel Yu—For introducing me to the Web in the early 90s. It all began with Yu, man.

Ryan Keiffer and Gretchen Gaede—For the couple who take nonprofit marketing to the next level.

Chen Sun— For always working to perfect Web marketing.

Paul and Jennifer Nastu—For always working to evolve email marketing.

Jenifer Niles—For always providing positive, responsive, and encouraging feedback. If only every editor could be like you. You truly have made this book as painless as humanly possible.

For all those who helped contribute to this book: Jesse Herron, Linda Heuer, Tami Anderson, Belen Carmichael, Graham Carter, Boon, Lisa Murillo, Coren Printing, and the staff at Saxby's (Julia, Scott, Cory, Joey, Anabel, Alex, Alyssa, Christine, Brook, Ian, and Seth) who juiced me with chai and smoothies and let me camp out until my brain was numb from writing, editing, and designing.

1 Creating Database-Driven Sites

Web Server

90 pages

Browser

In the mid to late 1990s, the purpose of most Web sites was to serve as "cool looking online brochures. This situation quickly evolved when some sites began to grow, soon having hundreds, even thousands, of pages. Developers needed to better manage rapidly growing amounts of content. A solution then began to appear throughout the Web—database-driven sites (db-driven sites), which could offer hundreds of pages of content with a small number (sometimes even one) of templates. The purpose of this chapter, as well as Chapters 2 and 3, is to give the reader a higher level of understanding about how the various components of db-driven sites work.

TERMINOLOGY

Terminology is one of the first things to understand when beginning to program. Without having a basic conceptual understanding of what the technical mumbo jumbo means, it is more difficult to understand the concepts they explain. The goal of the terminology in this section is to educate the reader with the basic concept of the terms, rather than getting too technical in the nuances and technicalities of their meanings.

Box: A physical server.

Call: Load or retrieve. For example, the page calls a template. In other words, the page retrieves another file, which in this case is a template.

Clause: Code in a Structured Query Language (SQL) statement that serves a specific purpose, such as telling the statement which table to pull data from or what conditions to pull the data from (e.g., SELECT, FROM, and WHERE).

Function: A section of code that performs a specific task. A function can be called from a single line of code that can, for example, do the work of 30 lines of code that are already programmed into the server or browser software.

Loop: A section of code that is repeated, using a condition or query results, to output and, possibly, manipulate data.

Module: A section of code that can be added, edited, or deleted autonomously from a larger amount of code, for example, a dynamic calendar that runs separately from a content-management system but can still be incorporated into it.

Modular: A term that refers to code that runs independently from a site or application it is written for.

Record (Data Record): One row in a database, where data from any number of columns in that row can be added, edited, deleted, manipulated, or displayed.

Recursive Page: A page that submits data back to itself, utilizing other code to process the data.

Server: The physical computer a Web site is run on. The term also refers to the software on the computer. Macromedia ColdFusion®, for example, is server software that can be run on a Microsoft® box.

Parse: Breaking up data so it can be manipulated or output in individual pieces. An example of parsing would involve separating "Van Gogh" from "Vincent Van Gogh."

Payment Gateway: A company that takes payments from a Web site and passes the data on to the credit-card interchange, which transmits credit-card data between the user merchant account and credit-card issuer.

Primary Key: A number in a database record that is used to uniquely identify that particular record or row of data. No other record in the table should have the same number.

Query: SQL code that is used to add, edit, and/or delete data from a database.

Usability: The ability of a user to view, use, and interpret a Web site's content, functionality, and design. An example of usability would be how easy a site's shopping cart is to use.

Variable: A container that includes a value that is changed programmatically. A variable, for example, can be called `family_name`, and it could contain the name `Eccher`. A shopping cart variable could be named `total`, containing the total dollar amount of the purchase.

HOW DB-DRIVEN SITES WORK

The overall concept of how a db-driven site works is not overly complicated (see Figure 1.1). While a developer can program such a site in different ways, the same basic process occurs for each request to a page when data is being added, edited, deleted, or output:

1. A user clicks a hyperlink or performs an action of a Web site, such as submitting a form.
2. The request is submitted to the Web server.
3. The server requests data from the database.
4. The data is returned, and the server processes the page. This could involve anything as basic as pulling a paragraph of text from a database record to performing a more complex query of several tables in the database and manipulating the results with server-side or client-side programming.

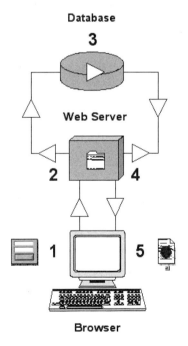

FIGURE 1.1   The process of how a db-driven site works.

Not all actions of a db-driven site require data from the database. Some actions, discussed later in the chapter, could be as simple as placing an include file into an-other file.

5. The server then serves up the page to the browser, using CSS, XHTML, and other possible languages.

STATIC SITES VERSUS DB-DRIVEN SITES

Static sites contain every page of content on separate pages. If a site has 10 pages and 90 news releases, the site is going to consist of 100 individual pages. One disadvantage of this system is that if a developer needs to change, for instance, the header of the news release, 90 separate pages are going to need to be changed (see Figure 1.2).

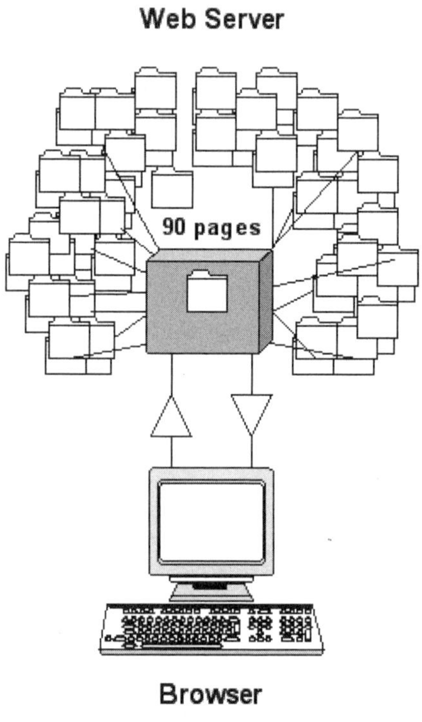

Web Server

90 pages

Browser

FIGURE 1.2   Static site where 90 files need to be edited if one item on every page needs to be changed.

While using "find and replace" functionality of an HTML editor can quickly change all the pages, this method can rapidly cause problems if the code being replaced is not consistent throughout all pages. Discovering that only 75 news releases were fixed becomes cumbersome because the developer knows the 15 pages that weren't changed are going to need to be found and, most likely, changed individually.

This is one of the advantages of db-driven sites. With a db-driven site, the content of all 90 pages is going to be stored in a database. The developer can use one template to display and/or edit each of the news releases (see Figure 1.3). Such functionality is used for various aspects of Web sites, such as forums, photo galleries, and content libraries.

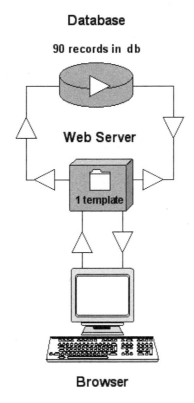

FIGURE 1.3   Db-driven site where 90 pages can be edited using one template file.

A common example of a db-driven template would be one that displays books in an online bookstore. In Figure 1.4, all the books in the center and right columns, when clicked, call for only one template (see Figure 1.5) to be output.

Because each book's data is stored in the database, the data can be selectively pulled and displayed on the page. The books in the center column have the same content as the books in the right column; however, the description field is not displayed in the right column. When clicked, though, each book opens the same template, which displays identical data elements.

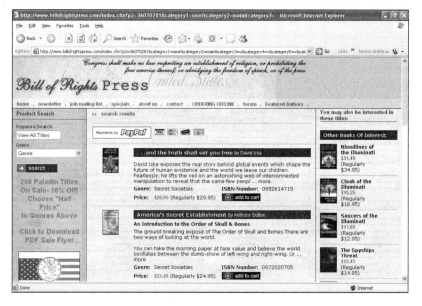

FIGURE 1.4   Db-driven lists (center and right columns) that use one template to display content. © 2006 Bill of Rights Press. Used with permission.

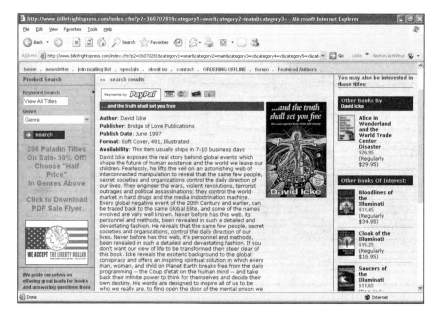

FIGURE 1.5   Db-driven template that is used to display content for all books.
© 2006 Bill of Rights Press. Used with permission.

SEPARATION OF DATA AND CODE

Db-driven functionality allows developers to build efficient Web sites because the data, in any amount, is separated from the code that processes and displays the information. Having the data separated from the code allows the developer to pull the data from a specified table(s) and display it on any number of pages in any number of ways.

An example of data being separated from code is how news releases are commonly displayed on Web sites. Figure 1.6 shows a `news_release` table in a Microsoft Access® (Access) database.

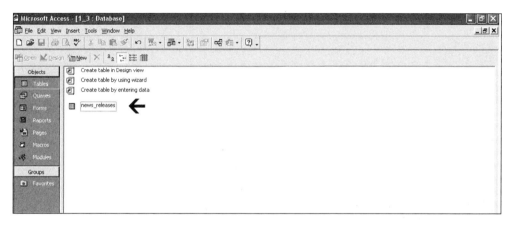

FIGURE 1.6   A `news_release` table included in an Access database. © 2006 Western Dairy Council. Used with permission.

In the table, the data is displayed in various columns and rows. A record, which is one row with columns of data, can be used however the developer chooses, such as being displayed, used for ordering output results, or determining whether that particular record should even be displayed (see Figure 1.7).

Various things should be considered when looking at the structure of the table in Figure 1.7:

■   The ID column is used as the *primary key*, which uniquely identifies that particular record or row of data. No other record in the table should have the same primary key because sometimes this will be the only data that can be used to pull that record, whereas other records may not have the same values. For example, a developer would not want to pull a record from a database using the `create_dt` (short for Create Date) field because other news releases may have been created on the same day. Instead, that record would need to be pulled using its ID number because that number would be assigned only to that particular record.

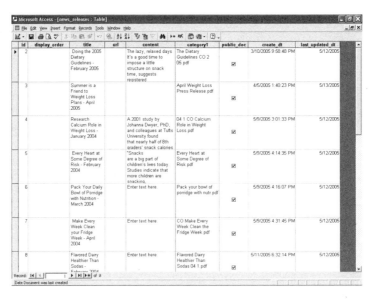

FIGURE 1.7 Data included in a `news_release` table in an Access database. © 2006 Western Dairy Council. Used with permission.

- The `title` column is separated from other data because it can be displayed by itself in a list or together with the data in the `content` column:

A common mistake developers make when creating database tables is to combine the `first_name` and `last_name` columns into one column called `name`. When data is stored this way and the developer needs to pull just the last names of people, the data then needs to be parsed. In this example, an underscore is used to replace spaces to ensure the name is one word. This limits possible problems the server may have with using names that use spaces or special characters.

- The `content` field can be output in its entirety or in limited fashion. It's possible for the developer, for example, to output 200 characters of the release on a News Release section page and/or the entire field on an individual news release template.
- The `url` or `category1` fields can both be used for hyperlinking. If the developer wanted to output the list of all records in the database and hyperlink them, the `category1` field could include an `<a href>` tag to open the PDF file listed in that field. The `url` field could also be used, if populated, to hyperlink to an external site.
- A `public_doc` record permits the developer to determine whether a record should be allowed for public viewing. Sometimes records can simply be flagged or marked for certain uses. In the example, when the `public_doc` checkbox is checked, the

record can be displayed on a page, but when it is not checked, it can be hidden from the output page.

■ Date fields are included with each record (`create_dt` and `last_updated_dt`). While the `last_updated_dt` field isn't overly useful in this example, the `create_dt` field is because it can be used for ordering. The records can be output from the most recent to oldest dates.

Not all records are output alphabetically or chronologically. Sometimes the developer may want to order records in a unique way, which is why the `display_order` field is added. By including the `display_order` field, the records can be ordered numerically.

Once the table is built and populated, the developer can use an SQL query to pull the data from the database so it can be output on a Web page, using CSS and/or XHTML. The query is typically written using a version of the parent SQL language that is modified for that particular server software. Various languages support SQL differently, so the syntax may differ. Following is an example of a query:

```
<cfquery datasource="sample_db" name="archived_news_releases">
    SELECT *
    FROM news_releases
    WHERE create_dt LIKE '%2005%'
    ORDER BY create_dt desc
</cfquery>
```

ColdFusion offers a <CFQUERY> tag that integrates SQL commands to add, edit, and delete data. Queries in other languages won't look exactly the same as this example.

The data pulled from the query joined with the CSS or XHTML code is then used to display the data in the Web browser (see Figure 1.8). Following is an example of code that loops over the data and structures it for the browser to output:

```
<cfloop query="nr" startrow="#output_start#" endrow="#output_end#">
    <tr>
        <td valign="top" colspan="2">
            <b>#dateformat(active_dt,'mm|dd|yy')# -</b> <a
href="#root#/Amend/images/
            newsreleases/#category1#" target="_new">#title#</a>
    </td>
        </tr>
        <tr>
            <td><img src="images/spacer.gif" width=1 height=5 alt=""
border="0"></td>
        </tr>
    </cfloop>
```

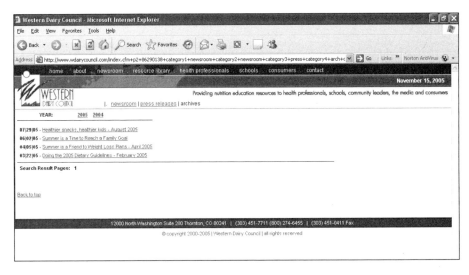

FIGURE 1.8   Data that has been pulled from a database and displayed using XHTML and CSS. © 2006 Western Dairy Council. Used with permission.

VARIOUS PROGRAMMING LANGUAGES

The db-driven examples in this book are written in CFML (ColdFusion Markup Language) code, but there are several other languages a developer can use when programming a db-driven site:

ASP and ASP.Net: These are Microsoft's development languages, which are used frequently by developers because many hosting platforms are Windows-based, which provides the server to run such pages.

JSP (Java Server Page): Developed by Sun, JSP pages are not platform specific, meaning they can be run from nearly any hosting server.

PHP (Hypertext Preprocessor): This is an open-source server-side language that is typically run on a Linux operating system, which is also open source.

Perl: This is an open-source scripting language that predates many current languages.

The thing to note about such languages is that each has its strengths and weaknesses. While some developers can become fanatical about a language, the important thing a beginning developer should remember is that there is never a solution that satisfies all needs when it comes to developing Web sites. Therefore, the first, and possibly only, language to be learned should be one with which the person feels most comfortable. Finding cost-effective, efficient hosting solutions for any of the aforementioned languages is no longer difficult.

VARIOUS DATABASES

Web developers typically use four common databases to create db-driven web sites:

Microsoft Access: An Access database is a cost-effective solution for smaller Web sites. It is not as powerful as other solutions but it satisfies the needs of many Web sites.

Microsoft SQL: Microsoft's version of an SQL database is robust enough to handle very large sites.

MySQL: This database is open-source and is typically run with a Linux or Microsoft OS.

Oracle: Oracle databases are powerful and expensive.

While Access databases are easy to learn and use, it is important that when working with them the developer make sure the database is locked down or located on a separate drive on a server. Otherwise, an Access database could be downloaded as easily as an image if a hacker were to discover the path and filename.

RELATIONAL DATABASES

When developing db-driven sites, the database a developer works with is called a "relational database." This means data can be separated into logical and manageable groupings in various tables in a database but then also can be easily associated together with data common to both. In other words, the data can be separated into various tables but then be combined together, based on a uniquely identifying piece of data common to the tables. To explain the process, a `contacts` table was added to the database already containing the `news_releases` table (see Figure 1.9).

The data has been broken up into two tables for several reasons:

Different groups of data will be reused with other tables: While the data in the `contacts` table will be used in association with individual news releases, it can and probably also will be used in other sections of the site, such as a Staff Listing page. Rather than run a more complex query to pull each unique contact listing from the `news_releases` table, it's easier to simply have the data separated into its own `contacts` table, which makes it easier to query.

When possible, it's a good practice to try to limit the number of columns: The `news_release` table already has nine columns of data. If the data from the `columns` table were added, the number of columns would increase by another seven columns. While there is no magic number of columns that should be used, the less complex a table is, the easier it is to manage.

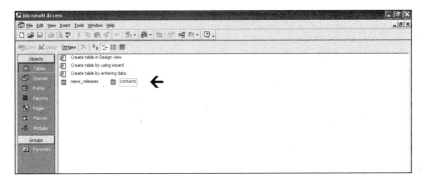

FIGURE 1.9   A `contacts` table that has been added to the database containing the `news_releases` table.

It's much less difficult to view, understand, and manipulate tables with easily discernable data: In other words, it's easier to view just the contact information by itself, rather than when it is being mixed with the `news_release` data.

Once different data groups, such as news releases and contact people, have been separated, the developer then needs to make the data "relational." This means each record in the `news_releases` table can be associated with at least one record in the `contacts` table. In Figure 1.10 a `contacts` column has been added to the `news_releases` table. The

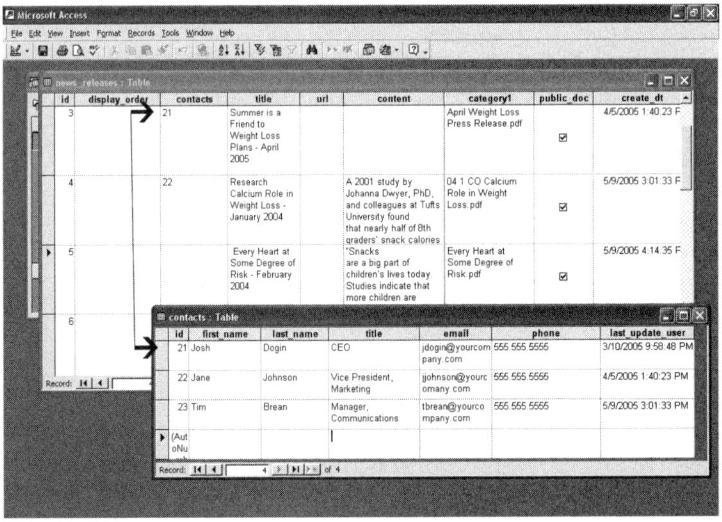

FIGURE 1.10   A relational database where the `news_releases` table is associated with the `contacts` table, based on them being associated with the `id` field in the `contacts` table. © 2006 Western Dairy Council. Used with permission.

numbers in this column are actually the unique identifiers in the `contacts` table. There-fore, in this example, the `21` in the `contacts` column of the `news_releases` table is the same number as the `id` of the first record in the `contacts` table. Therefore, when the developer uses a query to pull the "Doing the 2005 Dietary Guidelines—February 2005" news release, the query can also be written to pull "Josh Dogin's" contact information from the `contacts` page (see Figure 1.10). Thus, the two tables are related.

CLIENT-SIDE VERSUS SERVER-SIDE CODE

One of the problems with developing Web sites beyond basic CSS and XHTML is that there are too many browsers, versions of those browsers, operating systems, and versions of those operating systems. Such disparity makes it difficult for a developer to know what code is going to work consistently under all, or most, conditions, without very thorough and time-consuming testing.

Such variety in users' Web-surfing conditions results in the issue of client-side versus server-side code. With client-side code, the actual processing and manipulation of data occurs within the user's browser, relying on that particular computer for processing the code. This not only takes a load of work off the Web server's resources, but it also decreases the time it takes to receive results because the browser does not have to send a request to the Web server and wait for a response to be received and rendered onto the screen.

One issue with client-side code, however, is that not all code acts the same under all browsing conditions. One example is the use of the dropdown JavaScript menu in Figure 1.11. Because some users may choose to turn off the JavaScript functionality of their browsers, they are not going to be able to view the menu and navigate through the site. The question a developer must ask is, "Is the critical mass being served?" If 100% usability is the goal of the site, then using JavaScript is not an option. If critical mass is not 100%, then that number must be determined, using Web-usage statistics. One way to view this situation is that if only 2% of the desired audience is not using JavaScript, then they are probably going to run into similar issues on most other sites. Another consideration of client-side code is download time. While the menu in Figure 1.11 allows for quick and convenient usability, it also requires more than 15k of JavaScript to run.

Server-side code has its own pros and cons. The main con is that the user has to make a request to the site to receive the results, which takes time to be output back to the browser. The main pro, however, is that the developer is guaranteed that the processed results will be viewable by all users as long as they are output using CSS and XHTML. In other words, if it works on the server, then it will work everywhere else because it is simply outputting data that does not need further processing. An exception to this rule would be an instance where ColdFusion outputs server-generated JavaScript that is then run client-side. While the client-side code is created on the server's side, this doesn't mean the code will work when served up to the browser.

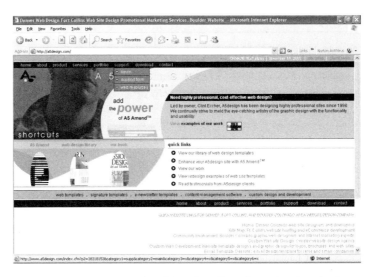

FIGURE 1.11   An example of functionality where the date in the top right corner could be generated either using client-side code or server-side code.

Figure 1.11 provides an example where either client-side or server-side code could be used. In the top right corner, the current date is displayed. This can either be accomplished using JavaScript, which would be loaded on the page, reading from the computer's date, or the date could simply be processed and output with the rest of the page as static data. During the latter, the output data will be created using the server's date.

Server time and dates can be easily modified using functions. The time, for instance, can be modified for the Mountain time zone if that is where the site is located, while the server is in the Eastern time zone.

CREATING PAGES THE SERVER CAN INTERPRET

Although a Web server outputs CSS and XHTML code the browser can interpret, the server itself needs to know when to process certain code. The developer needs to do three things to accomplish this:

1. Change the File Extension to the One the Programming Language Requires

In a static site a developer will typically name a file with an extension of .htm or .html. The following code will then be output as viewed in Figure 1.12:

```
<!DOCTYPE HTML PUBLIC "-//W3C//DTD HTML 4.01 Transitional//EN">
<html>
<head>
    <title>A5design</title>
</head>
<body>
This is a sample XHTML page.
</body>
</html>
```

FIGURE 1.12   A Web filename with an .htm file extension titled `sample.htm`.

The file extension needs to be changed, however, when the developer wants the server to process code in the page. Figure 1.13 is a sample ColdFusion page. Because it is programmed with CFML, a .cfm extension is used in the filename instead of .htm or .html, so the server knows to process and output the code. Notice that the file extension changed, but the way the page was output did not.

```
<!DOCTYPE HTML PUBLIC "-//W3C//DTD HTML 4.01 Transitional//EN">
<html>
<head>
    <title>A5design</title>
</head>
<body>
<cfoutput>
    This is a sample ColdFusion page that was viewed at
        #TimeFormat(Now(), "h:MM:SS tt")#
</cfoutput>
</body>
</html>
```

2. Wrap Output Tags Around Code That Is to Be Processed

As with other languages, such as Hypertext PreprocessorPHP (PHP), ColdFusion also requires the developer to wrap certain characters around programming code that is to be interpreted. With ColdFusion, these tags are <CFOUTPUT> and </CFOUTPUT>, the former being the opening tag and the latter being the closing tag (see example code for Figure 1.13).

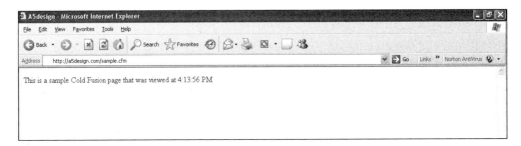

FIGURE 1.13 A Web filename with a .cfm file extension titled `sample.cfm`.

3. Wrap Designated Characters Around Items Such as Variables and Functions That Are to Be Processed

With ColdFusion, the pound (#) sign must be included on both sides. In the sample code for Figure 1.13, the pound signs are included on both sides of the `TimeFormat` function.

In case the pound sign needs to be output in the code, ColdFusion requires the developer to include another pound sign. For example, in the sentence, "He wore jersey #7," the sentence would need to read, "He wore jersey ##7." Another example is when an inline style is included that uses a HEX value, such as `color:##ffffff`.

FREQUENTLY USED SERVER-SIDE FUNCTIONS

One advantage of programming db-driven sites with ColdFusion is that it is designed for rapid application development. In other words, it offers very easy-to-use functions that remove much of the programming a developer will have to write for common functionality. The following are a few available functions. By no means does this cover the gamut of functions ColdFusion offers. They are merely included to show how easy and powerful they are to use.

Time/Date Formats

When a user hits a Web page, it can be programmed to show the exact time and/or date the request was made. This happens because the code takes the server's time/date at the time of the request and outputs it onto the Web page. Using the `TimeFormat` and `DateFormat` functions allows the developer to format how the variables are output. Figure 1.14 shows how the following code appears when output.

```
<!DOCTYPE HTML PUBLIC "-//W3C//DTD HTML 4.01 Transitional//EN">
<html>
<head>
    <title>A5design</title>
</head>
<body>
<cfoutput>
    The time this page was output to the browser was:
    <br /><br />
    #TimeFormat(Now(), "h:MM:SS tt")#
    <br /><br /><br />
    The date this page was output to the browser was:
    <br /><br />
    #DateFormat(Now(), "DDDD, MMMM DD, YYYY")#
</cfoutput>
</body>
</html>
```

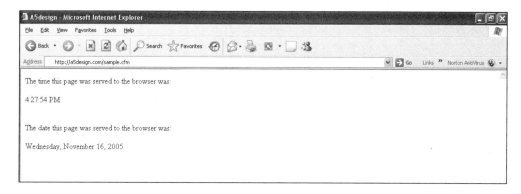

FIGURE 1.14 An output ColdFusion page, using the `TimeFormat` and `DateFormat` functions.

Include Files

Include files make life easier for a developer when creating db-driven sites. They allow for one file to be included in another, so when that particular piece of code or content needs to be revised, only one file needs to be edited. Saving copyright lines at the bottom of Web sites is a common use for an include file. Figure 1.15 shows how the following code is displayed as a file on its own.

```
<div style="padding:20px;background:#DDDDDD;">
    &copy; copyright 2005 | your company | all rights reserved
</div>
```

When saving code or content as an include file, the developer does not normally need to include the header and footer XHTML tags in the file. This is because the parent document that includes the other file should already contain the necessary XHTML tags, such as <html>, <head>, <title>, and <body>.

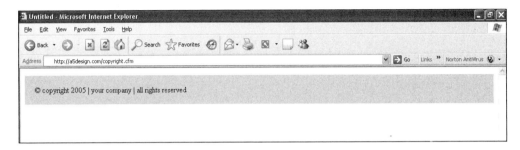

FIGURE 1.15 The include file `copyright.cfm` when displayed on its own.

To call the include file `copyright.cfm` into the parent page `sample.cfm`, the developer needs only to use the following line of code:

```
<cfinclude template="copyright.cfm">
```

Figure 1.16 shows what the page will look like when the code is added to the code from Figure 1.14.

```
<!DOCTYPE HTML PUBLIC "-//W3C//DTD HTML 4.01 Transitional//EN">
<html>
<head>
    <title>A5design</title>
</head>
<body>
<cfoutput>
    The time this page was output to the browser was:
    <br /><br />
    #TimeFormat(Now(), "h:MM:SS tt")#
    <br /><br /><br />
    The date this page was output to the browser was:
    <br /><br />
    #DateFormat(Now(), "DDDD, MMMM DD, YYYY")#
    <br /><br />
    <cfinclude template="copyright.cfm">
</cfoutput>
</body>
</html>
```

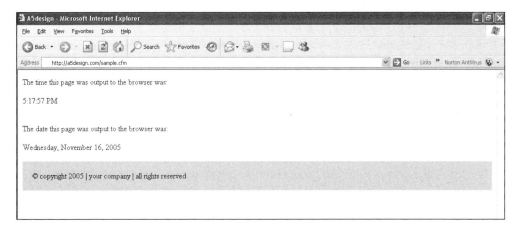

FIGURE 1.16   The include file `copyright.cfm` added into the `sample.cfm` page that also includes the `TimeFormat` and `DateFormat` functions.

Dollar Format

Many times when programming with numbers, a developer will enter data into the database with no formatting or calculations to keep the data clean and simple. When the data is output, though, calculations are run and the data is displayed with dollar signs. The `DollarFormat` function not only adds the dollar sign and proper placement of the decimal, but it also allows for calculations inside the function. Following is the syntax of the function, processing the variable `total_price`:

```
#DollarFormat(total_price)#
```

The output result is $154.08.

Following is the code that would be used to calculate the amount of sales tax to be added if the tax were calculated at 8.73%.

```
#DollarFormat(total_price * sales_tax)#
```

The output result is $13.45.

Although some databases will not allow it, the developer should be aware to not place dollar-formatted code back into the database if the data is not supposed to be formatted.

Mathematical Functions

Mathematical functions are surprisingly helpful when a developer is crunching numbers and, sometimes, when not crunching numbers, contradictory. Following are a couple functions included with ColdFusion and explanations on how they are helpful when programming db-driven sites:

`IncrementValue(number):` This function is particularly useful when looping through a list or output query (explained later in this chapter). After the developer sets a variable of 0 before beginning to loop through a specific piece of code, the `IncrementValue` function can be used to increase that number by one for every loop. This enables the developer to control the number of items of rows that are output.

`RandRange(number1, number2):` Sometimes clients want images to appear randomly. This function is very useful because you can include a range of numbers that will be randomly selected. What the developer can then do is name 10 photos with the same naming convention, with the only difference being the numbers 1 through 10 appended to each photo (e.g., `photo_1.jpg`, `photo_2.jpg`, `photo_3.jpg`, `photo_4.jpg`, and `photo_5.jpg`). To then have the page randomly change a photo, the developer simply includes this function at the end of the image name to make it dynamically change each time the page is selected and output to the browser. Following is an example of what the code would look like:

```
<cfoutput>
<img src=".images/photo_#RandRange(1, 10)#.jpg" width="250"
    height="100" alt="" border="0">
</cfoutput>
```

Round: When programming an application, numbers cannot always have decimal places. This function will save time that would have normally been spent programming code to do the same job. The functions `Ceiling` and `Int` can also round the number up or down, depending on their respective function.

Arithmetic Expressions: While these are not necessarily considered functions, the following expressions can be used with the varying mathematical functions: addition, subtraction, multiplication, division, etc.

Redirect

Redirecting a user automatically to a page is particularly useful when creating applications. If, for instance, the user has just added, edited, or deleted a record from the database, the developer may either offer the user a link to continue onto the next step or do it for them automatically. Following is the syntax for the `<CFLOCATION>` tag that automatically takes the user to another page in the site or to an external Web site:

```
<cflocation url="http://www.usatoday.com" addtoken="No">
```

Another use for the <CFLOCATION> tag is for redirecting users from directories made specifically to avoid URLs with long filenames or many variables. For instance, by creating a subfolder called sample under *http://www.a5design.com*, an index.cfm file could be included with the <CFLOCATION> tag pointed to *http://www.espn.com*. Therefore, when a user clicked on *http://www.a5design.com/sample*, the user would be redirected to *http://www.espn.com*.

VARIABLES

It's often said that db-driven sites are *dynamic*. This means parts of the site, whether content or design, are created on the fly each time a page is selected. Variables are essential to making a site dynamic. They are not just used in one way, though. There are a variety of different uses:

- Submitting data to pages that will process the information (e.g., adding, editing, and deleting data from the database).
- Determining which pieces of code a page will use (e.g., telling a page whether it should show a list or show an individual item).
- Passing user-selected values (e.g., telling a page what size of fonts to display).

Many times the terms "variable" and "parameter" are used interchangeably.

NOTE

Different Types of Variables

Several types of variables are included with each programming language. While the terminology may not be the same for every language, the functionality, for the most, is very similar. The following are a few types of variables and instances where they are used with ColdFusion (an entire list of variables can be found on Macromedia's site at *http://www.macromedia.com/v1/documents/cf31userguide/user/ug060001.htm*):

CGI variables: These variables, among other things, provide the developer with information provided by the server. Figure 1.17 shows the information that is displayed from the following code:

```
<cfoutput>
    Your IP address is: 62.184.183.14
    <br />
    Your server name is: #cgi.server_name#
    <br />
    The last page you just visited was: #cgi.http_referer#
    <br />
    The browser you're using is: #cgi.http_user_agent#
    <br />
```

```
The server software you're using is: #cgi.server_software#
</cfoutput>
```

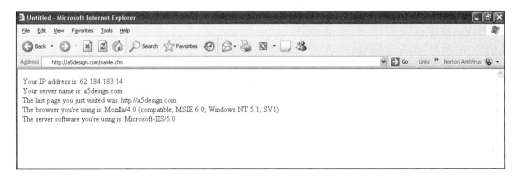

FIGURE 1.17   Information provided from the server using CGI variables.

Form variables: Form fields are considered variables. Therefore, once submitted, the following form would be passing, if the user were required to enter all the information, a department, first_name, email, and message variables.

```
<FORM NAME="sample_form" ACTION="http://www.a5design.com/sample.cfm"
    METHOD=POST>
    <b>Department You Wish to Contact:</b><br />
    <select name="department" class="black2">
        <option selected value="Sales">Sales/Marketing</option>
        <option value="Human Resources">Human Resources</option>
        <option value="IT">IT</option>
                <option value="Other">Other</option>
    </select>
    <br /><br />
    <b>First Name:</b><br />
    <INPUT TYPE="Text" NAME="first_name" SIZE="35" VALUE="">
    <br /><br />
    <b>E-mail Address:</b><br />
    <INPUT TYPE="Text" NAME="email" SIZE="35" VALUE="">
    <br /><br />
    <b>Message:</b><br />
    <textarea cols="30" rows="5" name="message" class="black2"></textarea></td>
    <br /><br />
    <input type="Submit" value="send" border="0" />
</FORM>
```

URL variables: Using a URL to pass variables is a commonly used technique. Figure 1.18 shows a URL with a long string of variables appended to it.

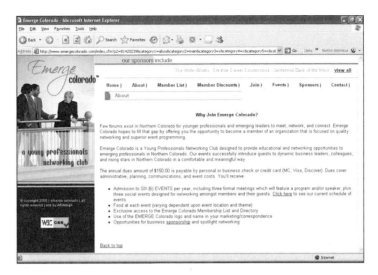

FIGURE 1.18   Page with variables being passed in the URL. © 2006
Emerge Colorado. Used with permission.

Session variables: Session variables are a commonly used type of variable because the developer needs to simply set them on a page, and they will reside on the server for a designated amount of time, determined by the default values of the server or by programmed settings. The developer, then, from nearly anywhere on the site can use, edit, or delete the variables. Because they are customizable for each user and because they don't need to be passed to every page, a good use for session variables is to store shopping-cart data while the user peruses various pages. Following is the code to set a session variable in ColdFusion:

```
<cflock scope="session" timeout="15" type="EXCLUSIVE">
    <cfset session.cart_oddcolor = "blue">
</cflock>
```

Application variables: This type of variable is usually set in the `Application.cfm` file in the root directory or subdirectory of a site. The variables can then be called from any page at any time, like session variables. The difference is that session variables can be assigned to each user, while the application variables are used for the entire site. An example of how an application variable could be used would be setting a contact email address for various email forms on the site. Therefore, if the address needs to be changed from *info@yourcompany.com* to *customersupport@ yourcompany.com*, the developer needs to do so in only one area—the `Application. cfm` file.

For each request to the ColdFusion server, the `Application.cfm` *file is called first before processing any other file. It is there that the developer can set variables that may be used throughout all the pages in that directory or subdirectories underneath that don't have an* `Application.cfm` *file included within themselves. If a subdirectory does have its own* `Application.cfm` *file, the variables from the parent directory will not be passed to the subdirectory.*

Default Values

When a developer passes variables to another page, that page expects to receive values for those variables if it is to process them. If the ColdFusion page does not receive data, the server will produce an error message. There are typically two ways of avoiding such error messages:

- Add conditional code on the next page that says that if the value is not defined or is not greater than 0, do not include the code that is going to use that variable. Such conditional statements are discussed later in this chapter.
- Set a default value for the variable that will allow the code to run with no adverse affects. The following is the code to set default parameters:

```
<cfparam name="first_name" default="Mikayla">
```

Or

```
<cfparam name="first_name" default="">
```

Setting Variables

Sometimes variables are automatically set when a form is submitted or a default parameter value has been defined; however, variables at other times need to be intentionally set. Following are ways to set various variables with ColdFusion:

Setting a Variable That Will Be Used on a Page

The following is the only line of code that needs to be used to set a variable on a page:

```
<cfset last_name = "Discoe">
```

A variable can also be set using another variable. The only difference is that the developer needs to remove the quotation marks around it:

```
<cfset last_name = form.last_name2>
```

Because the variable is contained within the <CFSET> tag, pound signs do not need to be included around the variable `form.last_name2`. Also, `form.` is appended to the last_name2 variable in the example to tell ColdFusion that it is being received from a submitted form. The form. can also be omitted, but it will require more server processing to figure out where the variable is coming from.

Setting an Application Variable

The process of declaring or setting an application variable in an Application.cfm page is the same as setting a regular variable on a page. The only difference is that to be able to set application, session, or client variables in ColdFusion, the developer must first add the <CFAPPLICATION> tag and the proper attributes and variables in the Application.cfm page. The tag not only allows the developer to tell the server which variables to enable, but it also allows for the timeout value to be set. In other words, if no activity (e.g., clicking on links or submitting forms) occurs, the variable will be deleted from the server. If products in a shopping cart are set using the following example, the cart will be emptied when no activity takes places in 30 minutes:

```
<cfapplication name="sample_application"
        clientmanagement="No"
    sessionmanagement="Yes"
        sessiontimeout=" #CreateTimeSpan(0,0,30,0)#"
    applicationtimeout=" #CreateTimeSpan(0,0,0,0)#">
```

A useful application variable to set is a root *variable. This variable contains the root path to be used for all images and internal hyperlinks. For example, the variable should be prepended to each image path or absolute hyperlink so that if the site needs to be moved from a development environment to a live environment, the developer need only change the one variable. Following is how the variable appears in the* Application.cfm *file and how it is used with images and hyperlinks:*

How the variable appears in the Application.cfm *page:*

```
<cfset root = "http://www.a5design.com/">
```

How the variable is used with images and hyperlinks on subsequent pages:

```
<img src="<cfoutput>#root#</cfoutput>/images/spacer.gif" width="1"
    height="5" alt="" border="0" />
<a href="<cfoutput>#root#</cfoutput>/documents/sample_form.pdf">
    Sample PDF document</a>
```

Setting a Session Variable

The process of setting session variables is the same as setting regular variables on a page or application variables in the Application.cfm file. To ensure that the server is not hung up by users setting variables simultaneously, the <CFLOCK> tag should be wrapped around the code that sets the variables. Also, "session." must be appended to the variable to identify it as a session variable. An example of how a session variable is set is:

```
<cflock scope="session" timeout="15" type="exclusive">
<cfset session.font_size = "small">
</cflock>
```

Passing Variables

Passing variables can be done a number of ways. Barring session and application variables that can be output whenever the developer needs, other variables need to actually be passed using forms (with visible and hidden values) and hyperlinks, which use URL strings:

Using forms to pass variables: Forms are a simple way to pass variables because the developer needs to name only the form field (see 1 in Figure 1.19). Once the form is submitted to the server (see 2 in Figure 1.19) and then output on a separate page (see 3 in Figure 1.19), the variables can be displayed and/or processed on the separate page.

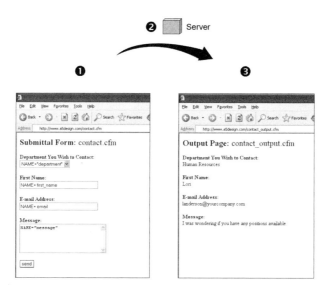

FIGURE 1.19 Page passing variables with form.

Using hyperlinks and URL strings to pass variables: One of the most common ways to pass variables from one page to the next is by using hyperlinks and URL strings. To do so, the developer needs only to append a question mark (?) after the filename, include the variable name, add an equals (=) sign, and post the variable value—all without any spaces between the various elements (see 1 in Figure 1.20). If additional variables are to be passed, an ampersand (&) needs to be included between them. Figure 1.20 illustrates the process:

A developer should always be cautious when passing information with forms or with hyperlinks and URL strings. This is because a hacker can easily see the variable names, which provides a tool to better understand how the Web site works and can be manipulated. Session variables are a safer means of passing variables because they are stored on the server, hidden from hackers.

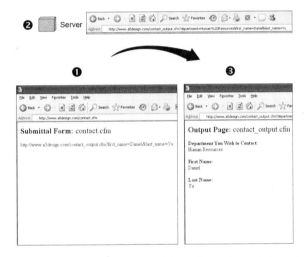

FIGURE 1.20   Passing variables using a hyperlink and a URL string.

ADDING, EDITING, AND DELETING DATA FROM A DATABASE

Adding, editing, and deleting data from a database is accomplished using queries. Queries are mainly written using SQL, a language designed specifically for working with databases. While entire books have been written on SQL, each db-driven programming language processes the language slightly differently. ColdFusion incorporates the language into its <CFQUERY> tag, which is better explained in the next three example queries, which explain how to add, edit, and delete data.

Adding Data

When adding data using the <CFQUERY> tag, the datasource must be identified so the server knows where to find the database. The tag should also contain a query name so the developer can reference the query in code that outputs results.

The developer must then tell the query which table the data is going to be inserted into, using the INSERT clause. In the following example, this is the contacts table. The query then needs to know which columns are going to have data added to them. While it is easier if the columns have the same names as the variables, in this example, the variables have submitted_ prepended to them to help differentiate between the two. The first column that is going to have data added to it is first_name, and the variable that will be added is called submitted_first_name.

```
<cfquery datasource="sample_datasource" name="insertrecord">
    INSERT
    INTO contacts
        (
    first_name
    ,last_name
    ,email
    )
    VALUES (
    '#submitted_first_name#'
    ,'#submitted_last_name#'
    ,'#submitted_email#'
    )
</cfquery>
```

When the data is passed to the query, the variables will have values associated with them, so the query will look like the following to the server:

```
<cfquery datasource="sample_datasource" name="insertrecord">
    INSERT
    INTO contacts
        (
    first_name
    ,last_name
    ,email
    )
    VALUES (
    'Daniel'
    ,'Yu'
    ,'danielyu@yourcompany.com'
    )
</cfquery>
```

Editing Data

When editing data using the <CFQUERY> tag, the datasource must be identified so the server knows where to find the database. The tag should also contain a query name so the developer can reference the query in code that outputs results.

The developer must then tell the query which table is going to be updated with the passed data. In the following example, this is the contacts table. It then needs to know which columns are going to have data updated in them and which variables will be used to accomplish this. While it is easier to have the columns have the same names as the variables, in this example, the variables have submitted_ prepended to them. The first column that is going to be updated, therefore, is called first_name, and the variable that is to be used is called submitted_first_name. If a WHERE clause is not declared, then the query will replace every first name, last name, and e-mail address value in the table with the submitted data. This is why it is necessary to include the submitted_id variable that will tell the query which record or row to update. In the following example, the record that is going to be updated will have the number 25 in its id column.

```
<cfquery datasource="sample_datasource" name="updaterecord">
    UPDATE contacts
    SET
    first_name = '#submitted_first_name#'
    ,last_name = '#submitted_last_name#'
    ,email = '#submitted_email#'
    WHERE id = #submitted_id#
</cfquery>
```

When passing data to an UPDATE *query, the developer usually needs to pass the unique identifier. This can be included as a "hidden" form field or as a variable in a URL string.*

When the data is passed to the query, the variables will have values, and the query will look like the following to the server:

```
<cfquery datasource="sample_datasource" name="updaterecord">
    UPDATE contacts
    SET
    first_name = 'Daniel'
    ,last_name = 'Yu'
    ,email = 'danielyu@yourcompany.com'
    WHERE id = 25
</cfquery>
```

Syntax is very important when writing SQL statements. Depending on the server, the syntax will sometimes be different. In ColdFusion, for example, numeric variables should not have single ticks around them (e.g., id = 25), but alpha variables should include the single ticks around them (e.g., id = 'twenty_five').

Deleting Data

When deleting data using the <CFQUERY> tag, the datasource must be identified so the server knows where to find the database. While it is optional, the query should also be given a name so the developer can reference the query in code that outputs query data and its variables.

The developer must then tell the query which table is going to have data deleted from it. In the following example, this is the contacts table. The query then needs to know which record or row to delete, which is why the WHERE clause is included. If the clause is not included, the query will delete every record in the database. In the following example, the record that is going to be updated will have the number 8 in its id column.

```
<cfquery datasource="sample_datasource" name="deleterecord">
    DELETE
FROM contacts
    WHERE id = #submitted_id#
</cfquery>
```

When passing data to a DELETE query, the developer usually needs to pass the unique identifier. This can be included as a hidden form field or as a variable in a URL string.

When the data is passed to the query, the variables will have values, and the query will look like the following to the server:

```
<cfquery datasource="sample_datasource" name="deleterecord">
    DELETE
FROM contacts
    WHERE id = 8
</cfquery>
```

OUTPUTTING DATA

As mentioned earlier, the ColdFusion server requires the developer to wrap any programming code (including variables) with the <CFOUTPUT> and </CFOUTPUT> tags so that the server knows it needs to output the processed data. The server also requires the pound (#) sign to be included on both sides of the variable. If the developer were to output the following variable, the code following it would need to look like the following:

```
<cfset message = "This is a test message I would like to output.">

<cfoutput>
    #message#
</cfoutput>
```

The output text would look like the following:

This is a test message I would like to output.

CFOUTPUT

The <CFOUTPUT> tag is not only used to output ColdFusion variables and code, but it also is used to loop through a query. All the developer has to do is enter the attribute query="query_name" inside the tag so it knows what query to output data from. Unlike the <CFLOOP> tag, the <CFOUTPUT> tag cannot be nested inside another <CFOUTPUT> tag. It also requires less server resources. An example of a query that is used to pull data, along with a <CFOUTPUT> tag used to loop through and output the results, is as follows:

```
<cfquery datasource="sample_datasource" name="sample_query">
SELECT first_name, last_name
    FROM contacts
    WHERE last_name <> 'Johnson'
</cfquery>

<cfoutput query="sample_query">
    #last_name#, #first_name# <br />
</cfoutput>
```

Following is a sample of what the query would output if the data was output from the table in Figure 1.10:

Dogin, Josh
Brean, Tim

Conditional Statements

Conditional statements are a useful tool when programming db-driven sites. The statements, for example, can be used to determine what code or content should be output or whether it should be interpreted. Following are several examples of how the statements help a developer control data output:

- Basic conditional statement with only one condition:

```
<cfif page_action IS "add">
    If the page_action variable is "add," this area would be
        interpreted by the server.
```

```
<cfelse>
    If the page_action variables is anything but "add," this area
        would be interpreted by the server.
</cfif>
```

■ Conditional statement with `cfelseif` condition:

```
<cfif department IS "Human Resources">
    If the department variable is "Human Resources," this area would
        be interpreted by the server.
<cfelseif department IS "IT">
    If the department variable is "IT," this area would be
        interpreted by the server.
<cfelseif department IS "Sales/Marketing">
    If the department variable is "Sales/Marketing," this area would
        be interpreted by the server.
<cfelse>
    If the department variable is "Human Resources," this area would
        be interpreted by the server.
</cfif>
```

■ Conditional statement that runs a piece a code if a variable exists:

```
<cfif isdefined("email")>
    If the "email" variable exists, meaning it has been set or passed
        to the page, then this code would be interpreted.
<cfelse>
    If the "email" variable doesn't exist, meaning it has not been
        set or passed to the page, then this code would be interpreted.
</cfif>
```

Loops

Loops are similar to the <CFOUTPUT> tag, but they offer the developer more control over how data is output. The developer, for instance, can loop through a list or a query, and the number of loops can be controlled. Loops are common among other programming languages. Following is an example of usage of the <CFLOOP> tag:

```
<cfquery datasource="sample_datasource" name="customers" >
SELECT *
    FROM customers
    WHERE first_name = 'Nancy'
</cfquery>

<cfloop query="customers">
    #first_name# #last_name#,
</cfloop>
```

This is how the code would appear once output:

Nancy Eccher, Nancy Johnson, Nancy Smith, Nancy Tulane, Nancy Willingsmith

With ColdFusion, one big advantage to the <CFLOOP> *tag is that it can be looped inside a* <CFOUTPUT> *or* <CFLOOP> *tag. This allows the developer to include queries inside of loops to pull more data for a particular record, especially if conditional statements are used.*

Arrays

Arrays are a more complex type of variable, which can store multiple pieces of data with multiple values for each piece. This makes them useful when building shopping carts. Such an array can be output with all the various pieces appearing however the developer chooses. Figure 1.21 shows three items in a shopping cart that were output from an array:

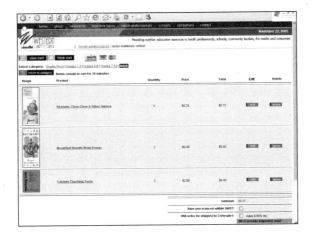

FIGURE 1.21   Items output in a shopping cart from an array. © 2006 Western Dairy Council. Used with permission.

The developer can use arrays in shopping carts because they can be saved as session variables (e.g., #session.shoppingcart#) and accessed from various sections of a site. While the array is saved as one session variable, it is considered a complex variable because it contains more than one piece of data. Figure 1.22 illustrates the complexity of an array that holds seven pieces of data for each item within it.

Emailing

Many db-driven Web sites use email form functionality to send emails through the server, such as sending an email from a Contact Us page or sending a purchase confirmation to a client. Whether an email is directed internally or externally, the code functions the same. With ColdFusion, the developer uses the <CFMAIL> tag to send an email. An example is:

```
<cfmail to="info@a5design.com"
from = "micheleDiscoe@yourcompany.com"
    subject = "E-mail from Web Site"
    server = "mail.yourcompany.com"
    type = "html"
    timeout=10>
From: #last_name#, #first_name#
E-mail Address: #from_email#
Message: #message#
</cfmail>
```

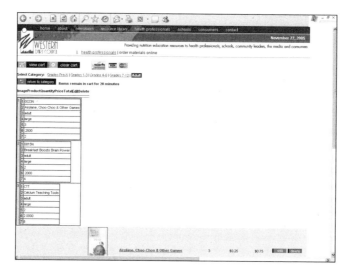

FIGURE 1.22 Array variable that contains seven pieces of data for three different items. © 2006 Western Dairy Council. Used with permission.

To better understand the code, a sample email form is included and explained in Chapter 2.

SUMMARY

Understanding the big picture of db-driven sites is the first step to understanding how to program them. Some of the things discussed in this chapter are how a page is processed in a db-driven site, how code and data are separated, how relational databases work, and various functions a developer can use to make programming the site much faster. Real-world examples, such as images and code, are used to help clarify concepts, thus helping the reader better understand how this process works.

2 Examples of Database Functionality

This chapter is designed to give the novice developer a more detailed understanding of how db-driven sites work, using more involved examples of code for commonly used functionality. There are two important things to remember about the code examples in this chapter:

Many of the examples can be reused in different ways: What is important to understand is that the general concepts can be applied in various situations. The conditional statements, for example, can be used to show or hide content, include code based on variables, and output dynamic links under certain conditions.

There are different methods of accomplishing the same goal when programming db-driven sites: This concept is analogous to a spoken language that has various ways of saying *hello*. While a novice may want to emulate more experienced developers, there also comes the point when he is going to have to program in a way that works for him. It is therefore good to explore the many options available.

GENERAL PAGE LAYOUT WITH INCLUDES

A couple strengths are associated with using include files. Not only are they not visible, so this is no disjuncture in a design, but they also make a developer's life much easier when managing db-driven sites. Similar to how stylesheets are used to effortlessly change the base font of an entire site, include files can be used to easily modify larger chunks of code. Figure 2.1 shows a Web site with the header area saved as an include file.

FIGURE 2.1   Web site with the header and copyright areas saved as include files.

Figure 2.2 illustrates what the Web site looks like when the lines of code that include the header and copyright areas are removed. While the missing copyright area is not as obvious, it is easy to see when the header include has been removed. Depending on how the site was built with XHTML table-based design, the body of the Web site would typically move up to replace the missing 126 pixels of height. Because the example site was programmed with CSS's absolute positioning, the Web site body remains in the same place.

Steps to Saving Code as an Include File

The following steps should be taken to save the header area as an include file:

1. **Cut code from the source file that is to be saved as an include file.** Following is the code for the design in Figures 2.1 and 2.2. Everything between the header comment tags should be removed:

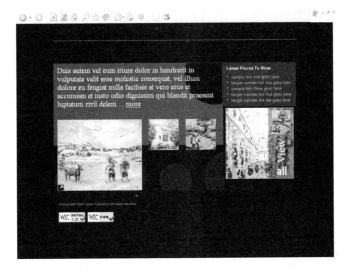

FIGURE 2.2 Web site with the `header` and `copyright` include files being removed.

```
<!DOCTYPE html PUBLIC "-//W3C//DTD XHTML 1.0 Transitional//EN"
    "DTD/xhtml1-transitional.dtd">
<html><head><title>Design</title>
<meta http-equiv="Content-Type" content="text/html;
    charset=iso-8859-1" />
<!-- link to main stylesheet that control text sizes and colors,
    among other things -->
<link rel="stylesheet" href="mainstyle.css" type="text/css" />
</head>
<body>
<div id="a5-body-center">
    <div id="a5-body">
<!-- ###### header start ###### -->
        <div id="a5-header">
            <div id="a5-logo">
                <a href="index.htm"><img src="images/logo.gif"
                    width="405" height="70" alt="" border="0" /></a>
            </div>
            <div id="a5-menu-box">
                <div id="a5-menu">
                    <a href="index.htm"><span style="color:#ffffff;
                        font-size:21px;font-weight:normal;">1 
                    </span> menu item 1</a>   
                    <a href="menu-item-2.htm"><span style="color:
                        #ffffff;font-size:21px;font-weight:normal;
                        ">2 </span> longer menu item 2
                        </a>   
                    <a href="menu-item-3.htm"><span style="color:
                        #ffffff;font-size:21px;font-weight:normal;
```

```
                              ">3 </span> menu item 3</a> 
                                
                     <a href="index.htm"><span style="color:#ffffff;
                              font-size:21px;font-weight:normal;">4 
                              </span> menu item 4</a>   
                     <a href="index.htm"><span style="color:#ffffff;
                              font-size:21px;font-weight:normal;">5 </span>
                              menu item
                                5</a>   
                  </div>
               </div>
               <div id="a5-phone">
                  555.555.5555
               </div>
               <img src="images/image-top-right.jpg" width="56"
                     height="43" alt="" border="0" style="position:
                     absolute; top:66px; right:32px;" />
            </div>
<!-- ###### header end ###### -->
            <div id="a5-main-content">
<!-- ###### column left start ###### -->
               <div id="a5-column-left">
                  <div id="a5-column-left-top">
Lorem ipsum dolor sit amet, consetetur sadipscing elitr, sed diam
   nonumy eirmod tempor invidunt ut labore et dolore magna aliquyam
   erat, sed diam voluptua. At vero eos et accusam et justo duo
   dolores et ea rebum. Stet clita kasd.
                  </div>
                  <div id="a5-column-left-bottom">
                     <div id="image-bottom-left">
                        <img src="images/image-bottom-left.jpg"
                           width="268" height="220" alt=""
                           border="0" />
                     </div>
                     <div id="image-bottom-center-left">
                        <img src="images/image-bottom-center-left.jpg"
                           width="95" height="95" alt="" border="0" />
                     </div>
                     <div id="image-bottom-center-right">
                        <img src="images/image-bottom-center-right.jpg"
                           width="95" height="95" alt="" border="0" />
                     </div>
                  </div>
<!-- ###### copyright start ###### -->
                  <div id="a5-copyright">
                     &copy; copyright 2006 | your company | all rights reserved
                     <p>
                     <a href="http://validator.w3.org/check?uri=
                        referer"><img
                           src="http://www.w3.org/Icons/valid-xhtml10"
                           alt="Valid XHTML 1.0 Transitional"
                           height="31" width="88" border="0" /></a>
                        <a href="http://jigsaw.w3.org/css-validator/">
                        <img style="border:0;width:88px;height:31px"
                              src="http://jigsaw.w3.org/
                              css-validator/images/vcss"
```

```
                                    alt="Valid CSS!" />
                            </a>
                            </p>
                    </div>
<!-- ###### copyright end ###### -->
            </div>
<!-- ###### column left end ###### -->
<!-- ###### column right start ###### -->
            <div id="a5-column-right">
                    <div id="a5-column-right-top">
                        <b>Latest Pieces To View</b>
                        <ul id="list-right-top">
                            <li><a href="index.htm" class="linklist1">
                                sample link one goes here</a></li>
                            <li><a href="index.htm" class="linklist1">
                                longer sample link two goes here</a></li>
                            <li><a href="index.htm" class="linklist1">
                                sample link three goes here</a></li>
                            <li><a href="index.htm" class="linklist1">
                                longer sample link four goes here</a></li>
                            <li><a href="index.htm" class="linklist1">
                                longer sample link five goes here</a></li>
                        </ul>
                    </div>
                    <div id="a5-column-right-bottom">
                        <img src="images/image-bottom-right.jpg"
                            width="216" height="220" alt="" border="0" />
                    </div>
            </div>
<!-- ###### column right end ###### -->
        </div>
    </div>
</div>
</body>
</html>
```

2. **Paste the code into blank file and save with a new filename.** The header code that is removed is saved as a new ColdFusion file called `header.cfm`.

```
        <div id="a5-header">
            <div id="a5-logo">
                <a href="index.htm"><img src="images/logo.gif"
                    width="405" height="70" alt="" border="0" /></a>
            </div>
            <div id="a5-menu-box">
                <div id="a5-menu">
                    <a href="index.htm"><span style="color:#ffffff;
                        font-size:21px;font-weight:normal;">1 
                        </span> menu item 1</a>   
                    <a href="menu-item-2.htm"><span style=
                        "color:#ffffff;font-size:21px;font-weight:
                        normal;">2 </span> longer menu item
                        2</a>   
                    <a href="menu-item-3.htm"><span style=
                        "color:#ffffff;font-size:21px;font-weight:
```

```
                        normal;">3 </span> menu item
                        3</a>   
                 <a href="index.htm"><span style="color:#ffffff;
                        font-size:21px;font-weight:normal;">4 
                        </span> menu item 4</a>   
                 <a href="index.htm"><span style="color:#ffffff;
                        font-size:21px;font-weight:normal;">5 
                        </span> menu item 5</a>   
          </div>
       </div>
       <div id="a5-phone">
          555.555.5555
       </div>
       <img src="images/image-top-right.jpg" width="56"
          height="43" alt="" border="0" style="position:absolute;
          top:66px; right:32px;" />
    </div>
```

Programming languages usually require the developer to save an include file with the file extension used with that language (e.g., .cfm, .jsp, or .aspx).

> **3. Add a line of code that tells the parent page where to find the include file.**
> The following line of code calls the header.cfm into the index.cfm file.

```
<cfinclude template="header.cfm">
```

When the line of code has been added, the index.cfm file will look like the following:

```
<!DOCTYPE html PUBLIC "-//W3C//DTD XHTML 1.0 Transitional//EN"
    "DTD/xhtml1-transitional.dtd">
<html><head><title>Design</title>
<meta http-equiv="Content-Type" content="text/html;
    charset=iso-8859-1" />
<!-- link to main stylesheet that controls text sizes and colors,
    among other things -->
<link rel="stylesheet" href="mainstyle.css" type="text/css" />
</head>
<body>
<div id="a5-body-center">
    <div id="a5-body">
<!-- ###### header start ###### -->
    <cfinclude template="header.cfm">
<!-- ###### header end ###### -->
        <div id="a5-main-content">
<!-- ###### column left start ###### -->
            <div id="a5-column-left">
                <div id="a5-column-left-top">
    Lorem ipsum dolor sit amet, consetetur sadipscing elitr, sed diam
        nonumy eirmod tempor invidunt ut labore et dolore magna
        aliquyam erat, sed diam voluptua. At vero eos et accusam et
        justo duo dolores et ea rebum. Stet clita kasd.
                </div>
                <div id="a5-column-left-bottom">
                    <div id="image-bottom-left">
```

```html
            <img src="images/image-bottom-left.jpg"
                width="268" height="220" alt=""
                border="0" />
        </div>
        <div id="image-bottom-center-left">
            <img src="images/image-bottom-center-left.jpg"
                width="95" height="95" alt="" border="0" />
        </div>
        <div id="image-bottom-center-right">
            <img src="images/image-bottom-center-right.jpg"
                width="95" height="95" alt="" border="0" />
        </div>
        </div>
<!-- ###### copyright start ###### -->
        <div id="a5-copyright">
            &copy; copyright 2006 | your company |
            all rights reserved
            <p>
            <a href="http://validator.w3.org/check?
            uri=referer"><img
                src="http://www.w3.org/Icons/valid-xhtml10"
                alt="Valid XHTML 1.0 Transitional"
            height="31" width="88" border="0" /></a>
            <a href="http://jigsaw.w3.org/css-validator/">
                <img style="border:0;width:88px;height:31px"
                    src="http://jigsaw.w3.org/css-validator/
                    images/vcss"
                        alt="Valid CSS!" />
                </a>
                </p>
        </div>
<!-- ###### copyright end ###### -->
        </div>
<!-- ###### column left end ###### -->
<!-- ###### column right start ###### -->
        <div id="a5-column-right">
            <div id="a5-column-right-top">
                <b>Latest Pieces To View</b>
                <ul id="list-right-top">
                    <li><a href="index.htm" class="linklist1">
                        sample link one goes here</a></li>
                    <li><a href="index.htm" class="linklist1">
                        longer sample link two goes here</a></li>
                    <li><a href="index.htm" class="linklist1">
                        sample link three goes here</a></li>
                    <li><a href="index.htm" class="linklist1">
                        longer sample link four goes here</a></li>
                    <li><a href="index.htm" class="linklist1">
                        longer sample link five goes here</a></li>
                </ul>
            </div>
            <div id="a5-column-right-bottom">
                <img src="images/image-bottom-right.jpg"
                    width="216" height="220" alt="" border="0" />
            </div>
        </div>
```

```
<!-- ###### column right end ###### -->
        </div>
    </div>
</div>
</body>
</html>
```

4. **Test the parent file.** In most instances, it is not possible to see if the page and its include file have been properly saved and programmed. Because it is a wise practice to test a site as it is being built, the developer should see if the page was saved correctly and that page includes the file because sometimes the source file may not have been overwritten, which means it will still contain the code that is to be saved as an include file, rather than just the line of code that calls the include file. To test the file, the border of the <DIV> container that contains the header file can be turned to a value of 1, or the line of code that is calling the include file can simply be removed.

NOTE   *Depending on the programming language, when an include is missing, the server will either produce an error message saying the file cannot be found, or the server will serve up the page with the file not being included.*

GENERAL CONTENT OUTPUT

Because db-driven sites are so flexible, clients frequently request the content of their sites be output in various ways. Following are just a few ways to modify content output.

Limiting the Number of Characters

Many times space requires developers to limit the amount of content that is viewable on a page, requiring the user to click to view the content, in its entirety, on another page. Home page content is a common use for such controlled output. In Figure 2.1 the main content on the page is output from the `example_content` table in the sample database in Figure 2.3.

The paragraph displayed in the design contains only 230 characters. It is designed to pull only the initial information of the 2,596 characters in the database record, which makes up the About the Work page (see Figure 2.4).

The query pulls the entire record, but the developer needs to limit the output text. This is where the following Mid function in ColdFusion is used:

```
Mid (string, start, count )
```

The function allows the developer to identify the variable being output, the starting point (in terms of number of characters) where the data should be pulled, and the

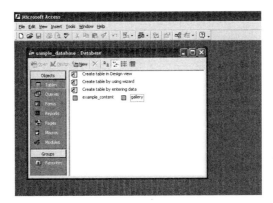

FIGURE 2.3   Sample database created with two tables. One is `example_content`, from which the homepage paragraph is pulled.

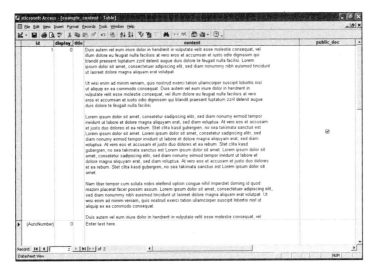

FIGURE 2.4   Content for the "about the work" record that is also output on the home page.

number of characters that should be pulled. The query and the function in the page look like the following:

```
<cfquery name="homepage_paragraph" datasource="sample_database">
SELECT *
FROM example_content
WHERE id = 1
</cfquery>
<cfoutput query="homepage_paragraph">#mid(content,1,230)#</cfoutput>
    ... <a href="about.cfm">more</a>
```

After the query pulls the data from the example_content table, the <CFOUTPUT> tag outputs the query results. The Mid function then pulls 230 characters from the content column, beginning with the first character, signified by the number 1, and ending with the 230th character. The "more" link is included after the paragraph so the user can link to the About the Work page, which contains all 2,596 characters.

The WHERE clause tells the query what row to pull the data from (i.e., the value is 1 in the id *column).*

NOTE

If the developer were to change the number of characters from 230 to 460, the last number in the function is all that would need to be changed to double the length of output text (see Figure 2.5).

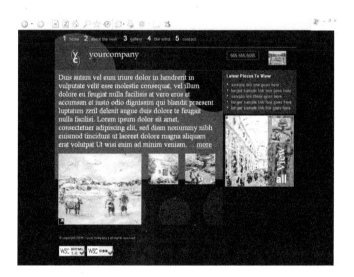

FIGURE 2.5 Home page paragraph that was doubled in length because the value of the last character pulled in the Mid function was doubled.

Looping Content That Is Dynamically Linked

Looping is used with all programming languages. It enables the developer to easily output results from a query and then display that content in a list or repeated layout. Figure 2.6 shows how the hyperlinks in the Latest Pieces to View section in the right column are output in a repeated vertical fashion:

When working with ColdFusion, a developer can loop through content using the <CFOUTPUT> or <CFLOOP> tag. Both will output the data pulled from a table, such as the Gallery table in Figure 2.7.

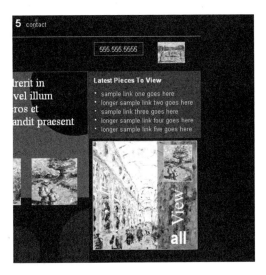

FIGURE 2.6 The Latest Pieces to View is the looped results of a query.

Microsoft Access - [gallery : Table]

id	display_ord	title	image	content	public_doc	create_dt
1	0	Tuscan Fountain	tuscany_fountain_tn.jpg	This is the sample text for "Tuscan Fountain." Duis autem vel eum iriure dolor in hendrerit in vulputate velit esse molestie consequat, vel illum dolore eu feugiat nulla facilisis at vero	☑	11/23/2005 2:42
2	0	Field Picnic	port_field_picnic_tn.jpg	This is the sample text for "Field Picnic." Duis autem vel eum iriure dolor in hendrerit in vulputate velit esse molestie consequat, vel illum dolore eu feugiat nulla facilisis at vero	☑	11/23/2005 2:42
3	0	Lake Como Couple	port_lake_como_couple_tn.jpg	This is the sample text for "Lake Como Couple." Duis autem vel eum iriure dolor in hendrerit in vulputate velit esse molestie consequat, vel illum dolore eu feugiat nulla facilisis at	☑	11/23/2005 2:44
4	0	Day of Boating	port_day_of_boating_tn.jpg	This is the sample text for "Day of Boating." Duis autem vel eum iriure dolor in hendrerit in vulputate velit esse molestie consequat, vel illum dolore eu feugiat nulla facilisis at vero	☑	11/23/2005 2:44
5	0	Red Couch	port_living_room_couch_tn.jpg	This is the sample text for "Red Couch." Duis autem vel eum iriure dolor in hendrerit in vulputate velit esse molestie consequat, vel illum dolore eu feugiat nulla facilisis at vero	☑	11/23/2005 2:44
6	0	Farm Tree	port_farm_tree_tn.jpg	This is the sample text for "Farm Tree." Duis autem vel eum iriure dolor in hendrerit in vulputate velit esse molestie consequat, vel illum dolore eu feugiat nulla facilisis at vero eros	☑	11/23/2005 2:45
7	0	Italian Market	port_italian_market_tn.jpg	This is the sample text for "Italian Market." Duis autem vel eum iriure dolor in hendrerit in vulputate velit esse molestie consequat, vel illum dolore eu feugiat nulla facilisis at vero	☑	11/23/2005 2:45
(AutoNumber)	0			Enter text here.		11/24/2005 10:22

Record: 8 of 8

Datasheet View

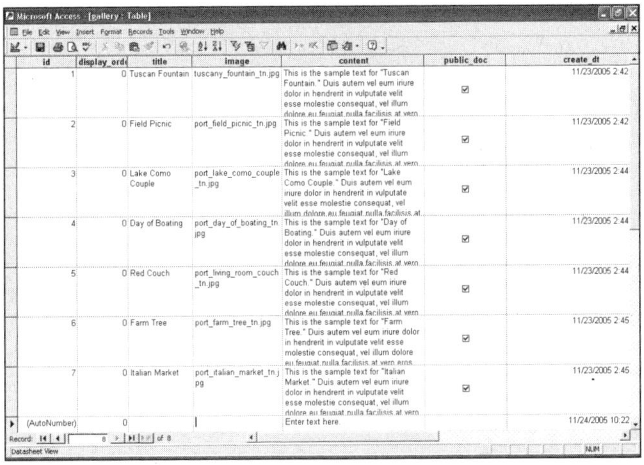

FIGURE 2.7 Data included in the Gallery table of the database titled `sample_database`.

Following is the query and code to output the data from the Gallery table using the `<CFLOOP>` tag. Notice the `Top 5` in the `SELECT` clause and the `create_dt DESC` in the `ORDER BY` clause. These two statements tell the query to pull the five oldest records from the table.

```
<cfquery name="latest_pieces" datasource="sample_database">
    SELECT Top 5 title, *
    FROM gallery
    ORDER BY create_dt DESC
```

```
    </cfquery>
    <cfoutput>
        <cfloop query="latest_pieces">
            <li><a href="gallery.cfm?id=#id#" class="linklist1">
                #title#</a></li>
        </cfloop>
    </cfoutput>
```

Another thing to note about the looped <LI> elements in this example is how the title and id variables for each record are dynamically output with that record. Each looped element links to the gallery.cfm page; however, an id variable is passed with each hyperlink that is clicked, allowing other code to pull data for that linked item and display it accordingly. Figure 2.8 shows how the data appears when the <LI> elements are repeatedly output between the <UL> XHTML tag.

FIGURE 2.8 Results of live data output using the <CFLOOP> tag.

Once the ColdFusion server processes the query and code, along with the rest of the page, everything is output to the browser in CSS and XHTML. When looking at the output results, it appears that everything was hard-coded instead of dynamically output.

```
    <!DOCTYPE html PUBLIC "-//W3C//DTD XHTML 1.0 Transitional//EN"
        "DTD/xhtml1-transitional.dtd">
    <html><head><title>Design</title>
    <meta http-equiv="Content-Type" content="text/html;
        charset=iso-8859-1" />
    <!-- link to main stylesheet that control text sizes and colors,
        among other things -->
    <link rel="stylesheet" href="mainstyle.css" type="text/css" />
    </head>
```

```
<body>
<div id="a5-body-center">
    <div id="a5-body">
<!-- ###### header start ###### -->
            <div id="a5-header">
            <div id="a5-logo">
                <a href="index.cfm"><img src="images/logo.gif"
                    width="405" height="70" alt="" border="0" /></a>
            </div>
            <div id="a5-menu-box">
                <div id="a5-menu">
                    <a href="index.cfm"><span style="color:#ffffff;
                        font-size:21px;font-weight:normal;">1 
                        </span> home</a>   
                    <a href="about.cfm"><span style="color:#ffffff;
                        font-size:21px;font-weight:normal;">2 
                        </span> about the work </a>   
                        <a href="gallery.cfm"><span style="color:
                        #ffffff;font-size:21px;font-weight:normal;
                        ">3 </span> gallery</a>  
                         
                    <a href="artist.cfm"><span style="color:#ffffff;
                        font-size:21px;font-weight:normal;">4 
                        </span> the artist</a>   
                    <a href="contact.cfm"><span style="color:#ffffff;
                        font-size:21px;font-weight:normal;">5 
                        </span> contact</a>   
                </div>
            </div>
            <div id="a5-phone">
                555.555.5555
            </div>
            <img src="images/image-top-right.jpg" width="56"
                height="43" alt="" border="0" style="position:absolute;
                top:66px; right:32px;" />
    </div>
<!-- ###### header end ###### -->
        <div id="a5-main-content">
<!-- ###### column left start ###### -->
            <div id="a5-column-left">
                <div id="a5-column-left-top">
                    Duis autem vel eum iriure dolor in hendrerit in
                        vulputate velit esse molestie consequat, vel
                        illum dolore eu feugiat nulla facilisis at
                        vero eros et accumsan et iusto odio
                        dignissim qui blandit praesent luptatum
                        zzril deleni ... <a href="about.cfm">more</a>
                </div>
                <div id="a5-column-left-bottom">
                    <div id="image-bottom-left">
                        <img src="images/image-bottom-left.jpg"
                            width="268" height="220" alt=""
                            border="0" />
                    </div>
                        <div id="image-bottom-center-left">
```

```
                          <img src="images/image-bottom-center-left.jpg"
                               width="95" height="95" alt=""
                               border="0" />
                </div>
                    <div id="image-bottom-center-right">
                    <img src="images/image-bottom-center-right.jpg"
                               width="95" height="95" alt=""
                               border="0" />
                </div>
            </div>
<!-- ###### copyright start ###### -->
            <div id="a5-copyright">
                &copy; copyright 2006 | your company |
                        all rights reserved
                <p>
                    <a href="http://validator.w3.org/
                    check?uri=referer"><img
                               src="http://www.w3.org/Icons/valid-xhtml10"
                        alt="Valid XHTML 1.0 Transitional"
                           height="31" width="88" border="0" /></a>
                    <a href="http://jigsaw.w3.org/css-validator/">
                    <img style="border:0;width:88px;height:31px"
                               src="http://jigsaw.w3.org/
                               css-validator/images/vcss"
                               alt="Valid CSS!" />
                    </a>
                    </p>
                </div>
<!-- ###### copyright end ###### -->
            </div>
<!-- ###### column left end ###### -->
<!-- ###### column right start ###### -->
            <div id="a5-column-right">
                <div id="a5-column-right-top">
                    <b>Latest Pieces To View</b>
                    <ul id="list-right-top">
                            <li><a href="gallery.cfm?id=7" class=
                                "linklist1">Italian Market</a></li>
                        .   <li><a href="gallery.cfm?id=6" class=
                                "linklist1">Farm Tree</a></li>
                            <li><a href="gallery.cfm?id=5" class=
                                "linklist1">Red Couch</a></li>
                            <li><a href="gallery.cfm?id=4" class=
                                "linklist1">Day of Boating</a></li>
                            <li><a href="gallery.cfm?id=3" class=
                                "linklist1">Lake Como Couple</a></li>
                    </ul>
                </div>
                <div id="a5-column-right-bottom">
                    <img src="images/image-bottom-right.jpg"
                        width="216" height="220" alt="" border="0" />
                </div>
            </div>
<!-- ###### column right end ###### -->
        </div>
    </div>
```

```
        </div>
        </body>
        </html>
```

Creating Dynamic Form Drop Downs

Dynamic drop downs are extremely powerful because they can be output using live data. Not only is all the data updated each time a page is hit, but it also allows the developer to pass data from a controlled form element so the query on the other end will have the correct data to process. Using the `<CFOUTPUT>` or `<CLOOP>` tag allows drop downs to be dynamically output, similarly to how the previous `<UL>` list in Figure 2.8 was created. Dynamic drop downs can be used in various ways. In the following example the dynamic Latest Pieces to View section is used with a drop-down menu instead of a `<UL>` list (see Figure 2.9).

```
<form method="post" action="gallery.cfm" name="latest_pieces">
<select name="individual_piece" size="1">
        <option value="All">Select All Pieces</option>
<cfquery name="latest_pieces" datasource="sample_database">
        SELECT *
        FROM gallery
        ORDER BY title
    </cfquery>
    <cfoutput query="latest_pieces">
            <option value="#id#">#title#</option>
            </cfoutput>
    </select>
</form>
```

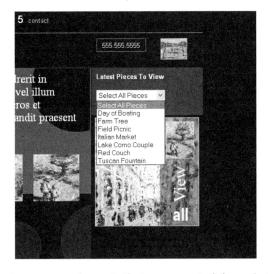

FIGURE 2.9   Output `<OPTION>` elements that were created dynamically by looping data.

There are several things to note about this example:

- The query is told to pull ALL data from the Gallery table because of the wildcard * in the SELECT clause.
- This query orders the items by title, which will output them alphabetically.
- The form is posting to the gallery.cfm page, using the action attributes in the form tag.
- The variable being passed is included in the value attributes in the looped <OPTION> elements in the <SELECT> form field.
- Both the id and title variables are being dynamically output with each item the query loops through the data results.
- The <CFQUERY> tag can be included inside or outside the <SELECT> form field, as long as the query is run in the code before it's called. If the query is run after the code that calls it, the ColdFusion server will output an error message because it won't have data to output.

Another advantage to using the drop down in this instance is that the developer can output many more items while taking up considerably less height. Many sites use dynamic drop downs to conserve space. Figure 2.10 displays the limited vertical height the drop down takes up compared to the output <UL> list:

FIGURE 2.10 Difference in height of an unordered list versus a <SELECT> form field.

Conditional Statements That Customize Content

Customizing content for different situations is another reason db-driven sites are so powerful. If, for instance, the developer wants to switch the small painting in the header with another painting that contains cross-selling text below it only on the About the Work page, an IF statement would work perfectly. To accomplish this, a condition must first be set so the server knows when the user is on the About the Work page. One way to do this is for each page to be saved on its own, with a variable called page set on the About the Work page. Following is the code to set such a variable:

```
<cfset page = "about">
```

This variable can be set anywhere on the page as long as it is above the code that requires it to be processed. In this example, it is placed above all other code.

Then, in the header.cfm include file, the developer can write a <CFIF> statement that says, "If the page called is the About the Work page, replace the existing image in this location with the other one." To do so, the developer would wrap a conditional statement around the code that normally calls the original image, such as in the following code:

```
<cfif page IS "about">
    <img src="images/sunflowers.jpg" width="56" height="58" alt=""
        border="0" style="position:absolute; top:66px; right:32px;" />
<br />View "Sunflowers"
<cfelse>
    <img src="images/image-top-right.jpg" width="56" height="43" alt=""
        border="0" style="position:absolute; top:66px; right:32px;" />
</cfif>
```

A little trick in writing conditional statements and queries is to first write out in English what the code is supposed to do. The developer then writes the code to do exactly as it is written. This allows the developer to make sure all the conditions are worked out in his mind before programming.

This replaces the image-top-right.jpg image with the sunflowers.jpg image, which is 15 pixels higher. Figure 2.11 shows the header on any page other than the About the Work page.

FIGURE 2.11   Header on any page other than the About the Work page.

Figure 2.12 shows the header when the user is on the About the Work page. If the developer wanted to replace the image with text, only the first <CFIF> statement would need to be replaced with whatever the developer wanted to show.

FIGURE 2.12   Header on the About the Work page, with the right image replaced and heightened by 15 pixels.

If the header.cfm include file were placed back into the About the Work page, the code, from the header area and above, would look like the following.

```
<cfset page = "about">
<!DOCTYPE html PUBLIC "-//W3C//DTD XHTML 1.0 Transitional//EN"
    "DTD/xhtml1-transitional.dtd">
<html><head><title>Design</title>
<meta http-equiv="Content-Type" content="text/html;
    charset=iso-8859-1" />
<!-- link to main stylesheet that controls text sizes and colors,
    among other things -->
<link rel="stylesheet" href="mainstyle.css" type="text/css" />
</head>
<body>
<div id="a5-body-center">
    <div id="a5-body">
<!-- ###### header start ###### -->
    <div id="a5-header">
        <div id="a5-logo">
            <a href="index.htm"><img src="images/logo.gif"
                width="405" height="70" alt="" border="0" /></a>
        </div>
        <div id="a5-menu-box">
            <div id="a5-menu">
                <a href="index.cfm"><span style="color:#ffffff;
                    font-size:21px;font-weight:normal;">1 
                    </span> home</a>   
                <a href="about.cfm"><span style="color:#ffffff;
                    font-size:21px;font-weight:normal;">2 
                    </span> about the work </a>   
                <a href="gallery.cfm"><span style="color:#ffffff;
                    font-size:21px;font-weight:normal;">3 
                    </span> gallery</a>   
                <a href="artist.cfm"><span style="color:#ffffff;
                    font-size:21px;font-weight:normal;">4 
                    </span> the artist</a>   
                <a href="contact.cfm"><span style="color:#ffffff;
                    font-size:21px;font-weight:normal;">5 
                    </span> contact</a>   
```

```
            </div>
        </div>
        <div id="a5-phone">
            555.555.5555
        </div>
        <cfif page IS "about">
            <img src="images/sunflowers.jpg" width="56" height="58"
                alt="" border="0" style="position:absolute;
                top:66px; right:32px;" />
            <br />View "Sunflowers"
        <cfelse>
            <img src="images/image-top-right.jpg" width="56"
                height="43" alt="" border="0" style="position:
                absolute; top:66px; right:32px;" />
        </cfif>
    </div>
<!-- ###### header end ###### -->
```

Incrementing Images

Because content can be dynamically changed on a db-driven site, designers and developers have great flexibility in how they can design sites. One frequently used type of functionality involves rotating images. Rotating images can either be selected randomly from a specified group or can be changed incrementally. When they are so changed, image 1 is displayed the first time the page is visited, image 2 the second time, image 3 the third time, and so on. The process then eventually loops back around to image 1. Rotating banner ads (see Figure 2.13) typically require more controlled output, which is why they are often changed incrementally.

FIGURE 2.13 Web page with rotating banner ad in the right column.

While there are different ways of incrementing images, using a session variable to keep track of the image number is an easy way. Following are the steps to this method:

1. **Save images with a consistent naming convention.** The developer is going to want to name all the images with the same base file name, except for a number, saved as a session variable, which is incremented with each image. For example, three separate images could be named:

   - `banner_right_bottom_1.jpg`
   - `banner_right_bottom_2.jpg`
   - `banner_right_bottom_3.jpg`

All three names are the same except for the number that is to be incremented. This number is the variable that is incremented each time the page is viewed.

2. **Set a default session variable for the number of the first image to be displayed.** The code is going to need a number to begin using and incrementing. The following code sets that number as a session variable, which can be accessed from any page that would include the rotating banner functionality:

```
<cflock scope="session" timeout="15" type="EXCLUSIVE">
    <cfparam name="session.image_number" default="1">
</cflock>
```

The session variable can be set either on the page that calls it or on the `Application.` `cfm` *page.*

3. **Add an image tag with a variable in the name.** By adding the `#session.image_number#` variable to the XHTML image tag, the image name will be created dynamically each time the page is viewed. Following is the code that dynamically changes the image name:

```
<cfoutput>
    <a href="gallery.cfm"><img src="images/banner-right-bottom-#session.
        image_number#.jpg" width="216" height="220" alt=""
        border="0" /></a>
<cfoutput>
```

When the code is interpreted, the resulting XHTML in the output page will look like the following:

```
<a href="gallery.cfm"><img src="images/banner-right-bottom-1.jpg"
    width="216" height="220" alt="" border="0" /></a>
```

4. **Write conditional code that determines whether to increment the variable by 1 or reset it to 1 if the final number has been reached.** If the developer wants to use three images, the incremented variable (`session.image_number`) cannot ever be 4

because no fourth image was created. Instead, once it changes to 3, it must be reset to 1. If the value is not 3 yet, it will be incremented by 1. Following is the code to increment and reset the variable value:

```
<cfif session.image_number IS "3">
    <cfset session.image_number = "1">
     <cfelse>
    <cfset session.image_number = incrementvalue(session.image_number)>
</cfif>
```

When the code has been completed, the `<IMG>` tag (`<img  src="images/banner-right-bottom-#session.image_number#.jpg" width="216" height="220" alt="" border="0" />`) will be replaced by the following code:

```
<cflock scope="session" timeout="15" type="EXCLUSIVE">
    <cfparam name="session.image_number" default="1">
</cflock>
<cfoutput>
    <a href="gallery.cfm"><img src="images/banner-right-bottom-
        #session.image_number#.jpg" width="216" height="220"
        alt="" border="0" /></a>
<cfif session.image_number IS "3">
        <cfset session.image_number = "1">
    <cfelse>
        <cfset session.image_number = incrementvalue
            (session.image_number)>
    </cfif>
</cfoutput>
```

Figure 2.14 illustrates how the codes works. The image is a screenshot of the banner ad in Figure 2.13, along with screenshots of the same page with the banner ad rotating after having been clicked two separate times.

FIGURE 2.14   Screenshots of a page with a rotating banner after having been clicked three times.

RECURSIVE PAGES

When submitting data or passing variables in db-driven sites, the developer can send and process the data either to a separate page (see Figure 2.15) or to the same page.

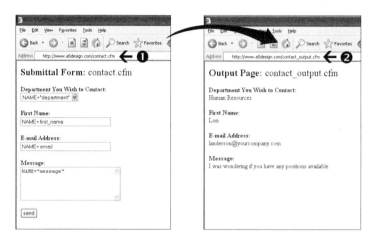

FIGURE 2.15   Db-driven page that passes data to a separate page (i.e., `contact.cfm` to `contact_output.cfm`).

A page that sends and processes data to itself is called a recursive page (see Figure 2.16). While such a page will have more code and become slightly more complex, it also reduces the number of pages in a Web site and can make managing a db-driven page simpler. When the page links or posts data to itself, it passes a variable that tells it which section of code to process and/or display. For example, a contact page with an email form can submit the data to itself with a variable called `section` with a value of `process_form`. When the page receives the form data, along with the variable value `process_form`, it will process a separate piece of code. If the variable value is different than `process_form`, a different piece of code will be processed.

There are only three basic steps to creating and processing a recursive page:

1. Create a page called `sample.cfm` and create a conditional statement that processes different code, depending on the value of a variable passed or a default variable:

```
<cfif section IS "showform">
    This section of the conditional statement shows the form when it
        hasn't been processed.
<cfelseif section IS "showmap">
    This section shows an enlarged version of the contact map,
        excluding the form.
```

```
<cfelse>
    This section will process the form if the value of the section
        variable is anything other than showform, the first condition
        of the page, or showmap, which is the second condition of
        the page.
</cfif>
```

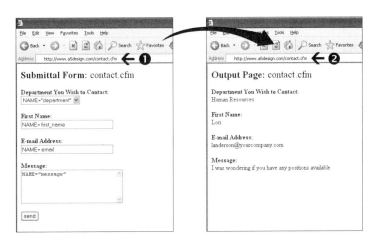

FIGURE 2.16   Recursive page that sends form data to itself to be processed.

2. Set a default variable the page can use to process if it doesn't receive the specified variable:

```
<cfparam name="section" default="showform">
<cfif section IS "showform">
    This section of the conditional statement shows the form when it
        hasn't been processed.
<cfelseif section IS "showmap">
    This section shows an enlarged version of the contact map,
        excluding the form.
<cfelse>
    This section will process the form if the value of the "section"
        variable is anything other than "showform," the first condition
        of the page, or "showmap," which is the second condition of
        the page.
</cfif>
```

Setting a default value ensures that the conditional statement will not produce an error statement if the variable is not passed from a form or URL.

3. Create a hyperlink or form on the page that passes the variable section to itself:

```
<a href="sample.cfm?section=showmap">Hyperlink that hits the page and
    processes the section that shows the map</a>
```

or

```
<form action="sample.cfm" method="post">
<input type="input" name="email" size="20" />
<input type="hidden" name="section" value="processform" />
    <input type="submit" value="submit form" />
</form>
```

When submitting a form on a recursive page, using a hidden form field is a good way to pass the variable to be processed without the user seeing it. While it acts like a normal <INPUT> field, it takes up no visible space on the page. This, in fact, is how many variables can be passed. The following code shows how such functionality can be included in a Web page:

```
<!DOCTYPE html PUBLIC "-//W3C//DTD XHTML 1.0 Transitional//EN"
    "DTD/xhtml1-transitional.dtd">
<html><head><title>Design</title>
<meta http-equiv="Content-Type" content="text/html;
    charset=iso-8859-1" />
<!-- link to main stylesheet that control text sizes and colors, among
    other things -->
<link rel="stylesheet" href="mainstyle.css" type="text/css" />
</head>
<body>
<div id="a5-body-center">
    <div id="a5-body">
<!-- ###### header start ###### -->
    <cfinclude template="header.cfm">
<!-- ###### header end ###### -->
        <div id="a5-main-content">
<!-- ###### column left start ###### -->
            <div id="a5-column-left">
                <div id="a5-column-left-top-sl">
                    <div id="a5-sl-title">
                        contact
                    </div>
<cfif section IS "showform">
    This section of the conditional statement shows the form when it
        hasn't been processed.
The following hyperlink would send the user to the map section of the
    page. <a href="sample.cfm?section=showmap">Hyperlink that hits the
    page and processes the section that shows the map</a>
The "hidden" value in the following form would send the user to the
    section that processes the form:
<form action="sample.cfm" method="post">
<input type="input" name="email" size="20" />
<input type="hidden" name="section" value="processform" />
                        <input type="submit" value="submit form" />
</form>
<cfelseif section IS "showmap">
    This section shows an enlarged version of the contact map,
        excluding the form.
<cfelse>
This section will process the form if the value of the "section"
    variable is anything other than "showform," which is the first
```

```
            condition or "showmap," which is the value of the second
            condition.
</cfif>
                            </div>
<!-- ###### copyright start ###### -->
                    <div id="a5-copyright">
                        &copy; copyright 2006 | your company |
                            all rights reserved
                        <p>
                            <a href="http://validator.w3.org/check?
                            uri=referer"><img
                                src="http://www.w3.org/Icons/valid-xhtml10"
                                alt="Valid XHTML 1.0 Transitional"
                                height="31" width="88" border="0" /></a>

                            <a href="http://jigsaw.w3.org/css-validator/">
                            <img style="border:0;width:88px;height:31px"
                                src="http://jigsaw.w3.org/css-
                                validator/images/vcss"
                                alt="Valid CSS!" />
                            </a>
                        </p>
                    </div>
<!-- ###### copyright end ###### -->
            </div>
<!-- ###### column left end ###### -->
<!-- ###### column right start ###### -->
            <div id="a5-column-right">
                <div id="a5-column-right-top">
                    <b>Latest Pieces To View</b>
                    <ul id="list-right-top">
                    <cfquery name="latest_pieces" datasource=
                        "sample_database">
                        SELECT Top 5 title, *
                        FROM gallery
                        ORDER BY create_dt DESC
                    </cfquery>

                    <cfoutput>
                        <cfloop query="latest_pieces">
                            <li><a href="gallery.cfm?id=#id#"
                                class="linklist1">#title#</a></li>
                        </cfloop>
                    </cfoutput>
                    </ul>
                </div>
                <div id="a5-column-right-bottom">
                    <cflock scope="session" timeout="15"
                        type="EXCLUSIVE">
                    <cfparam name="session.image_number" default="1">
                    </cflock>
                    <cfoutput>
                        <a href="gallery.cfm"><img src="images/banner-
                            right-bottom-#session.image_number#.jpg"
                            width="216" height="220" alt="" border="0"
                            /></a>
```

```
                            <cfif session.image_number IS "3">
                                <cfset session.image_number = "1">
                            <cfelse>
                                <cfset session.image_number =
                                    incrementvalue(session.image_number)>
                            </cfif>
                        </cfoutput>
                    </div>
                </div>
        <!-- ###### column right end ###### -->
                </div>
        </div>
        </div>
        </body>
        </html>
```

Some recursive pages don't have any XHTML or CSS code. Such a page may only add data to the database and then redirect the user to another page on the site.

NOTE

EMAIL FORM

Many db-driven sites offer email forms for users to submit comments or questions. All the previously mentioned languages provide the developer with the ability to use such functionality. It is very simple to program, using ColdFusion's <CFMAIL> tag. As long as the ColdFusion server is properly pointing to the email server, the developer simply needs to use the tag. Following are the steps involved with creating a recursive email form:

1. **Add the conditional code framework that allows the page to be recursive.** While making an email form recursive is not necessary, it does limit the number of pages a developer needs to create and maintain. Following is the framework for the example email form:

```
<cfparam name="section" default="showform">

<cfif section IS "showform">
    This is where the e-mail form goes.
<cfelse>
    This is where the <CFMAIL> tag is programmed, along with the text
        the user will see after the form is processed.
</cfif>
```

When the form is submitted, the conditional statement requires the value of the section variable to be anything except showform. In this example, the value of the variable will be submitform and be hidden in an XHTML element.

2. **Add the XHTML form to the default conditional statement.** A developer could add a more complex form that validates either client-side or server-side;

however, for the sake of simplicity this form contains only the basics (see Figure 2.17). The two things to note are that the form is submitting to itself in the action attribute of the <FORM> tag and the variable section is added as a hidden field right above the Submit button.

```
<form action="contact.cfm" method="post">
<b><span style="color:#DAF4FC;">Want to join our mailing list?
    </span></b>
<br />
Please fill out the following form to receive e-mails about upcoming
    shows and events:
<br />
<p>
<b>First Name:</b><br />
<input type="Text" name="first_name" size="35" />
</p>
<p>
<b>E-mail Address:</b><br />
<input type="Text" name="from_email_address" size="35" />
</p>
<p>
<b>Message:</b><br />
<textarea cols="30" rows="5" name="message"></textarea>
</p>
<p>
<input type="hidden" name="section" value="submitform" />
<input type="submit" value="send" border="0" />
</p>
</form>
```

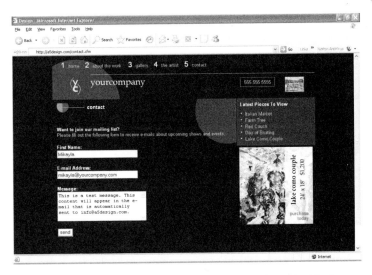

FIGURE 2.17 The form when output and populated inside the framework of the Web page.

3. **Add the <CFMAIL> tag and its appropriate code in the <CFELSE> condition.**
Following is a stripped-down version of the <CFMAIL> tag and how the text can be output and formatted in the tag. It is important to note that everything between the opening and closing <CFMAIL> tags is what is emailed. The content below the tag is what appears in the browser once the email is sent (see Figure 2.18).

```
<cfmail to="info@a5design.com"
        from = "#from_email_address#"
            subject = "E-mail from Web Site"
        type = "html"
        timeout=10>
First Name: #first_name#<br />
        E-mail Address: #from_email_address#<br />
        #message#
</cfmail>
    <cfoutput>
        Thank you for contacting us, #first_name#. We will contact
            you shortly.
    </cfoutput>
```

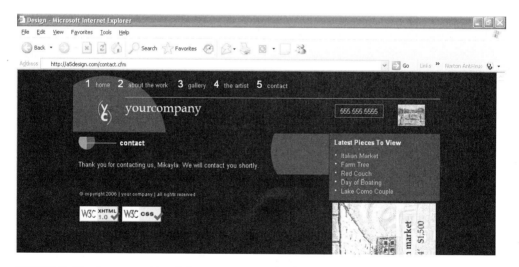

FIGURE 2.18 Output results of the <CFMAIL> tag in the recursive page.

The email that is sent from the ColdFusion server can be formatted using XHTML. It also can be sent similarly to how the <PRE> tag works, where the code is output exactly as it is included in the code. Figure 2.19 illustrates how the email will appear with the limited amount of XHTML code that is included in this example.

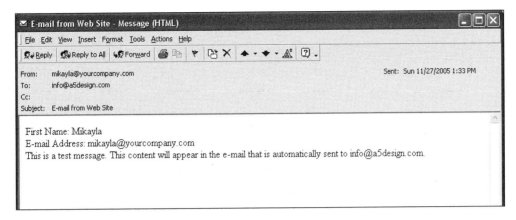

FIGURE 2.19   Results of email that was sent from the `<CFMAIL>` tag.

Following is the code for the entire email form page:

```
<!DOCTYPE html PUBLIC "-//W3C//DTD XHTML 1.0 Transitional//EN"
    "DTD/xhtml1-transitional.dtd">
<html><head><title>Design</title>
<meta http-equiv="Content-Type" content="text/html; charset=iso-8859-1" />
<!-- link to main stylesheet that controls text sizes and colors,
    among other things -->
<link rel="stylesheet" href="mainstyle.css" type="text/css" />
</head>
<body>
<div id="a5-body-center">
    <div id="a5-body">
<!-- ###### header start ###### -->
    <cfinclude template="header.cfm">
<!-- ###### header end ###### -->
        <div id="a5-main-content">
<!-- ###### column left start ###### -- >
            <div id="a5-column-left">
                <div id="a5-column-left-top-sl">
                    <div id="a5-sl-title">
                        contact
                    </div>
                    <cfparam name="section" default="showform">
                    <cfif section IS "showform">
                    <form action="2_17.cfm" method="post">
                        <b><span style="color:#DAF4FC;">Want to join
                            our mailing list?</span></b>
                        <br />
                            Please fill out the following form to
                            receive e-mails about upcoming shows and events:
                        <br />
                        <p>
```

```
                              <b>First Name:</b><br />
                              <input type="Text" name="first_name"
                                 size="35" />
                  </p>
                  <p>

                              <b>E-mail Address:</b><br />
                              <input type="Text" name="from_email_
                                 address" size="35" />
                  </p>
                  <p>

                              <b>Message:</b><br />
                              <textarea cols="30" rows="5"
                                 name="message"></textarea>
                  </p>
                  <p>

                                 <input type="hidden" name="section"
                                 value="submitform" />
                              <input type="submit" value="send"
                                 border="0" />
                  </p>
                  </form>

         <cfelse>
                  <cfmail to="info@a5design.com"
                      from = "#from_email_address#"
                      subject = "E-mail from Web Site"
                      type = "html"
                      timeout=10>
                      First Name: #first_name#<br />
                      E-mail Address: #from_email_address#<br />
                      #message#
                  </cfmail>
         <cfoutput>
                      Thank you for contacting us, #first_name#.
                         We will contact you shortly.
                  </cfoutput>
         </cfif>
      </div>
<!-- ###### copyright start ###### -->
            <div id="a5-copyright">
               &copy; copyright 2006 | your company |
                  all rights reserved
               <p>
                  <a href="http://validator.w3.org/check?uri=referer">
                   <img
                      src="http://www.w3.org/Icons/valid-xhtml10"
                      alt="Valid XHTML 1.0 Transitional"
                         height="31" width="88" border="0" /></a>

            <a href="http://jigsaw.w3.org/css-validator/">
               <img style="border:0;width:88px;height:31px"
                      src="http://jigsaw.w3.org/css-
                         validator/images/vcss"
                      alt="Valid CSS!" />
```

```
                                    </a>
                                    </p>
                            </div>
<!-- ###### copyright end ###### -->
                        </div>
<!-- ###### column left end ###### -->
<!-- ###### column right start ###### -->
                        <div id="a5-column-right">
                            <div id="a5-column-right-top">
                                <b>Latest Pieces To View</b>
                                <ul id="list-right-top">
                                <cfquery name="latest_pieces" datasource=
                                    "sample_database">
                                    SELECT Top 5 title, *
                                    FROM gallery
                                    ORDER BY create_dt DESC
                                </cfquery>

                                <cfoutput>
                                    <cfloop query="latest_pieces">
                                        <li><a href="gallery.cfm?id=#id#"
                                            class="linklist1">#title#</a></li>
                                    </cfloop>
                                </cfoutput>
                                </ul>
                            </div>
                            <div id="a5-column-right-bottom">
                                <cflock scope="session" timeout="15"
                                    type="EXCLUSIVE">
                                    <cfparam name="session.image_number"
                                        default="1">
                                </cflock>
                                <cfoutput>
                                <a href="gallery.cfm"><img src="images/
                                    banner-right-bottom-#session.image_
                                    number#.jpg" width="216" height="220"
                                    alt="" border="0" /></a>
                                    <cfif session.image_number IS "3">
                                        <cfset session.image_number = "1">
                                    <cfelse>
                                    <cfset session.image_number =
                                        incrementvalue(session.image_number)>
                                    </cfif>
                                </cfoutput>
                            </div>
                        </div>
<!-- ###### column right end ###### -->
                    </div>
                </div>
        </div>
    </body>
    </html>
```

SUMMARY

While db-driven programming can seem very complicated, nearly all such programming incorporates the fundamentals included in this chapter. Examples of these fundamentals include loops, conditional statements, include files, dynamic drop downs, incrementing images, recursive pages, and an email form. More important than the example code are the concepts, which can be used in a variety of creative ways when building db-driven sites.

3 Understanding E-Commerce Functionality

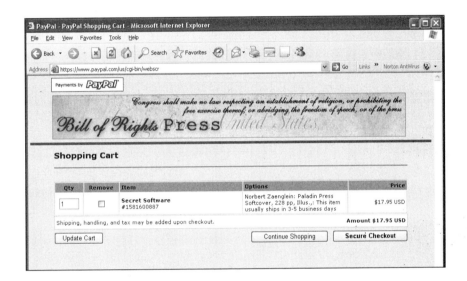

As Web development has evolved over the past decade, e-commerce sites have become very common. This is due, in large part, to the solutions that have been made available over the past several years. What used to require an experienced developer to program can now be accomplished by a novice within a matter of minutes or hours, depending on the developer's experience. That's not to say, though, that there are not more complicated solutions requiring more sophisticated programming. There simply are a growing number of solutions that range from the ease of using a service, such as PayPal®, to services that return data to a developer to add to a site's database. Thus, owing to the variety available, this chapter cannot adequately explain all options. Rather, it is designed to give the novice developer a basic understanding of the general spectrum of options available.

HOW THE E-COMMERCE PROCESS WORKS

Explaining the entire e-commerce process can quickly become involved. Because there are so many options available, it is easier to start with the high-level process. The three generic steps are:

1. The user submits an order to be processed.
2. The order is received, verified, and returned for further processing or denial.
3. The completed or rejected order is returned to the user.

These three steps were intentionally written to be overly general because there are a variety of options for each of them. For instance, a user can submit an order to a payment gateway either by a hyperlink or by a shopping cart. The order can be received by a payment gateway that sends the data on to another entity or it can be received by a business that does not necessarily identify itself as a payment gateway. While an order may appear to be completed, it may be entered into a pool of other orders that are processed later.

The two components to creating an e-commerce solution are:

- The Web site side of the equation, which usually involves a shopping cart
- The processing of a credit card number and order information

The shopping cart component is discussed in more depth later in this chapter. As for credit card and order processing, there are generally nine steps to successful processing (see Figure 3.1):

1. The user submits an order through a secure (https) connection to the Web site.
2. The Web site processes the order, which can include adding sales tax and shipping costs, among other things.
3. The Web site submits the order to a payment gateway, such as VeriSign® or Authorize.net.
4. The payment gateway then submits the credit card number to the client's merchant account for further processing.
5. The merchant account passes the credit card number to the credit card interchange.
6. The credit card interchange routes the data to the credit card issuer for approval or denial of funds withdrawal.
7. The credit card interchange deposits the money into the merchant account and informs the payment gateway of a successful transaction.
8. The payment gateway submits the confirmation back to the Web server. At this point, the order can be simply emailed or stored in a database on the payment gateway's server, the client's server, or both.
9. The Web server serves up the results to the user's browser.

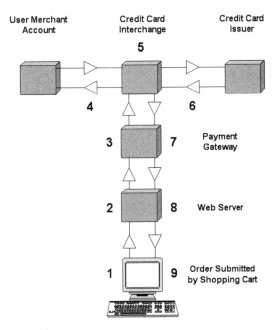

FIGURE 3.1   Nine general steps to submitting, confirming, and returning data for an e-commerce order.

If the order is denied by the credit card issuer at step 7, the credit card interchange sends back the reason(s) for denial to the payment gateway.

CREDIT CARD PROCESSING OPTIONS

Depending on site requirements, many e-commerce solutions are available to a developer. Barring programming considerations, a developer must answer three questions before selecting a solution or variety of options for a client:

- Does the client want data to be stored in their database or in the payment gateway's database?
- Does the client want the user to visually leave their site to process billing information (e.g., credit card information and personal information associated with that credit card)? While all orders physically leave the site, the user does not need to see a visual difference.
- Does the client want to pay for fees associated with online credit card processing?

The answers to these questions will help a developer decide between using one of the following three general processing solutions: transparent, semitransparent, or batched and/or terminal processing.

Transparent Processing

Sometimes a client wants the user to never leave the look and feel of a site so as to give a more professional complete shopping experience. One way to do this is to use an e-commerce solution that involves code and/or a processing engine from a payment gateway. When the user clicks to submit an order after entering billing information on the site, the data is sent to the payment gateway, where it handles the processing and returns the confirmation or denial code to a specified page on the site. That page is then programmed to process the results, which usually involves outputting the results, adding the data to the client's database, and finally, emailing a confirmation receipt of the order.

Many payment processors provide solutions for the various programming languages. Listing 3.1 is the code VeriSign has provided ColdFusion developers in the past, which is a custom tag that makes it easy to pass on the amount in the shopping cart to the processor:

LISTING 3.1   ColdFusion code provided by VeriSign

```
<CFX_PAYFLOWPRO QUERY        = "RESULT"
     HOSTADDRESS    = "payflow.verisign.com"
     HOSTPORT       = "443"
     TIMEOUT        = "30"
     PROXYADDRESS   = ""
     PROXYPORT      = ""
     PROXYLOGON     = ""
     PROXYPASSWORD  = ""
     TRXTYPE        = "S"
     TENDER         = "C"
     PARTNER        = "VeriSign"
     USER           = "Client Name Goes Here"
     PWD            = "Client Password Goes Here"
     ACCT           = "Predetermined Account Number Goes Here"
     EXPDATE        = "Expiration Date Goes Here"
     AMT            = "Amount Total Goes Here"
     COMMENT1       = "This is a comment - note that it is
        automatically escaped"
     COMMENT2       = "Embedded = and & work when escaped"
     CERTPATH   = "e:\cfpro\certs">
```

When configuring the account on VeriSign's side, the developer tells the gateway where to send the user after processing. The task is a simple redirect, so after the user enters billing information and clicks to check out (see Figure 3.2), the next page is the confirmation or denial page; between those two pages, the entire process of verifying a credit card occurs.

Allowing the user to enter credit card information on the Web site makes it is easy to maintain the look and feel of the site because it appears that the user has never left the site. Figure 3.3 is the confirmation/denial page the user is directed to after clicking Submit from the previous page (see Figure 3.2).

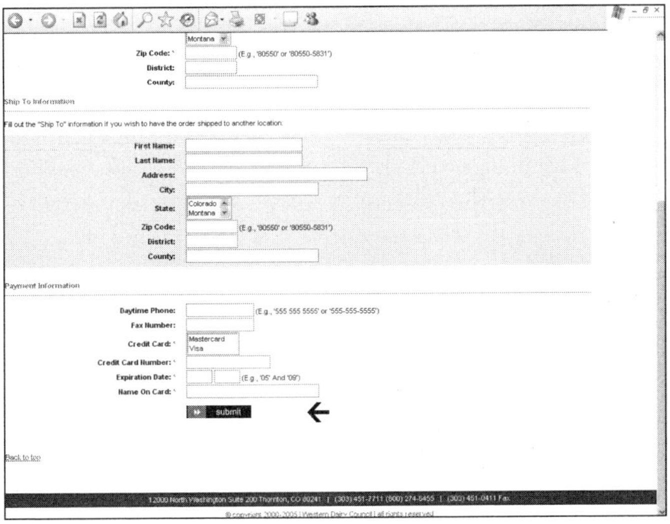

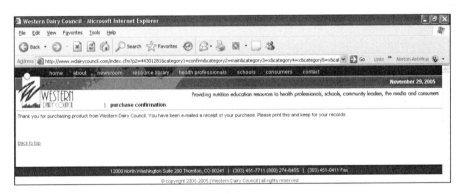

FIGURE 3.2   A page that collects billing information on a client's site. © 2006 Western Dairy Council. Used with permission.

FIGURE 3.3   Confirmation/denial page the user sees after submitting order and credit card information. © 2006 Western Dairy Council. Used with permission.

There are several advantages and disadvantages to transparent processing.

Advantages

■ The user remains within the framework of the site during the entire purchasing process.

■ Data is easily added to the client's database because the order information is already contained on the server. By having data in the client's database, the developer has full control to write additional code desired by the client, such as reporting pages.

Disadvantages

- It takes more time and expense to develop the code that submits and processes the orders.
- Payment gateways typically charge more for custom solutions than the less technical solutions they may offer.
- The client pays monthly expenses, such as usage fees for the payment gateway, credit card rates, and merchant account fees.
- The client needs to pay for a secure socket layer (SSL) certificate so the process is encrypted when the user enters billing information.

Semitransparent Processing

Sometimes it is good for some sites, such as startup mom-and-pop shops, to take baby steps when it comes to credit card processing. Until the site is showing critical-level usage and providing a return on the money, more expensive processing may not be the wisest use of resources. The money saved on processing fees can be used for marketing, which, in turn, may increase usage and then eventually be used for further development.

Some semitransparent processing solutions provide the perfect mix between the client being able to take credit card orders and not paying too much until the site is a proven success. One workable solution is when online companies offer to do all the processing and charge only on a per-transaction basis, rather than monthly fees in addition to a per-transaction basis. PayPal is such a company.

In the past if a user wanted to purchase a product using PayPal, that client had to set up a PayPal account. While the company still offers this solution, it now also offers the ability for the user to simply enter necessary billing information. This is where the *semi* part of the semitransparent processing occurs.

The way this process works is that when the user adds a product to purchase and/or wishes to check out, a link or form redirects the user to a customized page (see Figure 3.4) on that processor's server.

In some cases, such as one solution PayPal offers, the process involves outputting each item in the shopping cart and processing and storing the data. This is where the user can edit or delete items in the shopping cart or simply check out (see Figure 3.5).

The code involved with sending data to the cart is very basic. With PayPal, everything is based on the client's email address. The email address, along with other information, such as the price, is sent using the hyperlinked Add to Cart button. Following is the code required to submit information to PayPal, via a hyperlink:

```
<a href="https://www.paypal.com/cart/add=1&business=
    bob%40billofrightspress.com&item_name=Secret%20Software&item_number
    =1581600887&amount=17.95&on0=Norbert%20Zaenglein&os0=
    Paladin%20Press&on1=Softcover%2C%20228%20pp%2C%20Illus%2E%2C%20&os1
    =This%20item%20usually%20ships%20in%203%2D5%20business%20days
    " target="_new"><img src="http://www.billofrightspress.com/
```

```
inventory/images/button_add_to_cart.gif" width="100" height="19"
alt="" border="0"></a>
```

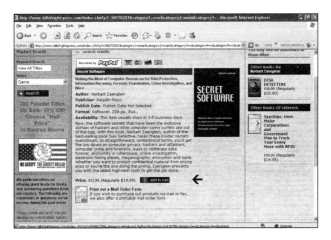

FIGURE 3.4   Add to Cart button that is a hyperlink that submits the product information to a PayPal account. © 2006 Bill of Rights Press. Used with permission.

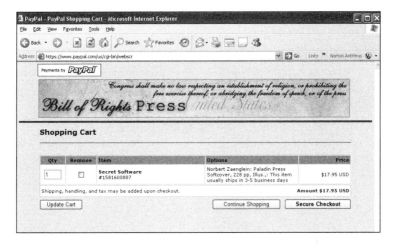

FIGURE 3.5   PayPal shopping cart that contains items after the user adds an item to the cart. © 2006   Bill of Rights Press. Used with permission.

Other solutions, such as VeriSign's PayFlow Link®, offer a similar, but slightly different solution. Rather than provide the shopping cart on its side, VeriSign allows for the site to pass the total dollar amount to be processed (see Figure 3.6), along with a description of items purchased.

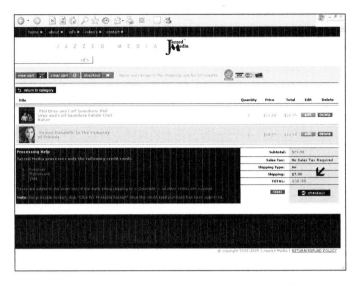

FIGURE 3.6   VeriSign's PayFlow Link solution allows the dollar amount to be passed to its servers to be processed. © 2006 Jazzed Media. Used with permission.

Once the order is processed, it is up to the developer to add order data to the client's database if that is a requirement of the site. Otherwise, VeriSign will simply store the order information, including a brief description of items and quantities purchased (see Figure 3.7), along with other information, on its own server.

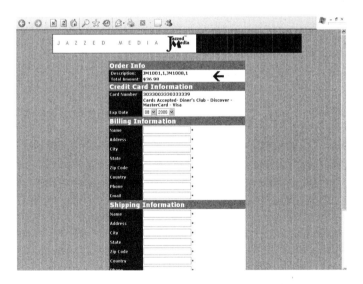

FIGURE 3.7   VeriSign's PayFlow Link allows for a brief description to be passed to and stored on its servers once an order is accepted. © 2006 Jazzed Media. Used with permission.

There are several advantages and disadvantages to semitransparent processing.

Advantages

- The client doesn't need to pay for an SSL certificate because the user is transferred to the site of the solution provider, such as PayPal or VeriSign, which provides a certificate.
- It takes very little time and expense to incorporate such a solution with an existing shopping cart.
- The costs involved with such solutions are considerably less than those of transparent processing.
- While data is stored in the provider's database, many existing tools are already available to the client, such as reporting functionality and shipping software that can print labels.

Disadvantages

- The user does not remain within the framework of the site during the entire purchasing process, resulting in the site looking less professional because such solutions are not as flexible in terms of design.
- Data is not as easily added to the client's database. In some instances it is not allowed, and other cases additional programming is required to provide such functionality.

Terminal-Processed and Batched Orders

Not all processing occurs instantaneously. A developer can design a site so that once the order is submitted, a temporary confirmation is sent to the client and the user. In this case the client, having received the order, can process the order via a credit card terminal or programmed batch that processes a large number of orders at once. Because this is a fully customized solution, the developer and client need to determine whether the expense of the additional customized programming is worth while in the long term.

SSL Certificate and Security

Whichever solution a developer offers, security should always be a priority. An SSL certificate needs to be purchased and loaded on a Web server so a developer can use the HTTPS scheme in all URLs.

To learn more about SSL certificates and their proper use, a developer can go to sites offering certificates, such as Thawte (*www.thawte.com*) and Network Solutions (*www.netsol.com*).

HOW A SHOPPING CART WORKS

It is easy to comprehend how a shopping cart works, just by clicking through the pages, but understanding how to program a cart first requires a basic overview of how the process works. A developer typically uses queries, loops, various content outputting methods, dynamic URLs, and session variables to build a cart. While there are different ways to program a shopping cart, following is an example of the general steps of one possible approach:

1. Output a list of products or one specific product (see number 1 in Figure 3.8) that the user can add to the cart. At this point, when the Add to Cart button is clicked, the developer can submit either all the information about that product or the `id` of that product to the next step, along with other specific user-selected information, such as quantity and size.

2. Add the item to an array that is saved as a session variable (see number 2 in Figure 3.8) and redirect the user back to wherever the developer chooses. The developer can either add all the information that was submitted or pull data from the database about that product, based on the `id` variable that was passed from the Add to Cart button. An array is a useful variable because it can store many data values under an individual index number (see Figure 3.9). When the array is saved as a session variable, it can be accessed from any page in the directory, allowing the developer to easily add, edit, delete, and output data.

3. Output the content of the completed array by looping over it on the page that lists the shopping cart items (see number 3 in Figure 3.8). The developer can either output data only from the final array variable (see number 4 in Figure 3.8) or pull and output additional data for each element by querying the database, using the product number saved for each indexed item in the array.

4. Calculate the subtotal and total based on various factors such as taxes, tax-exempt numbers, and shipping (see number 5 in Figure 3.8). This process can easily occur on one page or by a step-by-step process that occurs on several pages.

5. Submit the total dollar amount and any other order information to be processed to a payment gateway or other e-commerce solution (see number 6 in Figure 3.8).

When shopping-cart data is saved as an array, the developer needs to reference the index number to access elements in that indexed item. Figure 3.9 shows a close-up version of an array. Number 1 in the figure is the index number, and number 2 is a particular element (0502N) in that array.

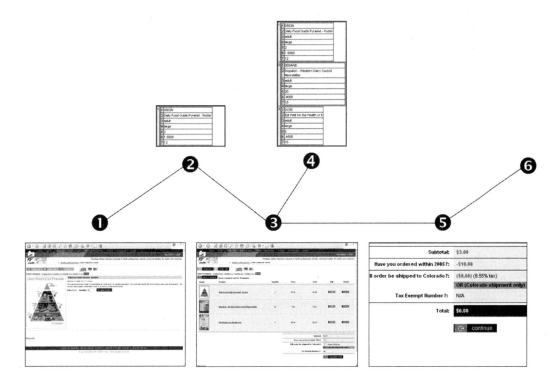

FIGURE 3.8   How data is collected and output using a shopping cart. © 2006 Western Dairy Council. Used with permission.

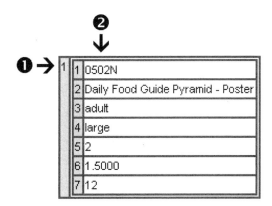

FIGURE 3.9   An array with the number 1 identifying the index number and the number 2 pointing toward the product number element, which in this example is 0502N. © 2006 Western Dairy Council. Used with permission.

SHOPPING CART OPTIONS

As with all Web technology, there seem to be too many possible solutions to problems unless a person has a checklist of required items. Shopping carts are no exceptions. By entering shopping cart software into a search engine, a developer can spend a week discovering all the choices there are, some of which include Miva, PayPal, and Yahoo® carts. Some questions a developer needs to consider when deciding on a shopping cart are:

- Is this software eventually going to be used for other clients with different technical requirements?
- Will it allow enough flexibility if the client asks for a more customized front end?
- Is it written in a language that will not require additional instruction?
- Are the process and coding style intuitive enough to avoid a high learning curve?
- How much does the software cost, and are subscription fees associated with it?

Each of these questions will lead a developer to either go with an out-of-the-box solution or make a case for writing a custom cart. If a custom cart is the answer, then the next section in this chapter will help provide a basic understanding of how code can be structured and written for various components of a shopping cart.

EXAMPLE PAGES OF A SHOPPING CART

Sometimes just seeing how a piece of code works can give a developer an idea of how to write a personalized version of the same functionality. The sample pages in this section are meant to do just that. Examples in this section are based on code used with *http://www.billofrightspress.com*.

Search Functionality

Not all sites have or need search functionality because they do not have many products in a cart. Rather, they can be dynamically created for pages with a limited number of products, such as a mom-and-pop shop with 20–30 products. For sites with many more categories, such as online bookstores, search functionality is usually necessary for the site's usability. Figure 3.10 shows the search functionality included in the top-left section of nearly every page on the site.

The search functionality allows for keyword searches, as well as searches by genre (see Figure 3.11). It is dynamically built, so any results that appear in the drop down contain at least one book in the database, guaranteeing results in the output page.

FIGURE 3.10   Home page with the search functionality included in the top-left section of nearly every page of the site. © 2006 Bill of Rights Press. Used with permission.

FIGURE 3.11   A drop-down menu that is dynamically populated each time the page is accessed, guaranteeing that the output page will produce results. © 2006 Bill of Rights Press. Used with permission.

Listing 3.2 is the section of code that is used create the search area:

LISTING 3.2   Search Area Code

```
<form method="post" action="search_parameters.cfm" name="search">
<tr>
    <td></td>
    <td align="left" valign="top" class="ochre2"><b>Keyword
        Search</b></td>
    <td></td>
</tr>
<tr>
    <td colspan="3"><img src="<cfoutput>#root#</cfoutput>/images/
        spacer.gif" width="1" height="2" alt="" border="0"></td>
</tr>
<tr>
    <td></td>
    <td align="left" valign="top">
        <input type="text" size="15" name="keywords" value="View
            All Titles">
    </td>
    <td></td>
</tr>
<tr>
    <td colspan="3"><img src="<cfoutput>#root#</cfoutput>/images/
        spacer.gif" width="1" height="5" alt="" border="0"></td>
</tr>
<tr>
    <td></td>
    <td align="left" valign="top" class="ochre2"><b>Genre</b></td>
    <td></td>
</tr>
<tr>
    <td colspan="3"><img src="<cfoutput>#root#</cfoutput>/images/
        spacer.gif" width="1" height="2" alt="" border="0"></td>
</tr>
<tr>
    <td></td>
    <td align="left" valign="top">
        <select name="genres" size="1">
            <option value="All">Genre</option>
            <cfquery datasource="freepress" name="search_categories">
                SELECT DISTINCT category1
                FROM store_inventory
                ORDER BY category1
            </cfquery>
            <cfoutput query="search_categories">
<option value="#category1#">#category1#</option>
</cfoutput>
        </select>
    </td>
    <td></td>
</tr>
<tr>
```

```
<td colspan="3"><img src="<cfoutput>#root#</cfoutput>/images/
    spacer.gif" width="1" height="15" alt="" border="0"></td>
</tr>
<tr>
    <td></td>
    <td align="left" valign="top">
    <input type="image" src="<cfoutput>#root#</cfoutput>/images/
        button-search.gif" border="0">
    </td>
    <td></td>
</tr>
</form>
```

Things to Note About the Code

- The form is sent to a page called search_parameters.cfm because all the search criteria are set up as session variables. This allows for various functionalities, such as providing the user the ability to go back to the last page, with the same search results appearing.

- The query called search_categories pulls distinct categories from the store_ inventory table. This outputs only one genre listing, such as Mind Control, for each particular class. Otherwise, if there were 50 titles under the Mind Control genre, the listing would appear 50 times in the dropdown.

- A <CFOUTPUT> tag is used to look up the results in an XHTML <SELECT> form element. This code is used to loop through the results.

As mentioned, the form is posted to the search_parameters.cfm page, which sets all the search items as session variables. Following is the code for the page:

```
<cfoutput>
    <cfparam name="keywords" default="All">
    <cfparam name="genres" default="All">
    <cflock scope="session" timeout="15" type="EXCLUSIVE">
        <cfset session.search_keywords = keywords>
        <cfset session.search_genres = genres>
</cflock>
    <cflocation url="search_output.cfm" addtoken="No">
</cfoutput>
```

Things to Note About the Code

- Default parameters are set in case the entire form or parts of the form were not filled out. While form-validation code, whether client-side or server-side, could have been added to the form to ensure all necessary fields were populated, such functionality is not necessary because of the default values. This helps ensure that users see results from the search, rather than error messages.

- The <CFLOCATION> tag is used to quickly redirect the user to the output page (search_ output.cfm). Because the purpose of this page is simply to set session variables and redirect the user, no XHTML code is necessary. It simply processes the code and sends the user onto the next page.

SEARCH OUTPUT AND CART ARRAY PAGES

After having submitted a search and having those values set as session variables, the user is redirected to the output page. Figure 3.12 illustrates how the page looks after a search is conducted and output in the `search_output.cfm` page.

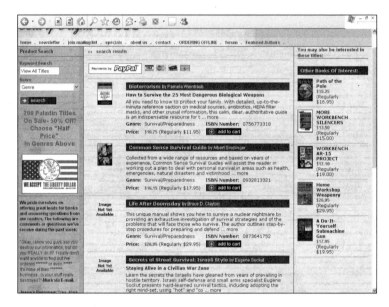

FIGURE 3.12   The center column shows the results from a search submitted from the search functionality in the upper left-hand corner.
© 2006 Bill of Rights Press. Used with permission.

While the right column is the result of different programming (i.e., cross-selling code), the center column outputs data pulled from the `store_inventory` table. Listing 3.3 is the code used to output the results:

LISTING 3.3   Code Used to Output Results from Figure 3.12

```
<!--- query that pulls search results from database start --->
<cfquery datasource="freepress" name="list">
    SELECT *
    FROM store_inventory
    WHERE
```

```
        product_id <> 999999
        <cfif session.search_keywords IS "All" OR
            session.search_keywords IS "View All Titles">
        <cfelse>
        AND
         (description LIKE '%#session.search_keywords#%'
            OR title_2 LIKE '%#session.search_keywords#%'
            OR title LIKE '%#session.search_keywords#%'
            OR data_5 LIKE '%#session.search_keywords#%'
            OR product_number LIKE '%#session.search_keywords#%'
            OR upload1 LIKE '%#session.search_keywords#%'
            )
        </cfif>
        <cfif session.search_genres IS "All"><cfelse>AND category1 =
            '#session.search_genres#'</cfif>
    ORDER BY title
</cfquery>
<!--- query that pulls search results from database end --->
<table width="100%" cellspacing="0" cellpadding="0" border="0">
<!--- values controlling the number of times the page loops
    start --->
    <cfoutput>
        <cfset row_output = "20">
        <!--- sets the number of search result page numbers --->
        <cfif list.recordcount LTE row_output>
            <cfset num_of_pages = "1">
        <cfelse>
            <cfset num_of_pages = ceiling(list.recordcount / row_output)>
        </cfif>
        <!--- sets default values for output query --->
        <cfif (list.recordcount LTE row_output) OR (not isdefined
            ("url.output_start"))>
            <cfset output_start = 1>
            <cfset output_end = row_output>
        <cfelse>
            <cfset output_start = url.output_start>
            <cfset output_end = url.output_end>
        </cfif>
    </cfoutput>
<!--- values controlling the number of times the page loops end --->
<tr>
    <td align="left" valign="top">
    <cfoutput>
        <cfset category_count = 1>
        <table width="100%" cellspacing="0" cellpadding="0" border="0">
<!--- conditional statement that displays if, by any chance, the search
    turns up no results start --->
        <cfif list.recordcount IS "0">
            <tr>
                <td align="center" valign="top" colspan="6"><br /><b>
                    There are no records that match your search</b><br
                    /><br /></td>
            </tr>
        </cfif>
```

```
<!--- conditional statement that displays if, by any chance, the search
    turns up no results end --->
<!--- loop that outputs search results start --->
        <cfloop query="list" startrow="#output_start#" endrow=
            "#output_end#">
        <cfparam name="loop_color_number" default="0">
            <tr>
                <td align="center" valign="top">
                    <cfif fileexists("r:\inventory\images\#product_
                        number#_tn.jpg")><a href="product_output.cfm?
                        product_id=#product_id#"><img src="#root#/
                        inventory/images/#product_number#_tn.jpg"
                        alt="" class="imageborder" /></a><cfelse><img
                        src="#root#/images/image-not-yet-available.gif"
                        alt="" /></cfif>
                </td>
                <td></td>
                <td align="left" valign="top">
                    <table width="100%" cellspacing="0"
                        cellpadding="0" border="0">
                    <tr>
                        <td align="left" valign="middle"
                            bgcolor="##650500" style="height:
                            22px">  <a href="product_output.
                            cfm?product_id=#product_id#" class=
                            "carttitle"><b>#list.title#</b></a> by
                            #author1_first# #author1_last#<cfif
                            author2_last GT "0">, #author2_first#
                            #author2_last#</cfif><cfif author3_last
                            GT "0">, #author3_first# #author3_last#
                            </cfif></span>
                        </td>
                    </tr>
                    <tr>
                        <td><img src="#root#/inventory/images/
                            spacer.gif" width="1" height="5" alt=""
                            border="0" /></td>
                    </tr>
                    <tr>
                        <td align="left" valign="top"><b>#list.
                            title_2#</b></td>
                    </tr>
                    <tr>
                        <td><img src="#root#/inventory/images/
                            spacer.gif" width="1" height="5" alt=""
                            border="0" /></td>
                    </tr>
                    <tr>
                        <td align="left" valign="top">#mid
                            (list.description, 1, 250)# <cfif
                            len(description) GT "250">... <a href=
                            "#root#/product_output.cfm?product_id=
                            #product_id#">more</a></cfif></td>
                    </tr>
                    <tr>
```

```
                    <td><img src="#root#/inventory/images/spacer.gif"
                        width="1" height="5" alt="" border="0"
                        /></td>
            </tr>
            <tr>
                <td align="left" valign="top">
                    <table cellspacing="0" cellpadding="0"
                        border="0">
                    <tr>
                        <td><b>Genre:</b>  </td>
                        <td>#list.category1#</td>
                        <td><img src="#root#/inventory/images/
                            spacer.gif" width="15" height="1"
                            alt="" border="0" /></td>
                        <td align="left" valign="top"><b>ISBN
                            Number:</b>  </td>
                        <td></td>
                        <td>#list.product_number#</td>
                    </tr>
                    <tr>
                        <td colspan="5"><img src="#root#/
                            inventory/images/spacer.gif" width="1"
                            height="5" alt="" border="0" /></td>
                    </tr>
                <tr>
                        <td><b>Price:</b>  </td>
                        <td><cfif list.discount GT "0"><b><span
                            class="red2">#dollarformat
                            (list.discount)#</span></b>
                            (Regularly #dollarformat
                            (list.price)#)<cfelse>
                            #dollarformat(list.price)#</cfif>
                            </td>
                        <td><img src="#root#/inventory/images/
                            spacer.gif" width="15" height="1"
                            alt="" border="0" /></td>
                        <td align="left" valign="top"
                            colspan="3">
<!--- form that sends data for this particular product to page that
    adds the product to the array session variable start --->
                        <form action="cart_array.cfm"
                            method="post">
                        <input type="hidden" name="order_
                            product_number" value=
                            "#list.product_number#">
                            <input type="hidden"
                                name="order_title" value=
                                "#list.title#">
                            <input type="hidden"
                                name="order_product_id"
                                value="#list.product_id#">
                            <input type="hidden" name=
                                "order_price" value="<cfif
                                list.discount GT "0">
                                #list.discount#<cfelse>#
                                list.price#</cfif>">
```

```
                                    <input type="hidden" name=
                                        "order_size" value="large">
                                    <input type="hidden"
                                        name="product_id"
                                        value="#product_id#">
                                    <input type="hidden" name=
                                        "action" value="add">
                                    <input type="image" src=
                                        "#root#/inventory/images/
                                        button_add_to_cart.gif">
                                </form>
            <!--- form that sends data for this particular product to page that
                adds the product to the array session variable end --->
                                            </td>
                            </table>
                        </td>
                    </tr>
                    </table>
                </td>
            </tr>
            </cfloop>
    <!--- loop that outputs search results end --->
            </table>
        </cfoutput>
        </td>
    </tr>
    </table>
```

Things to Note About the Code

- The query contains conditional code, depending on what variables and their values are passed from the search form. ColdFusion allows the developer to use conditional code because the server will recreate the query in the form it needs to correctly submit to the database.

- Notice the Order By clause in the query. The entire listing is sorted by the title field. A developer can not only change this value to sort the results differently, but the code can also be written so this value is a variable set by the user. In other words, the user can determine how the products are ordered.

- The code between the comment tags' values controlling the number of times the page loops sets the starting and ending values for how many times the code, which produces a row in the output page, should be looped over. These two variables, output_start and output_end, can also be used to create a list at the bottom of the page, which allows the user to click various output page numbers—similar to how a user can select different pages from search results in a search engine.

- The code included between the conditional statement that displays if the search turns up no results is added in case the search turns up no results. Although the query is designed to always find a book, sometimes there are certain conditions a developer has not tested for that will eventually occur. If this happens to be the case, the code will at least tell the user, "There are no records that match your search," rather than producing an error message.

■ Everything inside the comment tag loop that outputs search results is what outputs each row on the page.

■ Notice the FILEEXISTS function that is used in a conditional statement in the looping row. It will output an image that says "Image Not Yet Available" if no image matches the image #product_number#_tn.jpg. This code is calling for an image with the product number in the name, along with _tn.jpg appended to it, identifying it as a thumbnail image. This naming convention using _tn is completely arbitrary and left to the developer to create.

■ This page allows the developer to output all the required information about a product with no size restraints, unlike a looped list that has to output data for a lot of products at once. The image, title, and "more" text in the description paragraph for every product is hyperlinked to the product.cfm page.

■ Most variables have a list. prepended to them. This says to pull the data from query title list. Otherwise, if another variable of the same name exists, the server will pick it from one of the two queries, sometimes selecting it from the wrong query.

■ The form between the form that sends data to the page to add to array session variable comment tags is what sends the data for that particular product to the cart_array.cfm file, which adds the data to the array that is saved as a session variable.

■ Notice the hidden parameter in the form titled action. When the data is submitted to the cart_array.cfm page, this variable tells the server to process the conditional code that is in the add area because this is the value of the action parameter.

The cart_array.cfm file is a recursive page that allows the developer to add, edit, and delete items from the array. For the sake of simplicity, though, only the add condition is included in the following code:

```
<cflock scope="session" timeout="15" type="EXCLUSIVE">
    <cfset session.CartArray = ArrayNew(2)>
    <cfset session.CartArray[1][1] = "#order_product_number#">
    <cfset session.CartArray[1][2] = "#order_title#">
    <cfset session.CartArray[1][3] = "#order_color#">
    <cfset session.CartArray[1][4] = "#order_size#">
    <cfset session.CartArray[1][5] = "#order_quantity#">
    <cfset session.CartArray[1][6] = "#order_price#">
    <cfset session.CartArray[1][7] = "#order_product_id#">
</cflock>
<cflocation url="cart_output.cfm?action=add" addtoken="no">
```

Things to Note About the Code

■ There are seven items in the array, similar to the array in Figure 3.9.

■ Once the item is added to the array, the server redirects the user (although this page is not ever seen because it is processed only on the server) to the `cart_output.cfm` page.

PRODUCT PAGE

Because the search output page is limited in the amount of content it can show for each product, owing to the number of products it lists, the user is able to link to a `product.cfm` page for all the information on a product. Similar to the `search_output.cfm` page, this page is a template that is reused for every product in the database, making it easier for the developer to make changes to a large number of pages very quickly. Figure 3.13 is an example of how a product appears after being selected from the `search_output.cfm` page.

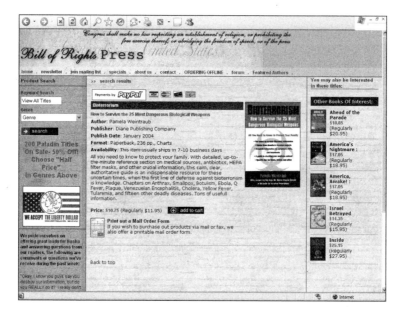

FIGURE 3.13   Product information that is output on the `product.cfm` page.
© 2006 Bill of Rights Press. Used with permission.

The code that is used to display an individual product is much less involved than a page that outputs looped data from a dynamic query. If the developer understands how the `search_output.cfm` page works, the code in Listing 3.4 for the `product.cfm` page will be much easier to grasp:

LISTING 3.4 Code for the `product.cfm` Page

```
<!--- query that pulls data for individual products from the database
    start --->
<cfquery datasource="freepress" name="product">
        SELECT *
    FROM store_inventory
    WHERE product_id = #product_id#
</cfquery>
<!--- query that pulls data for individual products from the database
    end --->
<!--- outputted product from data pulled from query start --->
<cfoutput query="product">
    <table width="100%" cellspacing="0" cellpadding="0" border="0">
            <tr>
            <td align="left" valign="top">
                <table cellspacing="0" cellpadding="0" border="0">
                <tr>
                    <td align="left" valign="middle" bgcolor=
                    "##62432E" style="height: 22px" class="white2">
                      <b>#product.title#</b></td>
                </tr>
                <tr>
                <td><img src="#root#/inventory/images/spacer.gif"
                        width="1" height="5" alt=""
                        border="0" /></td>
                </tr>
                <tr>
                    <td align="left" valign="top" class=
                    "burntorange2"><b>#product.title_2#</b>
                        </td>
                </tr>
                <tr>
                    <td><img src="#root#/inventory/images/
                        spacer.gif" width="1" height="5" alt=""
                        border="0" /></td>
                </tr>
                <cfif product.data_1 GT "0">
                <tr>
                    <td align="left" valign="top"><b>Author</b>:
                        #author1_first# #author1_last#<cfif
                        author2_last GT "0">, #author2_first#
                        #author2_last#</cfif><cfif author3_last GT
                        "0">, #author3_first# #author3_last#
                        </cfif></td>
                </tr>
                <tr>
                    <td><img src="#root#/inventory/images/
                        spacer.gif" width="1" height="5" alt=""
                        border="0" /></td>
            </tr>
            </cfif>
            <tr>
                    <td align="left" valign="top"><b>Publisher</b>:
                        #product.data_5#</td>
                </tr>
```

```
<tr>
    <td><img src="#root#/inventory/images/
        spacer.gif" width="1" height="5" alt=""
        border="0" /></td>
</tr>
<tr>
    <td align="left" valign="top"><b>Publish
        Date</b>: #product.data_6#</td>
</tr>
<tr>
    <td><img src="#root#/inventory/images/
        spacer.gif" width="1" height="5" alt=""
        border="0" /></td>
</tr>
<tr>
    <td align="left" valign="top"><b>Format</b>:
        #product.upload1#</td>
</tr>
<tr>
<td><img src="#root#/inventory/images/spacer.gif"
        width="1" height="5" alt="" border="0"
        /></td>
</tr>
<tr>
    <td align="left" valign="top"><b>Availability
        </b>: #product.upload2#</td>
</tr>
<tr>
    <td><img src="#root#/inventory/images/
        spacer.gif" width="1" height="5" alt=""
        border="0" /></td>
</tr>
<tr>
    <td align="left" valign="top">#product.
        description#</td>
</tr>
<tr>
    <td><img src="#root#/inventory/images/
        spacer.gif" width="1" height="15" alt=""
        border="0" /></td>
</tr>
<tr>
    <td align="left" valign="top">
        <table cellspacing="0" cellpadding="0"
            border="0">
        <tr>
            <td><b>Price:</b> </td>
            <td><cfif product.discount GT
                "0"><b><span class="red2">
                #dollarformat(product.discount)#
                </span></b> (Regularly
                #dollarformat(product.price)#)
                <cfelse><span class="black1">
                #dollarformat(product.price)
                #</span></cfif></td>
```

```
                    <td><img src="#root#/inventory/images/
                        spacer.gif" width="15" height="1"
                        alt="" border="0" /></td>

                    <td align="left" valign="top"
                    colspan="5">
<!--- form that sends data for this particular product to page that
    adds the product to the array session variable start --->
                        <form action="cart_array.cfm"
                            method="post">
                                <input type="hidden"
                                    name="order_
                                    product_number"
                                    value="#product.
                                    product_number#">
                                <input type="hidden"
                                    name="order_title"
                                    value="#product.
                                    title#">
                                <input type="hidden" name=
                                    "order_product_id"
                                    value="#product.
                                    product_id#">
                                <input type="hidden"
                                    name="order_price"
                                    value="<cfif
                                    product.discount GT
                                    "0">#product.
                                    discount#<cfelse>
                                    #product.price#
                                    </cfif>">
                                <input type="hidden"
                                    name="order_size"
                                    value="large">
                                <input type="hidden"
                                    name="product_id"
                                    value="#product_
                                    id#">
                                <input type="hidden"
                                    name="action"
                                    value="add">
                                <input type="image"
                                    src="#root#/
                                    inventory/images/
                                    button_add_to_
                                    cart.gif">
                        </form>
<!--- form that sends data for this particular product to page that
    adds the product to the array session variable end --->
                    </td>
                </tr>
            </table>
        </td>
    </tr>
    <tr>
```

```
                          <td><img src="#root#/inventory/images/
                                spacer.gif" width="1" height="10" alt=""
                                border="0" /></td>
                  </tr>
                  </table>
            </td>
            <td><img src="#root#/inventory/images/spacer.gif"
                  width="5" height="1" alt="" border="0" /></td>
            <td align="center" valign="top">
  <cfif fileexists("r:\inventory\images\#product_number#_full.jpg")><a
      href="#root#/inventory/images/#product_number#_full.jpg" target="_new">
      <img src="#root#/inventory/images/#product_number#_mid.jpg" alt=""
      border="0" class="imageborder" /></a><cfelse><img src="#root#/
      inventory/images/image-not-yet-available.gif" alt="" /></cfif>
            </td>
            <td><img src="#root#/inventory/images/spacer.gif"
                  width="5" height="1" alt="" border="0" /></td>
      </tr>
      </table>
  </cfoutput>
  <!--- outputted product from data pulled from query end --->
```

Things to Note About the Code

- The query is based solely on the `product_id` parameter that is passed from a hyperlink on the `search_output.cfm` page. All data then is subsequently pulled from the database record with that unique `id` number.

Even though the `id` value is passed in a parameter called `product_id`, the value is still derived from the `id` variable, no matter how it is named or renamed.

- Much of the same conditional code for content, such as when to include additional authors, is used from the `search_output.cfm` page. The form that submits the data is the same. The only difference is that some of the variables have `product.` prepended in front of them instead of `list.` because the query pulling the data on this page is named `product` instead of `list`.
- The product image on this page is based on the product number; however, it has `_mid.jpg` appended to it, because it is the mid-sized version of the product image. This naming convention is left to the developer to create. The image is even hyperlinked to an image with the same product number but with `_full.jpg` appended to the end of it, which links to a full-sized product image, giving the user a variety of options when viewing the product.
- The user is able to add the product from both the `search_output.cfm` page and the `product.cfm` pages for better usability.

CART OUTPUT PAGE

The flow of shopping carts is not always the same. In this example, whenever the user adds a product to the cart, the server redirects the person to the cart_output.cfm page, although technically, the person is coming from the cart_array.cfm page, which first sets the search variables. When the user is directed to the page, it is populated by the code looping over the CartArray session variable (i.e., session.CartArray). Figure 3.14 illustrates the initial view of the page.

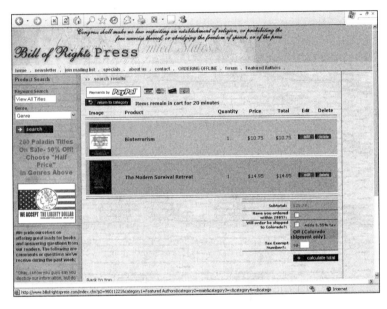

FIGURE 3.14   Output data on the cart_output.cfm page. © 2006 Bill of Rights Press. Used with permission.

Listing 3.5 is the code that outputs what is contained in the shopping cart. Because there is a lot of extra functionality on the page, which cannot be adequately explained in this book, such as editing and deleting items from the array, everything except the core essence of the page has been removed.

LISTING 3.5   Code That Outputs the Shopping Cart Contents

```
<!--- set defaults start --->
<cflock scope="session" timeout="15" type="EXCLUSIVE">
<!--- sets sub_total and total_quantity values to '0' start --->
    <cfset session.sub_total = "0">
    <cfset session.total_quantity = "0">
</cflock>
```

```
<!--- sets sub_total and total_quantity values to 'O' end --->
    <table width="100%" cellspacing="0" cellpadding="0" border="0">
    <tr>
        <td></td>
        <td><b>Image</b></td>
        <td><b>Product</b></td>
        <td align="center"><b>Quantity</b></td>
        <td align="center"><b>Price</b></td>
        <td align="center"><b>Total</b></td>
        <td class="black2" align="center"><b>Edit</b></td>
        <td align="center"><b>Delete</b></td>
</tr>
<!--- loops over and outputs array start --->
    <cfloop from="1" to="#ArrayLen(session.CartArray)#" index="idx">
        <cfoutput>
<!--- sets looping variables from array start --->
        <cfparam name="number" default="odd">
        <cfset output_data_1 = session.CartArray[idx][1]>
        <cfset output_data_2 = session.CartArray[idx][2]>
        <cfset output_data_3 = session.CartArray[idx][3]>
        <cfset output_data_4 = session.CartArray[idx][4]>
        <cfset output_data_5 = session.CartArray[idx][5]>
        <cfset output_data_6 = session.CartArray[idx][6]>
        <cfset output_data_7 = session.CartArray[idx][7]>
<!--- sets looping variables from array start --->
        <tr>
            <td><img src="#root#/inventory/images/spacer.gif" width="5"
                height="56" alt="" border="0" /></td>
            <td align="left" valign="middle">
                <a href="product_output.cfm?product_id=#product_id#">
                    <img src="#root#/inventory/images/products/#output_
                    data_1#_tn.jpg" width="60" alt="" border="0"
                    class="imageborder"></a>
            </td>
            <td align="left" valign="middle"><b><a href="product_
                output.cfm?product_id=#product_id#">#output_data_2#
                </a></td>
            <td align="center">#output_data_5#</td>
            <td align="center">
                #dollarformat(output_data_6)#
            </td>
            <td align="center">
                <cfset product_total = output_data_5 * output_data_6>
                #dollarformat(product_total)#
<!--- create a session variable for a running total start --->
                <cflock scope="session" timeout="15" type="EXCLUSIVE">
                    <cfset session.sub_total = session.sub_total +
                        product_total>
                </cflock>
<!--- create a session variable for a running total end --->
            </td>
            <td align="center">
```

```
        <img src="#root#/inventory/images/button_edit_off.gif"
            name="edit_#idx#" width="45" height="13" alt=""
            border="0">
    </td>
    <td align="center">
        <img src="#root#/inventory/images/button_delete_
            off.gif" name="delete_#idx#" width="45"
            height="13" alt="" border="0" /></a>
    </td>
</tr>
</cfoutput>
</cfloop>
<!--- loops over and outputs array end --->
</table>
</cfif>
```

Things to Note About the Code

■ Default values for session variables are set at the top of the page, between the `sets sub_total and total_quantity values to '0'` comment tags, using the `<CFSET>` tag rather than the `<CFPARAM>` tag because the user may have already visited the page, which means the values would be added to what already existed. Session variables are used because they allow the developer to keep track of array values as they are being looped over. The values can also be used with other cart functions after the order has been processed, such as sending a confirmation email to the user.

■ The code between the `sets looping variables from array` comment tags allows the developer to output data from the array. Those values are output during the looping process. Each of the variables, such as `output_data_1`, `output_data_2`, and `output_data_5`, could be named `product_number`, `title`, and `quantity`, respectively, if the developer chooses to do so.

■ The code between the `create a session variable for a running total` comment tags keeps a running tab of the total price each time the loop outputs a new array item. This total is then used in calculating the subtotal and total.

■ While the Edit and Delete functionality has been removed from this example of code, the buttons simply redirect the user back to the `cart_array.cfm` page, which has additional conditional code in it to edit and delete items from the cart.

One larger chunk of code that has been pulled from the `cart_output.cfm` for separate explanation is that which calculates the taxes, shipping, and other custom values that factor into the final total price (see Figure 3.15). When developing a shopping cart, the final total is not always calculated simply by multiplying the quantity by the item price and then adding each item to get a total price. Clients can have unique situations that need to be programmed into the code, such as adding city, county, and/or state taxes; not charging taxes if a tax-exempt number is supplied; adding shipping costs, both domestically and internationally; and not charging taxes on free gifts that are added to an order.

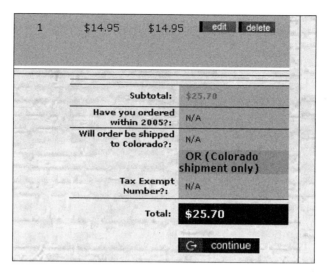

FIGURE 3.15   Elements of the `cart_output.cfm` page that are used to calculate the total before being sent for payment processing. © 2006 Bill of Rights Press. Used with permission.

To reduce liability, it is usually a wise practice for the developer to have the client be responsible for researching and documenting, usually in an email, such programming requirements. Considering that the client will need to know all this information to run the business anyway, it should not be too much of an additional burden. Listing 3.6 shows such code that was separated from the `cart_output.cfm` page. It helps collect the grand total that is then passed onto the payment gateway, which is VeriSign in this example.

LISTING 3.6   Code Handling the Final Total

```
<!--- default variable start --->
<cfparam name="total_calculated" default="no">
<!--- default variable end --->
<cfoutput>
    <table width="100%" cellspacing="0" cellpadding="0" border="0">
    <cfform action="cart_output.cfm" method="post"
        name="calculate_form">
    <tr>
        <td class="black1" valign="middle" align="right"><b>Subtotal:
            </b> </td>
    <td></td>
    <td valign="middle" class="black1"> 
    <cfset sub_total = session.sub_total>
    <span style="color: ##FF0000"><b>#dollarformat(sub_total)#</b>
            </span>
        </td>
```

```
        </tr>
        <tr>
        <td class="black1" valign="middle" align="right" colspan="3"><b>
                Have you ordered within #dateformat(Now(), "YYYY")#?:</b>
                 </td>
<!--- have you ordered calculation start --->
            <cfif total_calculated IS "no">
            <input type="checkbox" name="last_year">
            <cfelse>
                <cfif total_calculated IS "yes" AND isdefined("last_year")>
                    N/A
                <cfelse>
                    <cfset sub_total = session.sub_total - 10>
                    <span style="color: ##FF0000"><b>-$10.00</b></span>
                        </cfif>
            </cfif>
<!--- have you ordered calculation end --->
            </td>
        </tr>
        <tr>
            <td class="black1" valign="middle" align="right"><b>Will order
            be shipped to Colorado?:</b> </td>
            <td></td>
            <td align="left" valign="middle" class="black1"> 
<!--- colorado sales tax calculation start --->
            <cfif total_calculated IS "no">
                <input type="checkbox" name="colorado_tax">  
                <cfquery datasource="freepress" name="state_tax_rate">
                    SELECT *
                    FROM store_taxes
                    WHERE state = 'colorado'
                </cfquery>
                <cfset state_tax_rate = state_tax_rate.tax_rate>
                Adds #state_tax_rate#% tax
            <cfelse>
                <cfif isdefined("colorado_tax")>
                    <cfif tax_exempt GT "0">
                        N/A
                    <cfelse>
                        <cfset additional_tax_amount = sub_total * ".0855">
                        <span style="color: ##FF0000"><b>#dollarformat
                            (additional_tax_amount)#</b></span>
                            (8.55% tax)
                        <cfset sub_total = sub_total + additional_tax_amount>
                        </cfif>
                <cfelse>
                    N/A
                </cfif>
            </cfif>
<!--- colorado sales tax calculation end --->
            </td>
        </tr>
        <tr>
            <td></td>
            <td></td>
```

```
            <td align="left" valign="middle" bgcolor="##AAAAAA"> 
                 <b><span style="color: ##000000">OR (Colorado
                shipment only)</span></b></td>
        </tr>
        <tr>
            <td class="black1" valign="middle" align="right"><b>Tax Exempt
                Number?:</b>  </td>
            <td></td>
            <td valign="middle" class="black1"> 
<!--- tax exempt code start --->
            <cfif total_calculated IS "no">
                98-<input type="text" name="tax_exempt" class="black1"
                    size="2" maxlength="5">
            <cfelse>
                    <cfif tax_exempt GT "0">
                        #tax_exempt#
                        <input type="hidden" name="tax_exempt" value="
                            #tax_exempt#">
                    <cfelse>
                        N/A
                        <input type="hidden" name="tax_exempt" value="0">
                    </cfif>
            </cfif>
<!--- tax exempt code end --->
                </td>
        </tr>
<!--- recursive button start --->
        <cfif total_calculated IS "No">
        <tr>
            <td colspan="2"></td>
            <td align="left" valign="top">
                <input type="hidden" name="total_calculated" value="yes">
                  <input type="image" src="#root#/cart/images/
                    button_calculate_total.gif">
            </td>
            <td align="center" valign="middle"></td>
        </tr>
        </cfif>
<!--- recursive button end --->
        </cfform>
<!--- final processing start --->
        <cfif total_calculated IS "yes">
        <tr>
        <td class="black1" valign="middle" align="right"><b>Total:</b>
                 </td>
                <td></td>
            <td align="left" valign="middle" class="white8" style=
                "background-color: ##000000"> 
                <cflock scope="application" type="READONLY" timeout="30">
                    <cfif sub_total GT "0">
                        <cfset session.total = sub_total>
                    <cfelse>
<cfset session.total = "0">
                    </cfif>
                </cflock>
                <b>#dollarformat(session.total)#</b>
```

```
                    </td>
                </tr>
                <tr>
                    <td colspan="2"></td>
                    <td align="left" valign="top">
        <!--- form that submits data to payment gateway start --->
                        <FORM NAME="CFForm_1" ACTION="https://payments.verisign.com
                            /payflowlink" METHOD=POST>
                        <input type="hidden" name="amount" value=
                            "#session.process_total#">
                        <input type="hidden" name="LOGIN" value="This is where the
                            client's login id goes">
                        <input type="hidden" name="PARTNER" value="This is where
                            the merchant account abbreviation goes (such as,
                            'WFB,' which stands for 'Wells Fargo Bank'">
                        <input type="hidden" name="DESCRIPTION" value="#session.
                            verisign_desc_list#">
                        <input type="hidden" name="TYPE" value="S">
                        <input type="image" src="#root#/cart/images/
                            button_continue.gif">
                        </FORM>
        <!--- form that submits data to payment gateway end --->
                    </td>
                </tr>
                </cfif>
        <!--- final processing end --->
                </table>
        </cfoutput>
```

Things to Note About the Code

- This portion of the `cart_output.cfm` page operates under two conditions: (1) if the total has not been calculated and (2) if the total has been calculated. It is a recursive page, so after the user has selected the processing conditions in the bottom right-hand corner of Figure 3.14 and clicked the Calculate Total button, the variable `total_calculated` with the value of yes is passed back to the page, telling the server to process the various conditions. Because a default value must first be declared, the variable at the top of this code sets the page to no.

- The code between the comment tags that say `have you ordered calculation` is an example of how a section of code is processed differently, depending on whether the `total_calculated` variable is yes or no. The first condition provides a checkbox, and the second condition provides code that takes the running `sub_total` variable and adjusts it according to what it should be.

- The code between the `colorado sales tax calculation` comment tags calculates, if applicable, the appropriate tax and adds it to the subtotal. In the `<CFELSE>` statement the developer must first calculate how much the tax will be by multiplying the `sub_total` variable by the interest rate. This result will only give the developer the amount of tax. The `sub_total` variable must then be set again by adding the tax amount to the subtotal.

- The `total_calculated` variable, which can be set as `yes` or `no`, dictates whether the Calculate Total or Continue button will be displayed.
- Once the grand total has been calculated, the final function of the shopping cart is made available for the user to process. The code that is between the `form that submits data to payment gateway` comment tags is used to submit the necessary order information to the payment gateway. This code is what VeriSign's PayFlow Link product uses to pass on the total dollar amount to be processed. Each processor requires different information to be passed on so its servers know which client is processing a transaction. In this case, the `LOGIN` and `PARTNER` information are required. Another important field is `DESCRIPTION`, which allows the developer to pass on information about the product and quantities that are included in the order. Although this solution allows only for a comma-delimited list, it nonetheless will be stored in the payment gateway's database. The actual code that builds the `session.verisign_desc_list` variable during each loop has been removed from the example code; however, it functions the same as to how the running total of the total price is collected. Each time a product is looped over, its product number and quantity are added to the list.

SUMMARY

Understanding the big picture of how something works always makes learning the details easier. This chapter not only explains how the e-commerce process works, how credit cards are processed, and how shopping carts work, but it also provides example code. Explanations of the various pieces of the code are also given to help explain how the db-driven techniques explained in previous chapters are put into use.

4 **Creating CSS Designs**

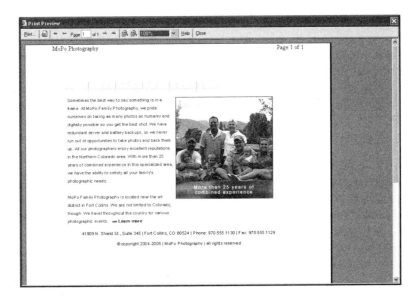

Since the inception of the Internet, the front-end design of Web sites has been built primarily using HTML. While back-end development such as db-driven programming and e-commerce functionality has made large strides over the years, so has the front-end design of sites. In the past to create a Web site that had the look and feel of traditional graphic design, the designer had to resort to using HTML, now XHTML, tables for the majority of content placement. The tables not only allowed the designer to mortise images together, but they also allowed for the layout of XHTML text that was styled using CSS. With the evolution of browsers over the past several years, nearly all layouts can now be accomplished using CSS. This chapter explains the basics of how CSS-designed sites work. It is necessary that the reader have a basic working knowledge of the language.

CSS-BASED DESIGN VERSUS XHTML TABLE DESIGN

The first question a designer usually asks when it comes to creating CSS designs is, "HTML has worked well for so many years, why is it not good enough now?" Unfortunately, there is not one answer to this question. Yes, HTML sites have been the main staple of designers since the mid-1990s. Yes, they are logical in the way they work. Yes, XHTML code, having replaced HTML as the standard, is compact enough, allowing for fast downloads, depending on included images and any extra code included. The bottom line, though, is nearly everything can be improved, and XHTML's table-based design is no exception. There are several advantages to creating CSS-based designs.

Advantages of CSS Designs

■ The outputted Web page, barring the stylesheet, is much cleaner and easier to follow, because it takes considerably less code to accomplish the same look and feel. This makes it easier for the designer to understand nested elements and how they relate to other content and containers. While nesting is still necessary to accomplish the same look and feel as XHTML-table design, the amount of code to do so is drastically reduced.

■ The combined download size, or weight, of the XHTML and CSS files is considerably smaller. Whether a user has a low- or high-speed connection, faster sites are always appreciated.

■ The structure and styling of the site can be easily added, edited, and deleted. Although this concept is not new to those who create db-driven sites, CSS allows for changes made to one page to cascade through an entire site.

■ Pages can be printed with much more control and consistency than can XHTML pages.

This is not to say that CSS is the perfect solution to coding Web sites. As with any Internet technology, there are going to be some disadvantages. However, it can be argued that the advantages outweigh the disadvantages, but the designer needs to be aware of these shortcomings.

Disadvantages of CSS Designs

■ There is a learning curve. Even if a designer is familiar with CSS, using the language to lay out an entire site takes longer to learn than just styling text. The main reason is that there are idiosyncrasies with how CSS elements interact in different browsers. The workarounds or hacks to solve many of these idiosyncrasies are explained in the following chapters, which mitigates this disadvantage.

■ CSS is not supported as consistently in browsers as XHTML is, so it requires more testing by the designer. Not only are there compliant and noncompliant browsers that handle CSS differently, but there also are different versions of such browsers. This means there are more bugs and thus more workarounds and hacks that a designer must be familiar with to fix the bugs.

Web design always seems to be evolving. An increasing number of Web sites are being programmed with CSS as the main layout method. It is just a matter of time before the industry, and thus clients, demand that sites be coded this way. While it is not a perfect solution, CSS design is much more powerful and efficient than XHTML table-based design. One of the goals of this book is to decrease the learning curve by explaining how the process works and how to avoid and/or correct issues when they arise.

The Basics of CSS-Based Design Versus XHTML Table-Based Design

With traditional Web design, the content of a homepage is mortised, or pieced, together using XHTML tables. This content may include text, images, or both. No matter what is included in the design, a minimum of one table is typically used to position the elements. CSS is then generally used to format the text. Figure 4.1 is an example of a site that uses one table to display the content. The table border is set to 3 to help show how the page is constructed.

FIGURE 4.1 Mortised XHTML homepage, with the border's value set to 3, that uses one table to display both text and images. © 2006 Onepartart.com. Used with permission.

Unfortunately, most XHTML sites that employ more visually and technically advanced design usually cannot be created with one table. The designer therefore must nest tables inside of tables to position the various elements of the site. Figure 4.2 is the combination of nested tables that are used to place all the elements together in a design.

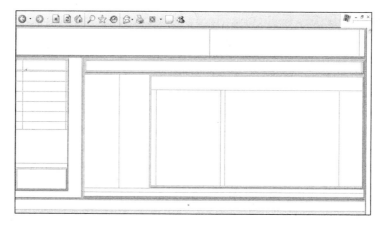

FIGURE 4.2   Table structure of a more complex table-based design, with the nested tables' borders set to 3 to display the framework.

Notice in Figure 4.2 that tables are nested inside one another. The purpose of this method is to place the content in various positions, down to the specific pixel, in some cases. This design is created to be a "liquid" design, which means it can flex to wider resolutions. Figure 4.3 shows what the design looks like when the images and text, along with the basic CSS formatting, are added.

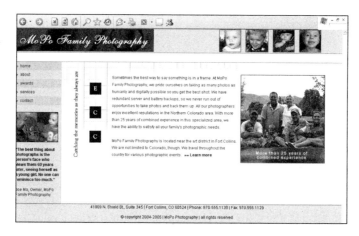

FIGURE 4.3   Design with table borders set to 0, and images, text, and CSS added to populate the table cells.

As complex as this design is, CSS can also be used to lay out the content. With relatively basic coding, a designer can make most sites look almost exactly like their table-based counterparts. Using a little more involved amount of code, the two can look exactly alike in most cases. Figure 4.4 is the same design as in Figure 4.3 but laid out using a limited amount of CSS.

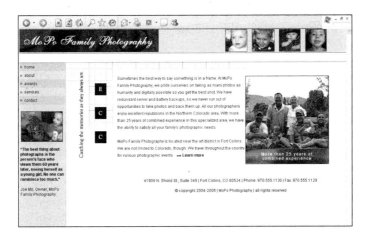

FIGURE 4.4 Design elements from Figure 4.3 laid out using CSS instead of XHTML tables.

In general, CSS sites work by using <DIV> and <SPAN> tags, in addition to a few other XHTML tags, such as <BR /> and <H1>, to format and position the content. The <DIV> and <SPAN> tags are wrapped around individual elements of content and then assigned rules in a stylesheet to position and style them. While the design in Figure 4.4 does not have tables that can have their borders set to 3 to show the layout, the borders or backgrounds of the tags can be set to 3 and assigned a color to differentiate them. Figure 4.5 shows the design with the borders "turned on" and the images and content removed.

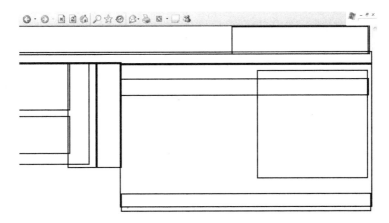

FIGURE 4.5 Borders turned on and content removed to show the basic structure of the site.

One thing to note about CSS coding is that it requires considerably less coding.
Listing 4.1 is the XHTML code that is used to lay out the design in Figure 4.3.

LISTING 4.1   XHTML Code for Figure 4.3

```
<!DOCTYPE html PUBLIC "-//W3C//DTD XHTML 1.0 Transitional//EN"
    "http://www.w3.org/TR/xhtml1/DTD/xhtml1-transitional.dtd">
<html>
<head>
    <title>MoPo Photography</title>
-- enter meta data here for search engines, such as the following example -->
    <meta HTTP-EQUIV="Content-Type" CONTENT="text/html; charset=iso-8859-1"
/>
    <meta content=" name="keywords" />
    <meta content=" name="description" />
<!-- link to javascript that enables any mouseovers on the page -->
<script src="mouseovers.js" type="text/javascript"></script>
<!-- link to main stylesheet that controls text sizes and colors,
    among other things -->
<link rel="stylesheet" href="mainstyle.css" type="text/css" />
</head>
<body style="background-color: #ffffff; margin: 0px">
<!-- Note: To make this page stretch to resolutions higher than
    800x600 or remain fixed at 800 x 600, change the width of the
    below table tag from "770" to "100%" and vice versa -->
<table width="100%" cellspacing="0" cellpadding="0" border="0">
<tr>
<!-- ###### header start ###### -->
    <td colspan="3" align="left" valign="top" style="background-image:
        url(images/bg_header.gif); background-repeat: repeat-x">
        <table width="100%" cellspacing="0" cellpadding="0" border="0">
        <tr>
            <td align="left" valign="top"><img src="images/
                header_left.jpg" width="431" height="73" alt=""
                border="0" /></td>
            <td align="center" valign="top"><img src="images/
                header_right.jpg" width="329" height="73" alt=""
                border="0" /></td>
            <td><img src="images/spacer.gif" width="10" height="1"
                alt="" border="0" /></td>
        </tr>
        </table>
    </td>
<!-- ###### header end ###### -->
</tr>
<tr>
    <td colspan="3" bgcolor="#919191"><img src="images/spacer.gif"
        width="1" height="1" alt="" border="0" /></td>
</tr>
<tr>
<!-- ###### menu column start ###### -->
    <td align="left" valign="top" bgcolor="#EDEAD1">
        <table width="144" cellspacing="0" cellpadding="0" border="0">
        <tr>
```

```
                        <td colspan="3" bgcolor="#ffffff"><img src="images/
                            spacer.gif" width="1" height="1" alt="" border="0"
                            /></td>
                    </tr>
                    <tr>
                        <td bgcolor="#ffffff"><img src="images/spacer.gif"
                            width="1" height="1" alt="" border="0" /></td>
                        <td align="left" valign="middle" bgcolor="#ffffff">
                             </td>
                        <td bgcolor="#ffffff"><img src="images/spacer.gif"
   name="menu_item_1"
                            width="3" height="26" alt="" border="0" /></td>
                    </tr>
                    <tr>
                        <td colspan="3" bgcolor="#909290"><img src="images/
                            spacer.gif" width="1" height="1" alt="" border="0"
                            /></td>
                    </tr>
                    <tr>
                        <td align="left" valign="middle" bgcolor="#E4E1C6"><img
                            src="images/bullet_menu_1_off.gif" name="homepage"
                            width="17" height="24" alt="" border="0" /></td>
                        <td align="left" valign="middle" bgcolor="#E4E1C6"><a
                            href="index.htm" onmouseover="document.homepage.src=
                            bullet_menu_1_on.src;"
   onmouseout="document.homepage.src=bullet_menu_1_off.src" style=
                            "text-decoration: none; color: #003366">home</a></td>

                        <td bgcolor="#E4E1C6"><img src="images/spacer.gif"
                            width="3" height="26" alt="" border="0" /></td>
                    </tr>
                <tr>
                        <td align="left" valign="middle" bgcolor="#EDEAD1"><img
                            src="images/bullet_menu_2_off.gif" name="about"
                            width="17" height="24" alt="" border="0" /></td>
                        <td align="left" valign="middle" bgcolor="#EDEAD1"><a
                            href="about.htm" onmouseover="document.about.src=
                            bullet_menu_2_on.src;"
                        onmouseout="document.about.src=bullet_menu_2_off.src"
                            style="text-decoration: none; color: #003366">about
                            </a></td>
                        <td bgcolor="#EDEAD1"><img src="images/spacer.gif"
                            width="3" height="26" alt="" border="0" /></td>
                    </tr>
                    <tr>
                        <td align="left" valign="middle" bgcolor="#E4E1C6"><img
                            src="images/bullet_menu_1_off.gif" name="bios"
                            width="17" height="24" alt="" border="0" /></td>
                        <td align="left" valign="middle" bgcolor="#E4E1C6"><a
                            href="awards.htm" onmouseover="document.bios.src=
                            bullet_menu_1_on.src;"
                        onmouseout="document.bios.src=bullet_menu_1_off.src"
                            style="text-decoration: none; color: #003366">awards
                            </a></td>
                        <td bgcolor="#E4E1C6"><img src="images/spacer.gif"
                            width="3" height="26" alt="" border="0" /></td>
```

```
    </tr>
    <tr>
        <td align="left" valign="middle" bgcolor="#EDEAD1"><img
            src="images/bullet_menu_2_off.gif" name="services"
            width="17" height="24" alt="" border="0" /></td>
        <td align="left" valign="middle" bgcolor="#EDEAD1"><a
            href="services.htm" onmouseover="document.services.src=
            bullet_menu_2_on.src;"
    onmouseout="document.services.src=bullet_menu_2_off.src"
        style="text-decoration: none; color: #003366">services</a></td>
        <td bgcolor="#EDEAD1"><img src="images/spacer.gif"
            width="3" height="26" alt="" border="0" /></td>
    </tr>
    <tr>
        <td align="left" valign="middle" bgcolor="#E4E1C6"><img
            src="images/bullet_menu_1_off.gif" name="contact"
            width="17" height="24" alt="" border="0" /></td>
        <td align="left" valign="middle" bgcolor="#E4E1C6"><a
            href="contact.htm" onmouseover="document.contact.src=
            bullet_menu_1_on.src;"
            onmouseout="document.contact.src=bullet_menu_1_off.src"
            style="text-decoration: none; color: #003366">contact
            </a></td>
        <td bgcolor="#E4E1C6"><img src="images/spacer.gif"
            width="3" height="26" alt="" border="0" /></td>
    </tr>
    <tr>
        <td><img src="images/spacer.gif" width="17" height="20"
            alt="" border="0" /></td>
        <td><img src="images/spacer.gif" width="124" height="1"
            alt="" border="0" /></td>
        <td><img src="images/spacer.gif" width="3" height="1"
            alt="" border="0" /></td>
    </tr>
    <tr>
        <td colspan="3"><a href="index.htm"><img src="images/
            photo_bottom_left.jpg" width="144" height="92" alt=""
            border="0" /></a></td>
    </tr>
    <tr>
        <td><img src="images/spacer.gif" width="1" height="10"
            alt="" border="0" /></td>
    </tr>
    <tr>
        <td colspan="3" align="left" valign="top">
            <table width="100%" cellspacing="0" cellpadding="4"
            border="0">
            <tr>
            <td align="left" valign="top"><b>"The best thing about
            photographs is the person's face who views them 60
            years later, seeing herself as a young girl. No one
            can reminisce too much."</b><br /><br />Joe Mo, Owner,
            MoPo Family Photography
<br /><br /></td>
            </tr>
            </table>
```

```
                    </td>
                </tr>
                </table>
        </td>
<!-- ###### menu column end ###### -->
<!-- ###### forces minimum height of body start ###### -->
        <td align="left" valign="top" bgcolor="#CAC9CA"><img src="images/
            spacer_white.gif" width="1" height="26" alt="" border="0"
            /></td>
<!-- ###### forces minimum height of body end ###### -->
<!-- ###### main content start ###### -->
        <td align="left" valign="top">
            <table width="100%" cellspacing="0" cellpadding="0" border="0">
            <tr>
<!-- ###### top center links start ###### -->
                <td colspan="3">
                    <table width="100%" cellspacing="0" cellpadding="0"
                        border="0">
                    <tr>
                        <td align="left"> </td>
                        <td><img src="images/spacer.gif" width="1"
                        height="26" alt="" border="0" /></td>
                    </tr>
                    <tr>
                        <td><img src="images/spacer.gif" width="500" height="1"
                            alt="" border="0" /></td>
                            <td><img src="images/spacer.gif" width="1"
                                height="1" alt="" border="0" /></td>
                    </tr>
                    </table>
                </td>
<!-- ###### top center links end ###### -->
            </tr>
            <tr>
                <td colspan="3" bgcolor="#909290"><img src="images/
                spacer.gif" width="1" height="1" alt="" border="0" /></td>
            </tr>
            <tr>
                <td align="left" valign="top"><img src="images/tagline.gif"
                    width="80" height="285" alt="" border="0" /></td>
                <td align="left" valign="top"><img src="images/image_left_
                    of_text.gif" width="69" height="285" alt="" border="0"
                    /></td>
<!-- ###### main text column start ###### -->
                <td align="left" valign="top">
                    <table width="100%" cellspacing="0" cellpadding="0"
                        border="0">
                    <tr>
                        <td colspan="5" align="left" valign="top"><img
                            src="images/image_above_text.gif" width="476"
                            height="36" alt="" border="0" /></td>
                    </tr>
                    <tr>
                        <td><img src="images/spacer.gif" width="1"
                            height="1" alt="" border="0" /></td>
```

```
                    <td align="left" valign="top" style="line-height:
                        16pt">
        Sometimes the best way to say something is in a frame. At MoPo Family
            Photography, we pride ourselves on taking as many photos as humanly
            and digitally possible so you get the best shot. We have redundant
            server and battery backups, so we never run out of opportunities to
            take photos and back them up. All our photographers enjoy excellent
            reputations in the Northern Colorado area.  With more than 25 years
            of combined experience in this specialized area, we have the
            ability to satisfy all your family's photographic needs.
        <br /><br />
        MoPo Family Photography is located near the art district in Fort
            Collins. We are not limited to Colorado, though. We travel
            throughout the country for various photographic events.
              <a href="x.htm" style="text-decoration:none"><b>&raquo;
            &raquo; Learn more</b></a></td>
                    <td><img src="images/spacer.gif" width="1"
                        height="1" alt="" border="0" /></td>
                    <td align="left" valign="top"><a href="x.htm"><img
                        src="images/photo_middle_right.jpg" width="260"
                        height="265" alt="" border="0" /></a></td>
    <!-- ###### forces minimum height of body start ###### -->
                    <td><img src="images/spacer.gif" width="1"
                        height="257" alt="" border="0" /></td>
    <!-- ###### forces minimum height of body end ###### -->
                </tr>
                <tr>
                    <td><img src="images/spacer.gif" width="10"
                        height="1" alt="" border="0" /></td>
                    <td><img src="images/spacer.gif" width="146"
                        height="1" alt="" border="0" /></td>
                    <td><img src="images/spacer.gif" width="8"
                        height="1" alt="" border="0" /></td>
                    <td><img src="images/spacer.gif" width="260"
                        height="1" alt="" border="0" /></td>
                    <td><img src="images/spacer.gif" width="52"
                        height="1" alt="" border="0" /></td>
                </tr>
                </table>
            </td>
    <!-- ###### main text column end ###### -->
        </tr>
        <tr>
            <td colspan="3" style="background-image: url(images/
                bg_bottom_line.gif); background-repeat: repeat-x"><img
                src="images/bottom_left_square.gif" width="80"
                height="9" alt="" border="0" /></td>
        </tr>
        <tr>
            <td colspan="3"><img src="images/spacer.gif" width="1"
                height="10" alt="" border="0" /></td>
        </tr>
        </table>
    </td>
    <!-- ###### main content end ###### -->
    </tr>
```

```
<tr>
    <td bgcolor="#7D7D7D"><img src="images/spacer.gif" width="144"
        height="1" alt="" border="0" /></td>
    <td bgcolor="#7D7D7D"><img src="images/spacer.gif" width="1"
        height="1" alt="" border="0" /></td>
    <td bgcolor="#7D7D7D"><img src="images/spacer.gif" width="625"
        height="1" alt="" border="0" /></td>
</tr>
<!-- ###### footer start ###### -->
<tr>
<td colspan="3" style="background-color: #CAC9CA;"><img src="images/
    spacer.gif" width="1" height="1" alt="" border="0" /></td>
</tr>
<tr>
    <td align="center" colspan="3" style="background-color: #EDEAD1;
        height:26px"><span style="color:#000000">41909 N. Shield St.,
        Suite 345  |  Fort Collins, CO 80524  |  Phone: 970.555.1130 |
        Fax: 970.555.1129
<br /><br />
© copyright 2004-2005 | MoPo Photography | all rights reserved
</span>
    </td>
</tr>
<tr>
    <td colspan="3" style="background-color: #EDEAD1;"><img
        src="images/spacer.gif" width="1" height="10" alt=""
        border="0" /></td>
</tr>
<!-- ###### footer end ###### -->
</table>
</body>
</html>
```

This code contains 7 tables and 185 lines of code to lay out the elements of the page. CSS-based design is much cleaner, reducing the weight, or download file size, of a page. The page contains only 67 lines of code. Listing 4.2 displays the code to produce the design in Figure 4.4.

LISTING 4.2   CSS Code for Figure 4.4

```
<!DOCTYPE html PUBLIC "-//W3C//DTD XHTML 1.0 Transitional//EN"
    "DTD/xhtml1-transitional.dtd">
<html>
<head>
<title>MoPo Photography</title>
<!--- link to main stylesheet that controls text sizes and colors,
    among other things --->
<link rel="stylesheet" href="mainstyle.css" type="text/css" />
</head>
<body>
<div id="a5-header">
    <span class="toprightimage"><img src="images/header-right.jpg"
        width="329" height="73" alt="" border="0" id="toprightimage"
        /></span>
```

```
        <img src="images/header-left.jpg" width="431" height="73" alt=""
            border="0" />
</div>
<div id="a5-title">
     
</div>
<!-- ###### left column start ###### -->
<div id="a5-column-left">
<!-- ###### menu start ###### -->
    <div id="a5-menu">
        <div class="a5-menu-odd">
            <a href="index.htm">home</a>
        </div>
        <div class ="a5-menu-even">
            <a href="about.htm">about</a>
        </div>
        <div class ="a5-menu-odd">
            <a href="awards.htm">awards</a>
        </div>
        <div class ="a5-menu-even">
            <a href="services.htm">services</a>
        </div>
        <div class ="a5-menu-odd">
            <a href="contact.htm">contact</a>
        </div>
    </div>
<!-- ###### menu end ###### -->
    <br />
    <div id="photo_bottom_left">
        <a href="index.htm"><img src="images/photo_bottom_left.jpg"
            width="144" height="92" alt="" border="0" /></a>
    </div>
    <div style="padding:12px 5px 0px 5px;"><b>"The best thing about
        photographs is the person's face who views them 60 years
        later, seeing herself as a young girl. No one can reminisce
        too much."</b><br /><br />Joe Mo, Owner, MoPo Family
        Photography</div>
</div>
<!-- ###### left column end ###### -->
<div id="a5-column-left-center">
    <img src="images/tagline.gif" width="80" height="285" alt=""
        border="0" />
</div>
<div id="a5-column-right-center">
    <img src="images/image-left-of-text.gif" width="69" height="285"
        alt="" border="0" />
</div>
<!-- ###### right column start ###### -->
<div id="a5-column-right">
    <img src="images/image-above-text.gif" width="476" height="36"
        alt="" border="0" />
    <div id="a5-column-right-bottom">
```

```
        <span class="photo"><img src="images/photo-middle-right.jpg"
            width="260" height="265" alt="" border="0" /></span>
Sometimes the best way to say something is in a frame. At MoPo Family
    Photography, we pride ourselves on taking as many photos as
    humanly and digitally possible so you get the best shot. We have
    redundant server and battery backups, so we never run out of
    opportunities to take photos and back them up. All our
    photographers enjoy excellent reputations in the Northern Colorado
    area.  With more than 25 years of combined experience in this
    specialized area, we have the ability to satisfy all your family's
    photographic needs.
<br /><br />
MoPo Family Photography is located near the art district in Fort
    Collins. We are not limited to Colorado, though. We travel
    throughout the country for various photographic events.
      <a href="x.htm" style="text-decoration:none"><b>&raquo;
    &raquo; Learn more</b></a>
    </div>
    <div id="copyright">
        41909 N. Shield St., Suite 345  |  Fort Collins, CO 80524  |
            Phone: 970.555.1130 | Fax: 970.555.1129
<br /><br />
© copyright 2004-2005 | MoPo Photography | all rights reserved
    </div>
</div>
<!-- ###### right column end ###### -->
</body>
</html>
```

Not only is the code much cleaner in Listing 4.2, but the file size is dramatically reduced, coming in at approximately 3.2 KB versus 11.2 KB for the table-based design in Listing 4.1. Because there is more CSS added to a stylesheet to create such a design, the stylesheet is going to be larger, but not by much. The stylesheet weight for Listing 4.1 is approximately 0.70 KB, while the weight for Listing 4.2 comes in around 3.6 KB. When the entire coding weight of each design is added up, the table-based design comes in around 12 KB, while the CSS-based design comes in at 6.8 KB, making a difference of nearly 50%. And this is only for one page. When the reduced file size for additional pages on the site is compounded, the reduction becomes much greater.

Understanding the Box Model

To design a CSS-based design such as in Figure 4.4, the designer needs to use the *box model* method. This method involves wrapping <DIV> and <SPAN> (at least with the style used in this book) tags around page elements to position and place them. These tags are commonly referred to as containers because they are used to style elements that are contained within them.

When thinking in terms of a table-based design, the box model's containers are analogous to individual tables being nested inside one another. Positioning with CSS-based design is different than with table-based design. The latter uses table elements, such as table rows, columns, and cells, many times in association with spacer.gifs, to determine where items are placed. The former uses CSS's absolute or relative positioning to tell the boxes exactly where they will be in terms of the top-left corner of the browser or in relation to a box or container in which it is nested.

Listing 4.3 displays a Web page with a stylesheet that tells the box with the id value of photo_bottom_left where it needs to be positioned in relation to the top-left corner of the page, with the X,Y coordinates being 0,0.

LISTING 4.3   Code for a Web Site That Uses the Box Model

```
<!DOCTYPE html PUBLIC "-//W3C//DTD XHTML 1.0 Transitional//EN"
    "DTD/xhtml1-transitional.dtd">
<html>
<head>
    <title>A5design</title>
    <style>
        body {
            margin:0px;
            padding:0px;
            background:#ffffff;
        }
        #logo {
            position:absolute;
            top:245px;
            left:160px;
border:1px solid #000000;
        }
    </style>
</head>
<body>
    <div id="logo"><a href="index.htm"><img src="images/logo.jpg"
        width="144" height="92" alt="" border="0" /></a></div>
</body>
</html>
```

Figure 4.6 illustrates how the image is placed 245 pixels from the top and 160 pixels from the left. The property border has been added with a value of 1 and a color of #000000. This turns on the border to allow the designer to better see the size of the box.

When two other <DIV> tags are added, for example, they also can have either absolute or relative positioning assigned to them. In Listing 4.4, the <DIV> tag with the id of box2 is given absolute positioning outside the photo_bottom_left box. The <DIV> tag with the id of box3 is given relative positioning inside the <DIV> tag with the id of box2.

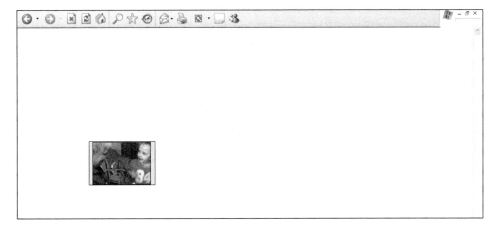

FIGURE 4.6   Box placed inside a Web page with absolute positioning forcing the image 245 pixels from the top and 160 pixels from the left.

LISTING 4.4   Relative Versus Absolute Positioning of Boxes

```
<!DOCTYPE html PUBLIC "-//W3C//DTD XHTML 1.0 Transitional//EN"
    "DTD/xhtml1-transitional.dtd">
<html>
<head>
    <title>A5design</title>
    <style>
        body {
            margin:0px;
            padding:0px;
            background:#ffffff;
            }
        #photo_bottom_left {
            position:absolute;
            top:245px;
            left:160px;
            border:1px solid #000000;
            }
        #box2 {
            position:absolute;
            top:400px;
            left:350px;
            width:100px;
            color:#ffffff;
            background:#000000;
            border:1px solid #000000;
            }
        #box3 {
            position:relative;
            top:0px;
            left:50px;
```

```
            height:100px;
            background:#D5C012;
            border:1px solid #000000;
            }
    </style>
</head>
<body>
    <div id="photo_bottom_left"><a href="index.htm"><img src="images/
        photo_bottom_left.jpg" width="144" height="92" alt=""
        border="0" /></a></div>
    <div id="box2">
        This is box 2
        <div id="box3">This is box 3</div>
    </div>
</body>
</html>
```

NOTE

The margin:0px; and padding:0px properties and values are added to the <BODY> tag in the stylesheet to ensure that the content is positioned in the top-left corner of the browser. If these attributes are not added, content will not always begin at the X,Y attributes of 0,0 in a browser. Depending on the browser, this distance can change. Similar to XHTML table-based designs, it is necessary to declare background page colors when creating CSS-based designs, which is why the background property is added. This is included to ensure that all browsers use the same background color, not leaving the option to be declared by their default values.

When the page is displayed, box2 is located 100 pixels from the top and 350 pixels from the left. box3 is then placed inside the box2 tag and positioned 50 pixels from the left. Both boxes are assigned background colors and have their borders turned on to better illustrate their shapes and positions (see Figure 4.7).

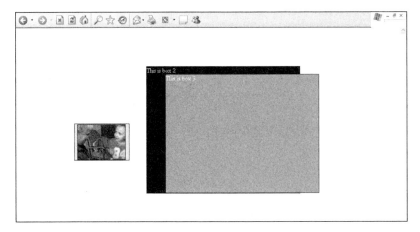

FIGURE 4.7   A box with relative positioning placed inside a box with absolute positioning.

Because box3 is positioned inside box2 using relative positioning, the latter stretches to the full height of both boxes. If, however, box3 is assigned absolute, instead of relative, positioning in the stylesheet (see Listing 4.5), it will react differently (see Figure 4.8).

- Following are three things to notice about how the relationship between the two boxes changes:
- Rather than position itself relative to box2, box3 positions itself from the top-left corner of box2. While using the z-index selector can change which box is on top of the other, it does not change the fact that overlapping now occurs.
- box2 will not recognize the combined height of the two boxes. Rather, it will recognize only its height. This is important to keep in mind because some sites require the designer to nest <DIV> tags in such a manner. However, the designer needs to know that if the height of the nested <DIV> is greater than the height of the parent <DIV>, the nested box will stretch past the parent box.

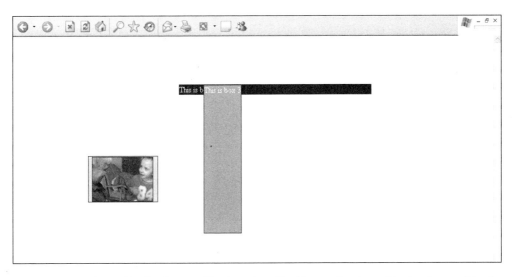

FIGURE 4.8   A box with absolute positioning placed inside another box with absolute positioning.

The nested box does not inherit the width of the parent box. It will now need to be forced in the stylesheet, using the width property.

LISTING 4.5   Box with the Height Forced

```
#box3 {
    position:relative;
    top:0px;
    left:50px;
    height:300px;
    background:#D5C012;
```

```
border:1px solid #000000;
}
```

These are just the overall concepts of the box model. Similar to XHTML tables, the box model, once understood at the basic level, can be used in more creative and advanced ways, such as the site shown in Figure 4.4. The case studies later in the book provide more detailed examples of building sites such as in this figure.

The box model is not interpreted the same between Internet Explorer® (IE) 5.0 and IE 5.5 browsers. One method of dealing with this bug is to use the Tantek Celik hack in the stylesheet (see Figure 4.11). This hack and the box model bug are explained in Chapter 5.

Adding elements with various properties and values can alter the way containers interact with each other, especially depending on the browser version and operating system. This requires the designer to always test a site in different browsers and sometimes even on different operating systems. IE 5.2 for Macs, for example, adds a narrow column of space between the right side of a design and the browser window when two <DIV>s with absolute positioning assigned to both of them are nested inside one another <DIV>.

WHEN TO USE TABLES

Some CSS purists believe CSS Web designs should include very little, if any, XHTML. While there are more advantages than disadvantages to creating CSS-based sites over table-based designs, this does not mean that there is no longer a need for tables.

Tables serve a practical purpose in Web design: handling columns and rows of data. While there are ways to handle such content using CSS, there is no reason XHTML cannot and should not be used in such circumstances, such as in Figure 4.9. In this example, 77 cells are used in the table. CSS would, in many cases, be too time-consuming to create and maintain.

LINKING TO CSS STYLESHEETS

While there are different ways to include a stylesheet, such as linking, embedding, and including inline, imported stylesheets offer one thing the others do not: they prevent older browsers that do not fully support CSS from crashing. While some browsers may not correctly display sites that use CSS, older browsers, such as Netscape® 4.7, can choke on the CSS. To avoid this problem, the designer needs to import the stylesheet (see Listing 4.6).

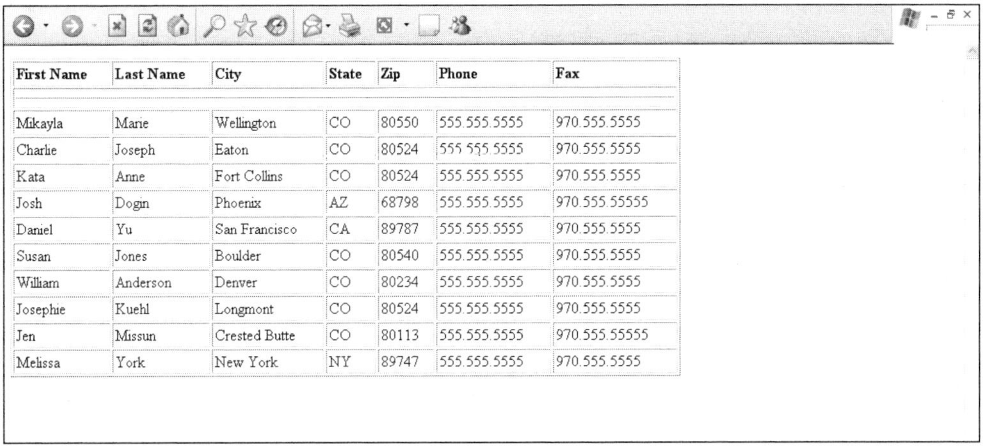

First Name	Last Name	City	State	Zip	Phone	Fax
Mikayla	Marie	Wellington	CO	80550	555.555.5555	970.555.5555
Charlie	Joseph	Eaton	CO	80524	555.555.5555	970.555.5555
Kata	Anne	Fort Collins	CO	80524	555.555.5555	970.555.5555
Josh	Dogin	Phoenix	AZ	68798	555.555.5555	970.555.55555
Daniel	Yu	San Francisco	CA	89787	555.555.5555	970.555.5555
Susan	Jones	Boulder	CO	80540	555.555.5555	970.555.5555
William	Anderson	Denver	CO	80234	555.555.5555	970.555.5555
Josephie	Kuehl	Longmont	CO	80524	555.555.5555	970.555.5555
Jen	Missun	Crested Butte	CO	80113	555.555.5555	970.555.55555
Melissa	York	New York	NY	89747	555.555.5555	970.555.5555

FIGURE 4.9 Example Web page where using an XHTML table is more practical than using CSS to position 77 cells of data.

LISTING 4.6 Code Used to Import Stylesheet

```
<style type="text/css" media="all">
    @import "mainstyle.css";
</style>
```

INCLUDING PRINT STYLESHEETS

A designer no longer has to create separate pages that are used specifically for printing a page. The following stylesheet link simply needs to be added to the page's code.

```
<link rel="stylesheet" href="print.css" type="text/css"
    media="print" />
```

Once this link has been added, the browser will call a separate stylesheet the browsers will use for printing purposes. Usually, the stylesheet is a copied version of the main stylesheet, which is then modified to display the page the way the designer desires. If the header, for example, does not need to be printed, the designer can change the stylesheet to hide that element of the page. Following are several things a designer should consider changing to make a page more printer-friendly:

- The font size could be changed to points for printing purposes. Otherwise, the page may not print sizes, such as pixels, clearly.
- Any section can be turned off by replacing all navigation rules in a `<DIV>` or `<SPAN>` tag with the rule `display:none;`. For example, the following style could have all its rules removed:

```
#a5-header {
    position:relative;
    top:0px;
    height:73px;
    background-image: url(images/bg-header.gif);
    voice-family: "\"}\""; voice-family:inherit;
    height:73px;
    }
    html>body #a5-header {
    height:73px;
    }
```
The display:none; rule could then be added to make the style look like:
```
#a5-header {
    display:none;
    }
```

By making this change, anything in the container with the id value of a5-header would be hidden from the printer. To test what the page will look like, the designer can select Print Preview in the browser, rather than actually having to print it (see Figure 4.10).

■ The text to be printed can be easily resized to fit the screen however the designer chooses.
■ Colors that may not print very well in gray scale, such as a yellow, can be changed to a darker color.

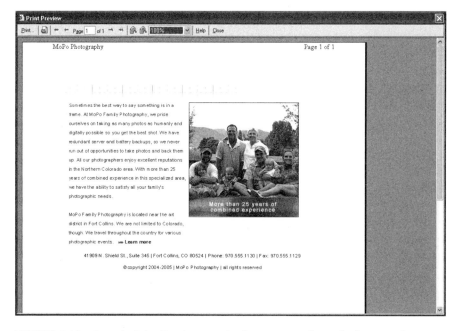

FIGURE 4.10 Page in Print Preview mode that uses a print stylesheet to change how it is printed, compared to how it looks in browser mode (see Figure 4.4).

Figure 4.10 illustrates how drastically a page can be changed when using a print stylesheet. Many of the elements of the page, including the header, menu, and content columns, were removed so only the necessary information would be printed. The figure is a screenshot of the Print Preview menu item in Internet Explorer.

UNDERSTANDING CSS TERMINOLOGY

As mentioned earlier, it is assumed that the designer has a working, if limited, knowledge of CSS. Recalling terminology, however, is not always the easiest thing to do, which is why Figure 4.11 was created. It provides a basic visual example of CSS elements and their terminology in a CSS stylesheet.

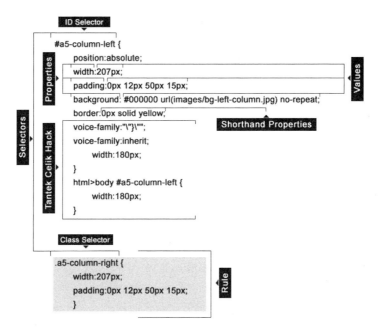

FIGURE 4.11   A visual reference of CSS terminology, including an example of the Tantek Celik hack.

Following are the various items to note about the code in Figure 4.11:

Selectors: These are used when declaring and calling a particular rule. Figure 4.11 identifies two types of selectors: an ID selector and a Class selector, both of which can be used with XHTML tags, such as <DIV> or <SPAN>.

Properties: Various aspects of a selector that can be used for different styles.

Values: The specific qualities of properties.

Shorthand Properties: A method of combining multiple related values for a property under one general property. An example would be combining `padding-top:10px; padding-right:15px; padding-bottom:25px; padding-left:30px` into one property that looks like `padding:10px 15px 25px 30px;`.

Rule: The entire grouping of a selector, a property (or properties), and value(s).

Tantek Celik Hack: While this is not necessarily considered CSS terminology, it is used enough by many designers that it is worth noting in a visual example.

CSS USED IN THIS BOOK

The CSS coding philosophy used in this book is to be creative with a limited number of CSS properties and values, rather than use those that do not necessarily function under all conditions. In other words, the goal is to be the most flexible with the smallest number of properties and values that are proven to work in the widest range of browsers and their versions. While there is a much wider array of possibilities for a designer, it is left to the designer to expand upon what is discussed in this book. Table 4.1 lists many properties that are used in this book. Many of them are shorthand examples, meaning one property is used to set the various values that could be broken up into other properties.

TABLE 4.1   Some of the CSS Properties Used in This Book

Example Property	Usage
`margin:0px 0px 0px 0px;`	Used for setting the distance between the outside border of a container and what it is nested inside of.
`padding:0px 0px 0px 0px;`	Used for setting the distance between the outside border of a container and what it is nested inside it.
`font:13px Arial, Helvetica, sans-serif;` `font-weight:bold;`	Used to set the size, face, and weight of a font. The bold value, however, does not work in all situations, which is why it is sometimes separated out as `font-weight:bold;` or included in the XHTML code.
`color:#000000;`	Used to set the text color.
`a:link { color:#FF7800; }`	Used to set a hyperlink color.
`a:visited { color:#FF5A00; }`	Used to set the hyperlink color of a visited, or previously clicked, link.

$\rightarrow$

Example Property	Usage
`a:active { color:#FFC600; }`	Used for defining the color of a link while it is being clicked and has not yet been released.
`a:hover { color:#000000; }`	Used for changing the color of a hyperlink when it is moused over but has yet to be clicked.
`a.linklist:link { text-decoration:none; color:#308DAE;}`	Used for setting the color of a link with an assigned class (e.g., `class="linklist"`).
`a.linklist:visited { text-decoration:none; color:#308DAE;}`	Used for setting the visited color of a link with an assigned class (e.g., `class="linklist"`).
`a.linklist:active { text-decoration:none; color:#308DAE;}`	Used for setting the active color of a link with an assigned class (e.g., `class="linklist"`).
`a.linklist:hover { text-decoration:underline; color:#FF7800;}`	Used for setting the hover color of a link with an assigned class (e.g., `class="linklist"`).
`border: 1px solid #000000;`	Used for setting the border of a CSS element to 1, with a specified color.
`text-align:left;` `text-align:right;` `text-align:center;`	Used to control the horizontal placement of content, whether the value `left`, `right`, or `center` is used.
`position:relative;` `position:absolute;`	Used to define whether a box, or container, in the box model will be assigned relative or absolute positioning.
`float:right;` `float:left;` `float:center;`	Used to position elements to the left or right in content.
`clear:both;`	Used to remove floating elements from the left and right sides of a container.
`width:100%;`	Used to set the width of an element, such as a box.
`margin-left:auto;` `margin-right:auto;` `left:0px;`	Used when centering a fixed-width Web page.
`right:0px;`	Used for setting how many pixels from the left or right side of the body or a parent box an element is placed.

→

Example Property	Usage
`top:0px;` `bottom:0px;`	Used for setting how many pixels from the top or bottom of the body or a parent box an element is placed.
`height:78px;`	Used for forcing the height of an element.

`width:88px;`
`voice-family:"\"}\";`
`voice-family:inherit;`
`width:78px;`
`}`
`html>body #a5-header {`
`    width: 78px;`	

`}`	Used for setting various properties and values for different browsers. It is called the Tantek Celik hack or Tantek hack and is explained in Chapter 5.
`line-height:42px;`	
`vertical-align:30%;`	Used for forcing the vertical positioning of text in an element. The line-height property needs to be included for the vertical-align property to be interpreted by the browser.

`background:#000000 url`
`(images/bg-menu.gif)`
`repeat-x 0px 0px;`
	Used for determining what background image is used, where it is placed, and how it is repeated. The HEX value sets what the background color of an element will be if the background does not fill the entire space.

UNDERSTANDING THE DOCTYPE DECLARATION

A DocType Declaration (DTD) is a line of code that should be included in the first line of every Web page, barring include files. The most basic explanation of a DTD is that it defines the rules of how a browser should render a Web page, based on World Wide Web Consortium (W3C) standards. Various types of declarations can be used, depending on how the designer wants a Web page to be interpreted by a browser and validated by the W3C. In other words, pages can be interpreted on their HTML, XHTML, or XML coding. The designs in this book are created using the following XHTML 1.0 transitional declaration:

```
<!DOCTYPE html PUBLIC "-//W3C//DTD XHTML 1.0 Transitional//EN"
    "DTD/xhtml1-transitional.dtd">
```

VALIDATING CODE

The W3C is the governing body when it comes to the creation of Web standards that help the Web "reach its true potential," according to the consortium. Over the years, an increasing number of designers and developers have begun adhering to such standards. They have become so prevalent that various search engines use whether a page is W3C compliant in their placement formulas.

During Web page design, both XHTML and CSS should be validated, using the W3C's free online validating services. They not only help a developer understand what code is not compliant, but they now provide explanations and examples of correctly written code. Following are the URLs for each validating service:

XHTML Markup Validation Service: *http://validator.w3.org/*

CSS Validation Service: *http://jigsaw.w3.org/css-validator/*. At the time of publication, some properties are validated differently if a URL, as opposed to an uploaded file, is submitted to the validator. Because the URL version of the software is used more often, it is probably wise for the designer to validate pages on servers beforehand.

The W3C also offers a downloadable version of its CSS Validator. The software can be found at *http://dev.w3.org/cvsweb/2002/css-validator/*

Once a page is validated, the W3C provides and encourages designers and developers to include a W3C validation image on the page, which verifies that the page has been validated for either XHTML or CSS or both.

TESTING DESIGNS IN VARIOUS BROWSERS

Because CSS is not interpreted as consistently as XHTML, it requires more testing. The designs in this book were tested using the following browsers:

- Internet Explorer (IE) 6.029
- Internet Explorer 5.5
- Internet Explorer 5.0
- FireFox® 1.0.7
- Netscape 7.1
- Opera 8.5

Based on Web-usage statistics by W3C Schools (*http://www.w3schools.com/browsers/browsers_stats.asp*), these browsers represent more than 99% of the users on the Web. Such statistics, obviously, fluctuate depending on whose statistics are considered and what their target audience is; however, it is safe to assume that these six browsers will represent the majority of users in the near future.

Downloading versions of non-Microsoft browsers can be accomplished by visiting their respective sites. Downloading older versions of IE is not so easy. A useful site for downloading various browsers is http://browsers.evolt.org/. The site offers various versions of IE, in addition to many other browsers. Because IE 6 is fully integrated into Micosoft operating systems, it is sometimes necessary to load modified versions of IE 5.5 and IE 5.0. It is important to note that this book's author and its publisher are not to be held accountable for any adverse effects of loading such software. The designer or developer does so at his or her own risk.

SUMMARY

While there is a learning curve that comes with changing a coding style from creating XHTML table-based designs to CSS-based designs, this chapter, along with Chapter 5, helps reduce the curve exponentially. In this chapter the designer learns the basics of creating such designs. Other useful pieces of information offered include how to create print stylesheets, the basic number of properties that are used with the designs in this book, and how to validate such code to make sure it is compliant with W3C standards.

5 Tips and Techniques

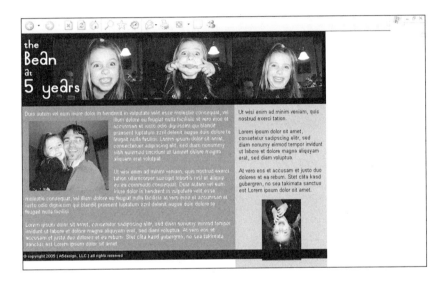

When first learning how to build Web sites, the most time-consuming aspect is not always creating the look and feel of the site in image-editing software such as Photoshop®. Rather, a designer can spend a lot of time figuring out how to code or program the site. The tips and techniques included in this chapter are offered to help save the reader time researching methods and workarounds for creating sites. While not all the tips will be useful while building one site, many of them will eventually arise if the reader builds many sites over time.

TANTEK OR BOX MODEL HACK

If it were not for the Tantek hack, also referred to as the Celik or Box Model hack, creating more complex pure CSS designs for both compliant and noncompliant browsers would be considerably more difficult—at least for most designers who are not experienced purists, who prefer to use only compliant code.

The main reason for the use of this hack is that versions of the IE 5 and 5.5 browsers treat the box model differently than other browsers. The way the box model is designed to work is that when the width property is assigned to a container, that width is supposed to represent only the width of the container. Borders, padding, and margin widths are not to be included in the total number of pixels. Thus, if the width of the box is set to 200px, with the left and right padding properties set to 50px, which adds 50 pixels to both the left and right sides, the total width of the box would grow to 300px (see Figure 5.1).

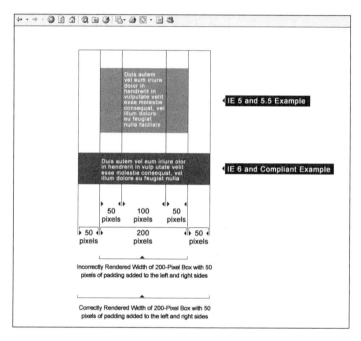

FIGURE 5.1 Example demonstrating how the box model is interpreted differently between IE 5 and 5.5 browsers and IE 6 and compliant browsers.

While newer browsers interpret the width property to W3C specifications, IE 5 and 5.5 do not. Rather than add the extra 100 pixels to the total, they include the extra pixels within the declared 200 pixels. This means the total width that is used for the content is reduced by the increased number of pixels. Thus, in Figure 5.1 the total width of the content area has 100 pixels subtracted from the total 200 pixels.

IE 6 will interpret the box model incorrectly if it is not in "quirks" mode, which means the page requires a valid DocType tag at the beginning of the documents (e.g., `<!DOCTYPE html PUBLIC "-//W3C//DTD XHTML 1.0 Transitional//EN" "http://www.w3.org/TR/xhtml1/DTD/xhtml1-transitional.dtd">`*).*

NOTE

Because of this bug, the designer needs to write code that works for two different environments. Some CSS purists feel stylesheets should not include hacks. To accomplish this, a designer needs to resort to various workarounds, such as branching JavaScript. The majority of designers, however, use the Tantek hack, which feeds different values for IE 5 and 5.5, IE 6, and compliant browsers. The nontechnical way the hack functions is a three-step method:

1. The CSS rule assigns the width, along with other styles, for the box element, from which all browsers read.

```
#tantek_hack_box {
position:relative;
background:#888787;
color:#ffffff;
padding-left:50px;
padding-right:50px;
width:200px;     }
```

2. The hack is added, which first reassigns the width for the IE 6 browser.

```
#tantek_hack_box {
position:relative;
background:#888787;
color:#ffffff;
padding-left:50px;
padding-right:50px;
width:200px;
voice-family:"\"}\"";
voice-family:inherit;
    width:100px;
}
html>body #tantek_hack_box {
}
```

3. The hack then assigns the width that will be read by compliant browsers. In this step the designer needs to add the same CSS selector to the new piece of code at the end.

```
#tantek_hack_box {
position:relative;
background:#888787;
color:#ffffff;
padding-left:50px;
padding-right:50px;
width:200px;
voice-family:"\"}\"";
voice-family:inherit;
    width:100px;
}
html>body #tantek_hack_box {
    width:100px;
}
```

Because there are other instances where various browsers treat CSS code differently, the Tantek hack can be used for other properties. A common use is to reposition elements that need to be altered when they have been nested inside other boxes and have inherited different values. The following code is used to position the two bottom-right columns of content in Figure 5.2 so that it appears the same in IE 5 and 5.5 browsers and other major browsers.

```
#a5-featured-center {
    position:relative;
    left:-5px;
    top:-57px;
    color:#DF7A1B;
    border:0px solid #000000;
    margin:38px 124px 0px 208px;
    padding:19px 10px 0px 0px;
    voice-family:"\"}\"";
    voice-family:inherit;
        margin:140px 158px 0px 180px;
        left:27px;
        top:-159px;
}
html>body #a5-featured-center {
        margin:41px 130px 0px 207px;
        padding:19px 10px 0px 0px;
        left:0px;
        top:-60px;
}
```

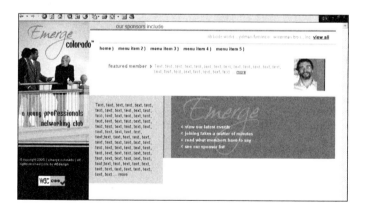

FIGURE 5.2 A design in IE 5.5 that uses the Tantek hack to correctly position the bottom-right columns of content in IE 5 browsers and other major browsers. © 2006 Emerge Colorado. Used with permission.

When the hack is not applied, the site will look completely different in other browsers. Figure 5.3 shows how different the positioning would end up in IE 6, for example.

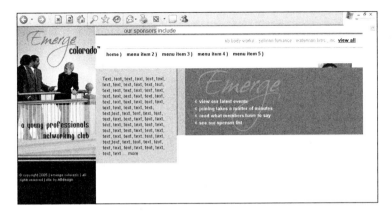

FIGURE 5.3 The design shown in Figure 5.2, viewed in IE 6 with the Tantek hack removed. © 2006 Emerge Colorado. Used with permission.

The Tantek hack is not always necessary. Sometimes the CSS code needs only to be cleaned up or reworked to accomplish the same look and feel.

While the Tantek hack is not considered pure form, the W3C CSS validator will validate the code with only a warning. A good place to learn more about the hack is to go to http://tantek.com/CSS/Examples/boxmodelhack.html.

NAMING RULES AND PROPERTIES CORRECTLY

Occasionally, the designer may add a style and either the page does not reflect the proper styling or the styling is incorrect. A few common errors can occur:

- The style on the page does not match the correct spelling in the stylesheet.

```
<style type="text/css">
    #samplestyle {
    color:#ffffff;
    }
</style>
<div id="sample_style">
    This is sample text
</div>
```

Should read as:

```
<style type="text/css">
    #samplestyle {
    color:#ffffff;
```

```
    }
  </style>
  <div id="samplestyle">
      This is sample text
  </div>
```

■   The style on the page may be referencing an ID selector when the selector in the stylesheet is actually a class or vice versa.

```
  <style type="text/css">
      .samplestyle {
      color:#ffffff;
      }
  </style>
  <div id="samplestyle">
      This is sample text
  </div>
```

Should read as:

```
  <style type="text/css">
      .samplestyle {
      color:#ffffff;
      }
  </style>
  <div class="samplestyle">
      This is sample text
  </div>
```

■   The syntax of a style may not be correct. Missing semicolons are an occasional reason for this error.

```
  <style type="text/css">
      #samplestyle {
      color:#ffffff;
      background:red
      }
  </style>
```

Should read as:

```
  <style type="text/css">
      #samplestyle {
      color:#ffffff;
      background:red;
      }
  </style>
```

Although it does not have anything to do with styling, another naming error a designer can make is to call the same ID class with two separate tags in the XHTML. While the page may still display correctly, the XHTML will not validate because an ID class can be referenced only once in a document.

Two other naming issues are more difficult to find. Sometimes, without removing code to test the problem, the designer will not find where the error is occurring.

■ **Two rules could have the same selector name.** Because it is easy to copy a rule and simply modify it to serve as another rule, the designer can sometimes forget to rename the new rule. If a new rule has been added but its properties are not being applied in the browser, the problem could be that it has the same name as another rule.

```
<style type="text/css">
    #style1 {
    color:yellow;
    background:black;
    }
    #style2 {
    color:white;
    background:blue;
    }
    #style1 {
    color:green;
    background:purple;
    }
</style>
<div id="style1">
    This is sample text
</div>
<div id="style3">
    This is sample text
</div>
```

Should read as:

```
<style type="text/css">
    #style1 {
    color:yellow;
    background:black;
    }
    #style2 {
    color:white;
    background:blue;
    }
    #style3 {
    color:green;
    background:purple;
    }
</style>
<div id="style1">
    This is sample text
</div>
<div id="style3">
    This is sample text
</div>
```

■ **A rule applies correctly to IE browsers but not to compliant browsers.** This problem is hidden within the Tantek hack. The designer has to be sure the selector in the compliant-browser portion of the hack has the same name as the selector of the rule it is associated with.

```
#samplestyle {
position:relative;
background:#414141;
color:#ffffff;
padding-left:50px;
padding-right:50px;
padding-top:10px;
width:400px;
voice-family:"\"}\"";
voice-family:inherit;
    width:300px;
}
html>body #style2 {
    width:300px;
}
```

Should read as:

```
#samplestyle {
position:relative;
background:#414141;
color:#ffffff;
padding-left:50px;
padding-right:50px;
padding-top:10px;
width:400px;
voice-family:"\"}\"";
voice-family:inherit;
    width:300px;
}
html>body #samplestyle {
    width:300px;
}
```

REMOVING BODY MARGINS AND PADDING

By default, browsers add top and left space between the browser window and the content that is output (see Figure 5.4). This space varies depending on the browser.

Removing the space is easily accomplished. The designer needs only to assign the style to the HTML and BODY selectors in the main stylesheet:

```
html, body {
    margin:0px;
    padding:0px;
    background:#ffffff;
    }
```

FIGURE 5.4 Web site with default margins that add space between the top and left edges of the Web window and the design.

For most browsers, setting the margin to 0px *removes the spacing. Opera, however, requires the designer to set the padding setting to* 0px.

Adding the margin and padding properties will make the page begin in the very top-left corner of the browser's window (see Figure 5.5). It is also always good form to define the background color.

FIGURE 5.5 Page with the margin and padding properties for the <HTML> and <BODY> tags set to 0px.

CREATING THE FRAMEWORK FOR A FIXED-WIDTH CSS DESIGN

The four case studies in Chapters 6, 7, 8, and 9 go into the specifics of creating fixed designs that can also be easily modified to be liquid layouts. This section, however, explains the basics of creating the framework for such a design. Following are the various stages of creating such a design:

1. Add basic XHTML framework and initial style rule.

Things to note about the code in this step:

■ As with table-based designs, the code in Listing 5.1 provides the basic structure that contains the DocType, character encoding labeling, embedded or linked stylesheet, and the code and content that are to be displayed on the page. A rule then defines the margins, padding, font, font color, and background color for the <HTML> and <BODY> tags.

LISTING 5.1   Code for Step 1

```
<!DOCTYPE html PUBLIC "-//W3C//DTD XHTML 1.0 Transitional//EN"
    "DTD/xhtml1-transitional.dtd">
<html><head><title>Fixed-Width Design</title>
<meta http-equiv="Content-Type" content="text/html;
    charset=iso-8859-1" />
<style type="text/css">
html, body {
    margin:0px;
    padding:0px;
    font: 13px Arial, Helvetica, sans-serif;
    color:#000000;
    background:#ffffff;
    }
</style>
</head>
<body>
</body>
</html>
```

2. Create body and header rules in the stylesheet and add code to the XHTML body (see Figure 5.6).

Things to note about the code in this step:

■ The a5-body rule is used as a container to restrain the width of the entire page to 770 pixels. The advantage of being able to control the width is that if the designer wants the design to expand to the full width of the screen, the value of the width property simply needs to be set to 100%.

<DIV> tags, by default, will stretch to 100% width of the screen when assigned relative positioning. If absolute positioning is assigned, the tag, by default, will expand only as wide as the content expands the container.

■ The `a5-header` rule sets the basic properties of the `<DIV>` tag that will be assigned to the content inside the tag (see Listing 5.2).

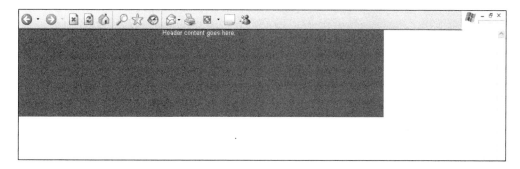

FIGURE 5.6 Design with header area added, along with a tag that restrains the width of the design to 770 pixels.

LISTING 5.2 Code for Step 2

```
<!DOCTYPE html PUBLIC "-//W3C//DTD XHTML 1.0 Transitional//EN"
    "DTD/xhtml1-transitional.dtd">
<html><head><title>Fixed-Width Design</title>
<meta http-equiv="Content-Type" content="text/html;
    charset=iso-8859-1" />
<style type="text/css">
html, body {
    margin:0px;
    padding:0px;
    font: 13px Arial, Helvetica, sans-serif;
    color:#000000;
    background:#ffffff;
    }
#a5-body {
    position: absolute;
    left:0px;
    top:0px;
    width: 770px;
    text-align:left;
    }
#a5-header {
    position:absolute;
    left:0px;
    top:0px;
    text-align:center;
    color:#ffffff;
```

```
        width:100%;
        background:red;
        height:180px;
        }
</style>
</head>
<body>
<div id="a5-body">
    <div id="a5-header">
        Header content goes here.
    </div>
</div>
</body>
</html>
```

3. Create rules in the stylesheet that not only create the left and right columns but also the rule they are nested inside of. Then add the code to the XHTML body (see Figure 5.7).

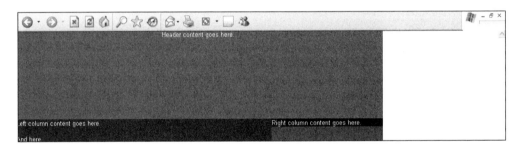

FIGURE 5.7 Design with the left and right columns added to a <DIV> tag that positions the content 180 pixels below the header <DIV>.

Things to note about the code in this step:

■ The a5-main-content rule is added to force the positioning of the left and right columns. It is positioned below the header, which is set to 180 pixels high. Therefore, the rule positions the <DIV> tag 180 pixels from the top. It also separates the nested left and right columns from the bottom footer area that will be added.

■ The a5-column-left rule is created to force the <DIV> to the top-left corner of the a5-main-content <DIV> tag. The left property tells the <DIV> tag to position itself 0 pixels from the left side. The margin-right property of the rule restricts its positioning by telling it that it must end its width at 232 pixels from the right-hand side of the page or <DIV> tag in which it is nested.

■ The a5-column-right rule is added to position the column on the right side of the page and force its width to 232 pixels. The right property tells the <DIV> tag that it is to be 0 pixels from the right side of the page.

Nesting <DIV> tags does not always function the same as nesting tables. Figure 5.7 shows that the background color of the right column does not stretch to the full height of the a5-main-content tag in which it is nested. While the designer can force the height of the right column, if the left column grows, the right column will not change its height. This situation presents a problem when repeating a background color or image. The figure shows how the background of the a5-main-content extends vertically beyond the right column but not the left column because the left column is forcing the height. Unlike with table-based design, this changes the way a designer can control the look and feel of the site (see Listing 5.3).

LISTING 5.3   Code for Step 3

```
<!DOCTYPE html PUBLIC "-//W3C//DTD XHTML 1.0 Transitional//EN"
    "DTD/xhtml1-transitional.dtd">
<html><head><title>Fixed-Width Design</title>
<meta http-equiv="Content-Type" content="text/html;
    charset=iso-8859-1" />
<style type="text/css">
html, body {
    margin:0px;
    padding:0px;
    font: 13px Arial, Helvetica, sans-serif;
    color:#000000;
    background:#ffffff;
    }
#a5-body {
    position: absolute;
    left:0px;
    top:0px;
    width:770px;
    text-align:left;
    }
#a5-header {
    position:absolute;
    left:0px;
    top:0px;
    text-align:center;
    color:#ffffff;
    width:100%;
    background:red;
    height:180px;
    }
#a5-main-content {
    position:absolute;
    left:0px;
    top:180px;
    color:#ffffff;
    width:100%;
    background:green;
    border:0px solid #ffffff;
    }
    #a5-column-left {
```

```
            position:relative;
            left:0px;
            top:0px;
            color:#ffffff;
            margin-right:232px;
            border:0px solid #ffffff;
            background:blue;
            }
        #a5-column-right {
            position:absolute;
            right:0px;
            top:0px;
            color:#ffffff;
            width:232px;
            background:black;
            border:0px solid #ffffff;
            }
</style>
</head>
<body>
<div id="a5-body">
    <div id="a5-header">
        Header content goes here.
    </div>
    <div id="a5-main-content">
        <div id="a5-column-left">
            Left column content goes here.<br /><br />And here.
        </div>
        <div id="a5-column-right">
            Right column content goes here.
        </div>
    </div>
</div>
</body>
</html>
```

4. Create a footer rule in the stylesheet and add the code to the XHTML body (see Figure 5.8).

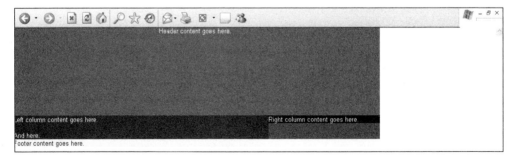

FIGURE 5.8 Design with a left column that has incorrectly assigned absolute positioning, allowing the footer area to move up and over the right column.

Things to note about the code in this step:

- The `a5-footer` rule is nested inside the `a5-main-content` tag. When the rule is assigned relative positioning, it is forced to the next line because the left and right columns fill the entire width of the page. If the `a5-column-left` rule were assigned absolute positioning without a width, the left and right columns together would not fill the entire width of the page, which would bump up the positioning of the `a5-footer` area, making the page look jumbled (see Figure 5.9).

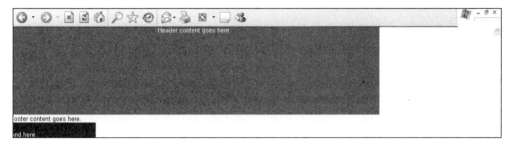

FIGURE 5.9   Completed framework of fixed-width design that includes two nested columns in a <DIV> tag that is positioned between the header and footer areas.

- The `a5-footer` rule does not need a width assigned because it is assigned relative positioning, which makes it fill 100% of the width by default (see Listing 5.4).

LISTING 5.4   Code for Step 4

```
<!DOCTYPE html PUBLIC "-//W3C//DTD XHTML 1.0 Transitional//EN"
    "DTD/xhtml1-transitional.dtd">
<html><head><title>Fixed-Width Design</title>
<meta http-equiv="Content-Type" content="text/html;
    charset=iso-8859-1" />
<style type="text/css">
html, body {
    margin:0px;
    padding:0px;
    font: 13px Arial, Helvetica, sans-serif;
    color:#000000;
    background:#ffffff;
    }
#a5-body {
    position: absolute;
    left:0px;
    top:0px;
    width:770px;
    text-align:left;
    }
```

```
#a5-header {
    position:absolute;
    left:0px;
    top:0px;
    text-align:center;
    color:#ffffff;
    width:100%;
    background:red;
    height:180px;
    }
#a5-main-content {
    position:absolute;
    left:0px;
    top:180px;
    color:#ffffff;
    width:100%;
    background:green;
    border:0px solid #ffffff;
    }
    #a5-column-left {
        position:absolute;
        left:0px;
        top:0px;
        color:#ffffff;
        margin-right:232px;
        border:0px solid #ffffff;
        background:blue;
        }
    #a5-column-right {
        position:absolute;
        right:0px;
        top:0px;
        color:#ffffff;
        width:232px;
        background:black;
        border:0px solid #ffffff;
        }
#a5-footer {
    position:relative;
    left:0px;
    top:0px;
    color:#000000;
    background:yellow;
    border:0px solid #ffffff;
    }
</style>
</head>
<body>
<div id="a5-body">
    <div id="a5-header">
        Header content goes here.
    </div>
    <div id="a5-main-content">
        <div id="a5-column-left">
            Left column content goes here.<br /><br />And here.
```

```
        </div>
        <div id="a5-column-right">
            Right column content goes here.
        </div>
        <div id="a5-footer">
            Footer content goes here.
        </div>
    </div>
</div>
</body>
</html>
```

Typically, the designer adds text, images, and additional code to the framework as it is being built. Figure 5.10 is a simplified example of how the page would look with content added and the stylesheet modified to not only make the page more attractive but to also customize various <DIV> tags.

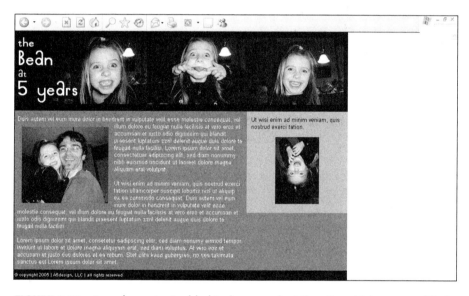

FIGURE 5.10   Sample content added to framework of the site, which was modified to accompany the content and to make it more attractive.

CONSIDER THE RESULTS OF INCREASING AND DECREASING COLUMN HEIGHTS

Although it is nice to include the footer row at the bottom of the design in Figure 5.10, there are a couple caveats to this design method, at least when including containers that use absolute positioning:

■ Because the positioning of the right column is set to absolute, if the content in the column were to be increased, it would not only stretch lower than the left column, but because the footer also has relative positioning assigned to it, the right column would also flow above or below it, depending on the browser (see Figure 5.11).

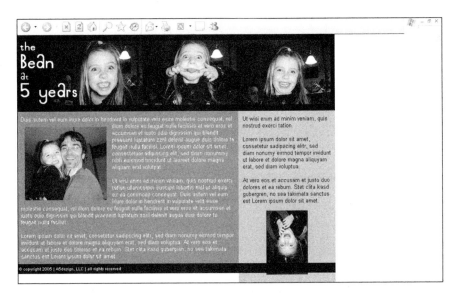

FIGURE 5.11   A problem with a container with absolute positioning (right column) running past a container with relative positioning (footer) that should, visually, remain below it.

■ If the content in the left column were to be decreased, not only would the right column extend below both it and the footer <DIV>, but the footer <DIV> would move up past the a5-main-content <DIV> (see Figure 5.12).

Because the photo in the left column of Figure 5.12 is floated, it is not included in the document flow, meaning other elements could pass above and below it, as well as in front of and behind it.

If the amount of content is going to change dynamically, this design structure may not be the best solution. The designer may consider not including a footer area and assigning different positions to the <DIV> tags, or the designer may want to use the design technique in Chapter 10 that provides a solution to creating equal column designs.

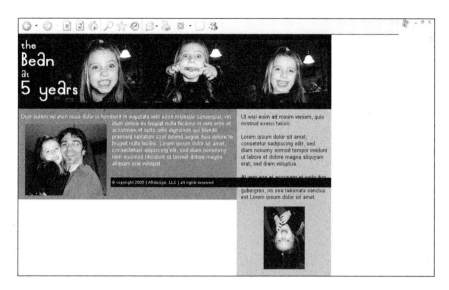

FIGURE 5.12 If content is decreased in the left column, not only does the right column move below the footer, but the footer moves up.

CENTERING A FIXED-WIDTH DESIGN

Depending on the requirements, some sites need to be designed with liquid layouts. That is, they fill the full width of the screen. Yet others require a fixed width. HTML and XHTML used to make the process simple, but with the varied browser support of CSS, the process is a little more involved. One way requires wrapping two different <DIV> tags around the body. Following are the steps to accomplish this task:

1. Add a rule to the stylesheet that centers the fixed-width design, which is set at 770 pixels for this example. This rule centers the body for IE 5 and 5.5.

    ```
    #a5-body-center {
        text-align:center;
        }
    ```

2. Add a second rule that sets the text-align property to left, assigns the left and right margins to auto, and defines the positioning as relative. Setting the positioning to relative will allow the design to be positioned relative to the <DIV> tag in which it is nested. The auto value of the margins will tell the browser to set the margins evenly on both sides, thus centering the code. The text-align:left; code is added because the a5-body-center rule that was added centers not only the body but also the text in that container by inheritance.

```
#a5-body-center {
    text-align:center;
    }

#a5-body {
    position: absolute;
    left:0px;
    top:0px;
    width:770px;
    text-align:left;
    }
```

3. Add the two <DIV> tags around the code between the <BODY> tags in the XHTML page. Listing 5.5 is the code that was used to create Figure 5.10.

LISTING 5.5   Code for Figure 5.10

```
<!DOCTYPE html PUBLIC "-//W3C//DTD XHTML 1.0 Transitional//EN"
    "DTD/xhtml1-transitional.dtd">
<html><head><title>Fixed-Width Design</title>
<meta http-equiv="Content-Type" content="text/html;
    charset=iso-8859-1" />
<style type="text/css">
html, body {
    margin:0px;
    padding:0px;
    font: 13px Arial, Helvetica, sans-serif;
    color:#000000;
    background:#ffffff;
    }
#a5-body-center {
    text-align:center;
    }
#a5-body {
    position: relative;
    margin-left:auto;
    margin-right:auto;
    width:770px;
    text-align:left;
    }
#a5-header {
    text-align:center;
    color:#ffffff;
    width:100%;
    padding-top:15px;
    background:black;
    height:180px;
    }
#a5-main-content {
    position:absolute;
    left:0px;
    top:180px;
    color:#ffffff;
    width:100%;
```

```
        background:#89766F;
        border:0px solid #ffffff;
        }
    #a5-column-left {
        position:relative;
        left:0px;
        top:0px;
        color:#ffffff;
        padding:10px;
        margin-right:232px;
        background:#7A7878;
        border:0px solid #ffffff;
        }
    #a5-column-right {
        position:absolute;
        right:0px;
        top:0px;
        color:#000000;
        height:100%;
        width:232px;
        background:#B0ADAD;
        border:0px solid #ffffff;
        }
#a5-footer {
    position:relative;
    left:0px;
    top:0px;
    font: 10px Arial, Helvetica, sans-serif;
    padding:5px;
    color:#ffffff;
    background:#000000;
    border:0px solid #ffffff;
    }
</style>
</head>
<body>
<div id="a5-body-center">
    <div id="a5-body">
        <div id="a5-header">
                <div><img src="images/photo_beanie_faces.jpg"
                width="750" height="150" alt="" border="0" /></div>
        </div>
        <div id="a5-main-content">
            <div id="a5-column-left">
                Duis autem vel eum iriure dolor in hendrerit in
                    vulputate velit esse <span  style="position:
                    relative;float:left;padding:10px;"><img
                    src="images/photo_beanie_daddy.jpg" width="200"
                    height="171" alt="" border="0" /></span>molestie
                    consequat, vel illum dolore eu feugiat nulla
                    facilisis at vero eros et accumsan et iusto odio
                    dignissim qui blandit praesent luptatum zzril
                    delenit augue duis dolore te feugait nulla
                    facilisi. Lorem ipsum dolor sit amet, consectetuer
                    adipiscing elit, sed diam nonummy nibh euismod
```

```
                              tincidunt ut laoreet dolore magna aliquam erat
                              volutpat
            <br /><br />
            Ut wisi enim ad minim veniam, quis nostrud exerci tation
                ullamcorper suscipit lobortis nisl ut aliquip ex ea commodo
                consequat. Duis autem vel eum iriure dolor in hendrerit in
                vulputate velit esse molestie consequat, vel illum dolore eu
                feugiat nulla facilisis at vero eros et accumsan et iusto
                odio dignissim qui blandit praesent luptatum zzril delenit
                augue duis dolore te feugait nulla facilisi.
            <br /><br />
            Lorem ipsum dolor sit amet, consetetur sadipscing elitr, sed diam
                nonumy eirmod tempor invidunt ut labore et dolore magna
                aliquyam erat, sed diam voluptua. At vero eos et accusam et
                justo duo dolores et ea rebum. Stet clita kasd gubergren, no
                sea takimata sanctus est Lorem ipsum dolor sit amet.
                    </div>
                    <div id="a5-column-right">
                        <div style="padding:10px;">
            Ut wisi enim ad minim veniam, quis nostrud exerci tation.
                        <br />
                        <div style="text-align:center;padding:15px 0px 10px
                            0px;"><img src="images/photo_beanie_right.jpg"
                            width="100" height="150" alt="" border="0"
                            /></div>
                        </div>
                    </div>
                    <div id="a5-footer">
                        © copyright 2005 | A5design, LLC | all rights
                            reserved  
                    </div>
                </div>
            </div>
        </div>
        </body>
        </html>
```

When the page is rendered, it would look like Figure 5.13. Notice that there is an even amount of space on both sides of the design.

CREATING A LIQUID DESIGN

Because of the way the fixed design was created, modifying it to be a liquid design is very simple. All the designer needs to do is change the 770px value of the a5-body rule to 100%. This is because the left column will always try to fill the screen because it is assigned relative positioning and it is included in a <DIV> tag, which together defaults to 100% width. There are two main reasons the design works the way it does:

■ The left column has relative positioning assigned to it, so it can expand and contract, depending on the resolution and/or width of the screen.

FIGURE 5.13   Fixed-width design that is centered using CSS.

■   While the positioning will stretch to 100% by default, it can also be controlled with the margin property. In this case, the margin-right property is set to 232px, which means the column will stretch within 232 pixels of the right side of the screen but no further.

Figure 5.14 shows how the page shown in Figure 5.13 expands when the value of the a5-body rule is changed from 770px to 100%.

FIGURE 5.14   Liquid design that fills the full width of the screen.

Chapters 6, 7, 8, and 9 provide additional examples and explanations of how designs can be created to be liquid. These chapters not only explain another two-column liquid design, but also three-column designs.

RENDERING THE `<HR />` TAG CONSISTENTLY

With XHTML table-based design, creating a line between content is very easy. The developer can either include the code `<HR />` or add a table row with a one-pixel image (or whatever height the designer chooses) with a background color assigned to the table cell:

```
<tr>
    <td bgcolor="#000000"><img src="images/ spacer.gif" alt=" " width="1"
    height="1" border="0" /></td>
</tr>
```

CSS design, however, does not interpret the `<HR>` tag consistently in all browsers. Figure 5.15 shows how the `<HR>` tag and the code in Listing 5.6 tag are displayed in various browsers.

LISTING 5.6   Code for Figure 5.15

```
<!DOCTYPE html PUBLIC "-//W3C//DTD XHTML 1.0 Transitional//EN"
    "http://www.w3.org/TR/xhtml1/DTD/xhtml1-transitional.dtd">
<html>
<head>
    <title>Untitled</title>
<style>
#samplebox {
    background:#000000;
    width:120px;
    height:50px;
    padding-bottom:15px;
    }
</style>
</head>
<body>
<div id="samplebox">
    <br />
        <hr />
    <br /><br />
</div>
</body>
</html>
```

There are a couple items to notice about Figure 5.15:

■ The `<HR>` line is not positioned at the same height in the browsers, which will affect pixel-specific placement of other elements.
■ The default color of the `<HR>` line is not consistent.

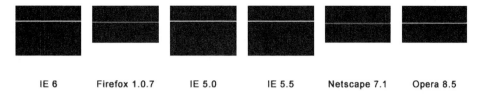

| IE 6 | Firefox 1.0.7 | IE 5.0 | IE 5.5 | Netscape 7.1 | Opera 8.5 |

FIGURE 5.15 Various ways the <HR /> tag, along with basic CSS formatting, will be displayed in different browsers.

This disparity in the rendering of the tag makes the designer have to use workaround code to maintain consistency among browsers. The code in Listing 5.7 can be used to provide a more consistent line in all six browsers tested for Figure 5.14.

LISTING 5.7 Code That Gives Line Consistency Across Browsers for Figure 5.14

```
<!DOCTYPE html PUBLIC "-//W3C//DTD XHTML 1.0 Transitional//EN"
    "http://www.w3.org/TR/xhtml1/DTD/xhtml1-transitional.dtd">
<html>
<head>
    <title>Untitled</title>
<style>
#samplebox {
    background:#000000;
    width:120px;
    height:50px;
    padding-bottom:15px;
    }
div.hrline {
    height:1px;
    background:url(images/sample-hr.gif) repeat-x scroll center;
}
div.hrline hr {
    display:none;
}
</style>
</head>
<body>
<div id="samplebox">
    <br />
    <div class="hrline"><hr /></div>
</div>
</body>
</html>
```

There are a couple things to notice about Figure 5.16:

■ The color of the line is now consistent among all browsers.
■ While the specific placement of the line is not at the exact same pixel height, the code renders the line in a more consistent manner in the different browsers.

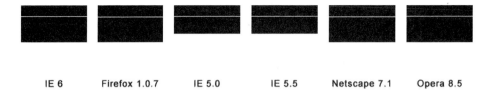

IE 6   Firefox 1.0.7   IE 5.0   IE 5.5   Netscape 7.1   Opera 8.5

FIGURE 5.16 A more consistent rendering of CSS code that makes use of an image that is repeated as a line.

USING BACKGROUND IMAGES AS DESIGN ELEMENTS

One disadvantage of designing table-based sites is that once three or more tables are nested inside each other, some browsers, such as Netscape 4.7, will not properly render the images and portions of the table cells they do not fill up. CSS-based design allows for full use of background images, which includes layering nested background images on top of one another. This change in design functionality allows for new types of designs. One example is using a background image for the entire site. While this has always been available with XHTML table-based design, there is no longer concern, for the designer, of running into browser issues as more and more background images are nested inside one another.

Figure 5.17 shows how background images can be used more extensively. There are three things to note about the design:

FIGURE 5.17 Design that uses background images as menu bullets, images for the left and right columns, and a repeating image for the entire page. © 2006 Innergy Coaching, LLC. Used with permission.

- The background in the right column (right side of the infinity loop) is broken up from the background in the left column (left side of the loop, along with the woman). This is because the right image is best saved as a GIF file, while the left image should be saved as a JPG.
- The entire left column of color is repeated as a background image in the page's <BODY> tag, so it will repeat endlessly down the left-hand side. It repeats underneath the background image of the left column. Because the bottom of the left background image looks exactly like the page background image, there is seamless repeating.
- Each menu item is assigned a background image to its left that serves as a bullet. The bullet changes when the menu item is moused over, which is explained in the next section.

CODING CSS MOUSEOVERS

Menu mouseovers used to require JavaScript to perform a simple image switch. Now, CSS allows the designer to simply replace the background image by assigning a different image when the user mouses over an item. The three-step process is:

1. The designer creates a rule that will be used to display the menu item when it is not moused over. The two main properties to pay attention to in the following code are display and background. The display property, when assigned a block value, tells the browser to vertically stack each hyperlinked menu item when it is included inside the a5-menu container. The background property, with its values, determines what image will be used for the menu item, including how it will be positioned and whether it will be repeated. In this example, the image will not be repeated, and it will be positioned in the top-left corner of the block.

```
#a5-menu a {
    display: block;
    background: url(images/bg-menu-off.gif) no-repeat 0px 0px;
    text-decoration:none;
    color:#ffffff;
    font-weight:normal;
    padding: 3px 5px 2px 25px;
}
```

2. The designer then adds the hover element to the hyperlinks. When the user mouses over a link, the background image is changed from bg-menu-off.gif to bg-menu-on.gif, with the same positioning of the image. The font is turned bold, so not only the image, but also the changing text color, identifies the link.

```
#a5-menu a:hover {
    background: url(images/bg-menu-on.gif) no-repeat 0px 0px;
```

```
            font-weight:bold;
            color:#ffffff;
    }
```

3. The menu items need to be added to a container with the ID value of a5-menu.

```
<div id="a5-menu">
    <a href="index.htm">home</a>
    <a href="about.htm">about</a>
    <a href="services.htm">services</a>
    <a href="ezine.htm">ezine</a>
    <a href="contact.htm">contact</a>
</div>
```

Figure 5.18 illustrates how the menu is displayed and how it appears when an item is moused over. Notice that the background image changes and the "services" link becomes bold.

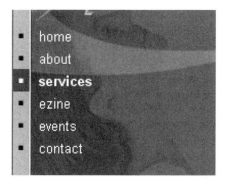

FIGURE 5.18   CSS-driven mouseover in the menu section of the site. © 2006 Innergy Coaching, LLC. Used with permission.

USING JAVASCRIPT DROP-DOWN MENUS

Often, a site requires more than a flat menu. Rather, it requires drop downs so the user can easily access the various levels of key pages by perusing the menu on one page. Figure 5.19 provides an example of such a menu.

Unless the designer or developer understands JavaScript, creating such a menu can be time-intensive. One solution is to purchase a system that will automatically create the menu. An example of such a system is EZ Menu. Included on the CD-ROM that comes with this book, the software allows the designer to create a menu by using a simple user interface. Once the various attributes are assigned, the software builds the code for the designer.

ON THE CD

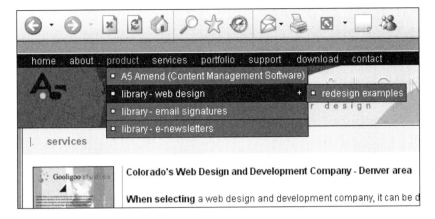

FIGURE 5.19   Example of a drop-down JavaScript menu.

REMEMBERING THE ORDER OF MARGIN AND PADDING SHORTCUTS

Writing shorthand CSS properties and values makes designing and managing sites much easier. Sometimes remembering the order of the shorthand methods, however, is not always as easy. There is a visual reminder for the value order of the two most commonly used properties: margin and padding. Because the values are ordered in clockwise motion, they can be visualized as being positioned around a box, starting with the top border (see Figure 5.20).

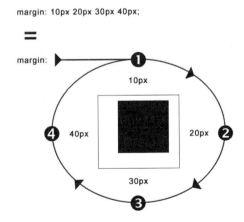

FIGURE 5.20   A visual reminder of how the values are ordered with the shorthand versions of the `margin` and `padding` properties.

USING THE BORDER AND BACKGROUND PROPERTIES FOR TROUBLESHOOTING

When developing CSS designs where containers of images and text are mortised together, it is important to know exactly where the boundaries of each box are. If this is not known, a simple process of adding a background color to a container can turn into a time-consuming task. Looking at Figure 5.21, it appears that the containers are properly positioned.

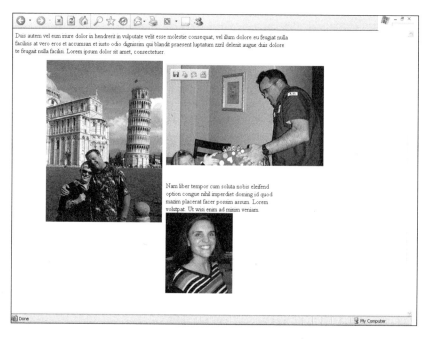

FIGURE 5.21   A page with three boxes laid out so no overlap or misplacement appears.

The truth, however, is while the text and images may be properly positioned, this does not mean the boxes that contain them are designed to be easily edited. Adding a background color to the top paragraph makes it readily apparent that the page's infrastructure is not as properly positioned as it may appear without the background color (see Figure 5.22).

Before a designer can correct such a problem with a design, it is necessary to understand where the boundaries are for the elements that are going to be modified. Two methods can be used to view the borders:

FIGURE 5.22   Results of adding a background color to the top container, which includes the text.

■ **Turn on the border of the elements by setting it to at least one pixel.** The code to do so is `border:1px solid #000000;`. When the designer is done testing the container, the value of the border size can be set to 0, such as `border:0px solid #000000;`. Much of the code in this book contains such lines. Because the extra code takes up a nominal amount of file size, it is easier to turn the border off than to remove the code. One advantage to this is that the designer can view the shapes of the containers and what is layered behind them because, other than the borders, they are transparent (Figure 5.23).

■ **Similar to the example in Figure 5.22, the background color can be set to contrast with the background of adjacent containers (Figure 5.24).** The code to do so is `background:red;`. The advantage of this method is that the designer understands the exact width a container will take up. If, on the other hand, a designer is trying to position two boxes to the exact pixel, turning on the borders of the boxes will be confusing because compliant browsers will add the extra width to the total width. Thus, if a box is 200 pixels wide, it will grow to 202 if the border is set to 1 because 1 pixel will be added to both the left and right sides.

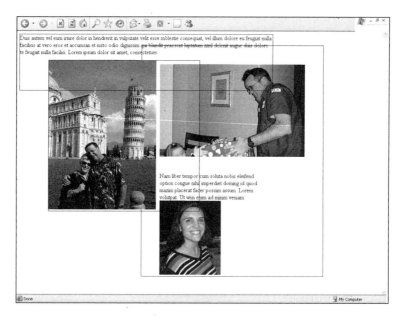

FIGURE 5.23 A page with the containers' borders set to 1 to view their boundaries.

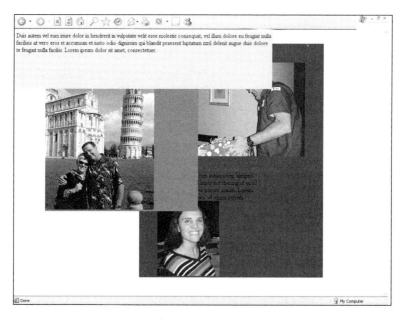

FIGURE 5.24 A page with the containers' backgrounds set to various colors to view their locations.

COMMENTING OUT CODE FOR TROUBLESHOOTING

Any novice designer or developer can create code. An experienced designer or developer, however, can fix things "under the hood." Being able to troubleshoot a page, whether it is XHTML, CSS, or a programming language, is a very useful skill to have. One helpful method for testing pages is to remove code to either see how a page will react in terms of layout or to see if the problem disappears when the code is removed.

While code can be cut and the page can be saved to perform such testing, the code can be lost if the computer crashes before the code can be reinserted and resaved. A safer method is to comment out the code. This is accomplished by using comment tags. The tags tell the browser or server to either not display or interpret the code, depending on the method used. For most languages, comment tags work similarly to XHTML tags, where an opening tag is added to the beginning and a closing tag is added to the end of the code that is to be excluded. Comment tags vary depending on the language, and the following are four examples of commonly used tags:

XHTML: The opening tag is `<!--` . The closing tag is `-->`. The second line of the following code would be output by the server but not displayed by the browser:

```
This is a sample line of text. <br />
<!-- This is the line that would be commented out <br /> -->
This is the line of code the browser would begin displaying again.
```

An XHTML page will not validate if the comment tags do not have the correct syntax. If the developer, for instance, has too many hyphens in a comment tag, it will not validate.

CSS: The opening tag is `/*`. The closing tag is `*/`. The second property of the following rule would be interpreted by the browser:

```
#photo2 {
    position:absolute;

    /* width:90px; */
    height:80px;
    }
```

ColdFusion: The opening tag is `<!---`. The closing tag is `--->`. The second line of the following code would not be output by the server; thus, it would not be visible in the page source.

```
This is a sample line of text. <br />
<!--- This is the line that would not be output by the
    server <br /> --->
This is the line of code the browser would begin displaying again.
```

JavaScript: This is one exception of using comment tags where the designer does not necessarily need to include a closing tag. The opening tag would merely be //. The second line of the following code would be output by the server but not interpreted by the browser:

```
bullet_text_on = new Image
// bullet_text_off = new Image
bullet_text_on.src = "http://www.a5design.com/images/
    bullet_text_on.gif"
```

If, however, the designer wanted to comment out the entire section of code, an opening /* could be used, along with a closing */. Following is how the code would look if it all were to be commented out:

```
/*
bullet_text_on = new Image
bullet_text_off = new Image
bullet_text_on.src = http://www.a5design.com/images/bullet_text_on.gif
*/
```

USING UNIQUE NAMING CONVENTIONS

When designing and developing code, whether it is XHTML, CSS, or a programming language, it is usually a smart practice to come up with a unique naming convention because there will be times when a developer's code has to be integrated with another developer's code. If naming conventions conflict, then errors will occur that will require time to troubleshoot.

When creating ID and class selectors in CSS, for example, most of the rules in this book will begin with a5-, which is short for A5design. This helps prevent integrating a stylesheet with another site's stylesheet. If both stylesheets contain a selector for the header, odds are that the other one will not be named a5-header. Instead, it may likely be header. A more difficult problem to unravel occurs when naming programming variables. If a variable such as path already exists on the server, the server not only may output its value, but may also not allow the developer to even set the variable, depending on how the server is configured.

CONTROLLING THE MARGINS IN FORM TAGS

Depending on the browser, form tags come with a different default margin setting. If the form does not follow inline text, it will react similarly across most browsers. Figure 5.25, on the other hand, shows how the code in Listing 5.8 would be interpreted if it were to follow inline text:

| IE 6 | Firefox 1.0.7 | IE 5.0 | IE 5.5 | Netscape 7.1 | Opera 8.5 |

FIGURE 5.25   How a `<FORM>` tag is interpreted differently in various browsers when it follows inline text.

LISTING 5.8   Code for Figure 5.25

```
<!DOCTYPE html PUBLIC "-//W3C//DTD XHTML 1.0 Transitional//EN"
    "http://www.w3.org/TR/xhtml1/DTD/xhtml1-transitional.dtd">
<html>
<head>
    <title>Untitled</title>
<style>
#a5-form {
    position:absolute;
    left:90px;
    top:80px;
    color:#ffffff;
    padding:10px;
    background:#000000;
    border:0px solid #000000;
    }
</style>
</head>
<body>
<div id="a5-form">
    This is a sample form:<br />
    <form action="test.cfm" method="post">
        <input type="text" size="15" name="test" />
    </form>
</div>
</body>
</html>
```

To make the margins consistent among the various tested browsers, the designer needs only to add the following style to the form: `style="margin:0px;"`. Figure 5.26 demonstrates how consistently the form (see Listing 5.9) will be interpreted after using the margin property in the following code:

LISTING 5.9   Code for Figure 5.26

```
<!DOCTYPE html PUBLIC "-//W3C//DTD XHTML 1.0 Transitional//EN"
    "http://www.w3.org/TR/xhtml1/DTD/xhtml1-transitional.dtd">
<html>
<head>
    <title>Untitled</title>
```

```
<style>
#a5-form {
    position:absolute;
    left:90px;
    top:80px;
    color:#ffffff;
    padding:10px;
    background:#000000;
    border:0px solid #000000;
    }
</style>
</head>
<body>
<div id="a5-form">
    This is a sample form:<br />
    <form action="test.cfm" method="post" style="margin:0px;">
        <input type="text" size="15" name="test" />
    </form>
</div>
</body>
</html>
```

If desired, the designer could also place the style in a general `<form>` rule in the stylesheet. If this is the case, the inline style does not need to be included in the XHTML `<form>` tag. The stylesheet would then look like the following:

```
<style>
form {
margin:0px;
}
#a5-form {
    position:absolute;
    left:90px;
    top:80px;
    color:#ffffff;
    padding:10px;
    background:#000000;
    border:0px solid #000000;
    }
</style>
```

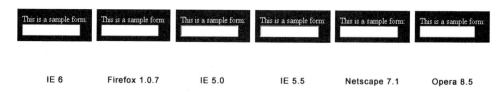

IE 6   Firefox 1.0.7   IE 5.0   IE 5.5   Netscape 7.1   Opera 8.5

FIGURE 5.26   The consistent manner in which a `<FORM>` tag will be displayed if a style is added that sets its margins to 0 pixels.

DESIGNING WITH THE LEAST AMOUNT OF REAL ESTATE POSSIBLE

When designing a page, it is usually best to avoid use of a horizontal scroll bar (see Figure 5.27). While some users already feel bothered to scroll vertically, scrolling horizontally, in many circles, is considered a cardinal sin. This is why a designer often wants to avoid making a page that is too wide, even if just by a few pixels, to make sure a design does not activate the horizontal bar.

The one exception to this rule is if the designer is creating a site for a higher resolution than that at which some users will have their monitors set.

FIGURE 5.27   A page with the horizontal scrollbar activated because the page was made too wide.

While page width must obviously be taken into consideration, a more subtle consideration is the browser the site is being designed in. Compliant browsers do not include the right scroll bar until the height of the page requires it, unlike IE, which always includes it. This means that if the designer creates a page in a compliant browser, an extra 18 pixels will be added to the page, which means the designer has 18 pixels less of horizontal space to work with. This is why it is a good practice to design sites initially in IE to ensure that the extra pixels are already included in the width. This avoids the need to test the page in compliant browsers because the extra width is already included in the screen real estate.

MORTISING IMAGES TOGETHER

One of the ways to make a site look and function in a professional manner is to mortise images together. Mortising involves positioning images together, usually with no visible separation. This can be done a couple of different ways with CSS sites:

Placing images together with absolute and/or relative positioning.   The designer can control placement of an image by wrapping a container around it and assigning the position, top, and left and right properties to it. Figure 5.28 shows how the first of three images is positioned in a container with the ID of a5-header. It is assigned absolute positioning, placing it 0 pixels from the top and 0 pixels from the left side.

The 627-pixel-wide container is assigned a black background to differentiate it from the white background of the page.

FIGURE 5.28   The first of three images positioned in the container.

After the first image has a <DIV> wrapped around it and is placed in the parent container, a second image is added. It also has a container wrapped around it. This image, however, is placed 247 pixels from the left, which positions the two images together (see Figure 5.29).

The third image is positioned 304 pixels from the left, which is the sum total width of the first two images (247 + 57 = 304 pixels). Depending on the instance of mortising, the right property can be used in place of the left property. Listing 5.10 is the code to build the completed mortised images in Figure 5.30.

LISTING 5.10   Code for Figure 5.30

```
<!DOCTYPE html PUBLIC "-//W3C//DTD XHTML 1.0 Transitional//EN"
    "DTD/xhtml1-transitional.dtd">
<html><head><title>Mortised Images</title>
<style>
    #a5-header {
        position:relative;
        top:0px;
        left:0px;
```

```
        width:627px;
        height:400px;
        background:black;
    }
    #a5-photo-left {
        position:absolute;
        top:0px;
        left:0px;
    }
    #a5-photo-center {
        position:absolute;
        top:0px;
        left:247px;
    }
    #a5-photo-right {
        position:absolute;
        top:0px;
        left:304px;
    }
</style>
</head>
<body>
<div id="a5-header">
    <div id="a5-photo-left"><img src="images/photo-left.jpg"
        width="247" height="400" alt="" border="0" /></div>
    <div id="a5-photo-center"><img src="images/photo-center.jpg"
        width="57" height="400" alt="" border="0" /></div>
    <div id="a5-photo-right"><img src="images/photo-right.jpg"
        width="323" height="400" alt="" border="0" /></div>
</div>
</body>
</html>
```

FIGURE 5.29   The second of three images positioned in the container.

FIGURE 5.30 All three images positioned in the container.

Use background images with images in the document flow. Placing background images in a container is another way to mortise images together. One reason a designer may want to do so is to place text over the image. Figure 5.31 shows how the left image of a container is added.

The 1000-pixel-wide container is assigned a black background to differentiate it from the white background of the page.

FIGURE 5.31 The left image added to the container.

Once the first image has been added, the second is inserted. In this example, the left text is saved as an image, so the process of mortising the two images together is the same as the previous example (figure 5.32).

FIGURE 5.32   The center image added to the container.

Adding the right container is where this example becomes more complex. The designer is going to size and position the a5-text-right <DIV>; however, the text is going to be added to another <DIV> that is nested inside. This allows for padding and line-height properties and values to be added at a local level. Listing 5.11 is the code used to create the final layout (see Figure 5.33).

LISTING 5.11   Code for Figure 5.33

```
<!DOCTYPE html PUBLIC "-//W3C//DTD XHTML 1.0 Transitional//EN"
    "DTD/xhtml1-transitional.dtd">
<html><head><title>Mortised Images</title>
<style>
    #a5-container {
        position:relative;
        top:0px;
        left:0px;
        width:1000px;
        height:500px;
        background:black;
    }
    #a5-image-left {
        position:absolute;
        top:0px;
        left:0px;
    }
    #a5-photo-center {
        position:absolute;
        top:0px;
```

```
        left:251px;
    }
    #a5-text-right {
        position:absolute;
        bottom:0px;
        right:0px;
        width:333px;
        height:500px;
        background:url("images/bg-right.jpg") no-repeat;
    }
</style>
</head>
<body>
<div id="a5-container">
    <div id="a5-image-left"><a href="x.htm"><img src="images/
        image-left.gif" width="251" height="500" alt="" border="0"
        /></a></div>
    <div id="a5-photo-center"><a href="x.htm"><img src="images/photo-
        center.jpg" width="416" height="500" alt="" border="0"
        /></a></div>
    <div id="a5-text-right">
        <div style="padding:250px 10px 10px 10px;line-height:60px;">
            This is sample text that can be added over the background
            image. While the background image cannot be hyperlinked,
            the <a href="x.htm">text can</a>.</div>
    </div>
</div>
</body>
</html>
```

When using background images, it is important that the designer consider whether a user is going to think it is clickable, because background images cannot be clicked. While this seems obvious, it is an easy mistake to make because when mortising images, using at least one background image can sometimes be tempting.

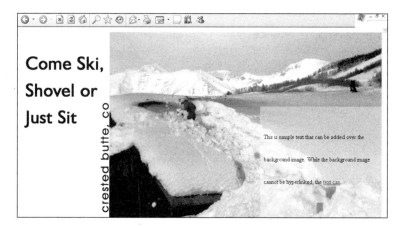

FIGURE 5.33   Background image and text added to the right column.

This is just a brief description of mortising. More thorough explanations and examples are included in the case studies in Chapters 6, 7, 8, and 9.

USING CSS SHORTCUTS

The goal of this book is not necessarily to produce the most efficient CSS coding possible. Rather, it is to make the examples as simple as possible, thus ensuring that the concepts are understood and retained. However, if more efficient coding is desired, one may also include the use of abbreviated HEX numbers, such as `#fff` instead of `#ffffff`, using descendent selectors, which makes use of CSS inheritance to streamline the amount of code used.

FONT UNITS

There are many considerations when it comes to what type of unit to use when sizing fonts on the Web. The options include pixels, points, ems, and percentages. Following are some things to consider when selecting a font:

- Will the text be viewed in a browser, printed, or both?
- What type of OS is the design primarily meant for?
- Do you want users to be able to resize the fonts using their browsers?

This subject requires thorough discussion, but it is being noted here for the designer to be aware of the various options for further possible investigation.

TEST CONTINUALLY AND CONSISTENTLY

It is a good practice to continually test pages as they are being created, rather than waiting until the coding is completed because coding problems can quickly compound themselves. If a container, for example, is assigned the wrong width, padding, or margins, other related `<DIV>` or `<SPAN>` tags may also be incorrectly adjusted. Once the initial problem is discovered, any number of changes may need to be made to make the design flow correctly.

Testing should also be done consistently. One method of testing consistently is to always open the same browsers in the same order. The designer can then easily click on each browser and refresh it to see how the site appears. By using some method of consistency, the designer will recall more readily how each browser handles the nuances of CSS.

SUMMARY

Understanding common roadblocks and issues with designing Web sites can make a designer or developer much more efficient. The tips and techniques included in this chapter will help in learning how to handle many of these issues. Some of these issues include using the Tantek hack to correctly render the box model bug, learning ways to make designs work for most browsers, discovering tricks to code more efficiently, and learning how to test code.

6 Case Study: Low Content CSS Design

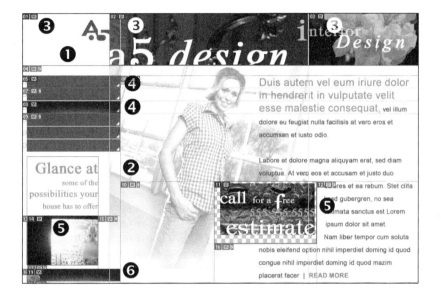

With the advent of CSS design, the visual complexity of designs has taken on a more simple look Web designers used nearly a decade ago before they started using more advanced table layouts. This look could be simply a design fad, which the industry experiences every few years, or it may be that designers simply do not know how to create the complex designs that give a site a more professional, creative look and feel. This chapter employs a simple CSS code base to demonstrate a more complex look by placing images and content outside the visual confines of linear (rectangular and square) containers. In other words, this chapter explains how to make designs look how the designer wants them to look, rather than having to make a design look like images were merely placed in columns because that is all that could technically be done. While the designer may choose not to create a visually complex design or fashion it for 800 × 600 resolution, techniques in this and the following three chapters can be uniquely employed to create nearly any type of design.

The design explained in this chapter is design 121 on the accompanying CD-ROM (photo credits: *www.idlerphotography.com*).

UNDERSTANDING THE DESIGN'S STRUCTURE

Before beginning to build a design, it is important that the designer understand the page's infrastructure. In this case study the end result can be viewed and absorbed before the elements are added individually. This design (see Figure 6.1) is a simple layout that uses a header and two columns below it to mortise the images together and therein place the content.

FIGURE 6.1   The low-content design explained in this chapter.

The Reasoning Behind Guides and Creating Slices in Photoshop Files

When building a design, one should usually create it in image-editing software, such as Photoshop, rather than spending time coding the actual design. Inversely, while creating a *comp*, or sample design, is time consuming, it will save time because most of the technical considerations are worked out during this phase of the process. It is also time-saving because the client is usually going to want to make changes to the design, and it is easier to make these changes when first creating the entire page. Then, once the design is approved, the designer simply needs to code it to appear as it does in the Photoshop file.

After a design is created in Photoshop, the designer is going to want to *break up*, or code, the design in XHTML and CSS. To begin this process, guides are placed to ensure that the elements are lined up in their correct positions. Slices, which are used to save pieces of the design as images, can then be easily fashioned once everything is correctly positioned.

Creating or customizing a design, which involves placing guides and creating slices, is explained in Chapter 9.

Figure 6.2 shows how the guides and slices are positioned. The numbers added to the design are used to point out the 10 most important guides and slices.

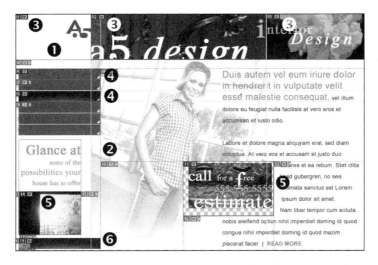

FIGURE 6.2 Guides and slices strategically placed within the design.

There are several things to note about the guides and slices in Figure 6.2:

- The horizontal guide just below number 1 is added to separate the header row from the lower part of the design.
- The vertical guide to the left of number 2 separates the left column, which includes the menu, from the right column, which contains the main content for the page.
- The three number 3s represent the slices that are used in the header area.

A slice is indicated by the small numbered rectangle in the top left corner of each outlined rectangle or square.

The two Number 4s indicate, to the left of them, the background images that are used in each menu item. The top Number 4 represents the menu item when the user has not selected that item. The lower Number 4 represents the background, when the hyperlinked menu item is in hover mode.

- The two number 5s represent slices used to save images for the design that are not mortised together with any others. The right image, which says, "call for a free estimate," has the background image removed from it. This is accomplished by cropping out the background, and any other images, below the slice. When saving the Photoshop file, the designer can designate the checkered background, which is the background of the file, as a transparent background. This allows the image to be easily layered over any background in the file, so that background can appear through the area that is checkered. The advantage of this technique is that the image can then be moved anywhere over the background image of the woman, without the "estimate" image containing remnants of her checkered shirt. It is a coincidence the Photoshop background and the woman's shirt are both checkered. If the image contained the woman's shirt, rather than that area being transparent, and was positioned differently, the image and background images would appear disjointed.

NOTE *If the image had a curve and that image was saved with a transparent background, the curve would have a jagged edge because of anti-aliasing, which blends colors to give the perception of one color being curved.*

- The slice to the left of number 6 represents the background image that is used for the page title row for second-level pages (see Figure 6.3). Often it is easier to save images that are not necessarily used on the home page with the source file that is used for the home page. This often eliminates the need to save a completely new .psd (Photoshop) file for just one image.

FIGURE 6.3 The page title <DIV> that uses a background image saved from the Photoshop file created for the homepage.

Because multiple images are layered and saved over the background image of the woman, it is necessary to duplicate the source .psd file and save it independently so the background can be saved. When the file has been duplicated, the extra images, all slices, and most guides can be removed, leaving only the background image. The designer then adds a slice around the portion of the file that will be saved as an individual image.

One advantage of duplicating the existing home page file and deleting excess images is that the background image's placement remains the same. Because the main slice, represented by number 2 in Figure 6.2, is not removed, the designer knows exactly where to place the new slice. Figure 6.4 shows the home page saved as a separate source file with all the original slices and excess images removed.

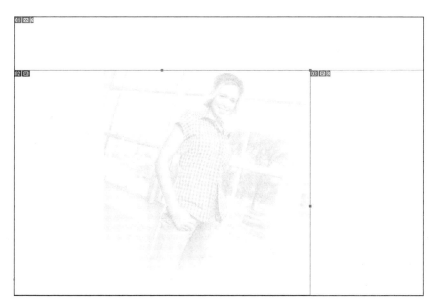

FIGURE 6.4   Homepage source file that is duplicated and saved as a separate file so the background image of the woman can be saved independently from the images layered over it.

Understanding the Placement of CSS Containers

More than 10 <DIV> tags are used to lay out the images saved from the Photoshop file and XHTML content. Figure 6.5 shows the <DIV>s with all the images and content removed and their borders "turned on" by setting them to 1px.

The <DIV> tags are used for different functions in the design, such as setting up the basic infrastructure of the design, providing containers to position content within, and styling the content. Following are explanations of the 10 most useful <DIV>s in Figure 6.5:

- The <DIV> tag above number 1 is used for centering the design in IE 5 and 5.5 if it is to have a fixed width. The container starts at the very top left corner of the browser window.
- The <DIV> tag below number 2 determines whether the design has a fixed width or is a liquid layout. It also begins in the top-left corner of the browser window.

- The <DIV> tag to the left of number 3 contains the images that are used in the header area.
- Numbers 4, 5, and 6 are images in the header area that are assigned absolute positioning.
- The <DIV> tag to the left of number 7 contains both the left and right columns of the body.
- Number 8 defines the left column, which contains, among other things, the menu.
- Number 9 represents the container that styles and positions the menu.
- Number 10 is the <DIV> that contains the content in the right column. It expands to the full width of the design when enough content is included to force the full width.

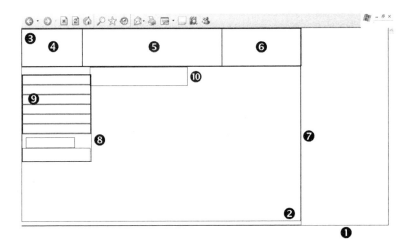

FIGURE 6.5   Design with images and content removed and various <DIV> tags turned on.

BUILDING THE STRUCTURE

Following are the steps for constructing the design, step by step. It is assumed that the Photoshop file has already been created or customized and the designer need only position the images and text.

Creating the XHTML and CSS Framework

The first step to building the design is to create the XHTML framework and initial CSS containers. Listing 6.1 is the code that is used to output the page in Figure 6.6.

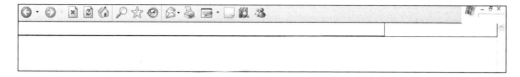

FIGURE 6.6 Basic XHTML and CSS framework for the design.

LISTING 6.1 Code for Figure 6.6

```
<!DOCTYPE html PUBLIC "-//W3C//DTD XHTML 1.0 Transitional//EN"
    "DTD/xhtml1-transitional.dtd">
<html><head><title>Design 121</title>
<meta http-equiv="Content-Type" content="text/html;
    charset=iso-8859-1" />
<style type="text/css">
/* ++++++++++ global general styles start ++++++++++*/
html, body {
    margin:0px;
    padding:0px;
    font: 13px Arial, Helvetica, sans-serif;
    color:#766D6D;
    background:#ffffff;
}
/* ++++++++++ global general styles end ++++++++++*/

/* ++++++++++ global structure styles start ++++++++++*/
#a5-body-center {
    text-align:left;
    border:1px solid #000000;
    }
#a5-body {
    position: relative;
    width: 770px; /* change this to a specific amount for a fixed
        design. E.g., 770px. */
/* remove these comment tags if the page is to be centered. The 'text-
    align' property in the 'a5-body-center' rule must also be changed
    from 'left' to 'center'
    margin-left: auto;
    margin-right: auto;*/
    text-align:left;
    padding-bottom:10px;
    border:1px solid #000000;
    }
/* ++++++++++ global structure styles end ++++++++++*/
</style>
</head>
<body>
<div id="a5-body-center">
    <div id="a5-body">
        Enter text here.
    </div>
</div>
</body>
</html>
```

There are several things to note about the code in Listing 6.1:

- The CSS stylesheet is commented into a couple different sections. The `global general styles` comment tags contain the general styles, such as the formatting of the `<HTML>` and `<BODY>` tags, hyperlinks, and fonts. The `global structure styles` comment tags include the styles used to define the structure of the design and elements included in that structure.

- Several rules define the `<HTML>` and `<BODY>` tags. The `margin` and `padding` properties are used to ensure that the design is placed in the very top-left corner of the browser, with no space between the design and the edges of the viewable area. The default font style for the site is set using the shorthand `FONT` property. The default font color is defined with the `COLOR` property. The background color also is assigned, even if it is only white (i.e., `#ffffff`). This guarantees that all browsers display the site with the same background color because the default color is not always the same among browsers.

- The `a5-body-center` and `a5-body` rules are used to force the design to the left side of the browser screen with a fixed width of 770 pixels. If the designer wanted the design to fill the full width of the screen, the value of `770px` would need to be changed to `100%`. If, however, the designer wanted to center the design, the value of the `text-align` property in the `a5-body-center` rule would need to be changed from `left` to `center`. The `margin-left` and `margin-right` properties in the `a5-body` rule would only need to have the comment tags around them removed. This system allows the designer flexibility when more than one site is going to be built using this same default code. By adding this code to every design, it does not take much effort to quickly change a design to fit a client's needs.

- Both the `a5-body-center` and `a5-body` rules have their borders turned on using the following code: `border:1px solid #000000;`. For demonstration purposes, the code was added to both rules to show what the structure of the `<DIV>` tags looks like with no content added. Turning on the borders also helps when building a site because it is not always apparent where elements are placed or expanding to. Rather than remove these rules, it is easier to change the value of `1px` to `0px`, turning the borders off, rather than removing them. Troubleshooting often involves turning the borders back on, thereby saving time and taking up very little download size by keeping them in the stylesheet.

- Because the `<div id="a5-body">` is nested inside the `<div id="a5-body-center">` tag, it is indented. This allows for quicker recognition of nested tags, which becomes a useful technique when the page has more code added to it later.

Adding the Header Content

Once the XHTML and basic CSS framework have been added, the header area is then added into the code. Listing 6.2 is the code that is used to output the page in Figure 6.7.

FIGURE 6.7   Design with all three header images added.

LISTING 6.2   Code for Figure 6.7

```
<!DOCTYPE html PUBLIC "-//W3C//DTD XHTML 1.0 Transitional//EN"
    "DTD/xhtml1-transitional.dtd">
<html><head><title>Design 121</title>
<meta http-equiv="Content-Type" content="text/html;
    charset=iso-8859-1" />
<style type="text/css">
/* ++++++++++ global general styles start ++++++++++*/
html, body {
    margin:0px;
    padding:0px;
    font: 13px Arial, Helvetica, sans-serif;
    color:#766D6D;
    background:#ffffff;
    }
/* ++++++++++ global general styles end ++++++++++*/
/* ++++++++++ global structure styles start ++++++++++*/
#a5-body-center {
    text-align:left;
    border:0px solid #000000;
    }
#a5-body {
    position: relative;
    width: 770px; /* change this to a specific amount for a fixed
        design. E.g., 770px. */
/* remove these comment tags if the page is to be centered. The 'text-
    align' property in the 'a5-body-center' rule must also be changed
    from 'left' to 'center'
    margin-left: auto;
    margin-right: auto;*/
    text-align:left;
    padding-bottom:10px;
    border:0px solid #000000;
    }
/* ++++++++++ global structure styles end ++++++++++*/
#a5-header {
    position:relative;
    left:0px;
    top:0px;
    height:98px;
    border:0px solid #000000;
    }
    #a5-header-left {
        width:169px;
        }
```

```
            #a5-header-center {
                position:absolute;
                left:169px;
                top:0px;
                }
            #a5-header-right {
                position:absolute;
                left:553px;
                top:0px;
                }
    </style>
    </head>
    <body>
    <div id="a5-body-center">
        <div id="a5-body">
    <!-- ###### header start ###### -->
            <div id="a5-header">
                <div><a href="index.htm"><img src="images/header-left.gif"
                    width="169" height="98" alt="" border="0" /></a></div>
                <div id="a5-header-center"><img src="images/
                    header-center.jpg" width="384" height="98" alt=""
                    border="0" /></div>
                <div id="a5-header-right"><img src="images/
                    header-right.jpg" width="217" height="98" alt=""
                    border="0" /></div>
            </div>
    <!-- ###### header end ###### -->
        </div>
    </div>
    </body>
    </html>
```

There are several things to note about the code in Listing 6.2:

■ Three images are being mortised together in the header area, rather than just one (see Figure 6.8).

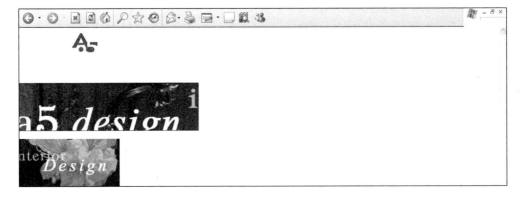

FIGURE 6.8   Three images that are mortised together in the header area.

- The a5-header rule is created to contain the three header images inside it. This container also allows the designer to easily move all those elements included inside it as one entity because their positioning is based off its top-left corner.

- Because it is assigned relative positioning, with the left and top properties set to 0px, the a5-header container begins at the very top-left corner of the Web browsers because the <DIV> tags it is nested inside also begin at the 0,0 X,Y coordinates of the page. The relative positioning also ensures that the <DIV> tag will stretch to the full width of the area it is occupying, which is 770 pixels. The height property of the rule, which is set to 98px, is added to ensure that the container collapses perfectly around the three images. Otherwise, different browsers may structure the container differently.

- <DIV> tags are wrapped around the header-left.gif image, which is the first image in the header area. This is to ensure that no additional space is added around the image, stretching the a5-header container too high, such as in Figure 6.9, which is a result of an entirely different cause, as noted.

Often, spaces or carriage returns in XHTML code can alter the way <DIV> tags are interpreted. The image in the a5-header-left tag is a perfect example of this. If a space or carriage return is added after the closing </a> tag, the a5-header container will add extra space below the image(s) in IE 6 (see Figure 6.9). The background color of the container was set as black to show the difference in the image.

FIGURE 6.9 Extra space added below the header area because of a carriage return in the XHTML code.

To ensure that the space around the image appears like it does in Figure 6.7, the code must look like the following:

```
<div><a href="index.htm"><img src="images/header-left.gif" width="169"
    height="98" alt="" border="0" /></a></div>
```

Rather than:

```
<div><a href="index.htm"><img src="images/header-left.gif" width="169"
    height="98" alt="" border="0" /></a>
</div>
```

■ Both the a5-header-center and a5-header-right rules are added to the stylesheet to position the other two images in the header area. Both of these rules use absolute positioning. This makes the left and top properties particularly important because they assign where the top-left corner of the container will be positioned. Because the first image is 169 pixels wide, the a5-header-center tag must start 169 pixels from the left—thus the 169px value. Because the center image is 384 pixels wide, that width added to the width of the first image determines that the third image must start 553 pixels from the left (384 + 169 = 553 pixels). This positioning, however, works only if the borders are turned off, so they are not entered into the equation in some browsers. To guarantee that both images begin at the top of the a5-header container, the top property, with a value of 0px, is added to both rules.

Adding <DIV> in Which to Nest Left and Right Columns

Before the left and right columns of the design can be added, a <DIV> must be added that can contain the columns. In this case, the a5-body-content container serves two functions:

■ Once the left and right columns are nested inside the <DIV>, the entire area can be easily moved in relation to the header area. If, for example, the design is customized to be 150 pixels high, the top property of the a5-body-center container would need to be changed to 150px.
■ A background image can be applied specifically to this section. In this case, it is the image of the woman.

The background image can also be applied to the HTML, BODY rule and have its location controlled by the shorthand background rule: background: #ffffff url(images/bg-body-content.jpg) no-repeat 0px 98px;. The left (0px) and top (98px) properties at the end of the rule tell the background image where it should be displayed in relation to the top-left corner of the browser window.

Figure 6.10 shows what the image looks like when the <DIV> is added. Without content in the <DIV>, it would normally collapse and not show the background. The a5-body-content rule, however, has been assigned a height of 410px, which will guarantee that the entire image always shows, whether there is content included in the <DIV> or it expands to the full 410 pixels if not enough content is added.

This rule is also assigned a margin-right property with the value of 15px. This is to ensure that eventually, when text is added to the center column, it will not touch the right side and make its readability more difficult.

FIGURE 6.10   The page with the a5-body-content container added, which will not only contain the left and right columns, but will also display a background image.

Creating the Left Column

After the a5-body-content container has been added, the left column can be created. This column will contain the menu, the Glance At box, and the copyright areas. Listing 6.3 shows what the code looks like, which then displays the design, as shown in Figure 6.11.

FIGURE 6.11   The design with the left column added to the a5-body-content container.

LISTING 6.3   Code for Figure 6.11

```
<!DOCTYPE html PUBLIC "-//W3C//DTD XHTML 1.0 Transitional//EN"
    "DTD/xhtml1-transitional.dtd">
<html><head><title>Design 121</title>
<meta http-equiv="Content-Type" content="text/html;
    charset=iso-8859-1" />
<style type="text/css">
/* ++++++++++ global general styles start ++++++++++*/
html, body {
    margin:0px;
    padding:0px;
    font: 13px Arial, Helvetica, sans-serif;
    color:#766D6D;
    background:#ffffff;
    }
/* ++++++++++ global general styles end ++++++++++*/
/* ++++++++++ global structure styles start ++++++++++*/
#a5-body-center {
    text-align:left;
    border:0px solid #000000;
    }
#a5-body {
    position: relative;
    width: 770px; /* change this to a specific amount for a fixed
        design. E.g., 770px. */
/* remove these comment tags if the page is to be centered. The 'text-
    align' property in the 'a5-body-center' rule must also be changed
    from 'left' to 'center'
    margin-left: auto;
    margin-right: auto;*/
    text-align:left;
    padding-bottom:10px;
    border:0px solid #000000;
    }
/* ++++++++++ global structure styles end ++++++++++*/
#a5-header {
    position:relative;
    left:0px;
    top:0px;
    height:98px;
    background:#000000;
    }
    #a5-header-center {
        position:absolute;
        left:169px;
        top:0px;
        }
    #a5-header-right {
        position:absolute;
        left:553px;
        top:0px;
        }
#a5-body-content {
    position:relative;
    background: #ffffff url(images/bg-body-content.jpg) no-repeat;
```

```
        height:410px;
margin-right:15px;
        border:0px solid #000000;
        }
    #a5-column-left {
        position:absolute;
        left:0px;
        top:19px;
        width:190px;
        }
        #a5-menu {
        font:bold 13px Arial, Helvetica, sans-serif;
            }
        #a5-menu a {
            display:block;
            text-align:left;
            line-height:23px;
            vertical-align:50%;
            padding-left:15px;
            margin-bottom:1px;
            text-decoration:none;
            background: url(images/bg-menu-off.gif) no-repeat 0px 0px;
            color:#E9F92C;
            }
        #a5-menu a:hover {
            background: url(images/bg-menu-on.jpg) no-repeat 0px 0px;
            margin-bottom:1px;
            color:#E9F92C;
            }
        #a5-bottom-left-content {
            width:136px;
            font:bold 12pt times, garamond, serif;
            line-height:26px;
            text-align:right;
            margin:9px 0px 0px 10px;
            color:#DF9B05;
            border:1px solid #999A8D;
            }
        #a5-copyright {
            font-size:8pt;
            padding:10px 50px 10px 10px;
            color:#766D6D;
            }
</style>
</head>
<body>
<div id="a5-body-center">
    <div id="a5-body">
<!-- ###### header start ###### -->
        <div id="a5-header">
            <div><a href="index.htm"><img src="images/header-left.gif"
                width="169" height="98" alt="" border="0" /></a></div>
            <div id="a5-header-center"><img src="images/
                header-center.jpg" width="384" height="98" alt=""
                border="0" /></div>
```

```
            <div id="a5-header-right"><img src="images/
                header-right.jpg" width="217" height="98" alt=""
                border="0" /></div>
        </div>
    <!-- ###### header end ###### -->

    <!-- ###### body content start ###### -->
        <div id="a5-body-content">
            <div id="a5-column-left">
                <div id="a5-menu">
                    <a href="index.htm">menu item 1</a>
                    <a href="menu-item-2.htm">longer menu item 2</a>
                    <a href="menu-item-3.htm">menu item 3</a>
                    <a href="index.htm">menu item 4</a>
                    <a href="index.htm">menu item 5</a>
                    <a href="index.htm">menu item 6</a>
                </div>

                <div id="a5-bottom-left-content">
                    <span style="font:bold 24pt times, garamond, serif;
                        ">Glance at</span><br />
                    some of the<br />
                    <span style="font:bold 13pt times, garamond, serif;
                        ">possibilities your</span><br />
                    house has to offer        <div style="padding-top:10px;">
                        <a href="index.htm"><img src="images/
                        photo-bottom-left.jpg" width="136"
                        height="93" alt="" border="0" /></a></div>
                </div>
                <div id="a5-copyright">
                    |  &copy; copyright 2006  
                        |<br />|  your company  |
                        <br />|  all rights reserved 
                         |
                </div>
            </div>
        </div>
    <!-- ###### body content start ###### -->
        </div>
    </div>
    </body>
    </html>
```

There are several things to note about the code in Listing 6.3:

■ The a5-column-left container is assigned absolute positioning. This guarantees that it will always be in the same location. The one disadvantage to absolute positioning is the a5-column-left container will fall outside the flow of the document, meaning it can end up vertically longer than the a5-column-left container. Fortunately, for this design, this would not be visible if it were the case because the column does not have a background color or image the content needs to remain over.

■ The a5-menu container contains the menu items that are styled to enable easy mouseovers. The column is given a specific width to guarantee that the first element is positioned correctly in all browsers.

■ The a5-menu a descendant rule is used to display and style each menu item. The display property with the block value will output each item in the <DIV> in its own row. The text is then left justified, assigning the text-align property a value of left. The line-height and vertical-align properties, which need to be used together for the vertical-align property to be interpreted, force the height of the menu item and how the text will be vertically aligned. The padding-left:15px; rule forces the menu items 15 pixels from the left so they do not fall on the circular image at the very left of the row. Because the menu is layered over the a5-body-content background image to the right, the margin-bottom:1px; rule is added to ensure that there is transparent spacing between the menu items so the layering effect is noticeable (see Figure 6.12).

One of the most important properties of this rule is the shorthand background property, which assigns a background image to a hyperlink and thus an item in the menu. This property works in conjunction with the a5-menu a:hover rule, which changes the background image when the user mouses over a menu item, avoiding the need for JavaScript (see Figure 6.13).

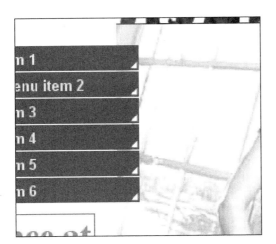

FIGURE 6.12   The menu items are assigned a margin-bottom value of 1px to ensure it is apparent that the menu is layered over the background image in the a5-body-content rule.

FIGURE 6.13   Background image that is switched using the code background: url(images/bg-menu-on.jpg) no-repeat 0px 0px;.

■   The a5-bottom-left-content rule is added to create a separate text section below the menu. It employs many of the properties already discussed in this chapter. What gives it a different appearance is that the border is turned on and given a different color. While default font styling is included in the rule, additional styling is used at a local level in the <DIV> tag to resize text such as "Glance at." The image in the container also is given local styling so that it has 10 pixels of padding between it and the text above it. If <DIV> tags are not added around the image, the border will not collapse around the image in IE 5, 5.5, and 6 browsers (see Figure 6.14).

FIGURE 6.14   An image in a container that will not allow the border to collapse around the bottom, in all browsers, unless additional <DIV> tags are added.

■   The only unique thing to note about the a5-copyright rule is where it is placed. If either the left or right columns or <DIV>s nested in them are assigned absolute positioning, then the copyright should probably not be included in a footer row across the bottom of the entire site because if the text runs too long in these absolute-positioned <DIV>s, they can extend below the footer, either over or under it.

Adding the Center (Right) Column

At this stage most of the coding has been accomplished for the home page. The designer needs to add only a column to the right. Because this design could always be turned into a three-column design, the column to the right is called a5-column-center, leaving the possibility of naming a right column a5-column-right. Listing 6.4 shows the completed code for the home page design, which is shown in Figure 6.15.

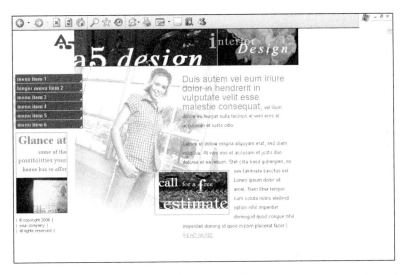

FIGURE 6.15   The completed design once the `a5-column-right` rule and content have been added.

LISTING 6.4   Code for Figure 6.15

```
<!DOCTYPE html PUBLIC "-//W3C//DTD XHTML 1.0 Transitional//EN"
    "DTD/xhtml1-transitional.dtd">
<html><head><title>Design 121</title>
<meta http-equiv="Content-Type" content="text/html;
    charset=iso-8859-1" />
<style type="text/css">
/* ++++++++++ global general styles start ++++++++++*/
html, body {
    margin:0px;
    padding:0px;
    font: 13px Arial, Helvetica, sans-serif;
    color:#766D6D;
    background:#ffffff;
    }
/* ++++++++++ global general styles end ++++++++++*/
/* ++++++++++ global structure styles start ++++++++++*/
#a5-body-center {
    text-align:left;
    border:0px solid #000000;
    }
#a5-body {
    position: relative;
    width: 770px; /* change this to a specific amount for a fixed
        design. E.g., 770px. */
/* remove these comment tags if the page is to be centered. The
    'text-align' property in the 'a5-body-center' rule must also be
    changed from 'left' to 'center'
```

```
    margin-left: auto;
    margin-right: auto;*/
    text-align:left;
    padding-bottom:10px;
    border:0px solid #000000;
    }
/* ++++++++++ global structure styles end ++++++++++*/
#a5-header {
    position:relative;
    left:0px;
    top:0px;
    height:98px;
    background:#000000;
    }
    #a5-header-center {
        position:absolute;
        left:169px;
        top:0px;
        }
    #a5-header-right {
        position:absolute;
        left:553px;
        top:0px;
        }
#a5-body-content {
    position:relative;
    background: #ffffff url(images/bg-body-content.jpg) no-repeat;
    height:410px;
    margin-right:15px;
    border:0px solid #000000;
    }
    #a5-column-left {
        position:absolute;
        left:0px;
        top:19px;
        width:190px;
        }
        #a5-menu {
            font:bold 13px Arial, Helvetica, sans-serif;
            }
        #a5-menu a {
            display:block;
            text-align:left;
            line-height:23px;
            vertical-align: 50%;
            padding-left:15px;
            margin-bottom:1px;
            text-decoration:none;
            background: url(images/bg-menu-off.gif) no-repeat 0px 0px;
            color:#E9F92C;
            }
        #a5-menu a:hover {
            background: url(images/bg-menu-on.jpg) no-repeat 0px 0px;
            margin-bottom:1px;
            color:#E9F92C;
            }
```

```
        #a5-bottom-left-content {
            width:136px;
            font:bold 12pt times, garamond, serif;
            line-height:26px;
            text-align:right;
            margin:9px 0px 0px 10px;
            color:#DF9B05;
            border:1px solid #999A8D;
            }
            #a5-copyright {
            font-size: 8pt;
            padding:10px 50px 10px 10px;
            color:#766D6D;
            }
    #a5-column-center {
        position:absolute;
        left:190px;
        top:0px;
        line-height:18pt;
        padding:24px 0px 0px 268px;
        }
</style>
</head>
<body>
<div id="a5-body-center">
    <div id="a5-body">
<!-- ###### header start ###### -->
        <div id="a5-header">
            <div><a href="index.htm"><img src="images/header-left.gif"
                width="169" height="98" alt="" border="0" /></a></div>
                <div id="a5-header-center"><img src="images/
                    header-center.jpg" width="384" height="98" alt=""
                    border="0" /></div>
                <div id="a5-header-right"><img src="images/
                    header-right.jpg" width="217" height="98" alt=""
                    border="0" /></div>
        </div>
<!-- ###### header end ###### -->

<!-- ###### body content start ###### -->
        <div id="a5-body-content">
            <div id="a5-column-left">
                <div id="a5-menu">
                    <a href="index.htm">menu item 1</a>
                    <a href="menu-item-2.htm">longer menu item 2</a>
                    <a href="menu-item-3.htm">menu item 3</a>
                    <a href="index.htm">menu item 4</a>
                    <a href="index.htm">menu item 5</a>
                    <a href="index.htm">menu item 6</a>
                </div>

                <div id="a5-bottom-left-content">
                    <span style="font:bold 24pt times, garamond,
                        serif;">Glance at</span><br />
                    some of the<br />
```

```
<span style="font:bold 13pt times, garamond,
 serif;">possibilities your</span><br />
house has to offer
<div style="padding-top:10px;"><a href="index.htm">
    <img src="images/photo-bottom-left.jpg"
    width="136" height="93" alt="" border="0" /></a></div>
</div>
<div id="a5-copyright">
|  &copy; copyright 2006  |<br />|
      your company  |<br />|
      all rights reserved  |
</div>
</div>
<div id="a5-column-center">
    <span class="color1text18">Duis autem vel eum iriure
        dolor in hendrerit in vulputate velit esse
        malestie consequat,</span> vel illum dolore eu
        feugiat nulla facilisis at vero eros et
        accumsan et iusto odio.<br /><br />
Labore et dolore magna aliquyam erat, sed diam voluptua. At vero eos et
    accusam et justo duo dolores et ea rebum. <span style="float:left;
    padding:10px; margin-left:-86px;"><a href="index.htm"><img src=
    "images/photo-center-middle.gif" width="199" height="117" alt=""
    border="0" /></a></span>Stet clita kasd gubergren, no sea takimata
    sanctus est Lorem ipsum dolor sit amet. Nam liber tempor cum
    soluta nobis eleifend option nihil imperdiet doming id quod congue
    nihil imperdiet doming id quod mazim placerat facer  | <a href=
    "index.htm">READ MORE</a>
        </div>
    </div>
<!-- ###### body content start ###### -->
    </div>
</div>
</body>
</html>
```

There are several things to note about the code in Listing 6.4:

■ Only one rule is added to style the right column: a5-column-center. It is given absolute positioning to ensure that the content does not fill the full width of the remaining screen. If the design were a liquid design, relative positioning would be the desired value.

■ The <DIV> tag uses the left property to position the text 190 pixels from the left.

■ The "call for a free estimate" image included in the container's text is assigned a local style that floats it to the left. The image is then assigned a margin-left property with the value of -86px. This forces the image to the left, partially outside the text flow (see Figure 6.16).

This is where the transparency of the image between the border and the main part of the image becomes useful. This image can be added wherever the designer chooses within the content area. This is possible because the area between the border and the main part of the image will show the actual area over which it is layered.

FIGURE 6.16 The design with the "call for a free estimate" image forced to the left, outside the main content flow.

CONSTRUCTING SECOND-LEVEL PAGES

A portion of the home page design can be reused many times with other pages to maintain consistency and to limit the additional download necessary for second-level pages (i.e., the user's browser can cache certain images so they do not have to be downloaded again, making the page load faster). When developing CSS sites, this process is much cleaner than with XHTML tables that can include many nested tables. Listing 6.5 shows the code used to create a second-level page after it has been customized from the homepage (see Figure 6.17).

FIGURE 6.17 A second-level page of the site constructed from the home page design and code.

LISTING 6.5   Code for Figure 6.17

```
<!DOCTYPE html PUBLIC "-//W3C//DTD XHTML 1.0 Transitional//EN"
    "DTD/xhtml1-transitional.dtd">
<html><head><title>Design 121</title>
<meta http-equiv="Content-Type" content="text/html;
    charset=iso-8859-1" />
<style type="text/css">
/* ++++++++++ global general styles start ++++++++++*/
html, body {
    margin:0px;
    padding:0px;
    font: 13px Arial, Helvetica, sans-serif;
    color:#766D6D;
    background:#ffffff;
    }
a:link { color:#CB951D; }
a:visited { color:#A8B32D; }
a:active { color:#A8B32D; }
a:hover { color:#000000; }
.color1text18 {
    font-family: arial, geneva, sans-serif;
    font-size: 18pt;
    color: #A8B32D;
    }
/* ++++++++++ global general styles end ++++++++++*/
/* ++++++++++ global structure styles start ++++++++++*/
#a5-body-center {
    text-align:left;
    }
#a5-body {
    position: relative;
    width: 770px; /* change this to a specific amount for a fixed
    design. E.g., 770px. */
/* remove these comment tags if the page is to be centered. The
    'text-align' property in the 'a5-body-center' rule must also be
    changed from 'left' to 'center'
    margin-left: auto;
    margin-right: auto;*/
    text-align:left;
    padding-bottom:10px;
    border:0px solid #000000;
    }
#a5-header {
    position:relative;
    left:0px;
    top:0px;
    height:98px;
    border:0px solid #000000;
    }
    #a5-header-center {
        position:absolute;
        left:169px;
        top:0px;
        }
```

```
#a5-header-right {
    position:absolute;
    left:553px;
    top:0px;
    }
#a5-body-content {
    position:relative;
    background: #ffffff url(images/bg-body-content.jpg) no-repeat;
    height:410px;
    margin-right:15px;
    border:0px solid #000000;
    }
#a5-column-left {
    position:absolute;
    left:0px;
    top:19px;
    width:190px;
    }
    #a5-menu {
        font:bold 13px Arial, Helvetica, sans-serif;
        }
    #a5-menu a {
        display:block;
        text-align:left;
        line-height:23px;
        vertical-align:50%;
        padding-left:15px;
        margin-bottom:1px;
        text-decoration:none;
        background: url(images/bg-menu-off.gif) no-repeat 0px 0px;
        color:#E9F92C;
        }
    #a5-menu a:hover {
        background: url(images/bg-menu-on.jpg) no-repeat 0px 0px;
        margin-bottom:1px;
        color:#E9F92C;
        }
    #a5-bottom-left-content {
        width:136px;
        font:bold 12pt times, garamond, serif;
        line-height:26px;
        text-align:right;
        margin:9px 0px 0px 10px;
        color:#DF9B05;
        border:1px solid #999A8D;
        }
    #a5-copyright {
        font-size: 8pt;
        padding:10px 50px 10px 10px;
        color:#766D6D;
        }
#a5-column-center {
    position:absolute;
    left:190px;
    top:0px;
```

```
            line-height:18pt;
            padding:24px 0px 0px 268px;
                }
/* ++++++++++ global structure styles end ++++++++++*/
/* ++++++++++ second level start ++++++++++*/
#a5-body-content-sl {
        position:relative;
        background: #ffffff url(images/bg-body-content-sl.jpg) no-repeat;
        height:410px;
        margin-right:15px;
        border:0px solid #000000;
        }
        #a5-column-center-sl {
            position:absolute;
            left:190px;
            top:0px;
            line-height:18pt;
            padding:18px 0px 0px 18px;
            }
        #a5-sl-title {
                height:24px;
                font:bold 14px Arial, Helvetica, sans-serif;
                background:#4E2124 url(images/bg-title.jpg) no-repeat
                    left top;
                color:#ffffff;
                padding:3px 0px 0px 40px;
                margin-bottom:10px;
                border:0px solid #000000;
                voice-family:"\"}\"";
                voice-family:inherit;
                    height:20px;
                }
                html>body #a5-sl-title {
                    height:20px;
                }
/* ++++++++++ second level end ++++++++++*/
</style>
</head>
<body>
<div id="a5-body-center">
    <div id="a5-body">
<!-- ###### header start ###### -->
        <div id="a5-header">
            <div><a href="index.htm"><img src="images/header-left.gif"
                width="169" height="98" alt="" border="0" /></a></div>
                <div id="a5-header-center"><img src="images/
                    header-center.jpg" width="384" height="98" alt=""
                    border="0" /></div>
                <div id="a5-header-right"><img src="images/
                    header-right.jpg" width="217" height="98" alt=""
                    border="0" /></div>
        </div>
<!-- ###### header end ###### -->
<!-- ###### body content start ###### -->
        <div id="a5-body-content-sl">
            <div id="a5-column-left">
```

```
            <div id="a5-menu">
                <a href="index.htm">menu item 1</a>
                <a href="menu-item-2.htm">longer menu item 2</a>
                <a href="menu-item-3.htm">menu item 3</a>
                <a href="index.htm">menu item 4</a>
                <a href="index.htm">menu item 5</a>
                <a href="index.htm">menu item 6</a>
            </div>
            <div id="a5-bottom-left-content">
                <span style="font:bold 24pt times, garamond,
                    serif;">Glance at</span><br />
                some of the<br />
                <span style="font:bold 13pt times, garamond,
                    serif;">possibilities your</span><br />
                house has to offer
                <div style="padding-top:10px;"><a href="index.htm">
                    <img src="images/photo-bottom-left.jpg"
                    width="136" height="93" alt="" border="0"
                    /></a></div>
            </div>
            <div id="a5-copyright">
                |  &copy; copyright 2006  
                    |<br />|  your company  |
                    <br />|  all rights reserved 
                     |
            </div>
        </div>
        <div id="a5-column-center-sl">
<!-- ###### title start ###### -->
            <div id="a5-sl-title">longer menu item 2</div>
<!-- ###### title end ###### -->
                Nam liber tempor cum soluta nobis eleifend option
                congue nihil imperdiet doming id quod mazim placerat
                facer possim assum. Lorem ipsum dolor sit amet,
                consectetuer adipiscing elit, sed diam nonummy nibh
                euismod tincidunt ut laoreet dolore magna aliquam erat
                volutpat. Ut wisi enim ad minim veniam, quis nostrud
                exerci tation ullamcorper suscipit lobortis nisl ut
                aliquip ex ea commodo consequat.
<br /><br />
Duis autem vel eum iriure dolor in hendrerit in vulputate velit esse
    molestie consequat, vel illum dolore eu feugiat nulla facilisis.
<br /><br />
At vero eos et accusam et justo duo dolores et ea rebum. Stet clita
    kasd gubergren, no sea takimata sanctus est Lorem ipsum dolor sit
    amet. Lorem ipsum dolor sit amet, consetetur sadipscing elitr, sed
    diam nonumy eirmod tempor invidunt ut labore et dolore magna
    aliquyam erat, sed diam voluptua. At vero eos et accusam et justo
    duo dolores et ea rebum. Stet clita kasd gubergren, no sea takimata
    sanctus est Lorem ipsum dolor sit amet. Lorem ipsum dolor sit amet,
    consetetur sadipscing elitr, At accusam aliquyam diam diam dolore
    dolores duo eirmod sed erat, et nonumy sed tempor et et invidunt
    justo labore Stet clita ea et gubergren, kasd magna no rebum.
    sanctus sea sed takimata ut vero voluptua. est Lorem ipsum
                </div>
        </div>
```

```
<!-- ###### body content end ###### -->
    </div>
</div>
</body>
</html>
```

There are several things to note about the code in Listing 6.5:

- The `a5-body-content` container is renamed `a5-body-content-sl` because the background image for the second-level pages is lightened, using Photoshop, to help make the text, which covers most of the image, more visible on the pages. The `a5-body-content-sl` rule then calls this new image.
- The `margin-right:15px;` code, as on the homepage, ensures that the text will never touch the right side of the browser window if it is a liquid design that expands to the full width of the screen.
- The `a5-sl-title` rule is added to allow the designer to place a title on every page so the user knows which page is selected. The main thing to note about this code is that because the container is given padding, the Tantek hack is used so the height of the row is the same in the tested browsers. A `margin-bottom` value of `10px` is also added to provide space between the title area and the text for that page.

Adding a Floating Container for Additional Content

In the case study designs in Chapters 7 and 8, a third column is added to allow for more layout options. In this design, however, a new `<DIV>` is merely added and floated to the right side of the text to allow for similar functionality. Figure 6.18 illustrates what the new code (outlined in Listing 6.6) will look like.

FIGURE 6.18 A right text block area is added to second-level pages to allow for more layout possibilities.

LISTING 6.6   Code for Figure 6.18

```
<!DOCTYPE html PUBLIC "-//W3C//DTD XHTML 1.0 Transitional//EN"
    "DTD/xhtml1-transitional.dtd">
<html><head><title>Design 121</title>
<meta http-equiv="Content-Type" content="text/html;
    charset=iso-8859-1" />
<style type="text/css">
/* ++++++++++ global general styles start ++++++++++*/
html, body {
    margin:0px;
    padding:0px;
    font: 13px Arial, Helvetica, sans-serif;
    color:#766D6D;
    background:#ffffff;
    }
a:link { color:#CB951D; }
a:visited { color:#A8B32D; }
a:active { color:#A8B32D; }
a:hover { color:#000000; }
.color1text18 {
    font-family: arial, geneva, sans-serif;
    font-size: 18pt;
    color: #A8B32D;
    }
/* ++++++++++ global general styles end ++++++++++*/
/* ++++++++++ global structure styles start ++++++++++*/
#a5-body-center {
    text-align:left;
    }
#a5-body {
    position: relative;
    width: 770px; /* change this to a specific amount for a fixed
        design. E.g., 770px. */
/* remove these comment tags if the page is to be centered. The
    'text-align' property in the 'a5-body-center' rule must also be
    changed from 'left' to 'center'
    margin-left: auto;
    margin-right: auto;*/
    text-align:left;
    padding-bottom:10px;
    border:0px solid #000000;
    }
#a5-header {
    position:relative;
    left:0px;
    top:0px;
    height:98px;
    border:0px solid #000000;
    }
    #a5-header-center {
        position:absolute;
        left:169px;
        top:0px;
        }
    #a5-header-right {
```

```
            position:absolute;
            left:553px;
            top:0px;
            }
#a5-body-content {
    position:relative;
    background: #ffffff url(images/bg-body-content.jpg) no-repeat;
    height:410px;
    margin-right:15px;
    border:0px solid #000000;
    }
#a5-column-left {
    position:absolute;
    left:0px;
    top:19px;
    width:190px;
    }
    #a5-menu {
        font:bold 13px Arial, Helvetica, sans-serif;
        }
    #a5-menu a {
        display:block;
        text-align:left;
        line-height:23px;
        vertical-align:50%;
        padding-left:15px;
        margin-bottom:1px;
        text-decoration:none;
        background: url(images/bg-menu-off.gif) no-repeat 0px 0px;
        color:#E9F92C;
        }
    #a5-menu a:hover {
        background: url(images/bg-menu-on.jpg) no-repeat 0px 0px;
        margin-bottom:1px;
        color:#E9F92C;
        }
    #a5-bottom-left-content {
        width:136px;
        font:bold 12pt times, garamond, serif;
        line-height:26px;
        text-align:right;
        margin:9px 0px 0px 10px;
        color:#DF9B05;
        border:1px solid #999A8D;
        }
    #a5-copyright {
        font-size: 8pt;
        padding:10px 50px 10px 10px;
        color:#766D6D;
        }
#a5-column-center {
    position:absolute;
    left:190px;
    top:0px;
    line-height:18pt;
```

```css
            padding:24px 0px 0px 268px;
        }
/* ++++++++++ global structure styles end ++++++++++*/
/* ++++++++++ second level start ++++++++++*/
#a5-body-content-sl {
    position:relative;
    background: #ffffff url(images/bg-body-content-sl.jpg) no-repeat;
    height:410px;
    margin-right:15px;
    border:0px solid #000000;
    }
    #a5-column-center-sl {
        position:absolute;
        left:190px;
        top:0px;
        line-height:18pt;
        padding:18px 0px 0px 18px;
        }
        #a5-sl-title {
            height:24px;
            font:bold 14px Arial, Helvetica, sans-serif;
            background:#4E2124 url(images/bg-title.jpg) no-repeat
                left top;
            color:#ffffff;
            padding:3px 0px 0px 40px;
            margin-bottom:10px;
            border:0px solid #000000;
            voice-family:"\"}\"";
            voice-family:inherit;
                height:20px;
            }
            html>body #a5-sl-title {
                height:20px;
            }
        #a5-content-right-sl {
            float:right;
            width:182px;
            font:bold 12pt times, garamond, serif;
            line-height:16px;
            text-align:right;
            padding:15px;
            margin:10px 10px 10px 15px;
            color:#ffffff;
            border:1px solid #999A8D;
            background:#C1C96A;
            voice-family:"\"}\"";
            voice-family:inherit;
                width:150px;
            }
            html>body #a5-content-right-sl {
                width:150px;
            }
/* ++++++++++ second level end ++++++++++*/
</style>
</head>
```

```
<body>
<div id="a5-body-center">
    <div id="a5-body">
<!-- ###### header start ###### -->
        <div id="a5-header">
            <div><a href="index.htm"><img src="images/header-left.gif"
                width="169" height="98" alt="" border="0" /></a></div>
            <div id="a5-header-center"><img src="images/
                header-center.jpg" width="384" height="98" alt=""
                border="0" /></div>
            <div id="a5-header-right"><img src="images/
                header-right.jpg" width="217" height="98" alt=""
                border="0" /></div>
        </div>
<!-- ###### header end ###### -->
<!-- ###### body content start ###### -->
        <div id="a5-body-content-sl">
            <div id="a5-column-left">
                <div id="a5-menu">
                    <a href="index.htm">menu item 1</a>
                    <a href="menu-item-2.htm">longer menu item 2</a>
                    <a href="menu-item-3.htm">menu item 3</a>
                    <a href="index.htm">menu item 4</a>
                    <a href="index.htm">menu item 5</a>
                    <a href="index.htm">menu item 6</a>
                </div>
                <div id="a5-bottom-left-content">
                    <span style="font:bold 24pt times, garamond,
                        serif;">Glance at</span><br />
                    some of the<br />
                    <span style="font:bold 13pt times, garamond,
                        serif;">possibilities your</span><br />
                    house has to offer
                    <div style="padding-top:10px;"><a href="index.htm">
                        <img src="images/photo-bottom-left.jpg"
                        width="136" height="93" alt="" border="0"
                        /></a></div>
                </div>
                <div id="a5-copyright">
                    |  &copy; copyright 2006  |
                        <br />|  your company  |
                        <br />|  all rights reserved 
                         |
                </div>
            </div>
            <div id="a5-column-center-sl">
<!-- ###### title start ###### -->
                <div id="a5-sl-title">longer menu item 2</div>
<!-- ###### title end ###### -->
                    Nam liber tempor cum soluta nobis eleifend option
                        congue nihil imperdiet doming id quod mazim
                        placerat facer possim assum. Lorem ipsum dolor sit
                        amet, consectetuer adipiscing elit, sed diam
                        nonummy nibh euismod tincidunt ut laoreet dolore
                        magna aliquam erat volutpat. Ut wisi enim ad minim
```

```
                                 <div id="a5-content-right-sl">Nam liber tempor cum
                                 soluta nobis eleifend option congue nihil imperdiet
                                 doming id quod mazim placerat facer possim assum.
                                 <br /><br />Duis autem vel eum iriure dolor in
                                 hendrerit in vulputate velit esse molestie
                                 consequat, vel illum dolore eu feugiat nulla
                                 facilisis.<br /><br />Nam liber tempor cum soluta
                                 nobis eleifend option congue nihil imperdiet doming
                                 id quod mazim placerat facer possim assum.</div>
                                 veniam, quis nostrud exerci tation ullamcorper
                                 suscipit lobortis nisl ut aliquip ex ea commodo
                                 consequat.
    <br /><br />
    Duis autem vel eum iriure dolor in hendrerit in vulputate velit esse
        molestie consequat, vel illum dolore eu feugiat nulla facilisis.
    <br /><br />
    At vero eos et accusam et justo duo dolores et ea rebum. Stet clita
        kasd gubergren, no sea takimata sanctus est Lorem ipsum dolor sit
        amet. Lorem ipsum dolor sit amet, consetetur sadipscing elitr, sed
        diam nonumy eirmod tempor invidunt ut labore et dolore magna
        aliquyam erat, sed diam voluptua. At vero eos et accusam et justo
        duo dolores et ea rebum. Stet clita kasd gubergren, no sea takimata
        sanctus est Lorem ipsum dolor sit amet. Lorem ipsum dolor sit amet,
        consetetur sadipscing elitr, At accusam aliquyam diam diam dolore
        dolores duo eirmod eos erat, et nonumy sed tempor et et invidunt
        justo labore Stet clita ea et gubergren, kasd magna no rebum.
        sanctus sea sed takimata ut vero voluptua. est Lorem ipsum
                    </div>
                </div>
    <!-- ###### body content end ###### -->
            </div>
        </div>
    </body>
    </html>
```

There are several things to note about the code in Listing 6.6:

■ The `a5-content-right-sl` rule uses the Tantek hack to ensure that the width is the same among all tested browsers. While none of the CSS is new at this point in the design, floating a `<DIV>` in the text can have varied results. Depending on where the container is included in the text, various browsers will render the line wraps and the line height (at least for one or two lines) differently. The designer should definitely test pages that use this layout technique.

Barring varied rendering issues, there are several noted bugs associated with floating various designed `<DIV>`s in content. Rather than use more complex floats, it is recommended that the designer use structured columns. If floats are used and the designer runs into problems, the Holly Hack and Peek-a-boo bug are two places to beginning researching a solution.

SUMMARY

The design built in this chapter is a two-column layout that allows for including a floating <DIV> area on second-level pages. The chapter explains how the design could work as a liquid design or as a fixed design. Other techniques such as using switching background images for mouseovers, mortising images, and using transparent GIFs in a layout are discussed. While a designer may not follow this exact coding method, all the techniques can be applied independently when creating other designs.

7 Case Study: Medium Content CSS Design

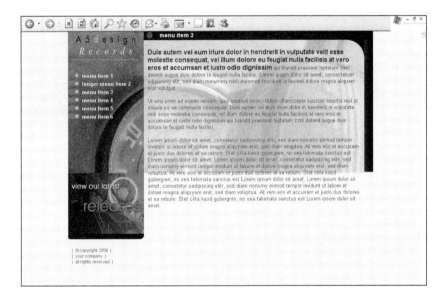

The complexity of a Web design can be deceptive. A design that looks simple can require more complex CSS coding, while a visually complex design may merely involve simple coding to achieve the proper mortising of images and content placement. The design in this chapter, while its look and feel appears similar to the design in Chapter 6, is more complex because it uses a three- rather than two-column design. Also, it is centered in the browser and uses mortised images on the top half of the home page so the user can not only view the images but also click on them. The second level uses a screened version as the background image. This allows the design to add content freely over the image.

The design explained in this chapter is design 122 on the accompanying CD-ROM (photo credits: *www.idlerphotography.com*).

UNDERSTANDING THE DESIGN'S STRUCTURE

Figure 7.1 is the design that is explained in this chapter. It involves two basic overall columns, one for the left side, which includes the menu, and one for the right, which includes additional nested <DIV>s to position and style the content on the right. This includes the "In the News" and "Purchase Online" text areas.

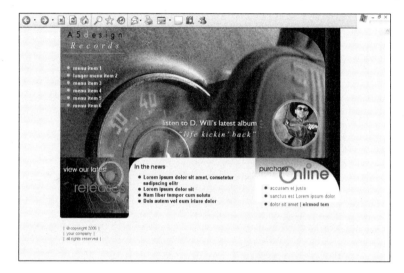

FIGURE 7.1   The medium-content CSS design explained in this chapter.

Reasoning Behind Guides and Creating Slices in Photoshop File

There are 10 slices included in this design (Figure 7.2), all deriving their positioning from the numerous guides that were added. Understanding these is the first step to better visualizing how to efficiently structure and style the various containers.

■ The guide to the left of number 1 is used to separate the design into left and right columns. The left column includes the menu, and the right column is a parent column that will have two columns, the center and right columns, nested inside it.

■ The guide below number 2 represents the guide that is used to not only outline the bottom of the background image in the menu, but also to separate the main graphical area on the right from the XHTML text, "In the News" and "Purchase Online"content, that is included below.

■ The guide to the left of number 3 is used to separate the center and right columns, both of which are nested inside the parent right column.

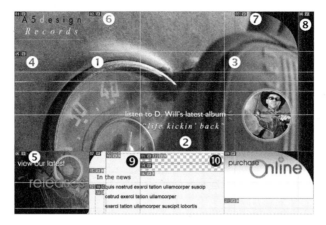

FIGURE 7.2   This image outlines 10 of the most important slices and guides the designer needs to understand. While some are used similarly in the design in Chapter 6, others offer additional ways to build mortised CSS sites.

- The slice indicated by number 4 is the background image that is used for the menu area of the design. One consideration in this type of design is that the background does not repeat vertically, because it is not designed to do so. This forces the designer to work within a specified height, which includes any height taken up by submenu items. By using a nonrepeatable background image, the designer can mortise it with the slice illustrated by number 5. If, however, the design were altered visually so that it did not matter if the two images were mortised together, the menu could be changed structurally to stretch down as far as the designer wanted.
- Number 5 shows the slice that creates an image placed below the menu in the left column.
- The images represented by numbers 6, 7, and 8 are mortised together to form the large image area of the right column. All three images are saved, so they can be hyperlinked or, for example, replaced by a Flash movie. Because they are nested in a fixed <DIV>, if the design were changed to be liquid, the background color on the right, which is black, would extend to the right of the images. The extension would be seamless because the right image is gradated into solid black.
- The slices to the right of number 9 are used for the background images of each menu item in normal and hover modes. The images are cut from them so their backgrounds can be saved as transparent. This enables the items to be moved over the menu's background image without containing the top image. This technique is explained in Chapter 6.
- Number 10 indicates the image that is used as the background of the bottom-right column text area. While text is layered over it, it cannot be hyperlinked because it is a background image.

Understanding the Placement of CSS Containers

The number of <DIV> tags used in this design is similar to the design in Chapter 6. The main difference is in how they are used. Figure 7.3 shows the structure of the designs with the borders of the <DIV>s turned on.

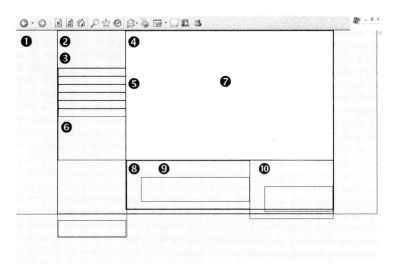

FIGURE 7.3   Ten of the most important containers used to build the design in this chapter.

The <DIV> tags are used for different functions in the design, such as setting up the basic infrastructure of the design, providing containers to position content within the infrastructure, and styling the content within the containers. Following are explanations for the 10 most useful containers in Figure 7.3:

- The <DIV> tag to the left of number 1 is used for centering the design in IE 5 and 5.5. It extends the full width of the screen.
- The <DIV> tag above number 2 determines whether the design has a fixed width or is a liquid layout.
- The <DIV> tag to the left of number 3 contains both the left and right parent columns of the body. They are considered parent columns because the right column contains the code for the visual center and right columns of the design. This container extends to the right edges of the <DIV> outlined by number 2.
- The <DIV> to the left of number 4 defines the right column, which contains everything to the right of the left column, which in this example, is for the sake of visual simplicity.
- The menu column lies to the left of number 5, which is included in the left column.

- Number 6 represents a `<DIV>` that contains the view of our latest releases image in the left column below the menu.
- Number 7 identifies the `<DIV>` that contains the top nested images in the right column.
- The `<DIV>` to the left of number 8 is used to contain the center and right content columns that begin below the `<DIV>` represented by number 7.
- Number 9 shows the bottom-center content column that is nested inside number 8.
- Number 10 represents the bottom-right content column nested inside number 8.

BUILDING THE STRUCTURE

Following are step-by-step instructions to building the design. It is assumed that the Photoshop file has already been created or customized and the designer only needs to position the images and text.

Creating the XHTML and CSS Framework

The first step to building the design is to create the XHTML framework and initial CSS containers. Listing 7.1 is the code that is used to output the page shown in Figure 7.4.

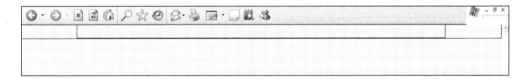

FIGURE 7.4   Basic XHTML and CSS framework for the design.

LISTING 7.1   Code for Figure 7.4

```
<!DOCTYPE html PUBLIC "-//W3C//DTD XHTML 1.0 Transitional//EN"
    "DTD/xhtml1-transitional.dtd">
<html><head><title>Design 122</title>
<meta http-equiv="Content-Type" content="text/html; charset=iso-8859-1" />
<style type="text/css">
/* ++++++++++ global general styles start ++++++++++*/
html, body {
    margin:0px;
    padding:0px;
    font: 13px Arial, Helvetica, sans-serif;
    color:#766D6D;
    background:#F8F4EB;
    }
/* ++++++++++ global general styles end ++++++++++*/
/* ++++++++++ global structure styles start ++++++++++*/
#a5-body-center {
```

```
        text-align:center;
        border:1px solid #000000;
        }
    #a5-body {
        position: relative;
        width: 770px; /* change this to a specific amount for a fixed design.
E.g., 770px. */
        margin-left: auto;
        margin-right: auto;
        text-align:left;
        padding-bottom:10px;
        border:1px solid #000000;
        }
    /* ++++++++++ global structure styles end ++++++++++*/
    </style>
    </head>
    <body>
    <div id="a5-body-center">
        <div id="a5-body">
         
        </div>
    </div>
    </body>
    </html>
```

There are several things to note about the code in Listing 7.1:

- The CSS stylesheet is commented into a couple different sections. The global general styles comment tags contain the general styles, such as the formatting of the <HTML> and <BODY> tags, hyperlinks, and fonts.
- Several rules define the <HTML> and <BODY> tags. The margin and padding properties are used to ensure that the design is placed in the very top-left corner of the browser, with no space between the design and the edges of the viewable area. The default font style is set using the shorthand FONT property. The default font color is defined with the COLOR property. The background color also is assigned (i.e., #F8F4EB). This guarantees that all browsers display the site with the same background color because they would not otherwise always necessarily be the same.
- The a5-body-center and a5-body rules are used to force the design to the left side of the browser screen with a fixed width of 770 pixels. If the designer wanted to fill the full width of the screen, the value of 770px would need to be changed to 100%. If, however, the designer wanted to simply justify the design to the left, the value of the text-align property in the a5-body-center rule would need to be adjusted from center to left. The margin-left and margin-right properties in the a5-body rule ensure that the extra white space is evenly split on both sides. This system allows more than one site to be built with ease and flexibility, using the same default code, allowing the designer to quickly adjust to a client's needs.
- Both the a5-body-center and a5-body rules have their borders turned on using the following code: border:1px solid #000000;. For demonstration purposes, the code

was added to both rules to show what the structure of the <DIV> tags looks like with no content added in them. Turning on the borders also helps a designer when building a site because it is not always apparent where elements are placed or to where they are expanding. Rather than remove these rules, it is easier to change the value of 1px to 0px, turning the borders off. Troubleshooting often involves turning the borders back on, because it saves times and takes up little download size to keep them in the stylesheet.

■ Because the <div id="a5-body"> tag is nested inside the <div id="a5-body-center"> tag, it is indented. This allows for quicker recognition of tags that are nested inside each other, which becomes useful when the page has more code added later.

Adding the Left Column

After the framework has been built, the left column needs to be added. This section includes the logo, menu, and bottom-left image of the design. Figure 7.5 shows what the design looks like after the code in Listing 7.2 has been added.

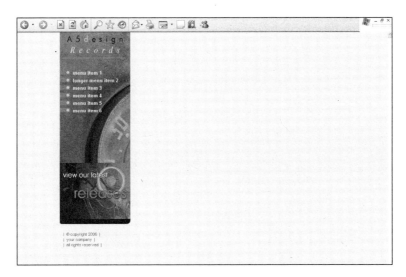

FIGURE 7.5   The design with the left column added.

LISTING 7.2   Code for Figure 7.5

```
<!DOCTYPE html PUBLIC "-//W3C//DTD XHTML 1.0 Transitional//EN"
    "DTD/xhtml1-transitional.dtd">
<html><head><title>Design 122</title>
<meta http-equiv="Content-Type" content="text/html;
    charset=iso-8859-1" />
<style type="text/css">
/* ++++++++++ global general styles start ++++++++++*/
```

```
html, body {
    margin:0px;
    padding:0px;
    font: 13px Arial, Helvetica, sans-serif;
    color:#766D6D;
    background:#F8F4EB;
    }
/* ++++++++++ global general styles end ++++++++++*/
/* ++++++++++ global structure styles start ++++++++++*/
#a5-body-center {
    text-align:center;
    }
#a5-body {
    position: relative;
    width: 770px; /* change this to a specific amount for a fixed
        design. E.g., 770px. */
    margin-left: auto;
    margin-right: auto;
    text-align:left;
    padding-bottom:10px;
    border:0px solid #000000;
    }
#a5-column-left {
    position:absolute;
    left:0px;
    top:0px;
    width:191px;
    border:0px solid #000000;
    }
    #a5-menu {
        font:bold 13px Arial, Helvetica, sans-serif;
        height:249px;
        background:url(images/bg-left-column.jpg) no-repeat;
        }
    #a5-menu a {
        display: block;
        text-align:left;
        line-height:20px;
        vertical-align: 30%;
        height:20px;
        padding-left:35px;
        text-decoration:none;
        background: url(images/bg-menu-off.gif) no-repeat 0px 0px;
        color:#ffffff;
        }
    #a5-menu a:hover {
        background: url(images/bg-menu-on.gif) no-repeat 0px 0px;
        color:#F9F68C;
        }
        #a5-menu-sl {
            width:191px;
            color:#000000;
            font:bold 12px Arial, Helvetica, sans-serif;
            text-align:left;
            }
```

```
            #a5-menu-sl a {
                display: block;
                text-align:left;
                line-height:18px;
                vertical-align: 50%;
                height:18px;
                padding-left:40px;
                font-weight:normal;
                text-decoration:none;
                background: url(images/bg-menu-off-sl.gif) no-repeat
                    0px 0px;
                color:#000000;
                }
            #a5-menu-sl a:hover {
                background: url(images/bg-menu-on-sl.gif) no-repeat
                    0px 0px;
                color:#4C5C6B;
                }
        #a5-copyright {
            font-size: 11px;
            padding:20px 50px 10px 10px;
            color:#978872;
            }
/* ++++++++++ global structure styles end ++++++++++*/
</style>
</head>
<body>
<div id="a5-body-center">
    <div id="a5-body">
<!-- ###### left column start ###### -->
        <div id="a5-column-left">
            <div><a href="index.htm"><img src="images/header-left.jpg"
                width="191" height="100" alt="" border="0" /></a></div>
            <div id="a5-menu">
                <a href="index.htm">menu item 1</a>
                <a href="menu-item-2.htm">longer menu item 2</a>
                <a href="menu-item-3.htm">menu item 3</a>
                <a href="index.htm">menu item 4</a>
                <a href="index.htm">menu item 5</a>
                <a href="index.htm">menu item 6</a>
            </div>
            <div><a href="index.htm"><img src="images/image-bottom-
                    left.jpg" width="191" height="162" alt=""
                    border="0" /></a></div>
            <div id="a5-copyright">
                |  &copy; copyright 2006  |<br />
                    |  your company  |<br />
                    |  all rights reserved  |
            </div>
        </div>
<!-- ###### left column end ###### -->
    </div>
</div>
</body>
</html>
```

There are several things to note about the code in Listing 7.2:

■ The a5-column-left rule has absolute positioning assigned to it. Its left and top properties are both assigned 0px to force the <DIV> into the top-left corner of the a5-body container it is nested within. The width of the column is fixed at 191 pixels, using the width property. This ensures that the column's width will not change, no matter what other content is included in the right column. It also forces the width of the left column so the menu items fill its full width.

■ When the logo is added as the first item in the a5-column-left container, it needs to have <DIV> tags wrapped around it to eliminate extra space between it and the menu area below in some browsers, such as IE 5, 5.5, and 6 (see Figure 7.6).

FIGURE 7.6   Space that is added between the logo and the menu area in IE 5, 5.5, and 6 because <DIV> tags were not wrapped around the image.

■ The a5-menu rule is assigned the height of 249 pixels, which forces it to be the full height of the background image, which also is 249 pixels. To call the background image, a version of the shorthand property for backgrounds is used: background:url(images/ bg-left-column.jpg) no-repeat;. Font size, boldness, and family also are assigned to this <DIV>, which will then cascade down to any nested or child containers.

■ The a5-menu a descendant rule is used to display and style each menu item. The display property with the block value will output each item in the <DIV> in its own row. The text is then left-justified by assigning the text-align property a value of left. The line-height is set to 20 pixels. Unlike the design in Chapter 6, the vertical-align property is not assigned here because it will move the text in relation to the background image, which is declared using the shorthand code: background: url(images/bg-menu-off.gif) no-repeat 0px 0px;.

■ The a5-menu a:hover rule is used to reassign the background image from bg-menu-off.gif to bg-menu-on.gif and the color of the text from #ffffff to #F9F68C when the user mouses over the text.

There is a case difference between the color of the a link and the hover link (i.e., #ffffff and #F9F68C). The reason for this is that #ffffff was entered manually while building the site, and #F9F68C was copied from Color Picker in Photoshop when grabbing the exact HEX color (see Figure 7.7).

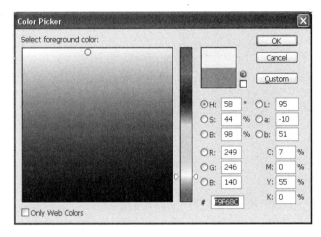

FIGURE 7.7   HEX color, #F9F68C, which was pulled from Color Picker in Photoshop.

■ The image-bottom-left.jpg image below the menu is added after the a5-menu <DIV> in the code. It has no styling added to it other than <DIV>s wrapped around it.

■ The a5-copyright rule positions the copyright text below the image-bottom-left.jpg image, using padding around the text. The padding:20px 50px 10px 10px; code adds 20 pixels of padding to the top of the text, 50 pixels to the right, 10 pixels to the bottom, and 10 pixels to the left.

Adding <DIV> to Nest Center and Inside Right Columns

An a5-body-content <DIV> is added to create a right column in which the top-right images, bottom-left content area, and bottom-right content area will be nested inside. Figure 7.8 shows what the design looks like with the a5-body-content <DIV> border turned on.

This container is added because it will contain a background image in the second-level pages. By building the design around it in the home page, the second-level pages, which are built from the home page, are easier to construct because it is already incorporated into the code. Following is the rule once it is added to the stylesheet:

```
#a5-body-content {
    position:relative;
```

```
margin-left:191px;
height:349px;
border:1px solid #000000;
}
```

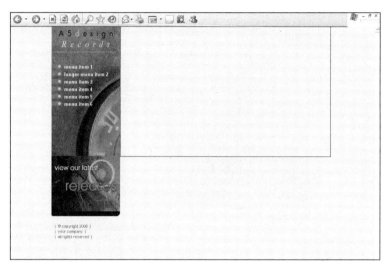

FIGURE 7.8   Page with the a5-body-content <DIV> added to form the right column.

There are three things to note about the code:

- The code has relative positioning so that it will flex to the full width of the a5-body container within which it is nested. This helps ensure that the design can also serve as a liquid design if the width of the a5-body rule is changed to 100%.
- The container is assigned a value of 191px to its margin-left property. This forces its left side 191 pixels from the left side of the design, so it is placed just past the left column.
- The height property is added to ensure that the container is 349 pixels high, which is the height of the background image that is added.

Adding the Top-Right Images

The first stage in adding the content in the right parent column is to add the top-right images. Figure 7.9 illustrates the design once the images are added into the code, which is included in Listing 7.3.

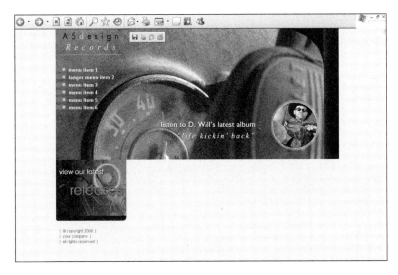

FIGURE 7.9   The first step to adding content to the right parent column is to add the mortised images.

LISTING 7.3   Code for Figure 7.9

```
<!DOCTYPE html PUBLIC "-//W3C//DTD XHTML 1.0 Transitional//EN"
    "DTD/xhtml1-transitional.dtd">
<html><head><title>Design 122</title>
<meta http-equiv="Content-Type" content="text/html; charset=iso-8859-1" />
<style type="text/css">
/* ++++++++++ global general styles start ++++++++++*/
html, body {
    margin:0px;
    padding:0px;
    font: 13px Arial, Helvetica, sans-serif;
    color:#766D6D;
    background:#F8F4EB;
    }
/* ++++++++++ global general styles end ++++++++++*/
/* ++++++++++ global structure styles start ++++++++++*/
#a5-body-center {
    text-align:center;
    }
#a5-body {
    position: relative;
    width: 770px; /* change this to a specific amount for a fixed
        design. E.g., 770px. */
    margin-left: auto;
    margin-right: auto;
    text-align:left;
    padding-bottom:10px;
    border:0px solid #000000;
    }
#a5-column-left {
```

```
        position:absolute;
        left:0px;
        top:0px;
        width:191px;
        border:0px solid #000000;
        }
        #a5-menu {
            font:bold 13px Arial, Helvetica, sans-serif;
            height:249px;
            background:url(images/bg-left-column.jpg) no-repeat;
            }
        #a5-menu a {
            display: block;
            text-align:left;
            line-height:20px;
            vertical-align: 30%;
            height:20px;
            padding-left:35px;
            text-decoration:none;
            background: url(images/bg-menu-off.gif) no-repeat 0px 0px;
            color:#ffffff;
            }
        #a5-menu a:hover {
            background: url(images/bg-menu-on.gif) no-repeat 0px 0px;
            color:#F9F68C;
            }
            #a5-menu-sl {
                width:191px;
                color:#000000;
                font:bold 12px Arial, Helvetica, sans-serif;
                text-align:left;
                }
                #a5-menu-sl a {
                display: block;
                text-align:left;
                line-height:18px;
                vertical-align: 50%;
                height:18px;
                padding-left:40px;
                font-weight:normal;
                text-decoration:none;
                background: url(images/bg-menu-off-sl.gif) no-repeat
                    0px 0px;
                color:#000000;
                }
            #a5-menu-sl a:hover {
                background: url(images/bg-menu-on-sl.gif) no-repeat
                    0px 0px;
color:#4C5C6B;
                }
        #a5-copyright {
            font-size: 11px;
            padding:20px 50px 10px 10px;
            color:#978872;
            }
    #a5-body-content {
```

```
            position:relative;
            margin-left:191px;
            border:0px solid #000000;
            }
#a5-top-row {
            position:relative;
            left:0px;
            top:0px;
            background:#000000;
            border:0px solid #000000;
            }
/* ++++++++++ global structure styles end ++++++++++*/
</style>
</head>
<body>
<div id="a5-body-center">
    <div id="a5-body">
<!-- ###### left column start ###### -->
        <div id="a5-column-left">
            <div><a href="index.htm"><img src="images/header-left.jpg"
                width="191" height="100" alt="" border="0" /></a></div>
            <div id="a5-menu">
            <a href="index.htm">menu item 1</a>
                <a href="menu-item-2.htm">longer menu item 2</a>
                <a href="menu-item-3.htm">menu item 3</a>
                <a href="index.htm">menu item 4</a>
                <a href="index.htm">menu item 5</a>
                <a href="index.htm">menu item 6</a>
            </div>
            <div><a href="index.htm"><img src="images/image-bottom-
                left.jpg" width="191" height="162" alt="" border="0"
                /></a></div>
            <div id="a5-copyright">
                |  &copy; copyright 2006  |<br />
                    |  your company  |<br />| 
                     all rights reserved  |
            </div>
        </div>
<!-- ###### left column end ###### -->
<!-- ###### body content start ###### -->
        <div id="a5-body-content">
            <div id="a5-top-row">
                <div><a href="x.htm"><img src="images/photo-center-
                    top.jpg" width="373" height="349" alt=""
                    border="0" /></a></div>
                <div style="position:absolute;left:373px;top:0px">
                    <a href="x.htm"><img src="images/photo-right-
                    top.jpg" width="164" height="349" alt=""
                    border="0" /></a></div>
                <div style="position:absolute;left:537px;top:0px;">
                    <a href="x.htm"><img src="images/image-right-
                    top.gif" width="42" height="349" alt="" border="0"
                    /></a></div>
            </div>
        </div>
<!-- ###### body content end ###### -->
```

```
        </div>
      </div>
    </body>
  </html>
```

There are several things to note about the code in Listing 7.3:

■   The only rule that is added to the page-level stylesheet is a5-top-row. This rule, how-
    ever, provides a container for the three images to be nested inside it. Because it is
    assigned relative positioning and a background value of #000000, a black background
    will expand to the right if the page is turned into a liquid design (see Figure 7.10).

FIGURE 7.10   The a5-top-row rule can be expanded to the full width
of the page if the design is changed to a liquid format.

■   Most of the styling in this container occurs at the local level. The first image is
    wrapped with <DIV> tags to ensure that no additional space is added to the bottom
    of the container in IE 5, 5.5, and 6, such as in Figure 7.11.

The other two images, however, are given absolute positioning, so they are mortised together. The first image is positioned 373 pixels from the left, using the following
style this is included in the local <DIV> tag: style="position:absolute;left:373px;
top:0px". This is 373 pixels because the coordinates of all images are based off the top-
left corner of the a5-top-row <DIV> in which they are nested. Since the first image is 373
pixels wide, the second image must begin 373 pixels from the left (see Figure 7.12).

FIGURE 7.11   Additional space added to the bottom of the container in IE 5, 5.5., and 6 when <DIV> tags are not wrapped around the first image when it is added.

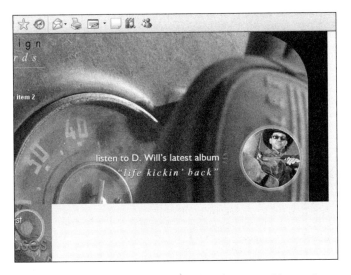

FIGURE 7.12   The top-right area after the second image is added 373 pixels from the left side of the container.

The third image is given absolute positioning that forces it 537 pixels from the left, which is the total width of the left image and center image: 373 pixels + 164 pixels = 537 pixels. Figure 7.9 shows what the design looks like with the addition of the third image, which, as with the other two images, is positioned 0 pixels from the top so they all touch the top of the browser window.

Adding the Bottom Center and Right Content Areas

The final step in creating the home page is to add the `a5-bottom-row` container and its contents. Figure 7.13 shows what the design looks like when the final code is added to the page (see Listing 7.4).

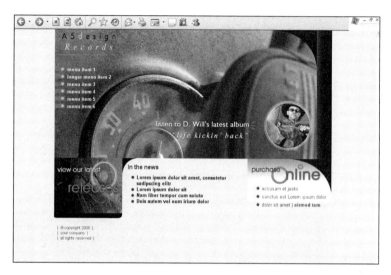

FIGURE 7.13 The design once the `a5-bottom-row` container and its contents are added.

LISTING 7.4   Code for Figure 7.13

```
<!DOCTYPE html PUBLIC "-//W3C//DTD XHTML 1.0 Transitional//EN"
"DTD/xhtml1-transitional.dtd">
<html><head><title>Design 122</title>
<meta http-equiv="Content-Type" content="text/html;
    charset=iso-8859-1" />
<style type="text/css">
/* ++++++++++ global general styles start ++++++++++*/
html, body {
    margin:0px;
    padding:0px;
    font: 13px Arial, Helvetica, sans-serif;
    color:#766D6D;
    background:#F8F4EB;
    }
a:link { color:#CB951D; }
a:visited { color:#A8B32D; }
a:active { color:#A8B32D; }
a:hover { color:#000000; }

a.linklist1:link { text-decoration:none;color:#191718;}
a.linklist1:visited { text-decoration:none;color:#064791;}
```

```
a.linklist1:active { text-decoration:none;color:#064791;}
a.linklist1:hover { text-decoration:underline;color:#0781E1;}

a.linklist2:link { text-decoration:none;color:#0762AD;}
a.linklist2:visited { text-decoration:none;color:#064791;}
a.linklist2:active { text-decoration:none;color:#064791;}
a.linklist2:hover { text-decoration:underline;color:#191718;}

.color-1-text-12 {
    font-family: arial, geneva, sans-serif;
    font-size: 12pt;
    color: #044465;
    }
/* ++++++++++ global general styles end ++++++++++*/
/* ++++++++++ global structure styles start ++++++++++*/
#a5-body-center {
    text-align:center;
    }
#a5-body {
    position: relative;
    width: 770px; /* change this to a specific amount for a fixed
        design. E.g., 770px. */
    margin-left: auto;
    margin-right: auto;
    text-align:left;
    padding-bottom:10px;
    border:0px solid #000000;
    }
#a5-column-left {
    position:absolute;
    left:0px;
    top:0px;
    width:191px;
    border:0px solid #000000;
    }
    #a5-menu {
        font:bold 13px Arial, Helvetica, sans-serif;
        height:249px;
        background:url(images/bg-left-column.jpg) no-repeat;
        }
    #a5-menu a {
        display: block;
        text-align:left;
        line-height:20px;
        vertical-align: 30%;
        height:20px;
        padding-left:35px;
        text-decoration:none;
        background: url(images/bg-menu-off.gif) no-repeat 0px 0px;
        color:#ffffff;
        }
    #a5-menu a:hover {
        background: url(images/bg-menu-on.gif) no-repeat 0px 0px;
        color:#F9F68C;
        }
```

```
#a5-menu-sl {
    width:191px;
    color:#000000;
    font:bold 12px Arial, Helvetica, sans-serif;
    text-align:left;
    }
#a5-menu-sl a {
    display: block;
    text-align:left;
    line-height:18px;
    vertical-align: 50%;
    height:18px;
    padding-left:40px;
    font-weight:normal;
    text-decoration:none;
    background: url(images/bg-menu-off-sl.gif) no-repeat
        0px 0px;
    color:#000000;
    }
#a5-menu-sl a:hover {
    background: url(images/bg-menu-on-sl.gif) no-repeat 0px 0px;
    color:#4C5C6B;
    }
#a5-copyright {
    font-size: 11px;
    padding:20px 50px 10px 10px;
    color:#978872;
    }
#a5-body-content {
position:relative;
margin-left:191px;
border:0px solid #000000;
}
#a5-top-row {
position:relative;
left:0px;
top:0px;
background:#000000;
border:0px solid #000000;
}
#a5-bottom-row {
position:relative;
left:0px;
top:0px;
height:100%;
border:0px solid #000000;
}
#a5-column-middle {
    position:relative;
    left:0px;
    top:0px;
    margin:0px 230px 0px 0px;
    font-weight:bold;
    background: url(images/bg-curve-bottom-middle.gif) no-repeat
        top left;
    border:0px solid #000000;
```

```
            }
        #list-1 {
            margin-top:10px;
            line-height:16px;
            vertical-align:top;
            list-style-image: url(images/bullet.gif);
            }
    #a5-column-right {
        position:absolute;
        right:-1px;/*explain this is a bug with IE */
        top:0px;
        width:230px;
        background: url(images/bg-right-column.jpg) no-repeat 0px 0px;
        border:0px solid #000000;
        voice-family:"\"}\"";
        voice-family:inherit;
            right:-1px;
            width:230px;
        }
        html>body #a5-column-right {
            right:0px;
            width:230px;
        }
        #list-2 {
            line-height:22px;
            vertical-align:top;
            list-style-image: url(images/bullet.gif);
            }
/* ++++++++++ global structure styles end ++++++++++*/
</style>
</head>
<body>
<div id="a5-body-center">
    <div id="a5-body">
<!-- ###### left column start ###### -->
        <div id="a5-column-left">
            <div><a href="index.htm"><img src="images/header-left.jpg"
                width="191" height="100" alt="" border="0" /></a></div>
            <div id="a5-menu">
                <a href="index.htm">menu item 1</a>
                <a href="menu-item-2.htm">longer menu item 2</a>
                <a href="menu-item-3.htm">menu item 3</a>
                <a href="index.htm">menu item 4</a>
                <a href="index.htm">menu item 5</a>
                <a href="index.htm">menu item 6</a>
            </div>
            <div><a href="index.htm"><img src="images/image-bottom-
                left.jpg" width="191" height="162" alt="" border="0"
                /></a></div>
            <div id="a5-copyright">
                |  &copy; copyright 2006  |<br />
                    |  your company  |<br />| 
                     all rights reserved  |
            </div>
        </div>
<!-- ###### left column end ###### -->
```

```
<!-- ###### body content start ###### -->
    <div id="a5-body-content">
        <div id="a5-top-row">
            <div><a href="x.htm"><img src="images/photo-center-
                top.jpg" width="373" height="349" alt=""
                border="0" /></a></div>
            <div style="position:absolute;left:373px;top:0px">
                <a href="x.htm"><img src="images/photo-right-
                top.jpg" width="164" height="349" alt="" border="0"
                /></a></div>
            <div style="position:absolute;left:537px;top:0px;">
                <a href="x.htm"><img src="images/image-right-
                top.gif" width="42" height="349" alt=""
                border="0" /></a></div>
        </div>
        <div id="a5-bottom-row">
            <div id="a5-column-middle">
                <div class="color-1-text-12" style="padding:15px
                0px 0px 15px;"><b>In the news</b></div>
                <ul id="list-1">
                    <li><a href="x.htm" class="linklist1">Lorem
                        ipsum dolor sit amet, consetetur sadipscing
                        elitr</a></li>
                    <li><a href="x.htm" class="linklist1">Lorem
                        ipsum dolor sit</a></li>
                    <li><a href="x.htm" class="linklist1">Nam
                        liber tempor cum soluta</a></li>
                    <li><a href="x.htm" class="linklist1">Duis
                        autem vel eum iriure dolor</a></li>
                </ul>
            </div>
            <div id="a5-column-right">
                <ul id="list-2" style="margin-top:70px;">
                    <li><a href="x.htm" class="linklist2">accusam
                        et justo </a></li>
                    <li><a href="x.htm" class="linklist2">sanctus
                        est Lorem ipsum dolor</a></li>
                    <li><a href="x.htm" class="linklist2">dolor sit
                        amet</a>  |  <a href="x.htm" class=
                        "linklist2"><b>eirmod tem</b></a></li>
                </ul>
            </div>
        </div>
    </div>
<!-- ###### body content end ###### -->
    </div>
</div>
</body>
</html>
```

There are several things to note about the code in Listing 7.4:

■ Rules are added between the `global general styles` comment tags for three types of links: the default links, the list in the bottom-center content area, and the list in the bottom-right content area. The default link style is added for all links without a specific class assigned to them. The `a.linklist1:link` rule is applied to the bottom-left list links, and the `a.linklist2:link` is assigned to the bottom-right list links. Both custom link rules were given general naming conventions so they could be assigned to lists that may be added elsewhere in the site.

■ The `color-1-text-12` rule is added between the global general styles comment tags. It is used to style the "In the News" headline of the bottom-center content area.

■ The `a5-bottom-row` rule and container are added to position the bottom-center and bottom-right content areas. They are assigned relative positioning with both the `left` and `right` properties set to `0px`. This positions the container below the `a5-top-row` `<DIV>`. It is assigned the `height` property with a value of 100% so larger amounts of content can be added to the column. Otherwise, the text will be cut off in IE 5, 5.5, and 6.

■ The `a5-column-middle` rule provides the container for the bottom center content area. Because it is assigned relative positioning, it will stretch to the far right edge of the design. A larger body of text is included in the area for Figure 7.14 to show how the text could fill the design without any padding or margin values set.

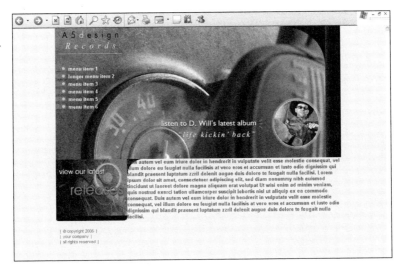

FIGURE 7.14   If given no constraints, the `a5-column-middle` rule would allow content to stretch the full width of the design, such as in this example, which includes a larger amount of dummied content.

The advantage of this structure is that the center column can stretch if the design is changed to a liquid design. Because the bottom-right column is 233 pixels wide, the `a5-column-middle` rule is assigned 240 pixels of margin to the right. This guarantees that the text in the center column will not only stop before it reaches the right column's area, but it will have 7 pixels of space between the two containers.

The a5-column-middle rule also has a background image declared in it, which provides the black curve in the top left corner of the design.

- The list-1 rule provides styling to the list that is included in the a5-column-middle container. The list-style-image is used in conjunction with the line-height rule and vertical-align rule to position the bullets in somewhat similar positions among the various tested browsers.

- Adding the a5-column-right rule and content is the final step in completing the design. The container is assigned the "Purchase Online" background image. Because of a positioning bug in IE, the Tantek hack must be used to position the container 1 pixel to the right of its default location so the entire container, and thus background image, lines up with the image in the top row. If the hack is not used, the page will be positioned incorrectly, as in Figure 7.15.

FIGURE 7.15 The Tantek hack must be used to position the bottom-right content area 1 pixel to the right or else there will be a 1-pixel difference between it and the above image.

- To prevent the list in the a5-column-right container from covering the text portion of the background image (i.e., "Purchase Online"), the list-2 rule is assigned a local style. This style sets the top margin to 70 pixels. The margin-top rule is separated from the list-2 rule in the page-level stylesheet to enable the designer to control the positioning of the list if the rule is reused elsewhere in the site. If the two rules were combined, this list would always be forced down 70 pixels from the top wherever it was included.

CONSTRUCTING SECOND-LEVEL PAGES

As with most sites, the second-level pages are based on the home page design. This allows images from the home page to be reused for subsequent pages, not only to provide visual consistency in the design, which improves usability, but also to allow browsers to cache the original images, making a page download quicker. In this design two second-level templates are created: one that contains three columns and one that contains two columns.

Constructing a Second-Level Page with Three Columns

The first second-level template that is created is the page that appears when the designer clicks on the menu item titled, Longer Menu Item 2. This page contains three columns. Such a design offers the ability to supplement pages with less content with a right column that could contain repetitive information, such as photos, announcements, and specials. Of course, this is not the only reason for a three-column design. The purpose, for example, could also be to provide a more advanced visual layout by adding another element, which, in turn, could have more elements added to it. Figure 7.16 shows what the design looks like when the final code (see Listing 7.5) is added to the page.

FIGURE 7.16   The three-column second-level template that is derived from the home page design.

LISTING 7.5   Code for Figure 7.16

```
<!DOCTYPE html PUBLIC "-//W3C//DTD XHTML 1.0 Transitional//EN"
    "DTD/xhtml1-transitional.dtd">
<html><head><title>Design 122</title>
<meta http-equiv="Content-Type" content="text/html;
    charset=iso-8859-1" />
<!-- link to main stylesheet that control text sizes and colors, among
    other things -->
<link rel="stylesheet" href="mainstyle.css" type="text/css" />
<style>
/* ++++++++++ global sl structure styles start ++++++++++*/
#a5-body-content-sl {
    position:relative;
    margin-left:191px;
    height:100%;
    background: url(images/bg-body-content-sl.jpg) no-repeat 0px 0px;
    border:0px solid #000000;
    }
    #a5-top-row-sl {
        position:relative;
        left:0px;
        top:0px;
        height:100%;
        border:0px solid #000000;
        }
    #a5-sl-title {
        height:24px;
        font:bold 14px italic Arial, Helvetica, sans-serif;
        background: #000000 url(images/bg-title.gif) no-repeat 0px 0px;
        color:#ffffff;
        padding:4px 0px 0px 40px;
        margin-bottom:10px;
        border:0px solid #000000;
        voice-family:"\"}\"";
        voice-family:inherit;
            height:20px;
        }
        html>body #a5-sl-title {
            height:20px;
        }
        #a5-column-middle-sl {
            position:relative;
            left:0px;
            top:10px;
            margin:0px 230px 0px 10px;
            padding-right:10pt;
            border:0px solid #000000;
            }
        #a5-column-right-sl {
            position:absolute;
            right:-1px;
            top:11px;
            width:230px;
            height:800px;
            text-align:right;
```

```
        background: url(images/bg-right-column-sl.gif) repeat-y
            0px 0px;
        border:0px solid #000000;
        voice-family:"\"}\"";
        voice-family:inherit;
            right:-1px;
            top:10px;
            width:230px;
        }
        html>body #a5-column-right-sl {
            right:0px;
            top:10px;
            width:230px;
        }
        #a5-column-right-content-sl {
            position:relative;
            right:0px;
            top:15px;
            width:230px;
            font: 14px italic Arial, Helvetica, sans-serif;
            color:#044465;
            padding:80px 30px 10px 20px;
            border:0px solid #000000;
            voice-family:"\"}\"";
            voice-family:inherit;
                width:180px;
            }
        html>body #a5-column-right-content-sl {
                width:180px;
            }
/* ++++++++++ global sl structure styles end ++++++++++*/
</style>
</head>
<body>
<div id="a5-body-center">
    <div id="a5-body">
<!-- ###### left column start ###### -->
        <div id="a5-column-left">
            <div><a href="index.htm"><img src="images/header-left.jpg"
                width="191" height="100" alt="" border="0" /></a></div>
            <div id="a5-menu">
                <a href="index.htm">menu item 1</a>
                <a href="menu-item-2.htm">longer menu item 2</a>
                <a href="menu-item-3.htm">menu item 3</a>
                <a href="index.htm">menu item 4</a>
                <a href="index.htm">menu item 5</a>
                <a href="index.htm">menu item 6</a>
            </div>
            <div><a href="index.htm"><img src="images/image-bottom-
                left.jpg" width="191" height="162" alt="" border="0"
                /></a></div>
            <div id="a5-copyright">
                |  &copy; copyright 2006  |<br />
                    |  your company  |<br />| 
                     all rights reserved  |
```

```
                </div>
            </div>
<!-- ###### left column end ###### -->
<!-- ###### body content start ###### -->
            <div id="a5-body-content-sl">
                <div id="a5-top-row-sl">
                    <div id="a5-sl-title">longer menu item 2</div>
                    <div id="a5-column-middle-sl">
<span class="color-1-text-12"><b>Duis autem vel eum iriure dolor in
    hendrerit in vulputate velit esse molestie consequat, vel illum
    dolore eu feugiat nulla facilisis at vero eros et accumsan et iusto
    odio dignissim</b></span> qui blandit praesent luptatum zzril
    delenit augue duis dolore te feugait nulla facilisi. Lorem ipsum
    dolor sit amet, consectetuer adipiscing elit, sed diam nonummy nibh
    euismod tincidunt ut laoreet dolore magna aliquam erat volutpat
<br /><br />
Ut wisi enim ad minim veniam, quis nostrud exerci tation ullamcorper
    suscipit lobortis nisl ut aliquip ex ea commodo consequat. Duis
    autem vel eum iriure dolor in hendrerit in vulputate velit esse
    molestie consequat, vel illum dolore eu feugiat nulla facilisis at
    vero eros et accumsan et iusto odio dignissim qui blandit praesent
    luptatum zzril delenit augue duis dolore te feugait nulla facilisi.
<br /><br />
Lorem ipsum dolor sit amet, consetetur sadipscing elitr, sed diam
    nonumy eirmod tempor invidunt ut labore et dolore magna aliquyam
    erat, sed diam voluptua. At vero eos et accusam et justo duo
    dolores et ea rebum. Stet clita kasd gubergren, no sea takimata
    sanctus est Lorem ipsum dolor sit amet. Lorem ipsum dolor sit amet,
    consetetur sadipscing elitr, sed diam nonumy eirmod tempor invidunt
    ut labore et dolore magna aliquyam erat, sed diam voluptua. At vero
    eos et accusam et justo duo dolores et ea rebum. Stet clita kasd
    gubergren, no sea takimata sanctus est Lorem ipsum dolor sit amet.
    Lorem ipsum dolor sit amet, consetetur sadipscing elitr, sed diam
    nonumy eirmod tempor invidunt ut labore et dolore magna aliquyam
    erat, sed diam voluptua. At vero eos et accusam et justo duo
    dolores et ea rebum. Stet clita kasd gubergren, no sea takimata
    sanctus est Lorem ipsum dolor sit amet.
                    </div>
                    <div id="a5-column-right-sl">
                        <div id="a5-column-right-content-sl">
<b>Duis autem vel eum iriure dolor in hendrerit in vulputate</b> velit
    esse molestie consequat, vel illum dolore eu feugiat nulla
    facilisis at vero eros et accumsan et iusto odio dignissim qui
    blandit praesent luptatum zzril delenit augue duis dolore te
    feugait nulla facilisi. Lorem ipsum dolor sit amet, consectetuer
    adipiscing elit, sed diam nonummy nibh euismod tincidunt ut laoreet
    dolore magna aliquam erat volutpat
                        </div>
                    </div>
                </div>
            </div>
<!-- ###### body content end ###### -->
        </div>
    </div>
</body>
</html>
```

There are several things to note about the code in Listing 7.5:

- A second stylesheet has been added for the second-level pages. For demonstration, the stylesheet for the home page has been saved as `mainstyle.css` and included a link to the page. The stylesheet for the second-level pages has been included as a page-level stylesheet, which will be interpreted after the first stylesheet.
- The `a5-body-content` rule has been renamed as the `a5-body-content-sl` rule. This enables the designer to include the background image `bg-body-content-sl.jpg` for the container. While the container was initially built into the home page design, it is not assigned a background image until this page because the top-right images in the home page need to be hyperlinked but do not need to have text flow over them. Saving the images together as one image and using it as a background image for this page maintains the look and feel of the top-right area of the home page. It is assigned 100% height to ensure that the text will fill its full height. Otherwise, it could get cut off in IE 5, 5.5, and 6.

The rules added in the second-level template have -sl appended to their names to signify that they are to be used for secondary pages. Otherwise, if the rules contain the same name in both the mainstyle.css and mainstyle-sl.css files, a browser may use the incorrect style for that page.

- Because the content is now nested inside what was the `a5-top-row` container, it has to be renamed `a5-top-row-sl` and have its background color of #000000 removed. The background image is now more transparent, so this `<DIV>` does not necessarily need to have a background color if it is changed to a liquid format.
- The `a5-sl-title` rule is added to include the page title for secondary pages at the top of the page. The height of the `<DIV>` is set at 24 pixels to guarantee that it expands to the specified height of the background image. Padding is used to position the title vertically in the container and 40 pixels from the left, which is taken up by the background image `bg-title.gif`. To ensure that the color of the `bg-title.gif` is continued across the screen, the shorthand background property is assigned a background color value of #000000. Because padding is used to position the text within the container, the Tantek hack is added to ensure that the height of the container is the same for both compliant and noncompliant browsers.
- Similar to the bottom two nested containers that were used in the home page (`a5-column-middle` and `a5-column-right`), the `a5-column-middle-sl` and `a5-column-right-sl` `<DIV>`s were added to provide the two right columns of the design. Because the `a5-column-right-sl` container is assigned an absolute positioning value, it also is assigned a height of 800 pixels to ensure that the text does not run beyond the container—not that there would be a visible difference because there is no repeating background image or color the text would run beyond. If the text were to

run farther down the page than 800 pixels and the column were to include a background color, for example, the designer might want to change the forced height of the column so the text did not pass the color.

■ The content included in the `a5-column-right-sl` container is nested inside the `a5-column-right-content-sl` `<DIV>` tag. The main thing to note about this rule is that it is assigned padding that forces it 80 pixels from the top, which guarantees the text will not be placed over the background image `bg-right-column-sl.gif` in the `a5-column-right-sl` column. This is done to avoid black text running over the black background of the image, which would make it appear invisible.

CONSTRUCTING A SECOND-LEVEL PAGE WITH TWO COLUMNS

The full-width second-level template included with this design is the page the designer comes to when clicking on the Menu Item 3 link in the menu. The purpose of this template is to provide a page where more content can be added. The designer, of course, may also choose to use the extra space to include a more customized layout on the page. Whatever the reason for using this template, the page allows more visual real estate with which to work. Figure 7.17 shows what the design looks like when the final code is added to the page (see Listing 7.6).

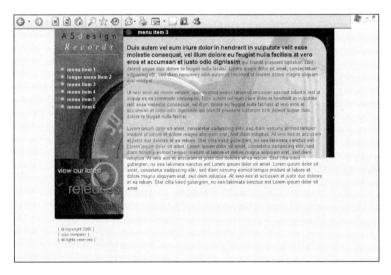

FIGURE 7.17 The two-column second-level template that is based on the home page design.

LISTING 7.5   Code for Figure 7.17

```
<!DOCTYPE html PUBLIC "-//W3C//DTD XHTML 1.0 Transitional//EN"
    "DTD/xhtml1-transitional.dtd">
<html><head><title>Design 122</title>
<meta http-equiv="Content-Type" content="text/html;
    charset=iso-8859-1" />
<!-- link to main stylesheet that control text sizes and colors, among
    other things -->
<link rel="stylesheet" href="mainstyle.css" type="text/css" />
<style>
/* ++++++++++ global sl structure styles start ++++++++++*/
#a5-body-content-sl {
    position:relative;
    margin-left:191px;
    height:100%;
    background: url(images/bg-body-content-sl.jpg) no-repeat 0px 0px;
    border:0px solid #000000;
    }
    #a5-top-row-sl {
        position:relative;
        left:0px;
        top:0px;
        border:0px solid #000000;
        }
    #a5-sl-title {
        height:24px;
        font:bold 14px italic Arial, Helvetica, sans-serif;
        background: #000000 url(images/bg-title.gif) no-repeat 0px 0px;
        color:#ffffff;
        padding:4px 0px 0px 40px;
        margin-bottom:10px;
        border:0px solid #000000;
        voice-family:"\"}\"";
        voice-family:inherit;
            height:20px;
        }
        html>body #a5-sl-title {
            height:20px;
        }
        #a5-column-middle-sl {
            position:relative;
            left:0px;
            top:10px;
            margin:0px 230px 50px 10px;
            padding-right:10pt;
            padding-bottom:20px;
            border:0px solid #000000;
            }
        #a5-column-right-sl {
            position:absolute;
            right:-1px;
            top:11px;
            width:230px;
            height:800px;
```

```
            text-align:right;
            background: url(images/bg-right-column-sl.gif) repeat-y
                0px 0px;
            border:0px solid #000000;
            voice-family:"\"}\"";
            voice-family:inherit;
                right:-1px;
                top:10px;
                width:230px;
            }
            html>body #a5-column-right-sl {
                right:0px;
                top:10px;
                width:230px;
                }
                #a5-column-right-content-sl {
                position:relative;
                right:0px;
                top:15px;
                width:230px;
                font: 14px italic Arial, Helvetica, sans-serif;
                color:#044465;
                padding:80px 30px 10px 20px;
                border:0px solid #000000;
                voice-family:"\"}\"";
                voice-family:inherit;
                    width:180px;
                }
                html>body #a5-column-right-content-sl {
                    width:180px;
                }
        #a5-column-full-sl {
            position:relative;
            left:0px;
            top:10px;
            margin:0px 20px 0px 10px;
            padding-right:10pt;
            border:0px solid #000000;
            }
/* ++++++++++ global sl structure styles end ++++++++++*/
</style>
</head>
<body>
<div id="a5-body-center">
    <div id="a5-body">
<!-- ###### left column start ###### -->
        <div id="a5-column-left">
            <div><a href="index.htm"><img src="images/header-left.jpg"
                width="191" height="100" alt="" border="0" /></a></div>
            <div id="a5-menu">
                <a href="index.htm">menu item 1</a>
                <a href="menu-item-2.htm">longer menu item 2</a>
                <a href="menu-item-3.htm">menu item 3</a>
                <a href="index.htm">menu item 4</a>
                <a href="index.htm">menu item 5</a>
```

```
                    <a href="index.htm">menu item 6</a>
            </div>
            <div><a href="index.htm"><img src="images/image-bottom-
                left.jpg" width="191" height="162" alt="" border="0"
                /></a></div>
            <div id="a5-copyright">
                |  &copy; copyright 2006  |<br />
                    |  your company  |<br />| 
                     all rights reserved  |
            </div>
        </div>
<!-- ###### left column end ###### -->
<!-- ###### body content start ###### -->
        <div id="a5-body-content-sl">
            <div id="a5-top-row-sl">
                <div id="a5-sl-title">menu item 3</div>
                <div id="a5-column-full-sl">
<span class="color-1-text-12"><b>Duis autem vel eum iriure dolor in
    hendrerit in vulputate velit esse molestie consequat, vel illum
    dolore eu feugiat nulla facilisis at vero eros et accumsan et
    iusto odio dignissim</b></span> qui blandit praesent luptatum
    zzril delenit augue duis dolore te feugait nulla facilisi. Lorem
    ipsum dolor sit amet, consectetuer adipiscing elit, sed diam
    nonummy nibh euismod tincidunt ut laoreet dolore magna aliquam
    erat volutpat
<br /><br />
Ut wisi enim ad minim veniam, quis nostrud exerci tation ullamcorper
    suscipit lobortis nisl ut aliquip ex ea commodo consequat. Duis
    autem vel eum iriure dolor in hendrerit in vulputate velit esse
    molestie consequat, vel illum dolore eu feugiat nulla facilisis at
    vero eros et accumsan et iusto odio dignissim qui blandit praesent
    luptatum zzril delenit augue duis dolore te feugait nulla facilisi.
<br /><br />
Lorem ipsum dolor sit amet, consetetur sadipscing elitr, sed diam
    nonumy eirmod tempor invidunt ut labore et dolore magna aliquyam
    erat, sed diam voluptua. At vero eos et accusam et justo duo
    dolores et ea rebum. Stet clita kasd gubergren, no sea takimata
    sanctus est Lorem ipsum dolor sit amet. Lorem ipsum dolor sit
    amet, consetetur sadipscing elitr, sed diam nonumy eirmod tempor
    invidunt ut labore et dolore magna aliquyam erat, sed diam
    voluptua. At vero eos et accusam et justo duo dolores et ea rebum.
    Stet clita kasd gubergren, no sea takimata sanctus est Lorem ipsum
    dolor sit amet. Lorem ipsum dolor sit amet, consetetur sadipscing
    elitr, sed diam nonumy eirmod tempor invidunt ut labore et dolore
    magna aliquyam erat, sed diam voluptua. At vero eos et accusam et
    justo duo dolores et ea rebum. Stet clita kasd gubergren, no sea
    takimata sanctus est Lorem ipsum dolor sit amet.
                </div>
            </div>
        </div>
<!-- ###### body content end ###### -->
    </div>
</div>
</body>
</html>
```

There are several things to note about the code in Listing 7.6:

- The only rule added to the second-level stylesheet is `a5-column-full-sl`. This rule forces the container to fill the full width of the page, barring the assigned padding and margin values.
- After the rule is added, the actual container replaces the `a5-column-middle-sl` and `a5-column-right-sl` `<DIV>`s in the code. Because it is assigned margin and padding settings, the text does not touch the right image.

SUMMARY

The design in this chapter is very different from the one in Chapter 6. It not only contains three columns in the home page, but it uses mortised images in the top-right section of the page. These images are then saved as one lighter background image that is included in the second-level pages. These pages use a second stylesheet that is assigned specifically to them. To avoid any interpretation issues between the two stylesheets, the rules in the second-level stylesheet have `-sl` appended to the end. The two- and three-column structures in the second-level pages offer the designer more content layout flexibility, depending on the amount of content included in the design.

8

Case Study: High Content CSS Design

The design explained in this chapter uses many of the same techniques as the layouts in Chapters 6 and 7; the key difference is that it contains more content. The technical structure is a hybrid of the two designs, in that it uses a header <DIV> across the top as in Chapter 6 and incorporates a three-column layout below, as does the design in Chapter 7. It is designed for product output in the center column, a layout method that can be used for a variety of purposes.

ON THE CD

The design explained in this chapter is design 123 on the companion CD-ROM (photo credits: *www.idlerphotography.com*).

UNDERSTANDING THE DESIGN'S STRUCTURE

Figure 8.1 illustrates the design explained in this chapter. It is designed to easily work as a fixed or liquid design. Because the header area stretches across the entire design, elements can be added, edited, or removed without having to modify other areas of the site.

FIGURE 8.1 The high-content CSS design explained in this chapter.

This book was written at a time when the resolution for which designers create sites was changing. Although only approximately 25% of users still have their browsers set for 800 × 600 resolution, more than 50% are using resolutions of 1024 × 768 or higher. Because there is still going to be a need for sites at 800 × 600 resolution even after this book is published, this design and those in Chapters 6 and 7 are created for this resolution. Similar to the transition from sites that were designed for both 640 × 480 and 800 × 600 resolutions, one method a designer may want to employ to satisfy both sets of users is to add a column to the right that appears approximately after the default 770 pixels of these designs. This design can include an extra column that does not necessarily contain vital information but can be partially seen by users with 800 × 600 resolution so they will know to scroll horizontally to view the full content if desired.

Another option is for the designer to simply widen the layout of the site. CSS design allows for the columns, such as the center and right column in the design in this chapter, to be easily widened for higher resolutions. This can be accomplished either by increasing the width, for example, of the right column, which is fixed, or by adding more products horizontally in the center column. Because the center column has relative sizing assigned to it, the rest of the design will stretch, as needed.

Reasoning Behind Guides and Creating Slices in Photoshop Files

There are 15 slices used in the main Photoshop file and 1 in a secondary file to create the images for the home page design. Figure 8.2 shows all the slices used in the home page file and outlines the 10 most important guides and slices necessary in constructing the design with XHTML and CSS.

FIGURE 8.2   Ten of the most important guides and slices used to build the design in this chapter.

Following are explanations of the 10 most important guides and slices used in Figure 8.2:

- The guide above number 1 is used to separate the header row from the bottom half of the design, which includes left, center, and right columns.
- The guide to the left of number 2 is used to separate the left column, which includes the menu, from the right column, which includes the nested center and right columns.
- The guide above number 3, which is difficult to differentiate from the black line it abuts, is used to separate the menu area from the content below.
- The slice to the top left of number 4 is used to save the `header-left` image, which includes the company's logo.
- The two images in the header row to the far right of number 5 are joined together, along with their text. The first image found to the right of number 5 is the background image that is repeated horizontally across the header file. This works even if the design is changed to a liquid format.
- Number 6 does not represent a slice in the home page file shown in Figure 8.2 but highlights the image behind the form that is saved as a background image in a separate file (see Figure 8.3). Similar to the Chapter 6 and 7 designs, a separate Photoshop file is used to save such an image. Although a slice could be created to save this background image in the main Photoshop file, a designer may want the image to run down the left column behind content other than the form. For this reason the image was created in a separate Photoshop file. Number 1 represents this slice in Figure 8.3.

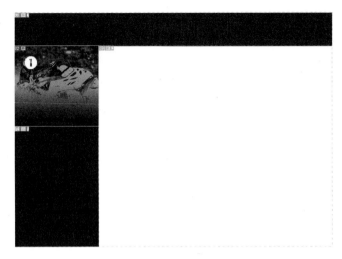

FIGURE 8.3 A Photoshop file that includes the background image behind the form, saved separately from the home page file.

- The slice to the top left of number 7 is used to save the Search button. If the designer were to continue building this e-commerce site, it would require additional buttons that would, most likely, be consistent with this image. Therefore, the designer might want to crop and save the button in a separate Photoshop file, which would make saving separate files easier.

- The slice to the top left of number 8 represents a banner ad saved from the home page file. The important thing to note about this image is that it is saved with padding on the left and right sides. This padding along the entire left column allows the banner ad to be easily placed in the document flow, without any items needing special placement in relation to the padded area.

- Number 9 represents a product used in the home page design. Although each of the four products are saved individually in this home page file, they could be saved as their own separate Photoshop files, for the same reason the button image could be saved individually.

- Number 10 represents two slices. The slice to the top left of the number is used to provide a line at the bottom of the right column to give it a sense of closure. Because the column is assigned absolute positioning, it will not automatically maintain the same height as the center column. The slice to the bottom left of number 10 is used as the background image of the title area for the second-level pages.

Understanding the Placement of CSS Containers

Slightly more <DIV> tags are used in this design than in the designs explained in Chapters 6 and 7 because more individual content elements are used in this design. Structurally,

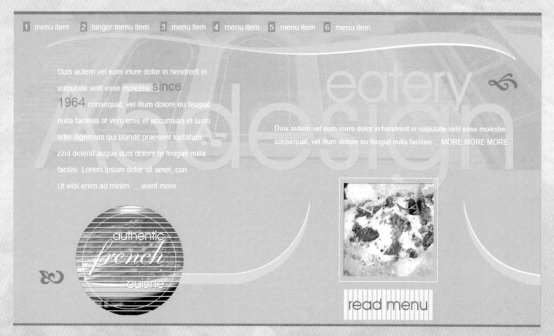

DESIGN 117   Non-coded 1024 × 768 Photoshop design (photo credits: idlerphotography.com)

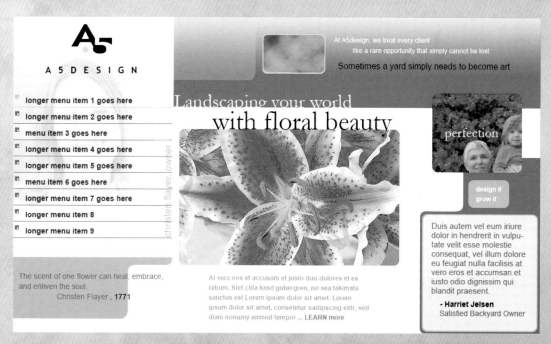

DESIGN 114   Non-coded 1024 × 768 Photoshop design (photo credits: idlerphotography.com, Joe Eccher)

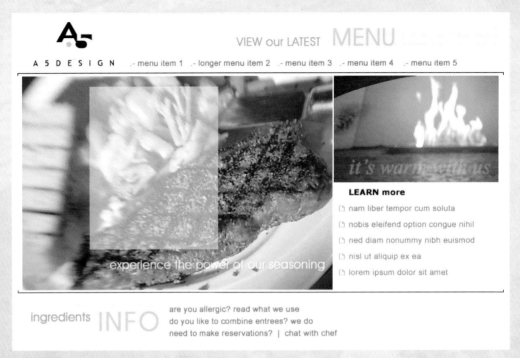

DESIGN 105 Non-coded 800 × 600 Photoshop design (photo credits: idlerphotography.com)

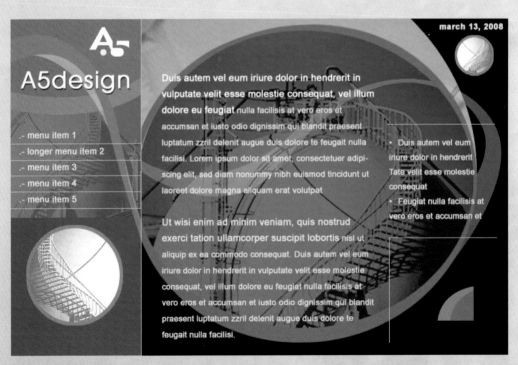

DESIGN 103 Non-coded 800 × 600 Photoshop design (photo credits: idlerphotography.com)

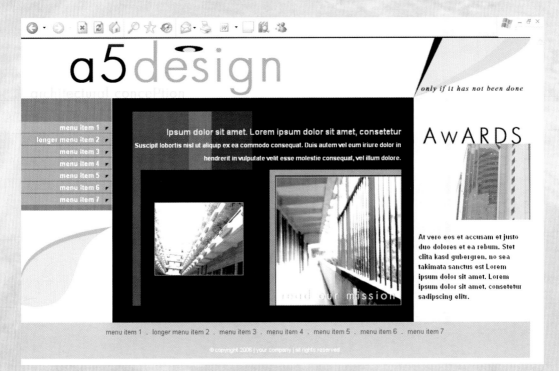

DESIGN 140 1024 × 768 default CSS design (photo credits: Justin Discoe)

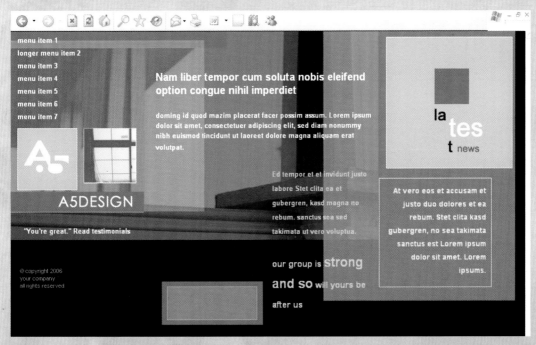

DESIGN 138 1024 × 768 default CSS design (photo credits: idlerphotography.com)

menu item 1   longer menu item 2   menu item 3   menu item 4   menu item 5   menu item 6   menu item 7

A5design Foundation

Nam liber tempor cum soluta nobis eleifend option congue nihil imperdiet doming id quod mazim pla facer possim assum. Lorem ipsum dolor sit amet, consectetuer

helping one life
save many

Nam liber tempor cum soluta nobis eleifend option congue nihil imperdiet doming id quod mazim placerat facer possim assum. Lorem ipsum dolor sit amet, consectetuer adipiscing elit, sed diam nonummy nibh euismod.

our mission

At vero eos et accusam et justo duo dolores et ea rebum. Stet clita kasd gubergren, no sea takimata sanctus est. Lorem ipsum dolor sit amet. Lorem ipsum dolor sit amet, consetetur sadipscing elitr, sed diam nonumy eirmod tempor.

golf
tournament

june 8-10
kuehling golf course

click to register

DESIGN 137   1024 × 768 default CSS design (photo credits: idlerphotography.com)

A5design PRINTING

MENU ITEM 1   LONGER MENU ITEM 2   MENU ITEM 3   MENU ITEM 4   MENU ITEM 5

. listed service 1
. longer listed service 2
. much longer listed service 3
. longer listed service 4
. much much longer listed service 5
. much much longer listed service 6
. longer listed service 7
. much longer listed service 8
. longer listed service 9

MAKING YOUR *RUSTY* SHINY

a gander

electronic

print

various

© copyright 2008 | your site | all rights reserved |

DESIGN 134   1024 × 768 default CSS design (photo credits: idlerphotography.com)

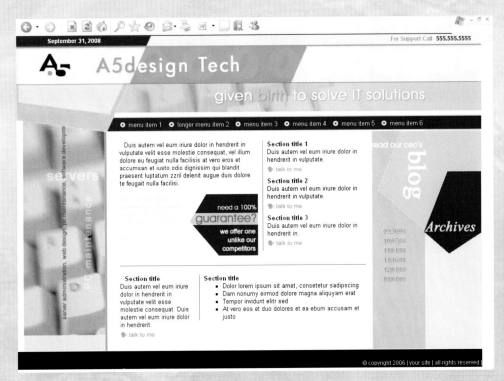

DESIGN 133   1024 × 768 default CSS design (photo credits: idlerphotography.com)

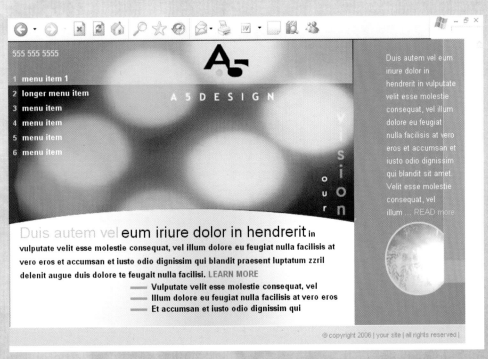

DESIGN 125   800 × 600 default CSS design (photo credits: A5design)

DESIGN 124 800 × 600 default CSS design (photo credits: Joe Eccher)

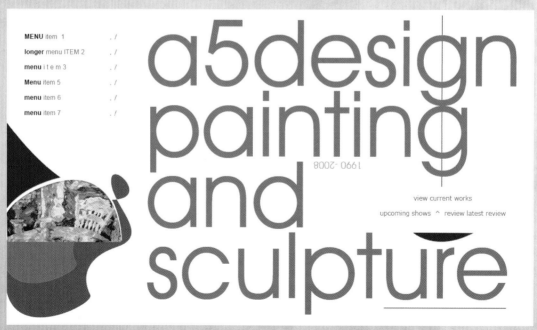

DESIGN 120 Non-coded 1024 × 768 Photoshop design (photo credits: A5design)

DESIGN 102 Non-coded 800 × 600 Photoshop design (photo credits: Joe Eccher, Justin Discoe)

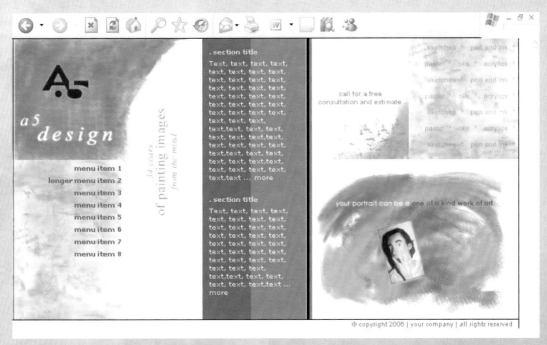

DESIGN 43 800 × 600 default XHTML design (photo credits: Lori Discoe)

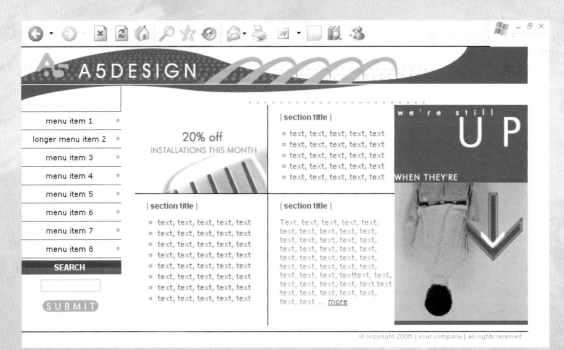

DESIGN 57 800 × 600 default XHTML design (photo credits: Lisa Murillo, A5design)

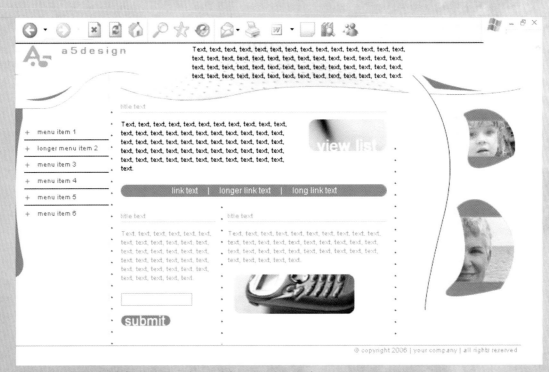

DESIGN 4 800 × 600 default XHTML design (photo credits: A5design)

all three designs require the same number of <DIV>s to build their infrastructures. They are merely placed differently. As mentioned earlier, this design, as shown in Figure 8.4 is a hybrid of those two designs in that it uses a horizontal header container and a three-column format below the header.

Following are explanations for 10 of the most useful containers in Figure 8.4:

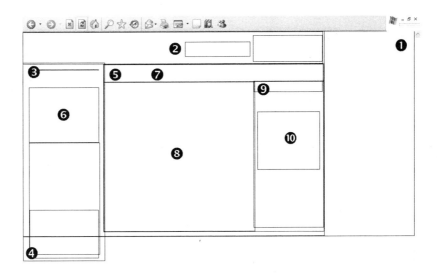

FIGURE 8.4 Ten of the most important containers used to build the design.

- The <DIV> tag to the right of number 1 is used for centering the design in IE 5 and 5.5.
- Number 2 represents the header <DIV>, which contains the nested content to the right of the number.
- The <DIV> tag to the top left of number 3 represents the left column's container.
- Number 4 represents the banner ad that is saved for the left column. It also shows how the left column, which is assigned absolute positioning, extends past the boundaries of the containers within which it is nested.
- The <DIV> to the top left of number 5 is the a5-column-right container, which includes the menu row and center and right columns.
- Number 6 points out the <DIV> in the left column that contains the search form.
- Number 7 represents the container within which the menu is nested.
- The center column of content is nested inside the container indicated by number 8.
- The right column container begins at the top-left corner of number 9.
- Number 10 represents a <DIV> tag that is used to nest additional content in the right column.

BUILDING THE STRUCTURE

Following are the step-by-step instructions to building the design. It is assumed that the Photoshop file has already been created or customized and the designer only needs to position the images and text.

Creating the XHTML and CSS Framework

The first step to building the design is to create the XHTML framework and initial CSS containers. Listing 8.1 is the code that is used to output the page in Figure 8.5.

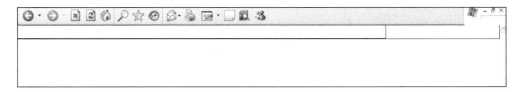

FIGURE 8.5   Basic XHTML and CSS framework for the design.

LISTING 8.1   Code for Figure 8.5

```
<!DOCTYPE html PUBLIC "-//W3C//DTD XHTML 1.0 Transitional//EN"
    "DTD/xhtml1-transitional.dtd">
<html><head><title>Design 123</title>
<meta http-equiv="Content-Type" content="text/html;
    charset=iso-8859-1" />
<style type="text/css">
/* ++++++++++ global general styles start ++++++++++*/
html, body {
    margin:0px;
    padding:0px;
    font: 13px Arial, Helvetica, sans-serif;
    color:#000000;
    background:#ffffff;
    }
/* ++++++++++ global general styles end ++++++++++*/
/* ++++++++++ global structure styles start ++++++++++*/
#a5-body-center {
    text-align:left;
    border:1px solid #000000;
    }
#a5-body {
    position: relative;
    width: 770px; /* change this to a specific amount for a fixed
        design. E.g., 770px. */
/* remove these comment tags if the page is to be centered
    margin-left: auto;
    margin-right: auto;*/
```

```
            text-align:left;
            padding-bottom:10px;
            border:1px solid #000000;
            }
            /* ++++++++++ global structure styles end ++++++++++*/
</style>
</head>
<body>
<div id="a5-body-center">
        <div id="a5-body">
             
        </div>
</div>
</body>
</html>
```

There are several things to note about the code in Listing 8.1:

- The CSS stylesheet is commented into a couple of different sections. The global general styles comment tags contain the general styles, such as the formatting of the <HTML> and <BODY> tags, hyperlinks, and fonts. The global structure styles comment tags include the styles used to define the structure of the design and elements included in that structure.

- Several rules define the <HTML> and <BODY> tags. The margin and padding properties are used to ensure that the design is placed in the very top-left corner of the browser, with no space between the design and the edges. The default font style for the site is set using the shorthand FONT property. Defining the default font color is accomplished with the COLOR property. The background color is assigned to ensure that all browsers display the same color because not all browsers show the same color.

- The a5-body-center and a5-body rules are used to force the design to the left side of the browser screen with a fixed width of 770 pixels. If the designer wanted to fill the full width of the screen, the value of 770px would need to be changed to 100%. If, however, the designer wanted to simply justify the design to the left, the value of the text-align property in the a5-body-center rule would need to be changed from center to left. The margin-left and margin-right properties in the a5-body rule ensure that the extra white space is split evenly on both sides. While this system tends to be more complex, it allows the designer flexibility when more than one site is going to be built. By adding this code to every design, it does not take much work to quickly modify a design to fit a client's needs.

- Both the a5-body-center and a5-body rules have their borders turned on using the following code: border:1px solid #000000;. For demonstration purposes, the code was added to both rules to show what the structure of the <DIV> tags looks like without content added. Turning on the borders helps a designer when building a site because it is not always apparent where elements are placed or expanding. Rather than remove these rules, it is easier to change the value of 1px to 0px, turning the borders off, rather than removing them. Troubleshooting often involves turning the borders back on, so it saves times and takes up very little download size to keep them in the stylesheet.

■ Because the `<div id="a5-body">` is nested inside the `<div id="a5-body-center">` tag, it is indented. This allows for quicker recognition of tags that are nested inside each other, which becomes a useful technique when the page has more code added to it.

Adding the Header Row

Once the XHTML and basic CSS framework have been added, the header area is then added into the code. Listing 8.2 is the code that is used to create the updated page in Figure 8.6.

FIGURE 8.6 The header row that is added to the design.

LISTING 8.2   Code for Figure 8.6

```
<!DOCTYPE html PUBLIC "-//W3C//DTD XHTML 1.0 Transitional//EN"
    "DTD/xhtml1-transitional.dtd">
<html><head><title>Design 123</title>
<meta http-equiv="Content-Type" content="text/html;
    charset=iso-8859-1" />
<style type="text/css">
/* ++++++++++ global general styles start ++++++++++*/
html, body {
    margin:0px;
    padding:0px;
    font: 13px Arial, Helvetica, sans-serif;
    color:#000000;
    background:#ffffff;
    }
a:link { color:#FF7800; }
a:visited { color:#FF5A00; }
a:active { color:#FFC600; }
a:hover { color:#000000; }

a.linklist1:link { text-decoration:none;color:#0EC0FF;}
a.linklist1:visited { text-decoration:none;color:#0EC0FF;}
```

```
    a.linklist1:active { text-decoration:none;color:#0EC0FF;}
    a.linklist1:hover { text-decoration:none;color:#D5EE03;}

/* ++++++++++ global general styles end ++++++++++*/
/* ++++++++++ global structure styles start ++++++++++*/
#a5-body-center {
    text-align:left;
    }
#a5-body {
    position: relative;
    width: 770px; /* change this to a specific amount for a fixed
        design. E.g., 770px. */
/* remove these comment tags if the page is to be centered
    margin-left: auto;
    margin-right: auto;*/
vvtext-align:left;
    padding-bottom:10px;
    border:0px solid #000000;
    }
#a5-header {
    position:relative;
    left:0px;
    top:0px;
    height:78px;
    background: #000000 url(images/bg-header.gif) repeat-x;
    border:0px solid #000000;
    }
    #a5-login {
        position:absolute;
        top:24px;
        right:186px;
        width:165px;
        font: 15px Arial, Helvetica, sans-serif;
        border:0px solid #ffffff;
        }
    #a5-call {
        position:absolute;
        top:8px;
        right:0px;
        width:177px;
        font: 13px Arial, Helvetica, sans-serif;
        color:#ffffff;
        border:0px solid #000000;
        }
/* ++++++++++ global structure styles end ++++++++++*/
</style>
</head>
<body>
<div id="a5-body-center">
    <div id="a5-body">
<!-- ###### header start ###### -->
        <div id="a5-header">
            <div><a href="index.htm"><img src="images/logo.gif"
                width="357" height="78" alt="" border="0" /></a></div>
            <div id="a5-login">
```

```
            <span style="float:left;"><a href="x.htm"><img
                src="images/reseller-button.gif" width="33"
                height="23" alt="" border="0" /></a></span>
            <a href="x.htm" class="linklist1"><b>Reseller Login
                </b><br />
            Forgot Password?</a>
        </div>
        <div id="a5-call">
            <span style="float:left;padding-right:6px;"><a href=
                "x.htm"><img src="images/photo-header-right.jpg"
                width="58" height="64" alt="" border="0"
                /></a></span>
            <div style="margin-top:8px;">
                <span style="font: 14px Arial, Helvetica, sans-
                    serif;"><b>Need Help?</b></span><br />
                Call us at<br />
                1-800-555-5555
            </div>
        </div>
    </div>
<!-- ###### header end ###### -->
    </div>
</div>
</body>
</html>
```

There are several things to note about the code in Listing 8.2:

■ Both the default link colors and linklist1 link rules are added. While the default colors are added before they will actually be used, the linklist1 style is used for the Reseller Login link.

■ The a5-header rule and code are added to provide a container for the nested elements. The rule has relative positioning assigned to it, so it expands to the full width of the screen. It is assigned a height of 78 pixels, which is the height of the images in the header. Using the background property, the bg-header.gif is repeated horizontally across the header.

■ The logo.gif file is included in a <DIV> tag (Figure 8.7). This ensures that the image will appear at the top-left corner of the header with no additional space around it in some browsers, such as IE 5, 5.5, and 6.

FIGURE 8.7 Header after the logo.gif image is added to the left side of the container.

■ The a5-login container is added after the logo.gif image in the header. The rule is given absolute positioning, locating the container 186 pixels from the right. This allows space for the final <DIV> to be added within those 186 pixels between it and the right side (see Figure 8.8).

FIGURE 8.8 The header after the a5-login container has been added to the right of the logo.gif image.

The reseller-button.gif image is floated to the left of the "Reseller Login. Forgot Password?" text. In this instance, the float property is assigned to the image using a <SPAN> tag at the local level in the code. Because the button image does not take up the full height of the header, the container is positioned 24 pixels from the top of the header, using the top property.

■ The final container in the header is included using the a5-call rule (see Figure 8.9). This rule is assigned absolute positioning, similar to the a5-login container. The former, however, is located 0 pixels from the right, with a width of 177 pixels. This not only guarantees that the <DIV> will abut the right side of the container, but it will also have 9 pixels of padding between it and the a5-login container because the a5-login <DIV> is located 186 pixels from the right (186 − 177 = 9 pixels).

FIGURE 8.9 After the final container, a5-call, is added, the header has all the elements added to it.

The layout of this content is a bit more involved than the previous containers in the a5-header row. It has two nested elements: the photo-header-right.jpg, which is floated to the left of the text, including 6 pixels of padding to the right, and a <DIV> that contains the text, which also has a <SPAN> tag styling the "Need Help" text. Barring the default font color and size, the majority of styling is completed at the local level.

Creating the Left Column

After the a5-header container has been added, the left column needs to be added. This column includes a search form, content area, and the image used as a banner ad. Figure 8.10 shows what the design looks like after the code in Listing 8.3 has been added.

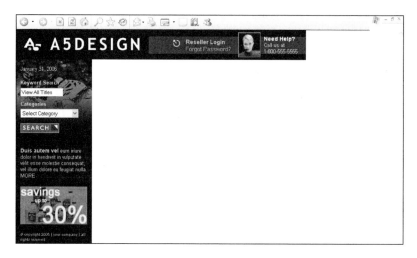

FIGURE 8.10 The design after the left column has been added under the header row.

LISTING 8.3 Code for Figure 8.10

```
<!DOCTYPE html PUBLIC "-//W3C//DTD XHTML 1.0 Transitional//EN"
"DTD/xhtml1-transitional.dtd">
<html><head><title>Design 123</title>
<meta http-equiv="Content-Type" content="text/html;
    charset=iso-8859-1" />
<style type="text/css">
/* ++++++++++ global general styles start ++++++++++*/
html, body {
    margin:0px;
    padding:0px;
    font: 13px Arial, Helvetica, sans-serif;
    color:#000000;
    background:#ffffff;
    }
a:link { color:#FF7800; }
a:visited { color:#FF5A00; }
a:active { color:#FFC600; }
a:hover { color:#000000; }

a.linklist1:link { text-decoration:none;color:#0ECOFF;}
a.linklist1:visited { text-decoration:none;color:#0ECOFF;}
a.linklist1:active { text-decoration:none;color:#0ECOFF;}
```

```
a.linklist1:hover { text-decoration:none;color:#D5EE03;}

.color-1-text-13 { font-family: arial, geneva, sans-serif; font-size:
    13px; color: #FFAE00;}
.color-1-text-14 { font-family: arial, geneva, sans-serif; font-size:
    14px; color: #FFAE00;}

.color-2-text-14 { font-family: arial, geneva, sans-serif; font-size:
    14px; color: #000000;}
/* ++++++++++ global general styles end ++++++++++*/
/* ++++++++++ global structure styles start ++++++++++*/
#a5-body-center {
    text-align:left;
    }
#a5-body {
    position: relative;
    width: 770px; /* change this to a specific amount for a fixed
        design. E.g., 770px. */
/* remove these comment tags if the page is to be centered
    margin-left: auto;
    margin-right: auto;*/
    text-align:left;
    padding-bottom:10px;
    border:0px solid #000000;
    }
#a5-header {
    position:relative;
    left:0px;
    top:0px;
    height:78px;
    background: #000000 url(images/bg-header.gif) repeat-x;
    border:0px solid #000000;
    }
    #a5-login {
        position:absolute;
        top:24px;
        right:186px;
        width:165px;
        font: 15px Arial, Helvetica, sans-serif;
        border:0px solid #ffffff;
        }
    #a5-call {
        position:absolute;
        top:8px;
        right:0px;
        width:177px;
        font: 13px Arial, Helvetica, sans-serif;
        color:#ffffff;
        border:0px solid #000000;
        }
#a5-column-left {
    position:absolute;
    left:0px;
    top:78px;
    width:207px;
```

```
        color:#ffffff;
        padding:0px 12px 50px 15px;
        background: #000000 url(images/bg-left-column.jpg) no-repeat;
        border:0px solid yellow;
        voice-family:"\"}\"";
        voice-family:inherit;
            width:180px;
        }
        html>body #a5-column-left {
            width:180px;
        }
        #date {
            position:relative;
            top:16px;
            left:0px;
            color:#ffffff;
            border:0px solid #ffffff;
            }
        #formsearch {
            position:relative;
            top:35px;
            left:0px;
            border:0px solid yellow;
            }
        #a5-column-left-content {
            position:relative;
            left:0px;
            top:35px;
            color:#ffffff;
            border:0px solid #ffffff;
            }
            #a5-copyright {
                position:relative;
                left:0px;
                top:10px;
                bottom:5px;
                font: 10px Arial, Helvetica, sans-serif;
                color:#9D9D9D;
                text-align:left;
                border:0px solid #000000;
                }
/* ++++++++++ global structure styles end ++++++++++*/
</style>
</head>
<body>
<div id="a5-body-center">
    <div id="a5-body">
<!-- ###### header start ###### -->
        <div id="a5-header">
            <div><a href="index.htm"><img src="images/logo.gif"
                width="357" height="78" alt="" border="0" /></a></div>
            <div id="a5-login">
                <span style="float:left;"><a href="x.htm"><img src=
                    "images/reseller-button.gif" width="33"
                    height="23" alt="" border="0" /></a></span>
```

```
            <a href="x.htm" class="linklist1"><b>Reseller Login
                </b><br />
            Forgot Password?</a>
        </div>
        <div id="a5-call">
            <span style="float:left;padding-right:6px;"><a href=
                "x.htm"><img src="images/photo-header-right.jpg"
                width="58" height="64" alt="" border="0" /></a>
                </span>
            <div style="margin-top:8px;">
                <span style="font: 14px Arial, Helvetica,
                    sans-serif;"><b>Need Help?</b></span><br />
                Call us at<br />
                1-800-555-5555
            </div>
        </div>
    </div>
</div>
<!-- ###### header end ###### -->
<!-- ###### left column start ###### -->
        <div id="a5-column-left">
            <div id="date">
                January 31, 2006
            </div>
            <div id="formsearch" class="color-1-text-13">
                <form method="post" action="x.htm" name="search"
                    style="margin-top:0px;">
                    <b>Keyword Search</b>
                    <div style="padding:5px 0px 10px 0px;"><input
                        type="text" size="15" name="keywords"
                        value="View All Titles" /></div>
                    <b>Categories</b>
                    <div style="padding:5px 0px 15px 0px;">
                    <select name="categories" size="1">
                        <option value="All">Select Category</
                            option>
                        <option value="sample">This is a sample
                            entry</option>
                    </select>
                    </div>
                    <input type="image" src="images/button-
                        search.gif" />
                </form>
        </div>
            <div id="a5-column-left-content">
                <div style="padding:15px 0px 10px 0px;color:
                    #ffffff;"><span class="color-1-text-14"><b>
                    Duis autem vel</b></span> eum iriure dolor in
                    hendrerit in vulputate velit esse molestie
                    consequat, vel illum dolore eu feugiat nulla.
                    MORE</div>
                <div style="padding:10px 0px 10px 0px;color:
                    #ffffff;"><a href="x.htm"><img src="images/
                    banner-left-bottom.jpg" width="180"
                    height="96" alt="" border="0" /></a></div>
                <div id="a5-copyright">
```

```
                              &copy; copyright 2006 | your company | all
                                        rights reserved
                            </div>
                        </div>
                    </div>
        <!-- ###### left column end ###### -->
            </div>
        </div>
        </body>
        </html>
```

There are several things to note about the code in Listing 8.3:

- The `a5-column-left` container, which contains all the content in the left column, is assigned absolute positioning. It remains on the left side of the design and begins 78 pixels from the top of the page, exactly below the header. It is assigned a width of 207 pixels. Using the `padding` property, the entire column is given padding on the left and right sides. Because of the box model bug, the Tantek hack must be used so the `left` and `right` padding is properly interpreted by both compliant and non-compliant browsers. This is why the width is changed to 180 pixels for compliant browsers—because 17 pixels need to be subtracted from the original specified width.

- The date container is the first content added. Although in this design the date is static text, scripts to output the date using JavaScript or a db-driven programming language can be easily added. Two more things to note about this container are that it is assigned relative positioning, which makes it take up the entire width of the column, and it is positioned 16 pixels from the top of the column using the `top` property.

- After the date container has been added, the `formsearch` <DIV> is added. It contains all the form elements, such as the "Keyword Search" text and input field, "Categories" text and drop-down menu, and the Search button. The positioning of the elements in the form occur at the local level. One style to note is `style="margin-top:0px;"`, which is included in the parent <FORM> tag. This helps override the default margin settings of some browsers so the form is positioned similarly among browsers. The `color-1-text-13` rule is added to style the text in the `formsearch` <DIV>.

- The `a5-column-left-content` <DIV> is added after the `formsearch` <DIV>. The first three words are not only styled with the `color-1-text-14` rule that was added to the stylesheet, but the container is assigned local padding to the top and bottom.

- Finally, the `a5-copyright` rule is added to the stylesheet to position and style the copyright statement at the bottom of the column.

Adding the Center Column

After the left column is completed, the right column is added to the design, completing it. Figure 8.11 shows what the design looks like after it has been completed (see Listing 8.4).

FIGURE 8.11 The design after the entire right column has been added.

LISTING 8.4 Code for Figure 8.11

```
<!DOCTYPE html PUBLIC "-//W3C//DTD XHTML 1.0 Transitional//EN"
    "DTD/xhtml1-transitional.dtd">
<html><head><title>Design 123</title>
<meta http-equiv="Content-Type" content="text/html;
    charset=iso-8859-1" />
<style type="text/css">
/* ++++++++++ global general styles start ++++++++++*/
html, body {
    margin:0px;
    padding:0px;
    font: 13px Arial, Helvetica, sans-serif;
    color:#000000;
    background:#ffffff;
    }
a:link { color:#FF7800; }
a:visited { color:#FF5A00; }
a:active { color:#FFC600; }
a:hover { color:#000000; }

a.linklist1:link { text-decoration:none;color:#0ECOFF;}
a.linklist1:visited { text-decoration:none;color:#0ECOFF;}
a.linklist1:active { text-decoration:none;color:#0ECOFF;}
a.linklist1:hover { text-decoration:none;color:#D5EE03;}

.color-1-text-13 { font-family: arial, geneva, sans-serif; font-size:
    13px; color: #FFAE00;}
.color-1-text-14 { font-family: arial, geneva, sans-serif; font-size:
    14px; color: #FFAE00;}

.color-2-text-14 { font-family: arial, geneva, sans-serif; font-size:
    14px; color: #000000;}
```

```
/* ++++++++++ global general styles end ++++++++++*/
/* ++++++++++ global structure styles start ++++++++++*/
#a5-body-center {
    text-align:left;
    }
#a5-body {
    position: relative;
    width: 770px; /* change this to a specific amount for a fixed
        design. E.g., 770px. */
/* remove these comment tags if the page is to be centered
    margin-left: auto;
    margin-right: auto;*/
    text-align:left;
    padding-bottom:10px;
    border:0px solid #000000;
    }
#a5-header {
    position:relative;
    left:0px;
    top:0px;
    height:78px;
    background: #000000 url(images/bg-header.gif) repeat-x;
    border:0px solid #000000;
    }
    #a5-login {
        position:absolute;
        top:24px;
        right:186px;
        width:165px;
        font: 15px Arial, Helvetica, sans-serif;
        border:0px solid #ffffff;
        }
    #a5-call {
        position:absolute;
        top:8px;
        right:0px;
        width:177px;
        font: 13px Arial, Helvetica, sans-serif;
        color:#ffffff;
        border:0px solid #000000;
        }
#a5-column-left {
    position:absolute;
    left:0px;
    top:78px;
    width:207px;
    color:#ffffff;
    padding:0px 12px 50px 15px;
    background: #000000 url(images/bg-left-column.jpg) no-repeat;
    border:0px solid yellow;
    voice-family:"\"}\"";
    voice-family:inherit;
        width:180px;
    }
    html>body #a5-column-left {
```

```
        width:180px;
    }
#date {
    position:relative;
    top:16px;
    left:0px;
    color:#ffffff;
    border:0px solid #ffffff;
    }
#formsearch {
    position:relative;
    top:35px;
    left:0px;
    border:0px solid yellow;
    }
#a5-column-left-content {
    position:relative;
    left:0px;
    top:35px;
    color:#ffffff;
    border:0px solid #ffffff;
    }
    #a5-copyright {
        position:relative;
        left:0px;
        top:10px;
        bottom:5px;
        font: 10px Arial, Helvetica, sans-serif;
        color:#9D9D9D;
        text-align:left;
        border:0px solid #000000;
        }
#a5-column-right {
    position:relative;
    right:0px;
    top:0px;
    margin-left:207px;
    border:0px solid #000000;
    }
#a5-menu-box {
    position:relative;
    top:0px;
    left:0px;
    height:42px;
    width:100%;
    color:#ffffff;
    line-height:42px;
    vertical-align:30%;
    background:url(images/bg-menu.gif) repeat-x 0px 0px;
    border:0px solid #000000;
    }
    #a5-menu a {
        display:inline;
        text-decoration:none;
        color:#94CCDE;
        font-weight:normal;
```

```
            }
        #a5-menu a:hover {
            font-weight:normal;
            color:#ffffff;
            }
    #a5-column-right-left {
        position:relative;
        left:0px;
        top:0px;
        padding:10px 10px 10px 10px;
        margin-right:177px;
        border:0px solid #000000;
        }
        .a5-products {
        height:300px;
        border: 0px solid #000000;
        }
        .a5-individual-product {
        float: left;
        margin:0px 2px 0px 2px;
        border:0px solid #000000;
        }
        .a5-individual-product p {
        border-top:1px solid #BFBFBF;
        width:170px;
        text-align: center;
        }

    #a5-column-right-right {
        position:absolute;
        right:0px;
        top:42px;
        width:177px;
        height:365px;
        color:#ffffff;
        padding:0px 9px 0px 9px;
        background:#215F5F url(images/bg-bottom-line-right-column.gif)
            no-repeat left bottom;
        border:0px solid red;
        voice-family:"\"}\"";
        voice-family:inherit;
            width:159px;
        }
        html>body #a5-column-right-right {
            width:159px;
        }
        .a5-title-right {
            font-family: arial, geneva, sans-serif;
            font-size: 13px;
            color: #D5EE03;
            line-height:25px;
            font-weight:bold;
            margin:0px -9px 0px -9px;
            padding-left:5px;
            margin-bottom:10px;
            background:#000000;
```

```
                border:0px solid #000000;
                }
          #a5-right-nested-box {
                position:relative;
                right:0px;
                top:23px;
                width:159px;
                padding:10px 10px 0px 10px;
                background:#000000;
                color:#ffffff;
                border:1px solid #0ECOFF;
                voice-family:"\"}\"";
                voice-family:inherit;
                    width:139px;
                }
          html>body #a5-right-nested-box {
                width:139px;
                }
/* ++++++++++ global structure styles end ++++++++++*/
/* ++++++++++ second level start ++++++++++*/
#a5-column-right-left-sl {
    position:relative;
    left:0px;
    top:0px;
    padding:0px 10px 0px 10px;
    margin-right:177px;
    border:0px solid #000000;
    }
#a5-sl-title {
    margin:0px -10px 10px -10px;
    padding:5px 0px 0px 40px;
    height:25px;
    color:#000000;
    background:#DBDBDB url(images/bg-sl-title.gif) no-repeat left top;
    border:0px solid #000000;
    font:bold 14px Arial, Helvetica, sans-serif;
    voice-family:"\"}\"";
    voice-family:inherit;
        height:20px;
    }
    html>body #a5-sl-title {
        height:20px;
    }
#a5-column-left-full {
    position:relative;
    left:0px;
    top:1px;
    color:#000000;
    padding:0px 10px 0px 10px;
    }
/* ++++++++++ second level end ++++++++++*/
</style>
</head>
<body>
<div id="a5-body-center">
    <div id="a5-body">
```

```
<!-- ###### header start ###### -->
        <div id="a5-header">
            <div><a href="index.htm"><img src="images/logo.gif" width=
                "357" height="78" alt="" border="0" /></a></div>
            <div id="a5-login">
                <span style="float:left;"><a href="x.htm"><img
                    src="images/reseller-button.gif" width="33"
                    height="23" alt="" border="0" /></a></span>
                <a href="x.htm" class="linklist1"><b>Reseller Login
                    </b><br />
                Forgot Password?</a>
            </div>
            <div id="a5-call">
                <span style="float:left;padding-right:6px;"><a
                    href="x.htm"><img src="images/photo-header-
                    right.jpg" width="58" height="64" alt=""
                    border="0" /></a></span>
                <div style="margin-top:8px;">
                    <span style="font: 14px Arial, Helvetica,
                        sans-serif;"><b>Need Help?</b></span><br />
                    Call us at<br />
                    1-800-555-5555
                </div>
            </div>
        </div>
<!-- ###### header end ###### -->
<!-- ###### left column start ###### -->
        <div id="a5-column-left">
            <div id="date">
                January 31, 2006
            </div>
            <div id="formsearch" class="color-1-text-13">
                <form method="post" action="x.htm" name="search"
                    style="margin-top:0px;">
                    <b>Keyword Search</b>
                    <div style="padding:5px 0px 10px 0px;"><input
                        type="text" size="15" name="keywords"
                        value="View All Titles" /></div>
                    <b>Categories</b>
                    <div style="padding:5px 0px 15px 0px;">
                    <select name="categories" size="1">
                        <option value="All">Select Category
                            </option>
                        <option value="sample">This is a sample
                            entry</option>
                    </select>
                    </div>
                    <input type="image" src="images/
                        button-search.gif" />
                </form>
            </div>
            <div id="a5-column-left-content">
                <div style="padding:15px 0px 10px 0px;color:
                    #ffffff;"><span class="color-1-text-14"><b>
                    Duis autem vel</b></span> eum iriure dolor in
                    hendrerit in vulputate velit esse molestie
```

```
                            consequat, vel illum dolore eu feugiat nulla.
                            MORE</div>
                    <div style="padding:10px 0px 10px 0px;color:
                        #ffffff;"><a href="x.htm"><img src="images/
                        banner-left-bottom.jpg" width="180"
                        height="96" alt="" border="0" /></a></div>
                    <div id="a5-copyright">
                        &copy; copyright 2006 | your company | all
                            rights reserved
                    </div>
                </div>
            </div>
<!-- ###### left column end ###### -->
<!-- ###### right column start ###### -->
            <div id="a5-column-right">
                <div id="a5-menu-box">
                    <div id="a5-menu">
                           
                        <a href="index.htm">menu item 1</a>  
                            .  
                        <a href="menu-item-2.htm">longer menu item 2
                            </a>  .  
                        <a href="menu-item-3.htm">menu item 3</a> 
                             .  
                        <a href="index.htm">menu item 4</a>  
                            .  
                        <a href="index.htm">menu item 5</a>  
                            .  
                    </div>
                </div>
<!-- ###### column right left start ###### -->
                <div id="a5-column-right-left">
                    <span class="color-2-text-14" style="padding-
                        bottom:5px;"><b>View Our Latest Products</b></span>
                    <br /><br />
                    <div class="a5-products">
                        <div class="a5-individual-product">
                            <a href="x.htm"><img src="images/
                                product-1.jpg" width="175" height="95"
                                alt="" border="0" /></a><br />
                            <p><a href="x.htm">Product 1 title</a></p>
                        </div>
                        <div class="a5-individual-product">
                            <a href="x.htm"><img src="images/
                                product-2.jpg" width="175" height="95"
                                alt="" border="0" /></a><br />
                            <p><a href="x.htm">Product 2 title</a></p>
                        </div>
                        <div class="a5-individual-product">
                            <a href="x.htm"><img src="images/
                                product-3.jpg" width="175" height="95"
                                alt="" border="0" /></a><br />
                            <p><a href="x.htm">Product 3 title</a></p>
                        </div>
                        <div class="a5-individual-product">
```

```
                                  <a href="x.htm"><img src="images/
                                      product-4.jpg" width="175" height="95"
                                      alt="" border="0" /></a><br />
                                  <p><a href="x.htm">Product 4 title</a></p>
                       </div>
                          </div>
                          <br />

                          <div class="color-2-text-14"><b>Learn About Our
                              Technical Classes</b></div>
                          Duis autem vel eum iriure dolor in hendrerit in
                              vulputate velit esse molestie consequat, vel
                              illum dolore eu feugiat nulla ... <a href=
                              "x.htm">MORE</a>


                       </div>
       <!-- ###### column right left end ###### -->
       <!-- ###### column right right start ###### -->
                       <div id="a5-column-right-right">
                           <div class="a5-title-right">
                               <b>View Our Specials</b>
                           </div>
                           <div>Duis autem vel eum iriure dolor in hendrerit
                               in vulputate velit esse molestie consequat.
                               </div>
                           <div id="a5-right-nested-box"><span class="color-1-
                               text-14"><b>Duis autem vel</b></span> eum
                               iriure dolor in hendrerit in vulputate velit
                               esse molestie consequat, vel illum dolore eu
                               feugiat nulla.
                           <div style="margin:24px 0px 20px 0px;"><img
                               src="images/banner-right-middle.jpg"
                               width="136" height="73" alt="" border="0"
                               /></div>
                           </div>
                       </div>
       <!-- ###### column right right end ###### -->
               </div>
       <!-- ###### right column end ###### -->
           </div>
       </div>
       </body>
       </html>
```

There are several things to note about the code in Listing 8.4:

■ All the content in the right column, including the menu; the center column, which includes the products; and the right column, are nested inside the a5-column-right container. It is assigned relative positioning, with a margin-left value of 207 pixels. This guarantees that the container will be positioned 207 pixels from the left, which is the width left column.

■   To ensure that the menu occurs consistently on every page, including the different second-level pages, the a5-menu-box container is added with relative positioning above the rest of the content in the <DIV>. Figure 8.12 shows what the design looks like with just the menu added.

FIGURE 8.12   The menu is the first element to be added to the right column.

One thing to consider about such a menu is it is limited in the amount of items that can be added because of limited horizontal space. This is where drop-down JavaScript menus can become useful because more menu items can be added when the user mouses over a menu item. The menu in this instance works fine because the site is created to be driven by the search form on the left, which can be used to navigate hundreds or thousands of pages. The menu itself is designed more for general sections, such as About, Customer Service, and Specials.

While the menu code looks the same as that in the designs in Chapters 6 and 7, it is styled slightly differently. The display property in the a5-menu a rule in this design is assigned a value of inline instead of block, meaning the items will be output horizontally across a line, as opposed to vertically.

■   The a5-column-right-left rule is used to output the content in the center column of the design. It is assigned relative positioning, with a margin-right value of 177 pixels, which keeps it from crossing over into the right column. One unique aspect of this container compared to any others in this design or in Chapters 6 or 7 is that it includes repeated floating <DIV>s, which contain each product. Normally handled with an XHTML table, these products wrap around to form separate columns and rows. If the width of the design were expanded to fill 1024 × 768 resolution, three products would appear in the first row, as opposed to two in the 800 × 600 version. While they do not have to expand, by doing so, they fill the extra white space of the design that would normally exist because only two products are used to fill it. This function is accomplished by adding a container that is assigned the a5-products rule. The one thing to note about this rule is that it is assigned a height of 300 pixels.

If this height is not set, the text below the images will randomly reposition itself in different browsers at 1024×768 resolution. Because the height value is assigned, the developer cannot output more products than the height will allow, which is four in this example. Each product is positioned and styled inside the `a5-products` container, using the `a5-individual-product` and `a5-individual-product p` rules. Figure 8.13 shows the design with the center column added with the border of the products table turned on to show the space it takes up.

Using comment tags to separate code makes finding particular sections much easier. Using an intuitive system is important for designers to understand their code. In this section of code the "right column" is the parent column, while "column right left" represents the left column of the right section. Visually, though, in the design, this column is the center column. The designer could also name this section the "center column," or name the "right column" the "parent right column," signifying that there will be a child right column.

NOTE

FIGURE 8.13   The center column added to the design, with the border of the products table turned on.

■   The content in the right column is nested inside the `a5-column-right` container. Because it is assigned absolute positioning, it is placed 42 pixels from the top of the container. These 42 pixels force the column down past the menu area. Otherwise, the column would begin in the area across which the menu runs (see Figure 8.14).

FIGURE 8.14   An image of how the right column would look if it were not positioned 42 pixels from the top.

Because the container is assigned absolute positioning, it is given a height value of 365 pixels to ensure that the nested content inside it does not run below the container. The <DIV> is assigned the `bg-bottom-line-right-column.gif` background image, which is the black line at the bottom of the column. No matter the height of the column, the background image will automatically place itself at the bottom because of the bottom value included in the shorthand `background` property.

■   The `a5-title-right` <DIV>, which is the first item nested in the right column, is placed at the top of the column. One of the most useful properties assigned to the rule is `margin-bottom`, which has a value of 10 pixels. This creates some visual space between the title area and the text below it.

■   The `a5-right-nested-box` rule is added to create the nested <DIV> in the column, which contains the text and image. Because padding is added to the container, the width of the <DIV> needs to be adjusted for various browsers, using the Tantek hack. The image is positioned using a local style that is included in the <DIV> tags wrapped around it.

CONSTRUCTING SECOND-LEVEL PAGES

As with the designs in Chapters 6 and 7, the home page is duplicated and modified for second-level templates. This design includes both three- and two-column versions to provide the design layout more flexibility.

Constructing a Second-Level Page with Three Columns

The first second-level template that is created is the page that appears when the designer clicks on the menu item titled Longer Menu Item 2. This page contains three columns.

Such a design offers the designer the ability to supplement content with a right column that could contain information that could be included on more than one page, such as photos and descriptions. Figure 8.15 shows what the design looks like when the final code is added to the page (see Listing 8.5).

FIGURE 8.15 A three-column second-level template created from a customized version of the home page design.

LISTING 8.5 Code for Figure 8.15

```
<!DOCTYPE html PUBLIC "-//W3C//DTD XHTML 1.0 Transitional//EN"
    "DTD/xhtml1-transitional.dtd">
<html><head><title>Design 123</title>
<meta http-equiv="Content-Type" content="text/html;
    charset=iso-8859-1" />
<style type="text/css">
/* ++++++++++ global general styles start ++++++++++*/
html, body {
    margin:0px;
    padding:0px;
    font: 13px Arial, Helvetica, sans-serif;
    color:#000000;
    background:#ffffff;
    }
a:link { color:#FF7800; }
a:visited { color:#FF5A00; }
a:active { color:#FFC600; }
a:hover { color:#000000; }

a.linklist1:link { text-decoration:none;color:#0ECOFF;}
a.linklist1:visited { text-decoration:none;color:#0ECOFF;}
```

```
a.linklist1:active { text-decoration:none;color:#0ECOFF;}
a.linklist1:hover { text-decoration:none;color:#D5EE03;}

.color-1-text-13 { font-family: arial, geneva, sans-serif; font-size:
    13px; color: #FFAE00;}
.color-1-text-14 { font-family: arial, geneva, sans-serif; font-size:
    14px; color: #FFAE00;}

.color-2-text-14 { font-family: arial, geneva, sans-serif; font-size:
    14px; color: #000000;}
/* ++++++++++ global general styles end ++++++++++*/
/* ++++++++++ global structure styles start ++++++++++*/
#a5-body-center {
    text-align:left;
    }
#a5-body {
    position: relative;
    width: 770px; /* change this to a specific amount for a fixed
    design. E.g., 770px. */
/* remove these comment tags if the page is to be centered
    margin-left: auto;
    margin-right: auto;*/
    text-align:left;
    padding-bottom:10px;
    border:0px solid #000000;
    }
#a5-header {
    position:relative;
    left:0px;
    top:0px;
    height:78px;
    background: #000000 url(images/bg-header.gif) repeat-x;
    border:0px solid #000000;
    }
    #a5-login {
        position:absolute;
        top:24px;
        right:186px;
        width:165px;
        font: 15px Arial, Helvetica, sans-serif;
        border:0px solid #ffffff;
        }
    #a5-call {
        position:absolute;
        top:8px;
        right:0px;
        width:177px;
        font: 13px Arial, Helvetica, sans-serif;
        color:#ffffff;
        border:0px solid #000000;
        }
#a5-column-left {
    position:absolute;
    left:0px;
    top:78px;
    width:207px;
```

```
color:#ffffff;
padding:0px 12px 50px 15px;
background: #000000 url(images/bg-left-column.jpg) no-repeat;
border:0px solid yellow;
voice-family:"\"}\"";
voice-family:inherit;
    width:180px;
}
html>body #a5-column-left {
    width:180px;
}
#date {
    position:relative;
    top:16px;
    left:0px;
    color:#ffffff;
    border:0px solid #ffffff;
    }
#formsearch {
    position:relative;
    top:35px;
    left:0px;
    border:0px solid yellow;
    }
#a5-column-left-content {
    position:relative;
    left:0px;
    top:35px;
    color:#ffffff;
    border:0px solid #ffffff;
    }
    #a5-copyright {
        position:relative;
        left:0px;
        top:10px;
        bottom:5px;
        font: 10px Arial, Helvetica, sans-serif;
        color:#9D9D9D;
        text-align:left;
        border:0px solid #000000;
        }
#a5-column-right {
    position:relative;
    right:0px;
    top:0px;
    margin-left:207px;
    border:0px solid #000000;
    }
#a5-menu-box {
    position:relative;
    top:0px;
    left:0px;
    height:42px;
    width:100%;
    color:#ffffff;
```

```
        line-height:42px;
        vertical-align:30%;
        background:url(images/bg-menu.gif) repeat-x 0px 0px;
        border:0px solid #000000;
        }
    #a5-menu a {
            display:inline;
            text-decoration:none;
            color:#94CCDE;
            font-weight:normal;
            }
    #a5-menu a:hover {
            font-weight:normal;
            color:#ffffff;
            }
#a5-column-right-left {
    position:relative;
    left:0px;
    top:0px;
    padding:10px 10px 10px 10px;
    margin-right:177px;
    border:0px solid #000000;
    }
    .a5-products {
    height:300px;
    border: 0px solid #000000;
    }
    .a5-individual-product {
    float: left;
    margin:0px 2px 0px 2px;
    border:0px solid #000000;
    }
    .a5-individual-product p {
    border-top:1px solid #BFBFBF;
    width:170px;
    text-align: center;
    }

#a5-column-right-right {
        position:absolute;
        right:0px;
        top:42px;
        width:177px;
        height:365px;
        color:#ffffff;
        padding:0px 9px 0px 9px;
        background:#215F5F url(images/bg-bottom-line-right-column.gif)
            no-repeat left bottom;
        border:0px solid red;
        voice-family:"\"}\"";
        voice-family:inherit;
            width:159px;
        }
        html>body #a5-column-right-right {
            width:159px;
```

```
            }
        .a5-title-right {
            font-family: arial, geneva, sans-serif;
            font-size: 13px;
            color: #D5EE03;
            line-height:25px;
            font-weight:bold;
            margin:0px -9px 0px -9px;
            padding-left:5px;
            margin-bottom:10px;
            background:#000000;
            border:0px solid #000000;
            }
        #a5-right-nested-box {
            position:relative;
            right:0px;
            top:23px;
            width:159px;
            padding:10px 10px 0px 10px;
            background:#000000;
            color:#ffffff;
            border:1px solid #0EC0FF;
            voice-family:"\"}\"";
            voice-family:inherit;
                width:139px;
            }
        html>body #a5-right-nested-box {
                width:139px;
            }
/* ++++++++++ global structure styles end ++++++++++*/
/* ++++++++++ second level start ++++++++++*/
#a5-column-right-left-sl {
    position:relative;
    left:0px;
    top:0px;
    padding:0px 10px 0px 10px;
    margin-right:177px;
    border:0px solid #000000;
    }
#a5-sl-title {
    margin:0px -10px 10px -10px;
    padding:5px 0px 0px 40px;
    height:25px;
    color:#000000;
    background:#DBDBDB url(images/bg-sl-title.gif) no-repeat left top;
    border:0px solid #000000;
    font:bold 14px italic Arial, Helvetica, sans-serif;
    voice-family:"\"}\"";
    voice-family:inherit;
        height:20px;
    }
    html>body #a5-sl-title {
        height:20px;
    }
#a5-column-left-full {
```

```
    position:relative;
    left:0px;
    top:1px;
    color:#000000;
    padding:0px 10px 0px 10px;
    }
/* ++++++++++ second level end ++++++++++*/
</style>
</head>
<body>
<div id="a5-body-center">
    <div id="a5-body">
<!-- ###### header start ###### -->
        <div id="a5-header">
            <div><a href="index.htm"><img src="images/logo.gif"
                width="357" height="78" alt="" border="0" /></a></div>
            <div id="a5-login">
                <span style="float:left;"><a href="x.htm"><img
                    src="images/reseller-button.gif" width="33"
                    height="23" alt="" border="0" /></a></span>
                <a href="x.htm" class="linklist1"><b>Reseller Login
                    </b><br />
                Forgot Password?</a>
            </div>
            <div id="a5-call">
                <span style="float:left;padding-right:6px;"><a href=
                    "x.htm"><img src="images/photo-header-right.jpg"
                    width="58" height="64" alt="" border="0" /></a>
                    </span>
                <div style="margin-top:8px;">
                    <span style="font: 14px Arial, Helvetica,
                        sans-serif;"><b>Need Help?</b></span><br />
                    Call us at<br />
                    1-800-555-5555
                </div>
            </div>
        </div>
<!-- ###### header end ###### -->
<!-- ###### left column start ###### -->
        <div id="a5-column-left">
        <div id="date">
            January 31, 2006
            </div>
            <div id="formsearch" class="color-1-text-13">
                <form method="post" action="x.htm" name="search"
                    style="margin-top:0px;">
                    <b>Keyword Search</b>
                    <div style="padding:5px 0px 10px 0px;"><input
                        type="text" size="15" name="keywords"
                        value="View All Titles" /></div>
                    <b>Categories</b>
                    <div style="padding:5px 0px 15px 0px;">
                    <select name="categories" size="1">
                        <option value="All">Select Category
                            </option>
```

```
                              <option value="sample">This is a sample
                                    entry</option>
                        </select>
                        </div>
                        <input type="image" src="images/
                              button-search.gif" />
                  </form>
            </div>
            <div id="a5-column-left-content">
                  <div style="padding:15px 0px 10px 0px;color:
                        #ffffff;"><span class="color-1-text-14"><b>
                        Duis autem vel</b></span> eum iriure dolor in
                        hendrerit in vulputate velit esse molestie
                        consequat, vel illum dolore eu feugiat nulla.
                        MORE</div>
                  <div style="padding:10px 0px 10px 0px;color:
                        #ffffff;"><a href="x.htm"><img src="images/
                        banner-left-bottom.jpg" width="180"
                        height="96" alt="" border="0" /></a></div>
                  <div id="a5-copyright">
                        &copy; copyright 2006 | your company | all
                              rights reserved
                  </div>
            </div>
      </div>
<!-- ###### left column end ###### -->
<!-- ###### right column start ###### -->
      <div id="a5-column-right">
            <div id="a5-menu-box">
                  <div id="a5-menu">
                           
                        <a href="index.htm">menu item 1</a> 
                               .  
                        <a href="menu-item-2.htm">longer menu item 2
                              </a>  .  
                        <a href="menu-item-3.htm">menu item 3</a> 
                               .  
                        <a href="index.htm">menu item 4</a>  
                              .  
                        <a href="index.htm">menu item 5</a>  
                              .  
                  </div>
            </div>
<!-- ###### column right left start ###### -->
            <div id="a5-column-right-left-sl">
                  <div id="a5-sl-title">
                        longer menu item 2
                  </div>
                  Enter text here.
            </div>
<!-- ###### column right left end ###### -->
<!-- ###### column right right start ###### -->
            <div id="a5-column-right-right">
                  <div class="a5-title-right">
                        <b>View Our Specials</b>
```

```
            </div>
            <div>Duis autem vel eum iriure dolor in hendrerit
            in vulputate velit esse molestie consequat.</div>
            <div id="a5-right-nested-box"><span class="color-
                1-text-14"><b>Duis autem vel</b></span> eum
                iriure dolor in hendrerit in vulputate velit
                esse molestie consequat, vel illum dolore eu
                feugiat nulla.
                <div style="margin:24px 0px 20px 0px;"><img
                    src="images/banner-right-middle.jpg"
                    width="136" height="73" alt="" border="0"
                    /></div>
            </div>
        </div>
<!-- ###### column right right end ###### -->
        </div>
<!-- ###### right column end ###### -->
    </div>
</div>
</body>
</html>
```

There are several things to note about the code in Listing 8.5:

■ The second level start and second level end comment tags are added to separate the rules specifically added for the second-level area from the rest of the stylesheet. Unlike the design in Chapter 6, the two stylesheets are included as one in this chapter.

The rules added in the second-level template have `-s1` appended to their names to signify that they are to be used for secondary pages.

■ The `a5-column-right-left-s1` rule is added to the stylesheet for the second-level template. It replaces the `a5-column-right-left` rule, which is the container for the center column on the homepage. The only difference between the two styles is that the content on the second-level page, which is styled by the `a5-column-right-left-s1` rule, adds 10 pixels of padding to the top and bottom of the container to position itself with the menu and to add extra spacing on the bottom.

■ The `a5-s1-title` rule is added to include the page title for secondary pages at the top of the page. This rule sets the height of the <DIV> at 25 pixels, using the `height` property. Padding also is used to position the title from the top and left sides in the container. To ensure that the color of the `bg-title.gif` is continued across the screen, the shorthand `background` property is assigned a background color value of #DBDBDB. Because padding is used to position the text within the container, the Tantek hack is added to ensure that the height of the container is the same for both compliant and noncompliant browsers.

Constructing a Second-Level Page with Two Columns

The full-width second-level template included with this design is the page the designer comes to when clicking on the Menu Item 3 link in the menu. The purpose of this template is to provide a page with more white space for the designer to work with. Figure 8.16 shows what the design looks like when the final code is added to the page and the right column is removed from the design in Figure 8.16 (see Listing 8.6).

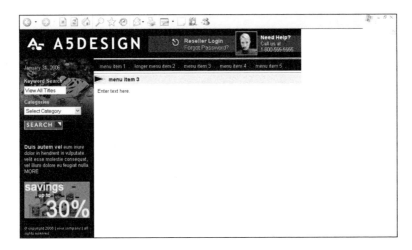

FIGURE 8.16   A two-column second-level template created from a customized version of the home page design.

LISTING 8.6   Code for Figure 8.16

```
<!DOCTYPE html PUBLIC "-//W3C//DTD XHTML 1.0 Transitional//EN"
    "DTD/xhtml1-transitional.dtd">
<html><head><title>Design 123</title>
<meta http-equiv="Content-Type" content="text/html;
    charset=iso-8859-1" />
<style type="text/css">
/* ++++++++++ global general styles start ++++++++++*/
    html, body {
    margin:0px;
    padding:0px;
    font: 13px Arial, Helvetica, sans-serif;
    color:#000000;
    background:#ffffff;
    }
a:link { color:#FF7800; }
a:visited { color:#FF5A00; }
a:active { color:#FFC600; }
a:hover { color:#000000; }
```

```
a.linklist1:link { text-decoration:none;color:#0ECOFF;}
a.linklist1:visited { text-decoration:none;color:#0ECOFF;}
a.linklist1:active { text-decoration:none;color:#0ECOFF;}
a.linklist1:hover { text-decoration:none;color:#D5EE03;}


.color-1-text-13 { font-family: arial, geneva, sans-serif; font-size:
    13px; color: #FFAE00;}
.color-1-text-14 { font-family: arial, geneva, sans-serif; font-size:
    14px; color: #FFAE00;}


.color-2-text-14 { font-family: arial, geneva, sans-serif; font-size:
    14px; color: #000000;}
/* ++++++++++ global general styles end ++++++++++*/
/* ++++++++++ global structure styles start ++++++++++*/
#a5-body-center {
    text-align:left;
    }
#a5-body {
    position: relative;
    width: 770px; /* change this to a specific amount for a fixed
        design. E.g., 770px. */
/* remove these comment tags if the page is to be centered
    margin-left: auto;
    margin-right: auto;*/
    text-align:left;
    padding-bottom:10px;
    border:0px solid #000000;
    }
#a5-header {
    position:relative;
    left:0px;
    top:0px;
    height:78px;
    background: #000000 url(images/bg-header.gif) repeat-x;
    border:0px solid #000000;
    }
    #a5-login {
        position:absolute;
        top:24px;
        right:186px;
        width:165px;
        font: 15px Arial, Helvetica, sans-serif;
        border:0px solid #ffffff;
        }
    #a5-call {
        position:absolute;
        top:8px;
        right:0px;
        width:177px;
        font: 13px Arial, Helvetica, sans-serif;
        color:#ffffff;
        border:0px solid #000000;
        }
#a5-column-left {
    position:absolute;
```

```
        left:Opx;
        top:78px;
        width:207px;
        color:#ffffff;
        padding:Opx 12px 50px 15px;
        background: #000000 url(images/bg-left-column.jpg) no-repeat;
        border:Opx solid yellow;
        voice-family:"\"}\"";
        voice-family:inherit;
            width:180px;
        }
        html>body #a5-column-left {
            width:180px;
        }
        #date {
            position:relative;
            top:16px;
            left:Opx;
            color:#ffffff;
            border:Opx solid #ffffff;
            }
        #formsearch {
            position:relative;
            top:35px;
            left:Opx;
            border:Opx solid yellow;
            }
        #a5-column-left-content {
            position:relative;
            left:Opx;
            top:35px;
            color:#ffffff;
            border:Opx solid #ffffff;
            }
            #a5-copyright {
                position:relative;
                left:Opx;
                top:10px;
                bottom:5px;
                font: 10px Arial, Helvetica, sans-serif;
                color:#9D9D9D;
                text-align:left;
                border:Opx solid #000000;
                }
#a5-column-right {
    position:relative;
    right:Opx;
    top:Opx;
    margin-left:207px;
    border:Opx solid #000000;
    }
    #a5-menu-box {
        position:relative;
        top:Opx;
        left:Opx;
```

```
        height:42px;
        width:100%;
        color:#ffffff;
        line-height:42px;
        vertical-align:30%;
        background:url(images/bg-menu.gif) repeat-x 0px 0px;
        border:0px solid #000000;
        }
        #a5-menu a {
            display:inline;
            text-decoration:none;
            color:#94CCDE;
            font-weight:normal;
            }
        #a5-menu a:hover {
            font-weight:normal;
            color:#ffffff;
            }
#a5-column-right-left {
        position:relative;
        left:0px;
        top:0px;
        padding:10px 10px 10px 10px;
        margin-right:177px;
        border:0px solid #000000;
        }
        .a5-products {
        height:300px;
        border: 0px solid #000000;
        }
        .a5-individual-product {
        float: left;
        margin:0px 2px 0px 2px;
        border:0px solid #000000;
        }
        .a5-individual-product p {
        border-top:1px solid #BFBFBF;
        width:170px;
        text-align: center;
        }
#a5-column-right-right {
        position:absolute;
        right:0px;
        top:42px;
        width:177px;
        height:365px;
        color:#ffffff;
        padding:0px 9px 0px 9px;
        background:#215F5F url(images/bg-bottom-line-right-column.gif)
            no-repeat left bottom;
        border:0px solid red;
        voice-family:"\"}\"";
        voice-family:inherit;
            width:159px;
        }
```

```
html>body #a5-column-right-right {
    width:159px;
    }
.a5-title-right {
    font-family: arial, geneva, sans-serif;
    font-size: 13px;
    color: #D5EE03;
    line-height:25px;
    font-weight:bold;
    margin:0px -9px 0px -9px;
    padding-left:5px;
    margin-bottom:10px;
    background:#000000;
    border:0px solid #000000;
    }
#a5-right-nested-box {
    position:relative;
    right:0px;
    top:23px;
    width:159px;
    padding:10px 10px 0px 10px;
    background:#000000;
    color:#ffffff;
    border:1px solid #0EC0FF;
    voice-family:"\"}\"";
    voice-family:inherit;
        width:139px;
    }
    html>body #a5-right-nested-box {
        width:139px;
    }
/* ++++++++++ global structure styles end ++++++++++*/
/* ++++++++++ second level start ++++++++++*/
#a5-column-right-left-sl {
    position:relative;
    left:0px;
    top:0px;
    padding:0px 10px 0px 10px;
    margin-right:177px;
    border:0px solid #000000;
    }
#a5-sl-title {
    margin:0px -10px 10px -10px;
    padding:5px 0px 0px 40px;
    height:25px;
    color:#000000;
    background:#DBDBDB url(images/bg-sl-title.gif) no-repeat left top;
    border:0px solid #000000;
    font:bold 14px italic Arial, Helvetica, sans-serif;
    voice-family:"\"}\"";
    voice-family:inherit;
        height:20px;
    }
    html>body #a5-sl-title {
        height:20px;
```

```
        }
#a5-column-left-full {
    position:relative;
    left:0px;
    top:1px;
    color:#000000;
    padding:0px 10px 0px 10px;
    }
/* ++++++++++ second level end ++++++++++*/
</style>
</head>
<body>
<div id="a5-body-center">
    <div id="a5-body">
<!-- ###### header start ###### -->
    <div id="a5-header">
            <div><a href="index.htm"><img src="images/logo.gif"
                width="357" height="78" alt="" border="0" /></a></div>
            <div id="a5-login">
                <span style="float:left;"><a href="x.htm"><img src=
                    "images/reseller-button.gif" width="33"
                    height="23" alt="" border="0" /></a></span>
                <a href="x.htm" class="linklist1"><b>Reseller Login
                    </b><br />
                Forgot Password?</a>
            </div>
            <div id="a5-call">
                <span style="float:left;padding-right:6px;"><a
                    href="x.htm"><img src="images/photo-header-
                    right.jpg" width="58" height="64" alt=""
                    border="0" /></a></span>
                <div style="margin-top:8px;">
                    <span style="font: 14px Arial, Helvetica,
                        sans-serif;"><b>Need Help?</b></span><br />
                    Call us at<br />
                    1-800-555-5555
                </div>
            </div>
        </div>
    </div>
<!-- ###### header end ###### -->
<!-- ###### left column start ###### -->
            <div id="a5-column-left">
                <div id="date">
                    January 31, 2006
                </div>
                <div id="formsearch" class="color-1-text-13">
                    <form method="post" action="x.htm" name="search"
                        style="margin-top:0px;">
                        <b>Keyword Search</b>
                        <div style="padding:5px 0px 10px 0px;"><input
                            type="text" size="15" name="keywords"
                            value="View All Titles" /></div>
                        <b>Categories</b>
                        <div style="padding:5px 0px 15px 0px;">
                        <select name="categories" size="1">
```

```
                                <option value="All">Select Category
                                    </option>
                                <option value="sample">This is a sample
                                    entry</option>
                            </select>
                            </div>
                            <input type="image" src="images/
                                button-search.gif" />
                        </form>
                    </div>
                    <div id="a5-column-left-content">
                        <div style="padding:15px 0px 10px 0px;color:
                            #ffffff;"><span class="color-1-text-14"><b>
                            Duis autem vel</b></span> eum iriure dolor in
                            hendrerit in vulputate velit esse molestie
                            consequat, vel illum dolore eu feugiat nulla.
                            MORE</div>
                        <div style="padding:10px 0px 10px 0px;color:
                            #ffffff;"><a href="x.htm"><img src="images/
                            banner-left-bottom.jpg" width="180"
                            height="96" alt="" border="0" /></a></div>
                        <div id="a5-copyright">
                            &copy; copyright 2006 | your company | all
                                rights reserved
                        </div>
                    </div>
                </div>
<!-- ###### left column end ###### -->
<!-- ###### right column start ###### -->
                <div id="a5-column-right">
                    <div id="a5-menu-box">
                        <div id="a5-menu">
                               
                            <a href="index.htm">menu item 1</a>  
                                .  
                            <a href="menu-item-2.htm">longer menu item 2
                                </a>  .  
                            <a href="menu-item-3.htm">menu item 3</a> 
                                 .  
                            <a href="index.htm">menu item 4</a>  
                                .  
                            <a href="index.htm">menu item 5</a>  
                                .  
                        </div>
                    </div>
<!-- ###### column right left start ###### -->
                    <div id="a5-column-left-full">
                        <div id="a5-sl-title">
                            menu item 3
                        </div>
                            Enter text here.
                    </div>
<!-- ###### column right left end ###### -->
                </div>
<!-- ###### right column end ###### -->
```

```
        </div>
      </div>
    </body>
  </html>
```

There are two things to note about the code in Listing 8.6:

- All the code between the `column right right start` and `column right right end` comment tags is removed from the source code.
- Once the right column is removed, the center column can expand to the full width of the screen. Before it can do this, though, the `a5-column-right-left-sl` container needs to be duplicated and named `a5-column-left-full`. The style then needs to be changed by removing the `margin-right` property so the new container can expand all the way to the right edge of the screen. The left and right padding properties and values need to remain in the rule so the text in the container does not touch the left and right edges.

SUMMARY

Overall, the structure and CSS used in this design is a hybrid of the designs explained in Chapters 6 and 7. Several characteristics make it unique. With considerably more content, this design requires more rules to be created. Another difference is the home page outputs products, which uses a technique that can be used in various sites and circumstances. The final major difference of this design from the other chapters is that the menu is given a limited amount of space and is aligned horizontally, rather than vertically. Therefore, the design relies on the search form in the left column to drive the majority of content. While not all sites will look and function similarly to the one in this chapter, elements of such an involved design can always be used.

9

Case Study: Full-Height Three-Column Layout

For more than a decade, creating a three-column table-based layout in XHTML, where all three columns have the same color, has been an easily accomplished, widely used, technique. As one column is increased in height, the other two change accordingly, maintaining the same colors. In CSS, however, it takes some maneuvering to modify the code because elements that are assigned absolute positioning or are floated fall outside the normal document flow, meaning they are not controlled by parent elements. Fortunately, there is a solution to this problem.

This chapter outlines the unique design structure A5design has created for its clients, building upon the core knowledge of many CSS gurus, including Eric Meyer, Big John, Holly Bergevin, and the group at *www.alistapart.com*. It is a simple, clean, hack-free solution that is used in many of the CSS designs included in this book. Following are some of the requirements it satisfies:

- The design can be easily changed from a fixed to liquid design and vice versa. The design explained in this chapter was created for 1024 × 768 resolution.
- A footer is included at the bottom of the three columns.
- No matter the height of any column, the colors of all three columns will run from the top of the page down to the footer.

 As with all CSS design, it does not take much to break the code, so it does not function similarly within all browsers. Therefore, the challenge is to modify the main structure of this design so it will continue to work. Several designs included with this book use a modified version of this design, the most advanced probably being design 133.

 The design explained in this chapter is design 131 on the CD-ROM (photos credits: *www.idlerphotography.com* and *www.gooligoo.com*).

UNDERSTANDING THE DESIGN'S STRUCTURE

Figure 9.1 illustrates the design explained in this chapter. As with the previous three case studies, it is created to function as a fixed or liquid design. Basic fundamental differences, however, allow it to work unlike many other CSS templates. These differences, which include a couple more <DIV> containers and a new core framework, are explained later in this chapter.

FIGURE 9.1   The full-height three-column design explained in this chapter.

Reasoning Behind Guides and the Creating of Slices in Photoshop File

There are 15 slices used from the Photoshop file to create the images for the homepage design. Figure 9.2 shows all the slices used in the file. It also outlines the 10 most important guides and slices necessary in constructing the design with XHTML and CSS.

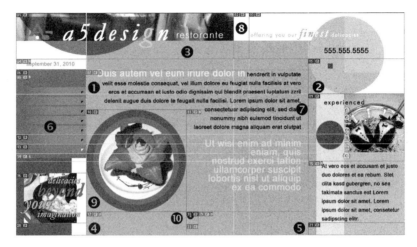

FIGURE 9.2   Ten of the most important guides and slices used to build the design in this chapter.

Following are explanations of the guides and slices illustrated in Figure 9.2:

- The guide to the left of number 1 is used to separate the left column from the center column.
- The guide to the left of number 2 is used to separate the center column from the right column.
- The guide below number 3 is used to differentiate the header from the content below it.
- The slice to the left of number 4 is very important in understanding this new design technique because it will be repeated as a background image behind the entire height of the left column.
- The slice to the right of number 5 is similar to the slice represented in number 4. It will be repeated on the right side from the top of the design, all the way to the footer. It illustrates the flexibility of this design technique because the background color does not necessarily have to extend the full column width, which is represented by number 2. This technique allows for the text to appear as though it is layered over the center column's color, even though, technically, it is included in the right column.

- The two slices below number 6 are used as the background images of the "on" and "off" states of the menu items.
- The slice to the right of number 7 creates an image that is included in the right column. This image is noteworthy because it includes the background image, so when the image is layered over the background, the change between the two is seamless.
- The slice represented by number 8 is used to save a background image for the header. It repeats horizontally in the design for both fixed and liquid formats.
- The slice to the left of number 9 is similar to the slice to the right of number 7 in that it includes the background image, which is repeated for the full height of the left column.
- The slice to the right of number 10 is used as the background image in the title area for the second-level pages (see Figure 9.3).

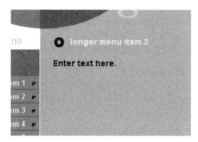

FIGURE 9.3   The background image of second-level titles that is saved from the home page design.

Understanding the Placement of CSS Containers

There are 20 <DIV> tags used in this design. The number is higher than in the previous case studies in this book, mainly because this design structure requires a few more to accomplish its flexibility and functionality.

Following are explanations of the 10 most useful containers, shown in Figure 9.4:

- The <DIV> tag to the top left of number 1 is used for centering the design in IE 5 and 5.5.
- The <DIV> nested inside number 1, represented by number 2, illustrates the a5-body container that is used to control, among other things, the width of the design.
- Number 3 illustrates the a5-bg-left <DIV> that is nested inside the a5-body <DIV>. This container is used to run a background image down the left side of the entire design.
- Number 4 represents the a5-bg-right container that runs a background image down the right side of the entire design.
- The <DIV> that contains number 5 represents the header row that is positioned across the top of the design.
- Number 6 illustrates the left column of the design.

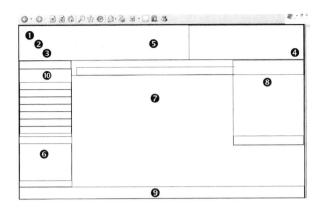

FIGURE 9.4 Ten of the most important containers used to build the design.

- Number 7 points out the <DIV> that is used for the entire area to the right of the left column. This area contains both the center and right columns.
- Number 8 is the right column that is nested inside the number 7 container. It is then floated to the right.
- The container represented by number 9 is used as the footer area.
- Number 10 represents a <DIV> tag that is used for the most complex nested container, which is used for the menu.

BUILDING THE STRUCTURE

Following are the steps to building the design. It is assumed that the Photoshop file has already been created or customized and the designer needs only to position the images and text.

Creating the XHTML and CSS Framework

The first step in building the design is to create the XHTML framework and initial CSS containers. Listing 9.1 is the code that is used to output the page shown in Figure 9.5.

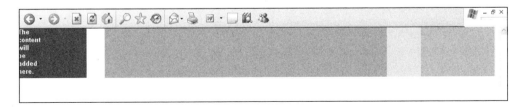

FIGURE 9.5 Basic XHTML and CSS framework for the design.

LISTING 9.1 Code for Figure 9.5

```
<!DOCTYPE html PUBLIC "-//W3C//DTD XHTML 1.0 Transitional//EN"
    "DTD/xhtml1-transitional.dtd">
<html><head><title>Design 131</title>
<meta http-equiv="Content-Type" content="text/html;
    charset=iso-8859-1" />
<style type="text/css">
/* ++++++++++ global general styles start ++++++++++*/
html, body {
    margin:0px;
    padding:0px;
    font: 9.8pt arial, helvetica, sans-serif;
    color:#000000;
    }
/* ++++++++++ global general styles end ++++++++++*/
/* ++++++++++ global structure styles start ++++++++++*/
.a5-bg-left {
    width:100%;
    margin-bottom:-10px;
background:url(images/bg-left-column.gif) repeat-y left top;
    }
.a5-bg-right {
    width:100%;
    background:url(images/bg-right-column.gif) repeat-y right top;
    }
#a5-body-center {
    text-align:left;
    }
#a5-body {
    position: relative;
    width: 1000px; /* change this to a specific amount for a fixed
    design. E.g., 1000px. Or, it can be changed to a percentage, which
    will allow the design to be liquid */

/* remove these comment tags if the page is to be centered
    margin-left: auto;
    margin-right: auto;*/
    text-align:left;
    background:#7ED0D4 url(images/bg-right-column.gif) repeat-y right
        top;
    border:0px solid #000000;
    }
/* ++++++++++ global structure styles end ++++++++++*/
</style>
</head>
<body>
<div id="a5-body-center">
    <div id="a5-body">
        <div class="a5-bg-left">
        <div class="a5-bg-right">
            <b><span style="color:#ffffff;">The<br />
            content<br />
            will<br />
            be<br />
            added<br />
```

```
            here.</b><br /> </span>
        </div>
    </div>
</div>
</body>
</html>
```

There are several things to note about the code in Listing 9.1:

■ The CSS stylesheet is commented into two sections. The `global general styles` comment tags contain the general styles, such as the formatting of the `<HTML>` and `<BODY>` tags, hyperlinks, and fonts. The `global structure styles` comment tags include the styles used to define the structure of the design and elements included in that structure.

■ Several rules define the `<HTML>` and `<BODY>` tags. The `margin` and `padding` properties are used to ensure that the design is placed in the very top-left corner of the browser, with no space between the design and the edges. The default font style for the site is set using the shorthand `FONT` property. Defining the default font color is accomplished with the `COLOR` property. The background color also is assigned to ensure that all browsers display the same color, which is not always the case.

■ The `a5-body-center` and `a5-body` rules are used to force the design to the left side of the browser screen with a fixed width of 1000 pixels. If the designer wants to fill the full width of the screen, the value of `1000px` needs to be changed to `100%`. If, however, the designer wants to simply justify the design to the left, the value of the `text-align` property in the `a5-body-center` rule needs to be changed from `center` to `left`. The `margin-left` and `margin-right` properties in the `a5-body` rule ensure that the extra white space is split evenly on both sides.

■ The big difference at this stage, compared to the previous case studies, is the addition of the `a5-bg-left` and `a5-bg-right` classes and `<DIV>` containers. These provide relatively positioned containers for the entire site to be nested within. The `a5-bg-left` `<DIV>` runs its background image down the left side, while the `a5-bg-right` runs its background image down the right side. Thus, rather than using browser-generated colors, the background images, which are found at the bottom-left and right-hand corners (see Figure 9.6) of the Photoshop design, are repeated.

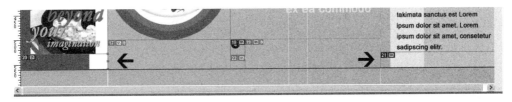

FIGURE 9.6 Slices, indicated by the left and right arrows, that are used to create the left and right background images.

The a5-bg-left rule has the margin-bottom property added with a value of -10px. This ensures that the background images will not extend past the footer in some browsers. When the content is added to the core area, without any columns or positioning, it shows that the background images repeat vertically (see Figure 9.5). If the length of the content is increased, the background images repeat accordingly (see Figure 9.7).

■ A background color is added to the a5-body container to give the center column color, as well as guaranteeing that the right background image is repeated correctly for all tested browsers. In other words, the right background is not correctly repeated in all instances for all browsers when it is simply included with the a5-bg-right <DIV>. Therefore, it is included in the a5-body container, as well.

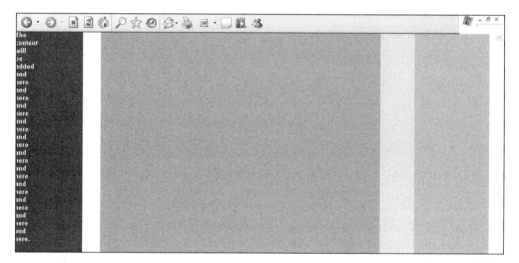

FIGURE 9.7 Text added to the design to illustrate how both background images will repeat vertically.

Adding the Rows and Columns to the Framework

Unlike in the previous case studies, the row and column framework of this design is explained upfront because it all works together to create a flexible design. Once understood, the content just needs to be added into these containers. Listing 9.2 is the code that is added to create the updated page in Figure 9.8.

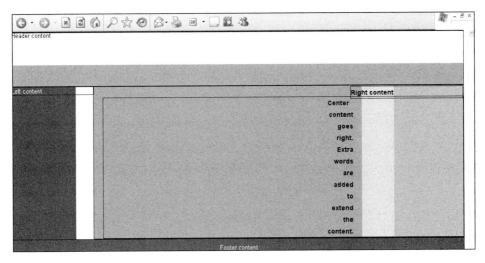

FIGURE 9.8   Row and column framework without content added to it.

LISTING 9.2   Code for Figure 9.8

```
<!DOCTYPE html PUBLIC "-//W3C//DTD XHTML 1.0 Transitional//EN"
    "DTD/xhtml1-transitional.dtd">
<html><head><title>Design 131</title>
<meta http-equiv="Content-Type" content="text/html;
    charset=iso-8859-1" />
<style type="text/css">
/* ++++++++++ global general styles start ++++++++++*/
html, body {
    margin:0px;
    padding:0px;
    font: 9.8pt arial, helvetica, sans-serif;
    color:#000000;
    }
/* ++++++++++ global general styles end ++++++++++*/
/* ++++++++++ global structure styles start ++++++++++*/
.a5-bg-left {
    width:100%;
    margin-bottom:-10px;
    background:url(images/bg-left-column.gif) repeat-y left top;
    }
.a5-bg-right {
    width:100%;
    background:url(images/bg-right-column.gif) repeat-y right top;
    }
#a5-body-center {
    text-align:left;
    }
#a5-body {
    position: relative;
```

```
        width: 1000px; /* change this to a specific amount for a fixed
            design. E.g., 1000px. Or, it can be changed to a percentage,
            which will allow the design to be liquid */

/* remove these comment tags if the page is to be centered
    margin-left: auto;
    margin-right: auto;*/
    text-align:left;
    background:#7ED0D4 url(images/bg-right-column.gif) repeat-y right
        top;
    border:0px solid #000000;
    }
#a5-header {
    position:relative;
    left:0px;
    top:0px;
    height:117px;
    background: url(images/bg-header.gif) repeat-x;
    border:1px solid #000000;
    }
#a5-column-left {
    float:left;
    width:181px;
    height:auto;
    border:1px solid #000000;
    }
#a5-body-content {
    position:relative;
    margin-left:181px;
    border:1px solid #000000;
    }
    #a5-column-center {
        position:relative;
        left:0px;
        top:0px;
        margin:23px 0px 0px 20px;
        font: bold 10.8pt arial, helvetica, sans-serif;
        line-height:19pt;
        border:1px solid #000000;
        }
    #a5-column-right {
        float:right;
        width:250px;
        margin-top:-23px;
        text-align:left;
        border:1px solid #000000;
        }
#a5-footer {
    clear:both;
    text-align:center;
    line-height:35px;
    background:#4A7A7D;
    border:1px solid #000000;
    }
```

```
/* ++++++++++ global structure styles end ++++++++++*/
</style>
</head>
<body>
<div id="a5-body-center">
    <div id="a5-body">
        <div class="a5-bg-left">
        <div class="a5-bg-right">
<!-- ###### header start ###### -->
            <div id="a5-header">
            Header content
            </div>
<!-- ###### header end ###### -->
<!-- ###### left column start ###### -->
            <div id="a5-column-left">
                <span style="color:#ffffff;">Left content</span>
            </div>
<!-- ###### left column end ###### -->
<!-- ###### body content start ###### -->
            <div id="a5-body-content">
                <div id="a5-column-center">
                    <div id="a5-column-right">
                        Right content
                    </div>
                    <div style="margin-right:246px;text-align:right;">
                        Center<br />content<br />goes<br />right.<br />
                            Extra<br />words<br />are<br />added<br />
                            to<br />extend<br />the<br />content.
                    </div>
                </div>
            </div>
<!-- ###### footer start ###### -->
            <div id="a5-footer"><span style="color:#ffffff;">Footer
                content</span></div>
<!-- ###### footer end ###### -->
<!-- ###### body content end ###### -->
        </div>
        </div>
    </div>
</div>
</body>
</html>
```

There are several things to note about the code in Listing 9.2:

- The a5-header row is the first structural element to be added. It is given relative positioning so it expands the full width of the page. It also is assigned a height of 117 pixels so the container collapses perfectly around the contents in all browsers. A horizontally repeating background is added to fill the space between the images and fill extra space if the design is changed to a liquid format.

- The a5-column-left rule floats the left column to the left side, under the header row. The width of the column is set to 181 pixels.

The border of the various containers is set to 1 for demonstration purposes for this step. They are reset to 0 in the final code.

■   The a5-body-content is added under the header area to contain the center and right columns. It is given relative positioning to fill the width of the page. It is assigned a left margin of 181 pixels, so any content in it abuts the left column. One of the tricks to this design is to set the right margin of the center content at the local level. This ensures that the content does not cross over into the right column because it is nested inside this container. The right margin for the center area is set at 246 pixels. To position the content that will be added to this container, the top margin is set to 23 pixels, and the left is set to 20 pixels.

Technically, the right column is 250 pixels wide, so the right margin of the center content should be set to 250, instead of 246, to avoid overlapping. In this design, however, 246 pixels is acceptable.

■   As mentioned in the previous note, the a5-column-right container is floated to the right inside the a5-column-center <DIV>. By floating it to the right and positioning the bg-right-column.gif image in the a5-bg-right container to the right, the background image of the column and the background of the image will always align with one another, whether the design is fixed or liquid. Because the center container is given a top-margin of 23 pixels, the right column has the top margin set to −23 pixels, so it will be mortised with the header row. This is why the words "center content" and "right content" are set at different heights in Figure 9.8. The words also are not aligned vertically because the right column is set to 250 pixels, while the right margin of the center content is set to 246 pixels, as mentioned earlier.

■   The a5-footer row is added outside the a5-body-content container, with the clear property set to both. This keeps the content in the a5-left-column and a5-center-column containers from crossing over the row.

Populating the Header, Footer, and Columns with Content

Once the framework of the design has been added, the designer need only populate the areas with the appropriate content. Because this styling is very similar to the previous three case studies, the discussion for this Listing 9.3 is limited to unique aspects to this design. Figure 9.9 is the completed home page design that is outlined in Listing 9.3.

FIGURE 9.9   The completed design after the various containers have been populated and styled.

LISTING 9.3   Code for Figure 9.9

```
<!DOCTYPE html PUBLIC "-//W3C//DTD XHTML 1.0 Transitional//EN"
    "DTD/xhtml1-transitional.dtd">
<html><head><title>Design 131</title>
<meta http-equiv="Content-Type" content="text/html;
    charset=iso-8859-1" />
<style type="text/css">
/* ++++++++++ global general styles start ++++++++++*/
html, body {
    margin:0px;
    padding:0px;
    font: 9.8pt arial, helvetica, sans-serif;
    color:#000000;
    }
a:link { color:#D0FAFC; }
a:visited { color:#D0FAFC; }
a:active { color:#D0FAFC; }
a:hover { color:#000000; }

a.linklist1:link { text-decoration:none;color:#E9DF40;}
a.linklist1:visited { text-decoration:none;color:#E9DF40;}
a.linklist1:active { text-decoration:none;color:#E9DF40;}
a.linklist1:hover { text-decoration:underline;color:#ffffff;}

.color-1-text-98 {
    font-family:arial, helvetica, sans-serif;
```

```
    font-size:9.8pt;
    color: #16C7C1;
    }

.color-2-text-8 {
    font-family:arial, helvetica, sans-serif;
    font-size:8pt;
    color: #D0FAFC;
    }
.color-2-text-10 {
    font-family:arial, helvetica, sans-serif;
    font-size:10pt;
    color: #D0FAFC;
    }
.color-2-text-18 {
    font-family:arial, helvetica, sans-serif;
    font-size:18pt;
    color: #D0FAFC;
    }
.color-3-text-88 {
    font-family:arial, helvetica, sans-serif;
    font-size:8.8pt;
    color: #ffffff;
    }
/* ++++++++++ global general styles end ++++++++++*/
/* ++++++++++ global structure styles start ++++++++++*/
.a5-bg-left {
    width:100%;
    margin-bottom:-10px;
    background:url(images/bg-left-column.gif) repeat-y left top;
    }
.a5-bg-right {
    width:100%;
    background:url(images/bg-right-column.gif) repeat-y right top;
    }
#a5-body-center {
    text-align:left;
    }
#a5-body {
    position: relative;
    width: 1000px; /* change this to a specific amount for a fixed
        design. E.g., 1000px. Or, it can be changed to a percentage,
        which will allow the design to be liquid */
/* remove these comment tags if the page is to be centered
    margin-left: auto;
    margin-right: auto;*/
    text-align:left;
    background:#7ED0D4 url(images/bg-right-column.gif) repeat-y right
        top;
    border:0px solid #000000;
    }
#a5-header {
    position:relative;
    left:0px;
    top:0px;
```

```
        height:117px;
        background: url(images/bg-header.gif) repeat-x;
        border:0px solid #000000;
        }
    #a5-header-right {
        position:absolute;
        right:0px;
        top:0px;
        height:117px;
        border:0px solid #000000;
        }
#a5-column-left {
    float:left;
    width:181px;
    border:0px solid #000000;
    }
        #a5-date {
            text-align:center;
            background:#ffffff;
            vertical-align:50%;
            line-height:26px;
            }
        #a5-menu {
            width:181px;
            padding:44px 0px 10px 0px;
            font:bold 9.8pt arial, helvetica, sans-serif;
            background: url(images/bg-menu.gif) repeat-y 0px 0px;
            }
        #a5-menu a {
            display:block;
            text-align:left;
            line-height:23px;
            vertical-align:50%;
            text-align:right;
            padding:0px 25px 0px 10px;
            text-decoration:none;
            background: url(images/bg-menu-off.jpg) no-repeat 0px 0px;
            color:#DEEFF0;
            }
        #a5-menu a:hover {
            background: url(images/bg-menu-on.jpg) no-repeat 0px 0px;
            color:#ffffff;
            }
        #a5-photo-bottom-left {
            margin:23px 0px 20px 0px;
            border:0px solid #000000;
            }.
#a5-body-content {
    position:relative;
    margin-left:181px;
    border:0px solid #000000;
    }
    #a5-column-center {
        position:relative;
        left:0px;
```

```
        top:0px;
        margin:23px 0px 0px 20px;
        font: bold 10.8pt arial, helvetica, sans-serif;
        line-height:19pt;
        border:0px solid #000000;
        }
    #a5-column-right {
        float:right;
        width:250px;
        margin-top:-23px;
        text-align:left;
        border:0px solid #000000;
        }
    #a5-bottom-right-text {
        font: bold 9.8pt arial, helvetica, sans-serif;
        line-height:14pt;
        padding:0px 10px 10px 30px;
        }
#a5-footer {
    clear:both;
    text-align:center;
    line-height:35px;
    background:#4A7A7D;
    border:0px solid #000000;
    }
/* ++++++++++ global structure styles end ++++++++++*/
</style>
</head>
<body>
<div id="a5-body-center">
    <div id="a5-body">
        <div class="a5-bg-left">
        <div class="a5-bg-right">
<!-- ###### header start ###### -->
            <div id="a5-header">
                <div><img src="images/header-left.jpg" width="557"
                    height="117" alt="" border="0" /></div>
                <div id="a5-header-right"><a href="index.htm"><img
                    src="images/header-right.gif" width="403"
                    height="117" alt="" border="0" /></a></div>
            </div>
<!-- ###### header end ###### -->
<!-- ###### left column start ###### -->
            <div id="a5-column-left">
                <div id="a5-date" class="color-1-text-98">September
                    31, 2010</div>
                <div id="a5-menu">
                    <a href="index.htm">menu item 1</a>
                    <a href="menu-item-2.htm">longer menu item 2</a>
                    <a href="menu-item-3.htm">menu item 3</a>
                    <a href="index.htm">menu item 4</a>
                    <a href="index.htm">menu item 5</a>
                    <a href="index.htm">menu item 6</a>
                    <a href="index.htm">menu item 7</a>
                </div>
```

```
                    <div id="a5-photo-bottom-left"><a href="index.htm">
                        <img src="images/photo-bottom-left.jpg"
                        width="180" height="125" alt="" border="0"
                        /></a></div>
                </div>
<!-- ###### left column end ###### -->
<!-- ###### body content start ###### -->
                <div id="a5-body-content">
                    <div id="a5-column-center">
                        <div id="a5-column-right">
                            <div><img src="images/image-right-column-
                                top.gif" width="250" height="88" alt=""
                                border="0" /></div>
                            <div><img src="images/image-right-column-
                                middle.jpg" width="250" height="169"
                                alt="" border="0" /></div>
                            <div id="a5-bottom-right-text">
At vero eos et accusam et justo duo dolores et ea rebum. Stet clita
    kasd gubergren, no sea takimata sanctus est Lorem ipsum dolor sit
    amet. Lorem ipsum dolor sit amet, consetetur sadipscing elitr.
                            </div>
                        </div>
                        <div style="margin-right:246px;text-align:right;">
<span class="color-2-text-18">Duis autem vel eum iriure dolor in
    </span> hendrerit in vulputate velit esse molestie consequat, vel
    illum dolore eu feugiat nulla facilisis at vero eros et accumsan
    et iusto odio dignissim qui blandit praesent luptatum <span
    style="float:left;padding:10px 10px 10px 0px;margin-left:-20px;">
    <img src="images/photo-center-middle.jpg" width="256" height="256"
    alt="" border="0" /></span>zzril delenit augue duis dolore te
    feugait nulla facilisi. Lorem ipsum dolor sit amet, consectetuer
    adipiscing elit, sed diam nonummy nibh euismod tincidunt ut
    laoreet dolore magna aliquam erat olutpat. <span class="color-2-
    text-18">Ut wisi enim ad minim eniam, quis nostrud exerci tation
    ullamcorper suscipit lobortis nisl ut aliquip ex ea commodo</span>
                        </div>
                    </div>
                </div>
<!-- ###### footer start ###### -->
                <div id="a5-footer"><div style="margin:0px 0px 10px 0px;
                    font-weight:bold;" class="color-2-text-10">
                        <a href="index.htm" class="linklist1">menu item 1
                            </a>  .  <a href="menu-
                            item-2.htm" class="linklist1">longer menu item
                            2</a>  .  <a href="menu-
                            item-3.htm" class="linklist1">menu item 3</a>
                              .  <a href="index.htm"
                            class="linklist1">menu item 4</a>  
                            .  <a href="index.htm" class=
                            "linklist1">menu item 5</a>  . 
                             <a href="index.htm" class="linklist1">
                            menu item 6</a>  .  <a
                            href="index.htm" class="linklist1">menu
                            item 7</a><br />
```

```
<span class="color-2-text-8">&copy; copyright 2006 | your company |
     all rights reserved</span></div></div>
<!-- ###### footer end ###### -->
<!-- ###### body content end ###### -->
        </div>
        </div>
     </div>
</div>
</body>
</html>
```

There are several things to note about the code in Listing 9.3:

■ The linklist1 rules are added to style the second menu that runs horizontally in the footer. This is the same menu that is included in the left column. It is added to increase usability of the design by providing navigation at the bottom of the page so the user does not have to scroll back up the page.

■ The a5-menu container is given a background image that is layered over the image that is repeated for the entire left column. Then, each menu item is assigned yet another background image when an item is moused on and off. Not only is this layering seamless, but it requires less download time because all three images are of nominal file size. This layering of background images provides the design with more flexibility than with XHTML table-based designs because Netscape 4.7 always had difficulty with more than two nested background images.

■ The a5-bottom-right-text container is assigned a left margin of 30 pixels to position the text to the right of the background color in the center column. Because this color is included in the right column background, which creates an overlapping effect, the text needs to be positioned differently if it is to remain over just the right two colors.

CONSTRUCTING SECOND-LEVEL PAGES

Similar to the previous three case studies, the home page is reused and customized for secondary pages. The technique is the same, except for a couple differences. One difference is that the 246-pixel right margin of the center column is removed so the text will run the full width of the content area. The second modification is that the a5-bg-right container is renamed a5-bg-right-sl for the full-page version, which is the Menu Item 3 page. Once it is renamed, the a5-bg-right-sl rule is added, which uses a background color, rather than an image, to populate the body of the page (see Figure 9.10).

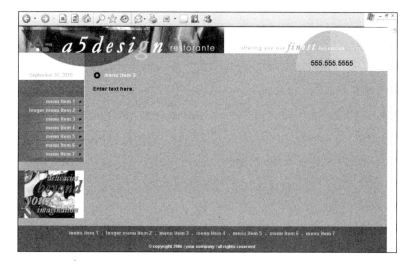

FIGURE 9.10   The Menu Item 3 template that has the repeating right background image replaced with a CSS-generated color that fills the page.

SUMMARY

The design explained in this case study is a succinct way to create one that has the background colors extended throughout all three columns. The coding is simple to understand and use, requiring no hacks or JavaScript. Not only are background images used to accomplish this technique, but the core structure of the design is written to allow for content that is scalable and will not run beyond the footer. As with other designs in this book, it allows for the page to be either a fixed-width or liquid design. Of all the design structures explained and included in this book, this one will, most likely, be the most widely used because of its flexibility and scalability.

10 Customizing the Designs Included in This Book

There are 140 templates included with this book, which contains both pure CSS and table-based XHTML Web designs; email signatures, e-newsletters, and Photoshop designs that do not have code written for them. All the files are constructed in a similar fashion, which makes understanding and customizing more than one of them a consistent process. This chapter not only explains how to customize such templates, but also provides basic Photoshop tips that can be used to quickly customize the templates.

STEPS TO CUSTOMIZING A TEMPLATE

There are six basic steps to customizing a template. The basic process involves customizing and saving a Photoshop file, which outputs .gif and .jpg files that preprogrammed XHTML (HTML), Cascading Stylesheets, and, possibly, JavaScript files then use to display, along with text. Following are the six steps:

Step 1: Open the main Photoshop file.

Step 2: Customize images and colors in the Photoshop file(s).

Step 3: Optimize and save necessary images used by a preprogrammed XHTML (HTML), CSS, and, possibly, JavaScript file(s).

Step 4: Open an XHTML (HTML), CSS, or JavaScript file(s) with an HTML editor.

Step 5: Customize text and any other code, all of which is open source.

Step 6: Test the design.

The example used for this chapter is Web template 57 on the CD-ROM (see Figure 10.1). While most of the designs have only one .psd file used for both the home page and a secondary template(s), some may have an additional file(s) for secondary pages. The same steps are to be applied for these files because they are created in and function the same as the main Photoshop file.

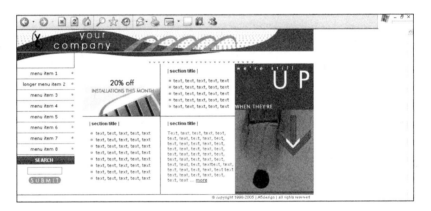

FIGURE 10.1   The design that is customized is this chapter.

Step 1: Open the Main Photoshop File

After copying the files from the CD-ROM and pasting them on the computer, the designer needs to locate and open the main design file (`design_57.psd`) in Photoshop (see Figure 10.2).

The templates included with this book are saved in Photoshop versions 6 or higher. Adobe has continually changed how its software handles text, and Photoshop 8 (Photoshop CS) is no exception. When opening a file in a more recent version, Photoshop will ask if the reader wants to update the file (see Figure 10.3). Selecting Update, will cause the vector-based text to have its positioning slightly readjusted.

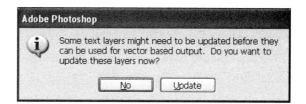

FIGURE 10.3   Photoshop dialog box asking if a file should have text updated.

FIGURE 10.2   The location of the files on the CD-ROM.

Step 2: Customizing Images and Colors in the Photoshop File(s)

Making and saving changes in Photoshop (see Figure 10.4) will change all the images in a design and many of the colors, as well. Colors that are not changed when saving a Photoshop file can be changed in the XHTML or CSS files.

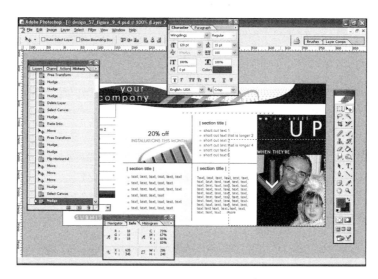

FIGURE 10.4   Design in Photoshop, with its colors and photos customized.

Step 3: Optimize and Save Necessary Images Used by a Preprogrammed XHTML (HTML), CSS, and/or JavaScript File(s)

Once changes have been made to the Photoshop file, the designer will need to save the file so the necessary .gif and .jpg images are saved from the sliced Photoshop file. Following are the steps to do so:

1. Select the Save For Web option from the File drop down in Photoshop's menu (see Figure 10.5).

FIGURE 10.5 Design being optimized with Photoshop's Save For Web function.

2. Click on the Slice Select Tool from the menu on the left (see Figure 10.6).
3. Select a slice to be optimized and select the compression on the right side of the window (see Figure 10.7).

NOTE

If the designer changes the type of image a slice is saved as, such as .gif to .jpg, the file extension must be changed in the CSS or XHTML template as well. For example, if photo_middle_right *is changed from a .jpg file to a .gif file, all references to* photo_middle_right.jpg *in the template must be changed to* photo_middle_right.gif.

4. Ensure that all changed slices of the template are still compressed to the proper level possible.
5. Select Save in the top-right area of the Save For Web window.
6. Select Replace in the Replace Files window.

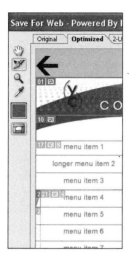

FIGURE 10.6 Slice Select Tool selected in the Save For Web window.

FIGURE 10.7 The slice that has its file type and compression assigned in the Save For Web window.

Once a user clicks on Replace, Photoshop will save all slices as either .gifs or .jpgs from the file and place them in an Images subdirectory below where the design_57.html *file is saved.*

Step 4: Open an XHTML (HTML), CSS, and/or JavaScript File(s) Included with the Design

All three file types can be opened in any HTML editor. In Figure 10.8 the sample file is opened in Macromedia's ColdFusion Studio.

Step 5: Customize Text and, Possibly, XHTML (HTML), CSS, or JavaScript Code

Once a template file has been opened in an HTML editor, it can be easily modified and saved however the designer may choose. Following are suggestions for customizing such files:

- Always save a backup to revert to or pull original pieces of code from, if necessary.
- Check pages in a browser frequently (Step 6).
- Switch the CSS or table border value to 1 where code is being customized. This allows the designer to better understand how the design is constructed.
- Ensure that the location and image name for each menu item is consistent when working with XHTML templates that use mouseovers in the menu (see Listing 10.1). No two menu items can have the same location and image names.

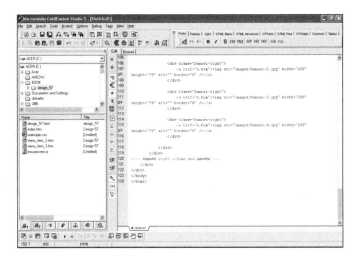

FIGURE 10.8   A file opened in Macromedia's ColdFusion Studio HTML Editing software.

LISTING 10.1   Unique JavaScript Names for Mouseover Code

```
<tr>
    <td valign="top"><img src="images/bullet_menu_off.gif" width="18"
        height="20" alt="" border="0" name="menu_item_1"></td>
    <td class="white2"><a href="index.htm" style="text-decoration:
        none; color: #ffffff" onmouseover="document.menu_item_1.src=
        bullet_menu_on.src;"
onmouseout="document.menu_item_1.src=bullet_menu_off.src"><b>menu
    item 1</b></a></td>
</tr>
```

Step 6: Test the Design

As soon as a designer makes a change to a template, it should be opened in a browser or, better yet, in various browsers, depending on how thorough the designer wants the testing to be. Then, as changes are made to the template from the HTML editor, the user should continually refresh the browser(s) to ensure that the changes were made correctly. To open a design in IE, for example, the user follows six steps:

1. Click File from the browser's menu items.
2. Click Open.
3. Click Browse.
4. Click on index.htm, which is the home page for the design in Figure 10.9.
5. Click on Open to open the file in a browser.
6. Click OK to confirm opening the file.

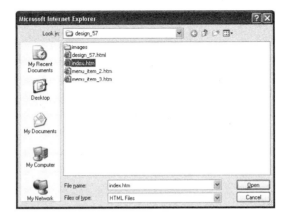

FIGURE 10.9   A locally saved index.htm file that is opened in IE 6.

TUTORIAL   PHOTOSHOP

This section includes tutorials on basic techniques a designer or developer will usually need to know to customize a design. They include replacing photos, resizing photos, changing colors, and undoing or redoing actions.

Replacing Photos

Not all designs can have photos in them replaced in the code. With many mortised designs, the process of replacing a photo first begins with the Photoshop file, using masks. Following are instructions on replacing a photo in a Photoshop template, using the original photo as a mask:

1. Make sure the Layers window is visible (see Figure 10.10).
2. Click on the Layers option in the drop down menu (see Figure 10.11).
3. Make sure the Layers tab is selected in the window. If it is not, click on it (see Figure 10.11).
4. Open the image to be inserted into the existing image.
5. Select the entire image (Ctrl-A for Windows; Cmd-A for Macintosh) and then copy that image (Ctrl + C for Windows; Cmd-C for Macintosh) (see Figure 10.12).
6. Select the layer of the photo in the design (in this example, it is the upside-down photo of the man) that is going to be replaced.

FIGURE 10.10   The Layers window in Photoshop where different layers may be selected. Click on the Window menu item in the top menu bar.

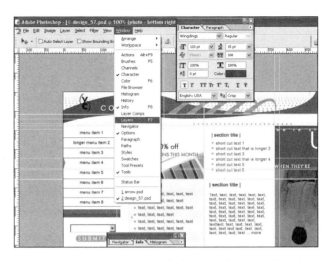

FIGURE 10.11   The Layers window can be turned on from the Window drop-down menu item.

FIGURE 10.12   The image selected that will be used in the design.

NOTE

Windows users can right-click the photo to be replaced and then select the layer's name, which will send the user directly to that layer (see Figure 10.13). The user may have more than one option to select, so if they are not already named, it might be necessary to click on the various layers until the correct one is selected.

7. Click on the layer in the Layers window. Once this layer has been selected, the content on the layer will be available to be edited.

A layer can be made to be visible or invisible by clicking the eye, located to the left of the layer name, on and off (see Figure 10.14). Toggling the eye on and off is a good way to test if the correct layer has been selected.

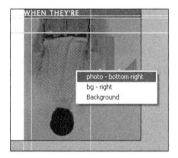

FIGURE 10.13 Possible layers to select if the user right-clicks on an image.

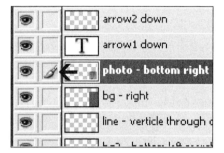

FIGURE 10.14 Toggling the eye on a layer will turn it off and on in the Photoshop file.

8. Activate the layer's image by selecting the entire layer area (Ctrl-A for Windows; Cmd-A for Macintosh) and move the layer up one pixel (one click) and down one pixel by using the up and down arrow keys (see Figure 10.15).

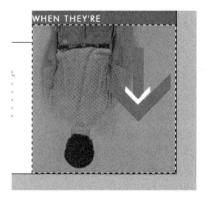

FIGURE 10.15 The image that will be used as a mask must first be selected.

The image is selected when the "marching ants" (moving dotted lines) are marching around that specific image or at least the part of the image that is viewable within the borders of the Photoshop file. Prior to moving the image up and down one pixel, ants will be marching around the border of the entire Photoshop file. If the marching ants are displayed in a square or rectangular shape that is larger than the image (see Figure 10.16), then the image is already set as a mask. If this occurs, the user must turn off the photo by turning off the eye for its layer and restarting this tutorial at step 3, this time selecting the correct layer (the square image that contains the actual photo).

9. Insert the image already copied in step 2 (Figure 10.12) by pressing Shift-Ctrl-V for Windows or Shift-Cmd-V for Macintosh. The image will then be placed inside the existing image (see Figure 10.17).

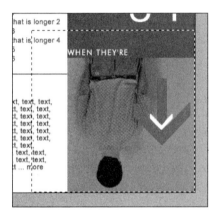

FIGURE 10.16   How the marching ants would appear if the image were already saved as a mask.

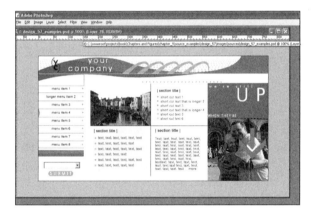

FIGURE 10.17   The design after both the selected image and the one in the center have been added into their respective masks.

TUTORIAL   **RESIZING PHOTOS**

Following are instructions on resizing a photo in Photoshop. Although this tutorial explains how to resize a photo in a mask, the same process occurs when resizing any photo or image on any layer.

1. Make sure the Layers window is visible (see Figure 10.10).

2. Select the layer of the photo in the design (in this example, it is the couple hugging) that is going to be replaced (see Figure 10.13).

3. Click on the layer in the Layers window. Once this layer has been selected, the content will be available to be edited.

4. Activate the layer's image by selecting the entire layer area (Ctrl-A for Windows; Cmd-A for Macintosh) and move the layer up one pixel (one click) and down one pixel by using the up and down arrow keys (see Figure 10.18).

The image in Figure 10.18 extends below and to the right of the design. The marching ants, however, will remain inside the Photoshop file.

5. Activate the outer frame of the image by hitting Ctrl-T for Windows or Cmd-T for Macintosh. Once the outer frame is active, small square handles in the corners will appear (see Figure 10.19).

6. Resize the image by clicking and dragging any of the corners on the frame that turn the mouse into an up or down arrow image.

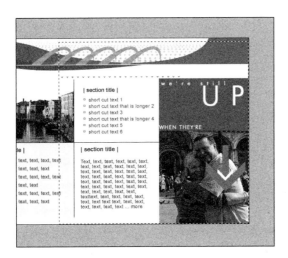

FIGURE 10.18 The photo after it has been activated in the window.

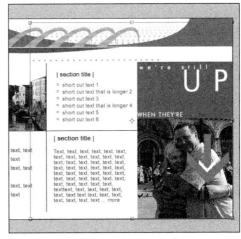

FIGURE 10.19 Small handles will appear when the image is ready to be resized.

Often the image will need to be resized proportionately. Holding the Shift key and the handles simultaneously, while dragging, will ensure that the image's proportions remain the same.

7. During the resizing process, the image can also be moved. To do so, select the Move Tool (see Figure 10.20) in the toolbar and click and drag the image rather than the handles.
8. Deactivate the marching ants by hitting Ctrl-D for Windows or Cmd-D for Macintosh once the image has been resized and located correctly (see Figure 10.21). The border and corners will then disappear.

FIGURE 10.20   The Move tool included in the menu bar.

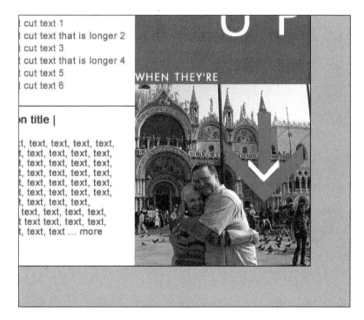

FIGURE 10.21   The photo after it has been resized and moved.

TUTORIAL   ## CHANGING COLORS

Changing the colors of a design often begins with the Photoshop file because the colors are saved as images, rather than browser-generated colors. Following are instructions on changing colors of solid objects in a Photoshop template:

1. Make sure the Layers window is visible (see Figure 10.10).
2. Select the layer of the photo in the design (in this example, it is the couple hugging) that is going to be replaced (see Figure 10.13).
3. Click on the layer in the Layers window. Once this layer has been selected, content on the layer will be available to be edited.
4. Select the layer of the photo in the design (in this example, the top-right corner) that is going to be changed (see Figure 10.22).

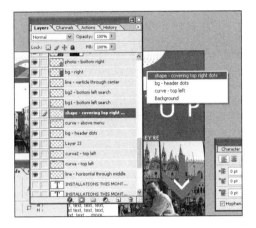

FIGURE 10.22 The layer, which represents the top-right curve of the design, to be recolored.

5. Click on the layer in the Layers window. Once this layer has been selected, the content on the layer will be available to be edited.
6. Activate the layer's image by selecting the entire layer area (Ctrl-A for Windows; Cmd-A for Macintosh) and move the layer up one pixel (one click) and down one pixel by using the up and down arrow keys (see Figure 10.23).

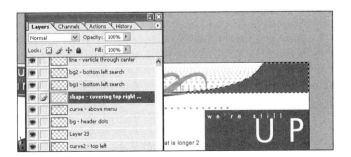

FIGURE 10.23 The image that will be recolored once it has been activated.

7. Click the Color Picker in the toolbar to pop open the Color Picker window and select a color to replace the color with (see Figure 10.24).

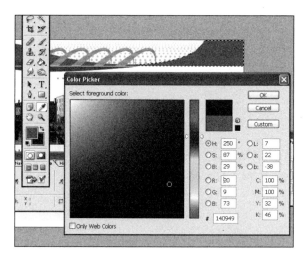

FIGURE 10.24   The color that is selected, using the Color Picker, which is selected from the menu bar.

8. Click OK to close the Color Picker window once the color has been selected.
9. Select Fill from the Edit drop down in the menu area (see Figure 10.25).
10. Click OK to confirm the fill (see Figure 10.26).

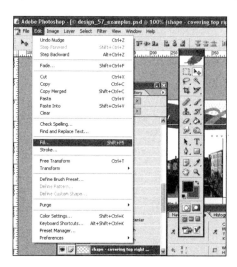

FIGURE 10.25   The Fill action in the Edit drop-down window.

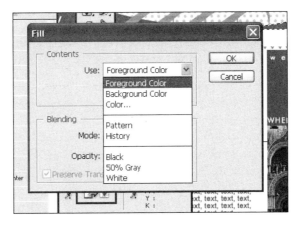

FIGURE 10.26   The Fill window, with the various possibilities the Use drop-down menu offers.

11. Deactivate the marching ants by hitting Ctrl-D for Windows or Cmd-D for Macintosh once the color has been replaced, or "filled." Figure 10.27 shows the design with many of the colors changed.

FIGURE 10.27   The design once many of the colors have been changed.

TUTORIAL   **UNDOING AND REDOING ACTIONS**

The designer can undo and redo actions in Photoshop. This tutorial outlines the hot keys for undoing actions, but, more importantly, it shows how to configure Photoshop to allow for actions to be undone.

Undoing Actions

To undo an action using hot keys, the user needs to select Ctrl-Alt-Z for Windows and Cmd-Alt-Z for Macintosh. By holding down the Ctrl (or Cmd) and Alt keys, the user can repeatedly click the letter Z to go back however many actions the program has been configured to allow.

Redoing Actions

After undoing actions, the user can click Ctrl-Z for Windows and Cmd-Z for Macintosh to redo all the actions. By repeatedly hitting this key combination, the user can toggle between the two different states of change. This is useful when deciding how a certain image or color will look compared to the older version.

Configuring the Undo Actions (History States) Setting

Undoing actions has a limit with the default settings of Photoshop, so the user needs to first change the settings to ensure that it will allow a certain number of changes. Following are instruction on how to do so:

1. Select the General selection under the Preferences selection under the Edit menu item (see Figure 10.28).

FIGURE 10.28   The General preferences menu item, selected from the Edit drop-down menu.

2. Change the History States setting to the number of changes Photoshop should be able to revert back to. The number of changes in this example is changed to 20 (see Figure 10.29).

In some versions of Photoshop, the number of changes a designer can make is one less than what is stated in the History States. Therefore, to be safe, the user should increase the number by one.

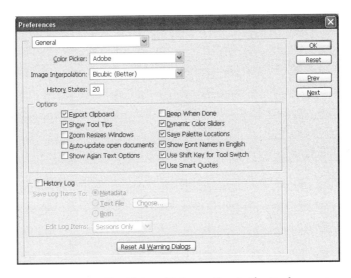

FIGURE 10.29   The History States option in the Preferences window, which is set at 20.

3. Click OK to confirm the changes.

SUMMARY

Because all the designs included in this book are built similarly, they also are customized in very much the same way. This chapter not only explains the steps to customizing a design, but it also provides brief Photoshop tutorials on how to make changes in the software. These tutorials include replacing photos, resizing photos, changing colors, and undoing and redoing actions. Filled with images, this chapter offers a quick read for fundamental Photoshop skills.

11 Designs Included on the CD-ROM

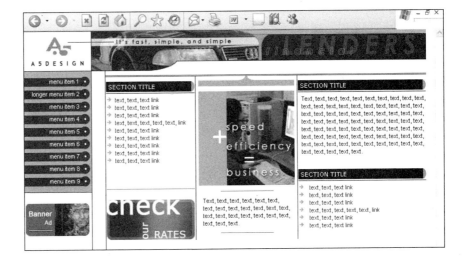

Of the 140 designs included on the CD-ROM that comes with the book, several types are included for various reasons. From designs that are created solely as Photoshop files to designs that not only include Photoshop files but also have been coded, the collection gives the reader many options that can simply serve as inspiration or be customized and used as working designs:

Designs 1–80: XHTML table-based designs that were originally created for 800 × 600 resolution but were also coded as liquid designs, which allows for them to expand to greater widths. One of the strengths of these designs is a large variety of potential layouts.

Designs 81–90: XHTML e-newsletters that can be either emailed from a browser or embedded into an email and then emailed. These designs incorporate very little CSS to ensure a higher rate of visual consistency among the many different email clients.

E-newsletters can be sent a number of ways. One of the simplest ways is to upload the file to a server and in IE 5, 5.5., or 6 select File/Send/Page by E-mail. The browser will then open the email software, such as Microsoft Outlook, and embed the file into a new email. The user then sends the email like any other email. It is important to note that all images included in such a file need to be stored on a server and given absolute addresses, such as <img src="http://www.a5design.com/ sample_newsletter/header.gif ">, rather than <img src="images/header.gif">. If assigned a relative address, the email will look for that image on the recipient's system, where the image will not exist.

Designs 91–100: XHTML signatures that can be embedded into email messages, many times working in conjunction with a Web site and/or e-newsletter to provide a consistent branding.

Emails with signature files can be sent in a variety of ways. One way is to save the XHTML file on the computer that contains the user's email software. Then in software, such as Microsoft Outlook, go to Tools/Options/Mail Format and select the file. The software will then embed the file into the email. It is important to note that all images included in such a file need to be stored on a server and given absolute addresses, such as <img src="http://www.a5design.com/sample_newsletter/header.gif">, rather than <img src="images/header.gif">. If assigned a relative address, the email will look for that image on the recipient's system, where the image will not exist. To send an email with a signature, the user should first read about how to do so with the email software that is being used to send email. Not all software offers the same functionality.

Designs 101–110: Photoshop designs created for 800 × 600 resolution but can be easily modified for 1024 × 768 resolution. These designs have not been coded.

Designs 111–120: Photoshop designs created for 1024 × 768 resolution. These designs have not been coded.

Designs 121–130: CSS designs created for 800 × 600 resolution. Because the designs are liquid, they can be easily modified to fit higher resolutions or be centered within the browser in a fixed format.

Designs 131–140: CSS designs created for 1024 × 768 resolution. Because the designs are liquid, they can be easily modified to fit higher resolutions or be centered within the browser in a fixed format.

On-line color versions of all the designs included with this book can be found at http://www.a5design.com/a5-book-designs.

When selecting a design, it is important for the reader to realize that the color and/or images can be easily modified. The layout is what should be the driving force behind selecting a design. Layout considerations include whether the title and logo are given the right placement and prominence, whether the menu is horizontal or vertical, how many initial text sections are provided, and how scalable the design is for future functionality and growth.

All designs have been validated by the W3C's CSS and XHTML validators.

The commented code in the mainstyle.css file of several CSS web designs should be disregarded: /*this value added for Holly Hack to position menu to the left 3 pixels */. The code is not used for the "Holly Hack."

DESIGN 1

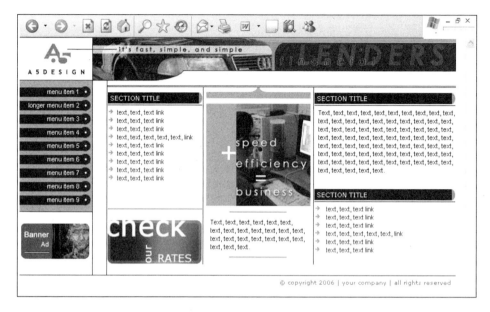

FIGURE 11.1   Design 1 home page design.

FIGURE 11.2   Design 1 second-level template for less content.

FIGURE 11.3   Design 1 second-level template for more content.

Photoshop source file name: Designs/1-80-xhtml-web/design_1/images/sources/design_1.psd

XHTML pages: index.htm, menu_item_2.htm, menu_item_3.htm

Photo credits: A5design

DESIGN 2

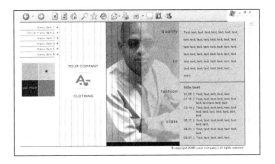

FIGURE 11.4   Design 2 home page design.

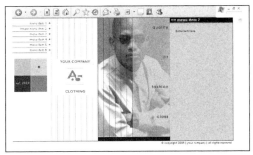

FIGURE 11.5   Design 2 second-level template for less content.

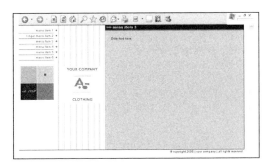

FIGURE 11.6   Design 2 second-level template for more content.

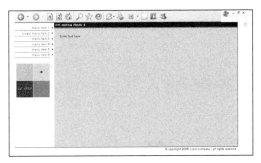

FIGURE 11.7   Design 2 second-level template for more content.

Photoshop source file name: `Designs/1-80-xhtml-web/design_2/images/sources/design_2.psd`

XHTML pages: `index.htm, menu_item_2.htm, menu_item_3.htm, menu_item_4.htm`

Photo credits: Lisa Murillo

DESIGN 3

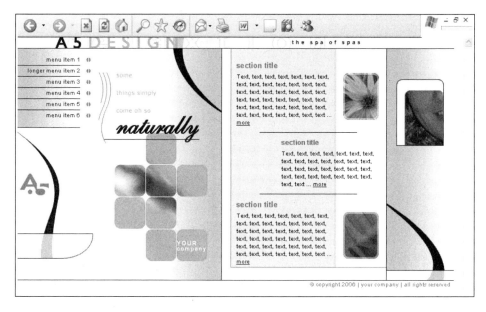

FIGURE 11.8 Design 3 home page design.

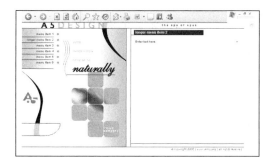

FIGURE 11.9 Design 3 second-level template for less content.

FIGURE 11.10 Design 3 second-level template for more content.

Photoshop source file names: Designs/1-80-xhtml-web/design_3/images/sources/design_3.psd, bg_center_column.psd

XHTML pages: index.htm, menu_item_2.htm, menu_item_3.htm

Photo credits: Justin Discoe

DESIGN 4

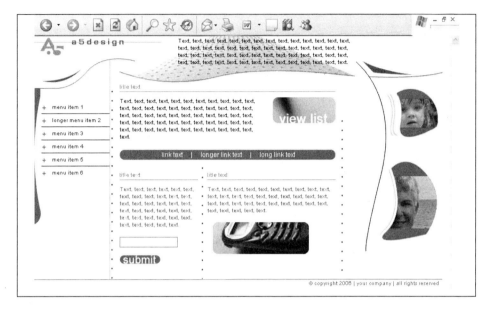

FIGURE 11.11   Design 4 home page design.

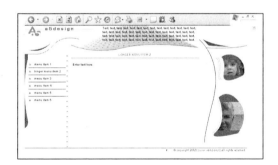

FIGURE 11.12   Design 4 second-level template for less content.

FIGURE 11.13   Design 4 second-level template for more content.

Photoshop source file names: `Designs/1-80-xhtml-web/design_4/images/sources/design_4.psd, bg_top_photo.psd`

XHTML pages: `index.htm, menu_item_2.htm, menu_item_3.htm`

Photo credits: A5design

DESIGN 5

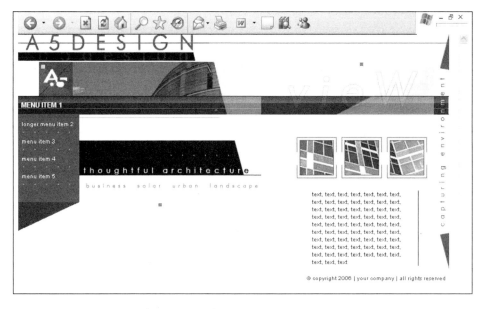

FIGURE 11.14 Design 5 home page design.

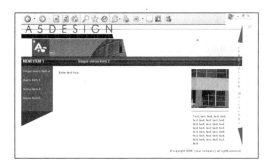

FIGURE 11.15 Design 5 second-level template for less content.

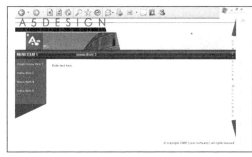

FIGURE 11.16 Design 5 second-level template for more content.

Photoshop source file name: Designs/1-80-xhtml-web/design_5/images/sources/design_5.psd

XHTML pages: index.htm, menu_item_2.htm, menu_item_3.htm

Photo credits: A5design

DESIGN 6

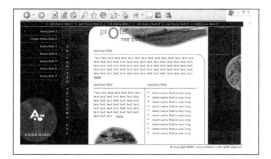

FIGURE 11.17 Design 6 home page design.

FIGURE 11.18 Design 6 second-level template for less content.

FIGURE 11.19 Design 6 second-level template for more content.

FIGURE 11.20 Design 6 second-level template for more content.

Photoshop source file name: `Designs/1-80-xhtml-web/design_6/images/sources/design_6.psd`

XHTML pages: `index.htm, menu_item_2.htm, menu_item_3.htm, menu_item_4.htm`

Photo credits: Joe Eccher

DESIGN 7

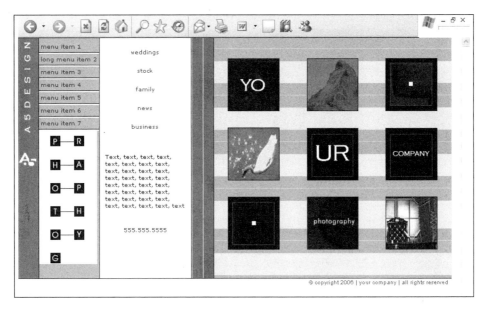

FIGURE 11.21 Design 7 home page design.

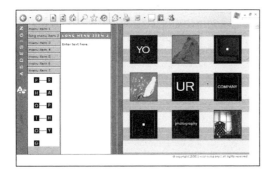

FIGURE 11.22 Design 7 second-level template for less content.

FIGURE 11.23 Design 7 second-level template for more content.

Photoshop source file name: Designs/1-80-xhtml-web/design_7/images/sources/
design_7.psd

XHTML pages: index.htm, menu_item_2.htm, menu_item_3.htm

Photo credits: Joe Eccher

DESIGN 8

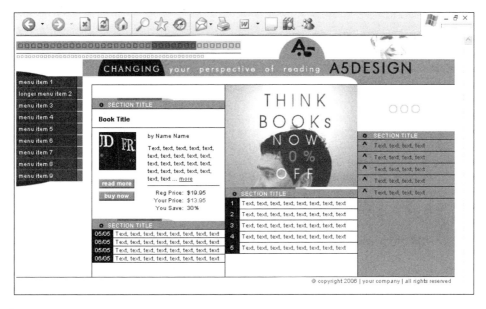

FIGURE 11.24 Design 8 home page design.

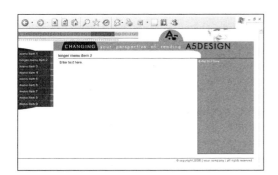

FIGURE 11.25 Design 8 second-level template for less content.

FIGURE 11.26 Design 8 second-level template for more content.

Photoshop source file name: `Designs/1-80-xhtml-web/design_8/images/sources/design_8.psd`

XHTML pages: `index.htm`, `menu_item_2.htm`, `menu_item_3.htm`

Photo credits: Lisa Murillo

DESIGN 9

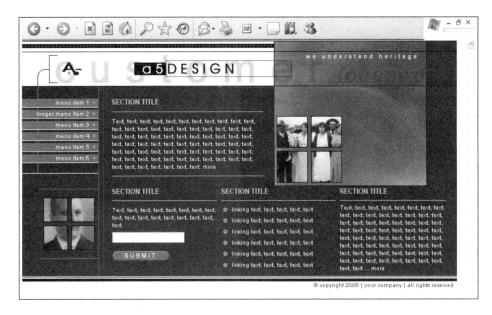

FIGURE 11.27   Design 9 home page design.

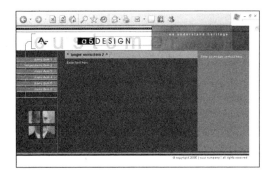

FIGURE 11.28   Design 9 second-level template for less content.

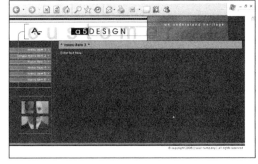

FIGURE 11.29   Design 9 second-level template for more content.

Photoshop source file name: Designs/1-80-xhtml-web/design_9/images/sources/design_9.psd

XHTML pages: index.htm, menu_item_2.htm, menu_item_3.htm

Photo credits: Joe Eccher

DESIGN 10

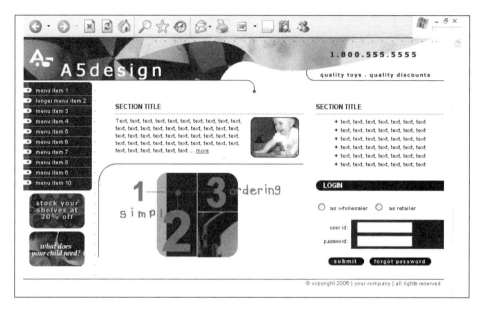

FIGURE 11.30   Design 10 home page design.

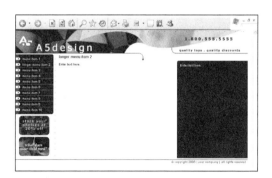

FIGURE 11.31   Design 10 second-level template for less content.

FIGURE 11.32   Design 10 second-level template for more content.

Photoshop source file name: `Designs/1-80-xhtml-web/design_10/images/sources/design_10.psd`

XHTML pages: `index.htm`, `menu_item_2.htm`, `menu_item_3.htm`

Photo credits: Lisa Murillo, A5design

DESIGN 11

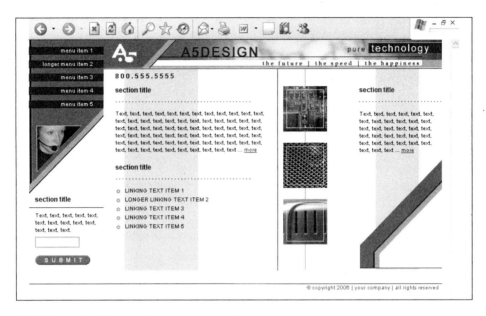

FIGURE 11.33 Design 11 home page design.

FIGURE 11.34 Design 11 second-level template for less content.

FIGURE 11.35 Design 11 second-level template for more content.

Photoshop source file name: `Designs/1-80-xhtml-web/design_11/images/sources/design_11.psd`

XHTML pages: `index.htm, menu_item_2.htm, menu_item_3.htm`

Photo credits: Lisa Murillo, A5design

DESIGN 12

FIGURE 11.36   Design 12 home page design.

FIGURE 11.37   Design 12 second-level template for less content.

FIGURE 11.38   Design 12 second-level template for more content.

Photoshop source file name: Designs/1-80-xhtml-web/design_12/images/sources/design_12.psd

XHTML pages: index.htm, menu_item_2.htm, menu_item_3.htm

Photo credits: Joe Eccher, A5design

DESIGN 13

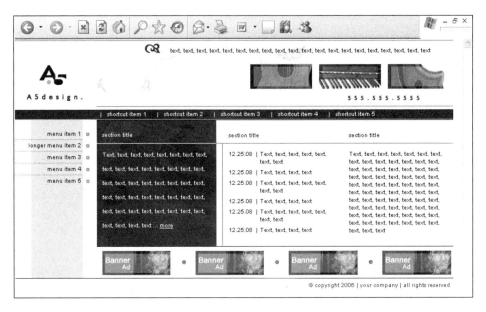

FIGURE 11.39   Design 13 home page design.

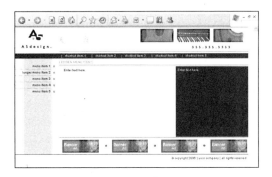

FIGURE 11.40   Design 13 second-level template for less content.

FIGURE 11.41   Design 13 second-level template for more content.

Photoshop source file name: Designs/1-80-xhtml-web/design_13/images/sources/design_13.psd

XHTML pages: index.htm, menu_item_2.htm, menu_item_3.htm

Photo credits: A5design

DESIGN 14

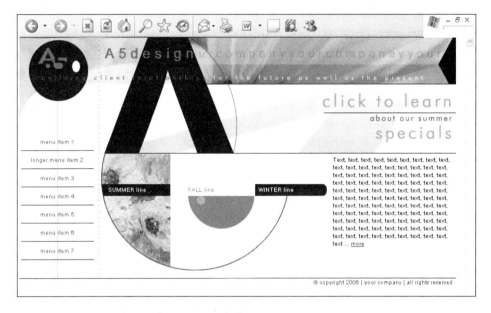

FIGURE 11.42   Design 14 home page design.

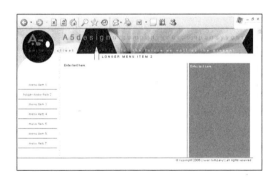

FIGURE 11.43   Design 14 second-level template for less content.

FIGURE 11.44   Design 14 second-level template for more content.

Photoshop source file name: Designs/1-80-xhtml-web/design_14/images/sources/
design_14.psd

XHTML pages: index.htm, menu_item_2.htm, menu_item_3.htm

Photo credits: A5design

DESIGN 15

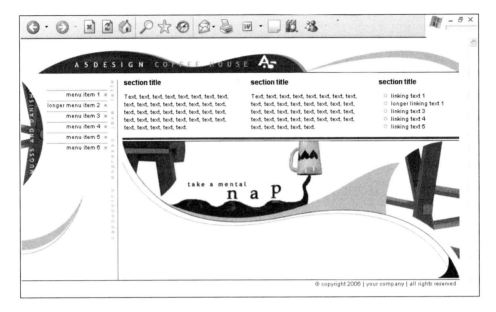

FIGURE 11.45 Design 15 home page design.

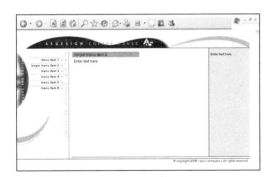

FIGURE 11.46 Design 15 second-level template for less content.

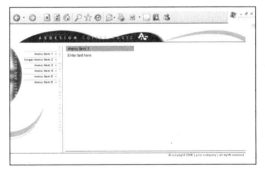

FIGURE 11.47 Design 15 second-level template for more content.

Photoshop source file name: Designs/1-80-xhtml-web/design_15/images/sources/design_15.psd

XHTML pages: index.htm, menu_item_2.htm, menu_item_3.htm

Photo credits: A5design

DESIGN 16

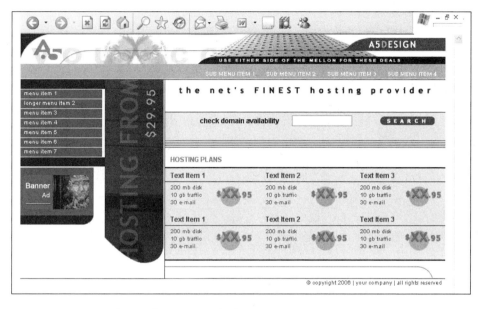

FIGURE 11.48   Design 16 home page design.

FIGURE 11.49   Design 16 second-level template for less content.

FIGURE 11.50   Design 16 second-level template for more content.

Photoshop source file name: `Designs/1-80-xhtml-web/design_16/images/sources/design_16.psd`

XHTML pages: `index.htm, menu_item_2.htm, menu_item_3.htm`

Photo credits: A5design

DESIGN 17

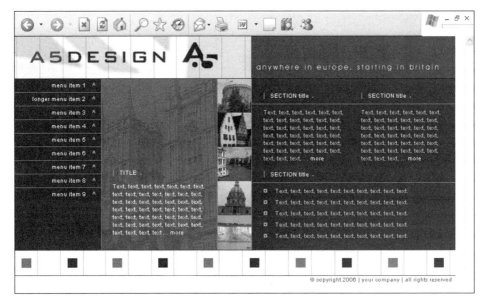

FIGURE 11.51   Design 17 home page design.

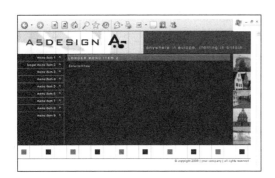

FIGURE 11.52   Design 17 second-level template for less content.

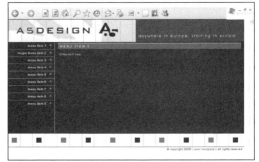

FIGURE 11.53   Design 17 second-level template for more content.

Photoshop source file name: `Designs/1-80-xhtml-web/design_17/images/sources/design_17.psd`

XHTML pages: `index.htm, menu_item_2.htm, menu_item_3.htm`

Photo credits: A5design

DESIGN 18

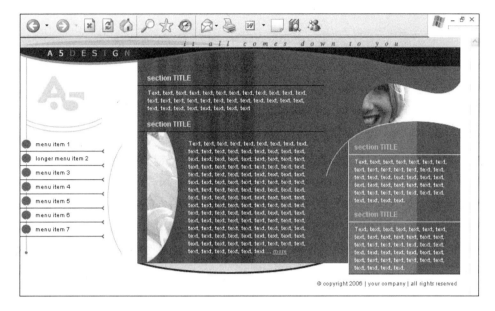

FIGURE 11.54   Design 18 home page design.

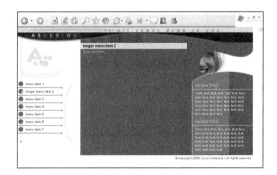

FIGURE 11.55   Design 18 second-level template for less content.

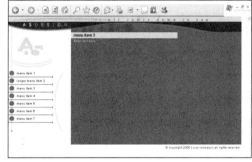

FIGURE 11.56   Design 18 second-level template for more content.

Photoshop source file names: `Designs/1-80-xhtml-web/design_18/images/sources/design_18.psd, bg_left_columnpsd`

XHTML pages: `index.htm, menu_item_2.htm, menu_item_3.htm`

Photo credits: A5design

DESIGN 19

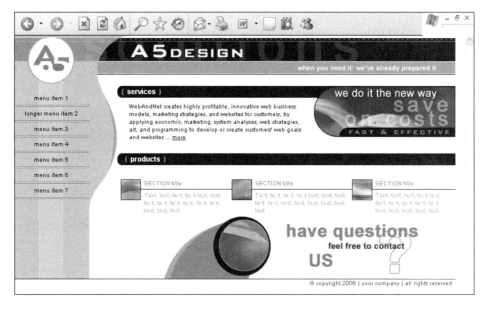

FIGURE 11.57 Design 19 home page design.

FIGURE 11.58 Design 19 second-level template for less content.

FIGURE 11.59 Design 19 second-level template for more content.

Photoshop source file name: Designs/1-80-xhtml-web/design_19/images/sources/design_19.psd

XHTML pages: index.htm, menu_item_2.htm, menu_item_3.htm

Photo credits: A5design

DESIGN 20

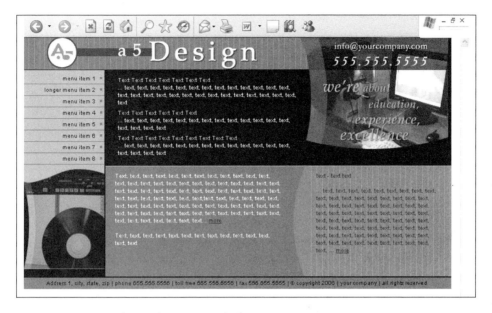

FIGURE 11.60   Design 20 home page design.

FIGURE 11.61   Design 20 second-level template for less content.

FIGURE 11.62   Design 20 second-level template for more content.

Photoshop source file name: Designs/1-80-xhtml-web/design_20/images/sources/design_20.psd

XHTML pages: index.htm, menu_item_2.htm, menu_item_3.htm

Photo credits: A5design

DESIGN 21

FIGURE 11.63 Design 21 home page design.

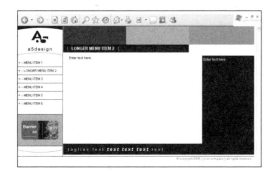

FIGURE 11.64 Design 21 second-level template for less content.

FIGURE 11.65 Design 21 second-level template for more content.

Photoshop source file name: Designs/1-80-xhtml-web/design_21/images/sources/design_21.psd

XHTML pages: index.htm, menu_item_2.htm, menu_item_3.htm

Photo credits: Joe Eccher

DESIGN 22

FIGURE 11.66   Design 22 home page design.

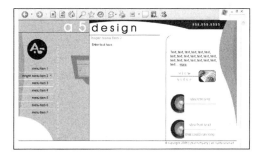

FIGURE 11.67   Design 22 second-level template for less content.

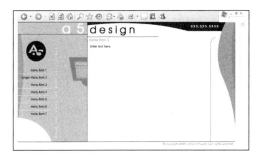

FIGURE 11.68   Design 22 second-level template for more content.

FIGURE 11.69   Design 22 second-level template for more content.

FIGURE 11.70   Design 22 second-level template for more content.

Photoshop source file names: Designs/1-80-xhtml-web/design_22/images/sources/design_22.psd, bg_menu.psd

XHTML pages: index.htm, menu_item_2.htm, menu_item_3.htm, menu_item_4.htm, menu_item_5.htm

Photo credits: A5design

DESIGN 23

FIGURE 11.71 Design 23 home page design.

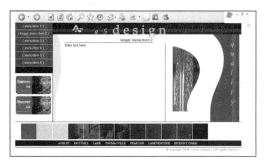

FIGURE 11.72 Design 23 second-level template for less content.

FIGURE 11.73 Design 23 second-level template for more content.

FIGURE 11.74 Design 23 second-level template for more content.

Photoshop source file name: Designs/1-80-xhtml-web/design_23/images/sources/design_23.psd

XHTML pages: index.htm, menu_item_2.htm, menu_item_3.htm, menu_item_4.htm

Photo credits: A5design

DESIGN 24

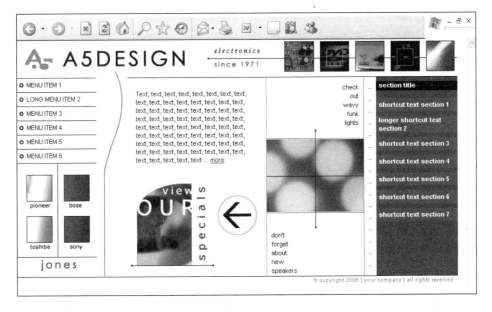

FIGURE 11.75   Design 24 home page design.

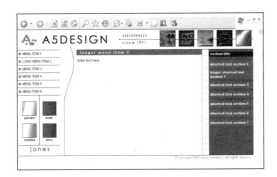

FIGURE 11.76   Design 24 second-level template for less content.

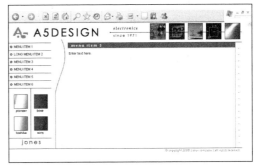

FIGURE 11.77   Design 24 second-level template for more content.

Photoshop source file name: `Designs/1-80-xhtml-web/design_24/images/sources/design_24.psd`

XHTML pages: `index.htm, menu_item_2.htm, menu_item_3.htm`

Photo credits: Lisa Murillo, A5design

DESIGN 25

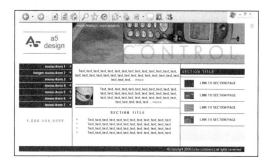

FIGURE 11.78 Design 25 home page design.

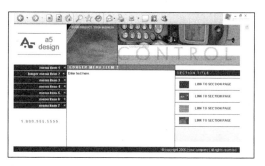

FIGURE 11.79 Design 25 second-level template for less content.

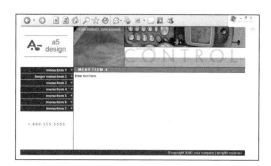

FIGURE 11.80 Design 25 second-level template for more content.

FIGURE 11.81 Design 25 second-level template for more content.

Photoshop source file name: Designs/1-80-xhtml-web/design_25/images/sources/design_25.psd

XHTML pages: index.htm, menu_item_2.htm, menu_item_3.htm, menu_item_4.htm

Photo credits: Lisa Murillo, A5design

DESIGN 26

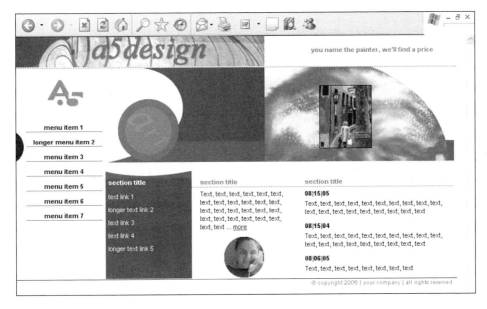

FIGURE 11.82   Design 26 home page design.

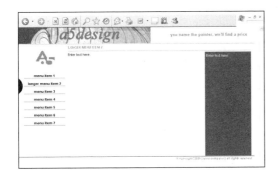

FIGURE 11.83   Design 26 second-level template for less content.

FIGURE 11.84   Design 26 second-level template for more content.

Photoshop source file name: `Designs/1-80-xhtml-web/design_26/images/sources/design_26.psd`

XHTML pages: `index.htm, menu_item_2.htm, menu_item_3.htm`

Photo credits: Justin Discoe, A5design

DESIGN 27

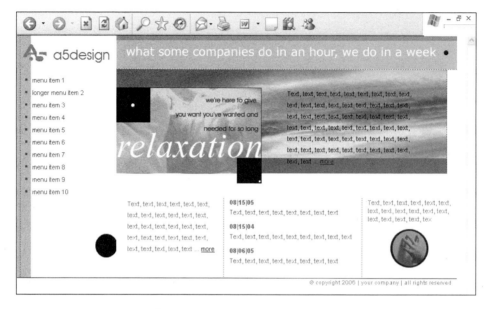

FIGURE 11.85 Design 27 home page design.

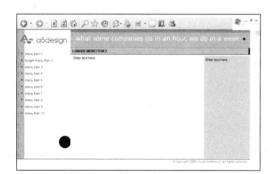

FIGURE 11.86 Design 27 second-level template for less content.

FIGURE 11.87 Design 27 second-level template for more content.

Photoshop source file name: Designs/1-80-xhtml-web/design_27/images/sources/design_27.psd

XHTML pages: index.htm, menu_item_2.htm, menu_item_3.htm

Photo credits: Joe Eccher, A5design

DESIGN 28

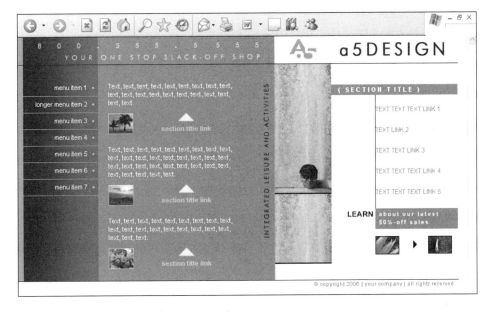

FIGURE 11.88   Design 28 home page design.

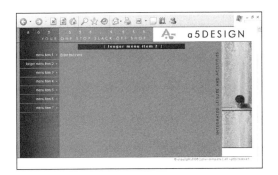

FIGURE 11.89   Design 28 second-level template for less content.

FIGURE 11.90   Design 28 second-level template for more content.

Photoshop source file name: `Designs/1-80-xhtml-web/design_28/images/sources/design_28.psd`

XHTML pages: `index.htm, menu_item_2.htm, menu_item_3.htm`

Photo credits: Joe Eccher

DESIGN 29

FIGURE 11.91 Design 29 home page design.

FIGURE 11.92 Design 29 second-level template for less content.

FIGURE 11.93 Design 29 second-level template for more content.

Photoshop source file name: Designs/1-80-xhtml-web/design_29/images/sources/design_29.psd

XHTML pages: index.htm, menu_item_2.htm, menu_item_3.htm

Photo credits: Joe Eccher

DESIGN 30

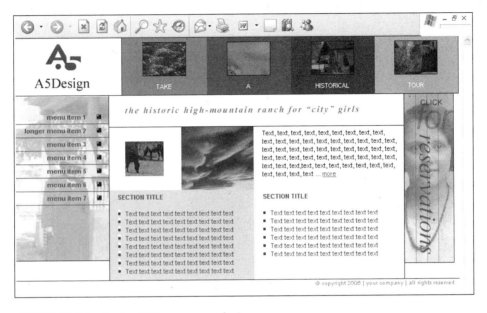

FIGURE 11.94 Design 30 home page design.

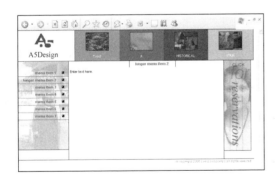

FIGURE 11.95 Design 30 second-level template for less content.

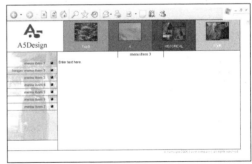

FIGURE 11.96 Design 30 second-level template for more content.

Photoshop source file names: Designs/1-80-xhtml-web/design_30/images/sources/
design_30.psd, bg_menu.psd

XHTML pages: index.htm, menu_item_2.htm, menu_item_3.htm

Photo credits: Joe Eccher

DESIGN 31

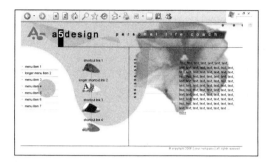

FIGURE 11.97 Design 31 home page design.

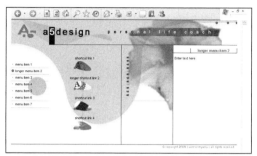

FIGURE 11.98 Design 31 second-level template for less content.

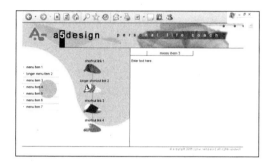

FIGURE 11.99 Design 31 second-level template for more content.

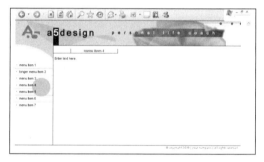

FIGURE 11.100 Design 31 second-level template for more content.

Photoshop source file names: Designs/1-80-xhtml-web/design_31/images/sources/design_31.psd, bg_images.psd

XHTML pages: index.htm, menu_item_2.htm, menu_item_3.htm, menu_item_4.htm

Photo credits: Joe Eccher, Justin Discoe

DESIGN 32

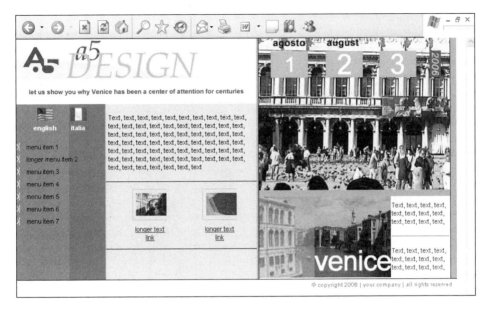

FIGURE 11.101 Design 32 home page design.

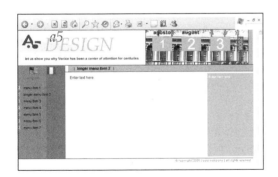

FIGURE 11.102 Design 32 second-level template for less content.

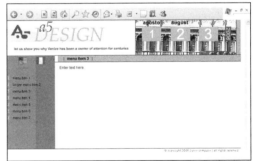

FIGURE 11.103 Design 32 second-level template for more content.

Photoshop source file name: Designs/1-80-xhtml-web/design_32/images/sources/design_32.psd

XHTML pages: index.htm, menu_item_2.htm, menu_item_3.htm

Photo credits: A5design

DESIGN 33

FIGURE 11.104 Design 33 home page design.

FIGURE 11.105 Design 33 second-level template for less content.

FIGURE 11.106 Design 33 second-level template for more content.

Photoshop source file names: Designs/1-80-xhtml-web/design_33/images/sources/ design_33.psd, bg_images.psd

XHTML pages: index.htm, menu_item_2.htm, menu_item_3.htm

Photo credits: A5design

DESIGN 34

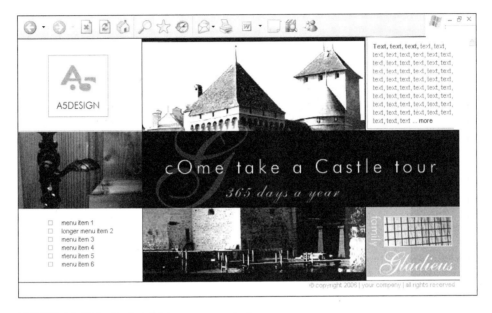

FIGURE 11.107   Design 34 home page design.

FIGURE 11.108   Design 34 second-level
template for less content.

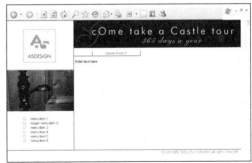

FIGURE 11.109   Design 34 second-level
template for more content.

Photoshop source file names: `Designs/1-80-xhtml-web/design_34/images/sources/`
`design_34.psd, sl_header.psd`

XHTML pages: `index.htm, menu_item_2.htm, menu_item_3.htm`

Photo credits: Joe Eccher

DESIGN 35

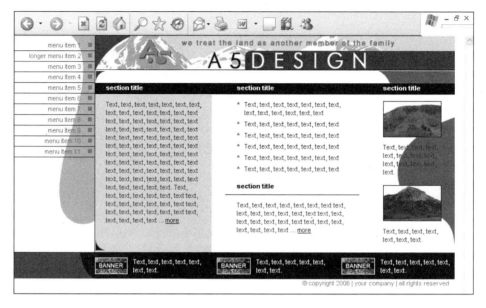

FIGURE 11.110 Design 35 home page design.

FIGURE 11.111 Design 35 second-level template for less content.

FIGURE 11.112 Design 35 second-level template for more content.

Photoshop source file names: Designs/1-80-xhtml-web/design_35/images/sources/ design_35.psd, bg_images.psd

XHTML pages: index.htm, menu_item_2.htm, menu_item_3.htm

Photo credits: Joe Eccher

DESIGN 36

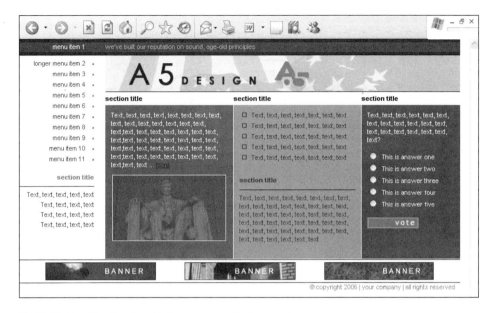

FIGURE 11.113   Design 36 home page design.

FIGURE 11.114   Design 36 second-level template for less content.

FIGURE 11.115   Design 36 second-level template for more content.

Photoshop source file names: `Designs/1-80-xhtml-web/design_36/images/sources/design_36.psd, bg_images.psd`

XHTML pages: `index.htm, menu_item_2.htm, menu_item_3.htm`

Photo credits: Justin Discoe, A5design

DESIGN 37

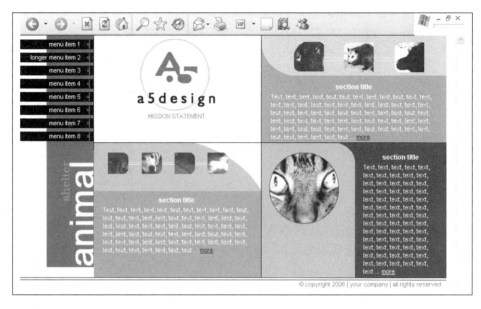

FIGURE 11.116   Design 37 home page design.

FIGURE 11.117   Design 37 second-level template for less content.

FIGURE 11.118   Design 37 second-level template for more content.

Photoshop source file names: `Designs/1-80-xhtml-web/design_37/images/sources/design_37.psd, design_37_sl.psd`

XHTML pages: `index.htm, menu_item_2.htm, menu_item_3.htm`

Photo credits: Lori Discoe

DESIGN 38

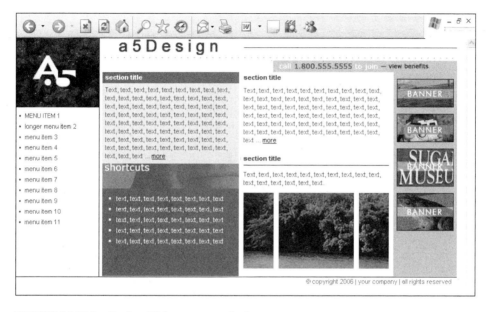

FIGURE 11.119   Design 38 home page design.

FIGURE 11.120   Design 38 second-level template for less content.

FIGURE 11.121   Design 38 second-level template for more content.

Photoshop source file name: Designs/1-80-xhtml-web/design_38/images/sources/
design_38.psd

XHTML pages: index.htm, menu_item_2.htm, menu_item_3.htm

Photo credits: A5design

DESIGN 39

FIGURE 11.122 Design 39 home page design.

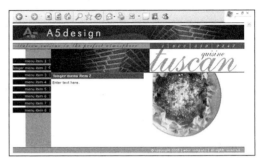

FIGURE 11.123 Design 39 second-level template for less content.

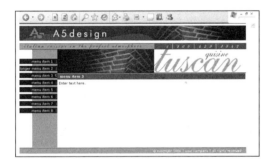

FIGURE 11.124 Design 39 second-level template for more content.

FIGURE 11.125 Design 39 second-level template for more content.

Photoshop source file name: Designs/1-80-xhtml-web/design_39/images/sources/design_39.psd

XHTML pages: index.htm, menu_item_2.htm, menu_item_3.htm, menu_item_4.htm

Photo credits: Lori Discoe

DESIGN 40

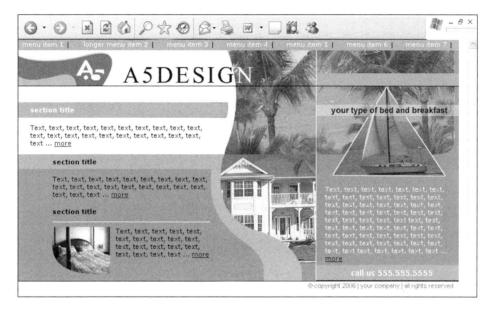

FIGURE 11.126 Design 40 home page design.

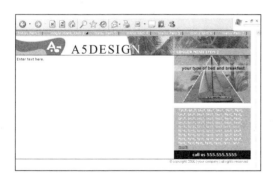

FIGURE 11.127 Design 40 second-level template for less content.

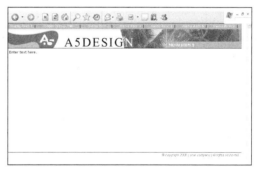

FIGURE 11.128 Design 40 second-level template for more content.

Photoshop source file name: Designs/1-80-xhtml-web/design_40/images/sources/design_40.psd

XHTML pages: index.htm, menu_item_2.htm, menu_item_3.htm

Photo credits: A5design

DESIGN 41

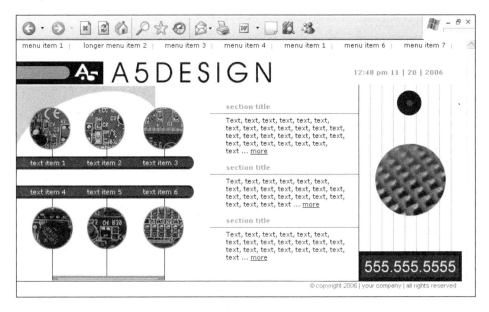

FIGURE 11.129 Design 41 home page design.

FIGURE 11.130 Design 41 second-level template for less content.

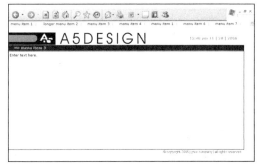

FIGURE 11.131 Design 41 second-level template for more content.

Photoshop source file name: `Designs/1-80-xhtml-web/design_41/images/sources/design_41.psd`

XHTML pages: `index.htm, menu_item_2.htm, menu_item_3.htm`

Photo credits: Lisa Murillo

DESIGN 42

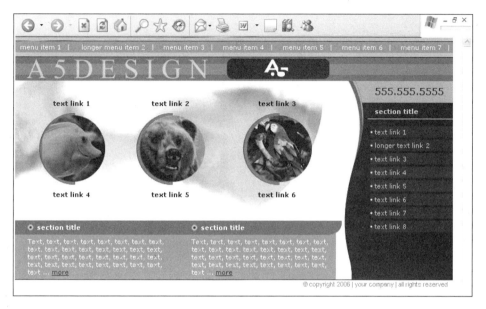

FIGURE 11.132   Design 42 home page design.

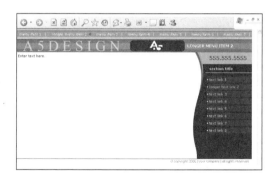

FIGURE 11.133   Design 42 second-level template for less content.

FIGURE 11.134   Design 42 second-level template for more content.

Photoshop source file name: Designs/1-80-xhtml-web/design_42/images/sources/design_42.psd

XHTML pages: index.htm, menu_item_2.htm, menu_item_3.htm

Photo credits: Lori Discoe

DESIGN 43

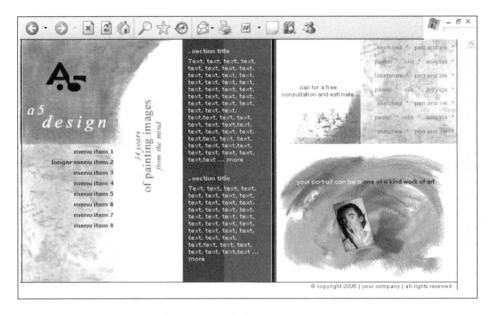

FIGURE 11.135   Design 43 home page design.

FIGURE 11.136   Design 43 second-level template for less content.

FIGURE 11.137   Design 43 second-level template for more content.

Photoshop source file name: Designs/1-80-xhtml-web/design_43/images/sources/design_43.psd

XHTML pages: index.htm, menu_item_2.htm, menu_item_3.htm

Photo credits: Lori Discoe

Chapter 11   Designs Included on the CD-ROM   **367**

DESIGN 44

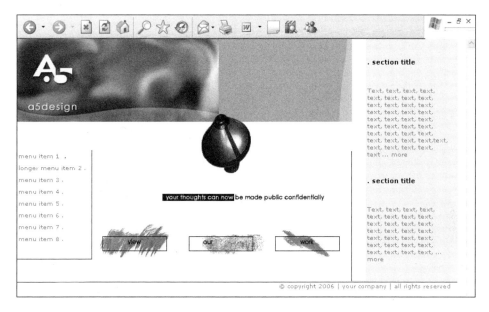

FIGURE 11.138   Design 44 home page design.

FIGURE 11.139   Design 44 second-level
template for less content.

FIGURE 11.140   Design 44 second-level
template for more content.

Photoshop source file name: Designs/1-80-xhtml-web/design_44/images/sources/
design_44.psd

XHTML pages: index.htm, menu_item_2.htm, menu_item_3.htm

Photo credits: A5design

DESIGN 45

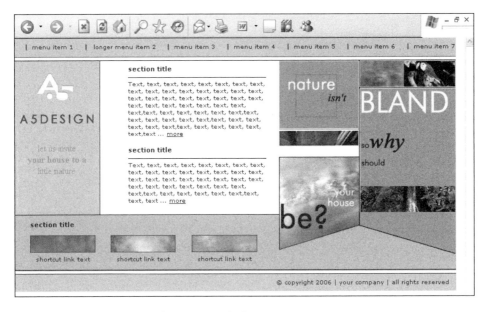

FIGURE 11.141 Design 45 home page design.

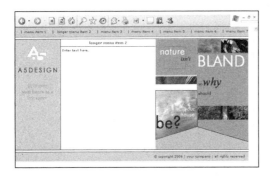

FIGURE 11.142 Design 45 second-level template for less content.

FIGURE 11.143 Design 45 second-level template for more content.

Photoshop source file name: Designs/1-80-xhtml-web/design_45/images/sources/design_45.psd

XHTML pages: index.htm, menu_item_2.htm, menu_item_3.htm

Photo credits: Joe Eccher, Lori Discoe

DESIGN 46

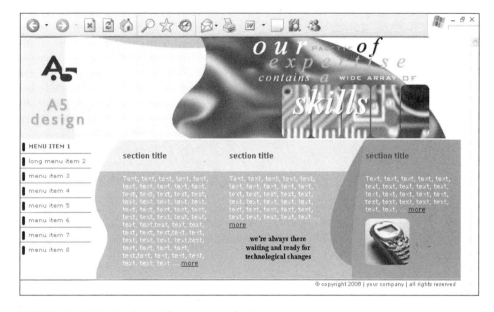

FIGURE 11.144   Design 46 home page design.

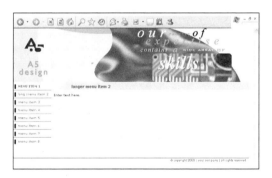

FIGURE 11.145   Design 46 second-level template for less content.

FIGURE 11.146   Design 46 second-level template for more content.

Photoshop source file names: Designs/1-80-xhtml-web/design_46/images/sources/design_46.psd, sl_image.psd

XHTML pages: index.htm, menu_item_2.htm, menu_item_3.htm

Photo credits: Lisa Murillo, A5design

DESIGN 47

FIGURE 11.147 Design 47 home page design.

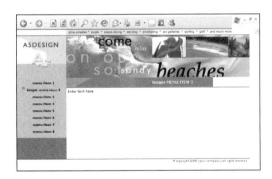

FIGURE 11.148 Design 47 second-level template for less content.

FIGURE 11.149 Design 47 second-level template for more content.

Photoshop source file name: Designs/1-80-xhtml-web/design_47/images/sources/design_47.psd

XHTML pages: index.htm, menu_item_2.htm, menu_item_3.htm

Photo credits: Joe Eccher

DESIGN 48

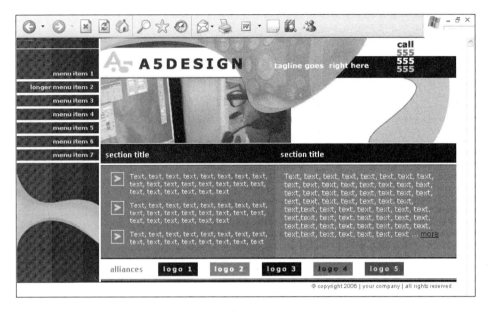

FIGURE 11.150   Design 48 home page design.

FIGURE 11.151   Design 48 second-level
template for less content.

FIGURE 11.152   Design 48 second-level
template for more content.

Photoshop source file name: Designs/1-80-xhtml-web/design_48/images/sources/
design_48.psd

XHTML pages: index.htm, menu_item_2.htm, menu_item_3.htm

Photo credits: A5design

DESIGN 49

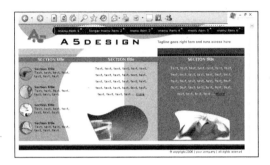

FIGURE 11.153 Design 49 home page design.

FIGURE 11.154 Design 49 second-level template for less content.

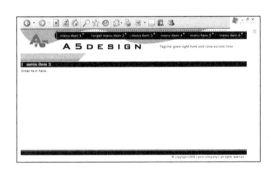

FIGURE 11.155 Design 49 second-level template for more content.

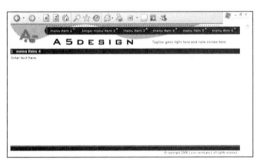

FIGURE 11.156 Design 49 second-level template for more content.

Photoshop source file names: Designs/1-80-xhtml-web/design_49/images/sources/ design_49.psd, bg_images.psd

XHTML pages: index.htm, menu_item_2.htm, menu_item_3.htm, menu_item_4.htm

Photo credits: A5design

DESIGN 50

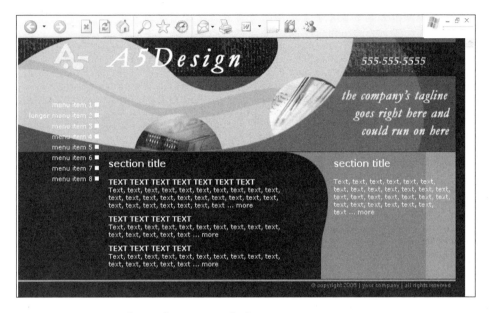

FIGURE 11.157   Design 50 home page design.

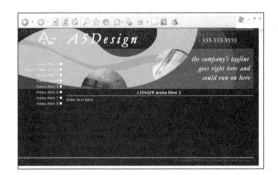

FIGURE 11.158   Design 50 second-level template for less content.

FIGURE 11.159   Design 50 second-level template for more content.

Photoshop source file names: `Designs/1-80-xhtml-web/design_50/images/sources/design_50.psd, bg_images.psd`

XHTML pages: `index.htm, menu_item_2.htm, menu_item_3.htm`

Photo credits: A5design

DESIGN 51

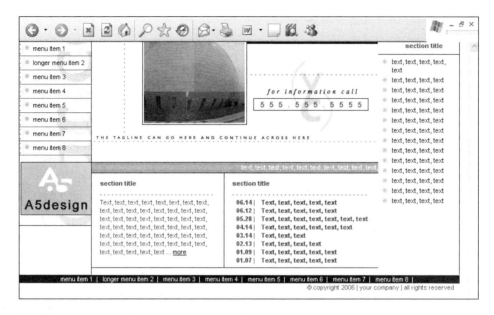

FIGURE 11.160   Design 51 home page design.

FIGURE 11.161   Design 51 second-level template for less content.

FIGURE 11.162   Design 51 second-level template for more content.

Photoshop source file names: Designs/1-80-xhtml-web/design_51/images/sources/ design_51.psd, bg_images.psd

XHTML pages: index.htm, menu_item_2.htm, menu_item_3.htm

Photo credits: Joe Eccher

DESIGN 52

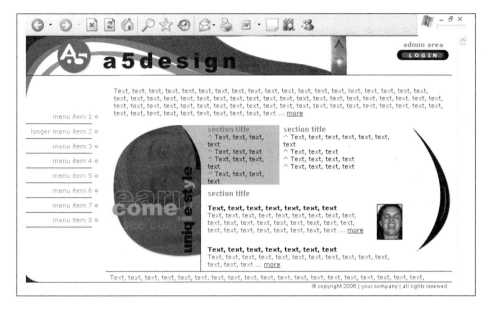

FIGURE 11.163 Design 52 home page design.

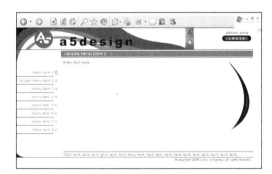

FIGURE 11.164 Design 52 second-level template for less content.

FIGURE 11.165 Design 52 second-level template for more content.

Photoshop source file name: Designs/1-80-xhtml-web/design_52/images/sources/design_52.psd

XHTML pages: index.htm, menu_item_2.htm, menu_item_3.htm

Photo credits: Justin Discoe, Lori Discoe

DESIGN 53

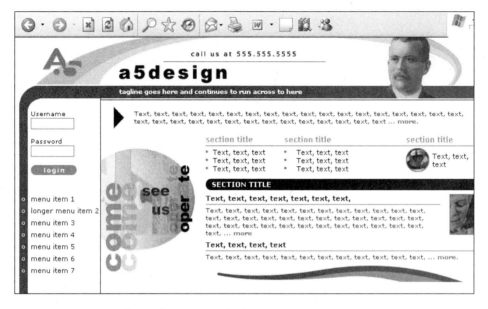

FIGURE 11.166 Design 53 home page design.

FIGURE 11.167 Design 53 second-level template for less content.

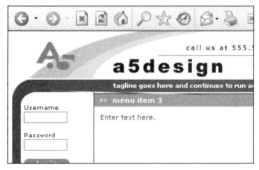

FIGURE 11.168 Design 53 second-level template for more content.

Photoshop source file name: Designs/1-80-xhtml-web/design_53/images/sources/design_53.psd

XHTML pages: index.htm, menu_item_2.htm, menu_item_3.htm

Photo credits: Lori Discoe

DESIGN 54

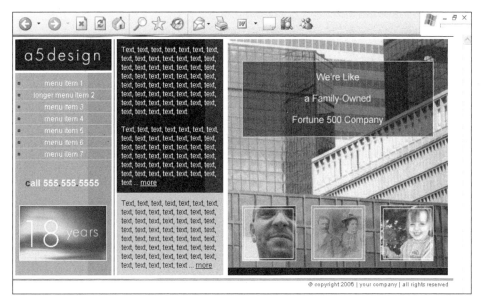

FIGURE 11.169 Design 54 home page design.

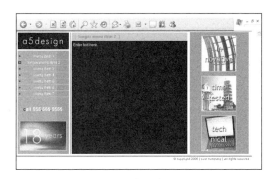

FIGURE 11.170 Design 54 second-level template for less content.

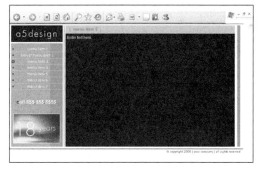

FIGURE 11.171 Design 54 second-level template for more content.

Photoshop source file names: Designs/1-80-xhtml-web/design_54/images/sources/design_54.psd, design_54_sl.psd

XHTML pages: index.htm, menu_item_2.htm, menu_item_3.htm

Photo credits: Joe Eccher, A5design

DESIGN 55

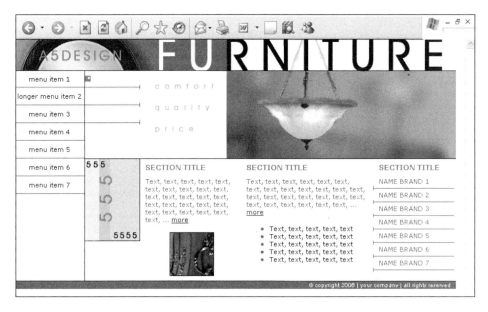

FIGURE 11.172 Design 55 home page design.

FIGURE 11.173 Design 55 second-level template for less content.

FIGURE 11.174 Design 55 second-level template for more content.

Photoshop source file name: Designs/1-80-xhtml-web/design_55/images/sources/design_55.psd

XHTML pages: index.htm, menu_item_2.htm, menu_item_3.htm

Photo credits: A5design

DESIGN 56

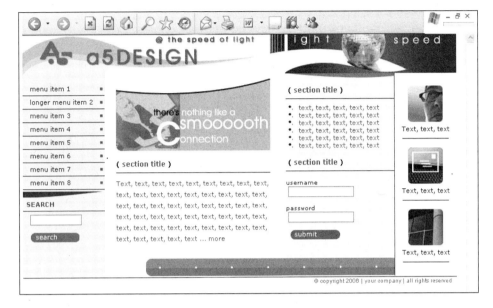

FIGURE 11.175 Design 56 home page design.

FIGURE 11.176 Design 56 second-level template for less content.

FIGURE 11.177 Design 56 second-level template for more content.

Photoshop source file name: `Designs/1-80-xhtml-web/design_56/images/sources/design_56.psd`

XHTML pages: `index.htm, menu_item_2.htm, menu_item_3.htm`

Photo credits: Lisa Murillo, A5design

DESIGN 57

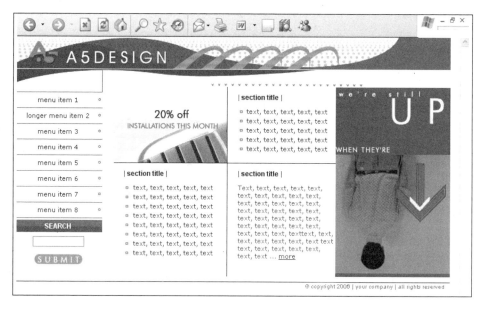

FIGURE 11.178   Design 57 home page design.

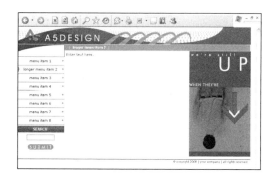

FIGURE 11.179   Design 57 second-level template for less content.

FIGURE 11.180   Design 57 second-level template for more content.

Photoshop source file name: Designs/1-80-xhtml-web/design_57/images/sources/design_57.psd

XHTML pages: index.htm, menu_item_2.htm, menu_item_3.htm

Photo credits: Lisa Murillo, A5design

DESIGN 58

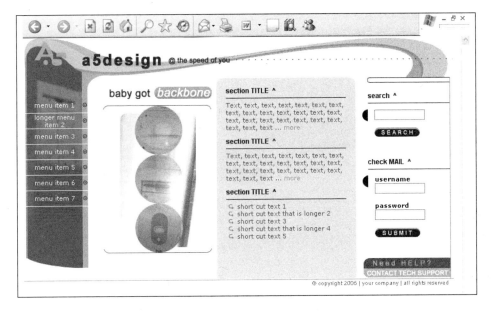

FIGURE 11.181   Design 58 home page design.

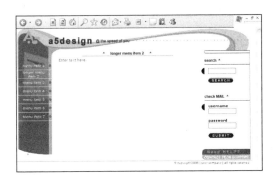

FIGURE 11.182   Design 58 second-level template for less content.

FIGURE 11.183   Design 58 second-level template for more content.

Photoshop source file names: `Designs/1-80-xhtml-web/design_58/images/sources/design_58.psd, bg_images.psd`

XHTML pages: `index.htm, menu_item_2.htm, menu_item_3.htm`

Photo credits: A5design

DESIGN 59

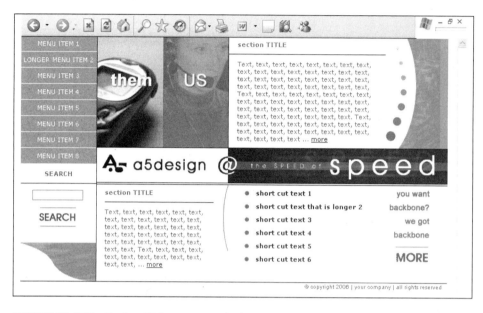

FIGURE 11.184   Design 59 home page design.

FIGURE 11.185   Design 59 second-level template for less content.

FIGURE 11.186   Design 59 second-level template for more content.

Photoshop source file name: `Designs/1-80-xhtml-web/design_59/images/sources/design_59.psd`

XHTML pages: `index.htm, menu_item_2.htm, menu_item_3.htm`

Photo credits: A5design

DESIGN 60

FIGURE 11.187   Design 60 home page design.

FIGURE 11.188   Design 60 second-level template for less content.

FIGURE 11.189   Design 60 second-level template for more content.

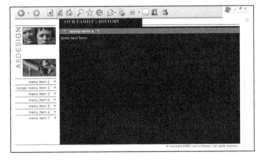

FIGURE 11.190   Design 60 second-level template for more content.

Photoshop source file name: `Designs/1-80-xhtml-web/design_60/images/sources/design_60.psd`

XHTML pages: `index.htm, menu_item_2.htm, menu_item_3.htm, menu_item_4.htm`

Photo credits: Joe Eccher, Lori Discoe, A5design

DESIGN 61

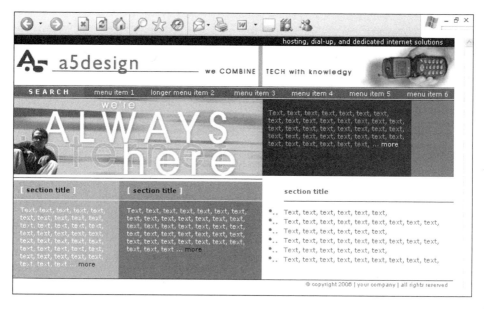

FIGURE 11.191   Design 61 home page design.

FIGURE 11.192   Design 61 second-level template for less content.

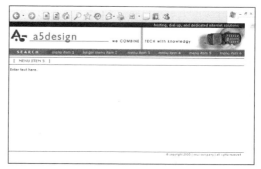

FIGURE 11.193   Design 61 second-level template for more content.

Photoshop source file name: Designs/1-80-xhtml-web/design_61/images/sources/design_61.psd

XHTML pages: index.htm, menu_item_2.htm, menu_item_3.htm

Photo credits: A5design

DESIGN 62

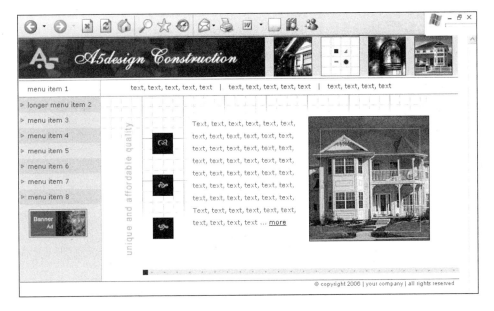

FIGURE 11.194   Design 62 home page design.

FIGURE 11.195   Design 62 second-level template for less content.

FIGURE 11.196   Design 62 second-level template for more content.

Photoshop source file name: `Designs/1-80-xhtml-web/design_62/images/sources/design_62.psd`

XHTML pages: `index.htm, menu_item_2.htm, menu_item_3.htm`

Photo credits: A5design

DESIGN 63

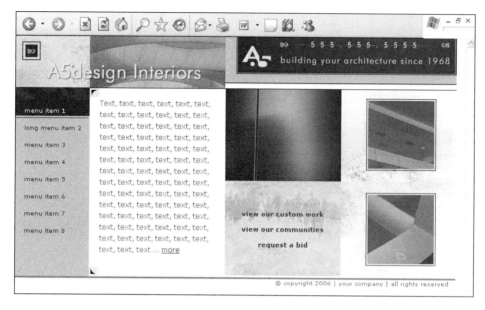

FIGURE 11.197   Design 63 home page design.

FIGURE 11.198   Design 63 second-level template for less content.

FIGURE 11.199   Design 63 second-level template for more content.

Photoshop source file name: Designs/1-80-xhtml-web/design_63/images/sources/
design_63.psd

XHTML pages: index.htm, menu_item_2.htm, menu_item_3.htm

Photo credits: Joe Eccher

DESIGN 64

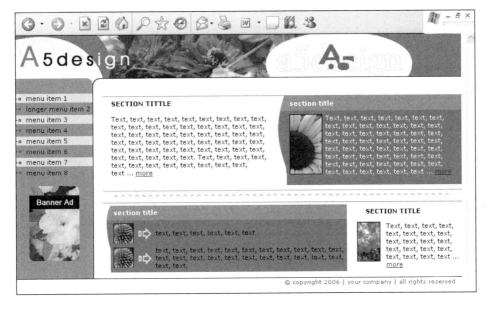

FIGURE 11.200   Design 64 home page design.

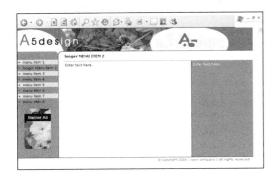

FIGURE 11.201   Design 64 second-level template for less content.

FIGURE 11.202   Design 64 second-level template for more content.

Photoshop source file name: Designs/1-80-xhtml-web/design_64/images/sources/design_64.psd

XHTML pages: index.htm, menu_item_2.htm, menu_item_3.htm

Photo credits: Joe Eccher

DESIGN 65

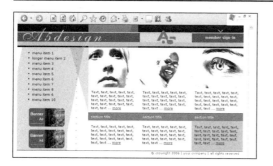

FIGURE 11.203 Design 65 home page design.

FIGURE 11.204 Design 65 second-level template for less content.

FIGURE 11.205 Design 65 second-level template for more content.

FIGURE 11.206 Design 65 second-level template for more content.

FIGURE 11.207 Design 65 second-level template for more content.

Photoshop source file name: Designs/1-80-xhtml-web/design_65/images/sources/design_65.psd

XHTML pages: index.htm, menu_item_2.htm, menu_item_3.htm, menu_item_4.htm, menu_item_5.htm

Photo credits: Lisa Murillo, A5design, Justin Discoe

DESIGN 66

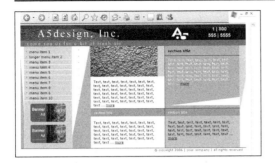

FIGURE 11.208   Design 66 home page design.

FIGURE 11.209   Design 66 second-level template for less content.

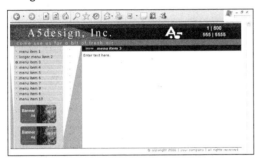

FIGURE 11.210   Design 66 second-level template for more content.

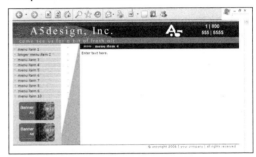

FIGURE 11.211   Design 66 second-level template for more content.

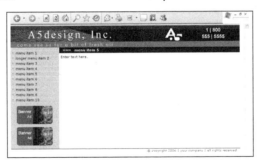

FIGURE 11.212   Design 66 second-level template for more content.

Photoshop source file name: Designs/1-80-xhtml-web/design_66/images/sources/ design_66.psd

XHTML pages: index.htm, menu_item_2.htm, menu_item_3.htm, menu_item_4.htm, menu_item_5.htm

Photo credits: Joe Eccher

DESIGN 67

FIGURE 11.213   Design 67 home page design.

FIGURE 11.214   Design 67 second-level template for less content.

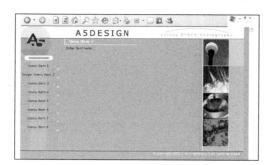

FIGURE 11.215   Design 67 second-level template for more content.

FIGURE 11. 216   Design 67 second-level template for more content.

Photoshop source file names: Designs/1-80-xhtml-web/design_67/images/sources/design_67.psd, bg_images.psd

XHTML pages: index.htm, menu_item_2.htm, menu_item_3.htm, menu_item_4.htm

Photo credits: Lisa Murillo, A5design

DESIGN 68

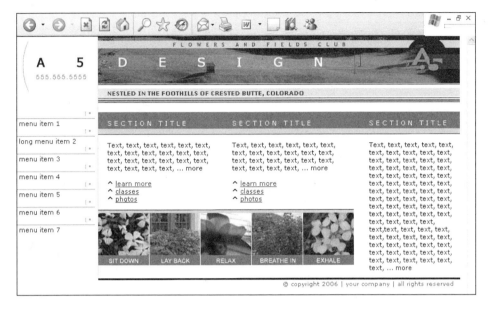

FIGURE 11.217 Design 68 home page design.

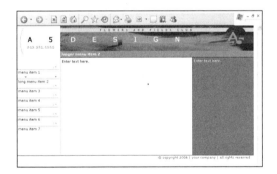

FIGURE 11.218 Design 68 second-level template for less content.

FIGURE 11.219 Design 68 second-level template for more content.

Photoshop source file name: Designs/1-80-xhtml-web/design_68/images/sources/design_68.psd

XHTML pages: index.htm, menu_item_2.htm, menu_item_3.htm

Photo credits: Joe Eccher

DESIGN 69

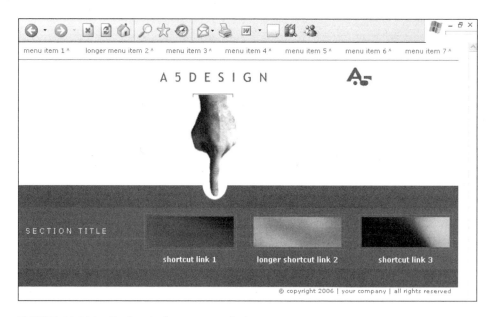

FIGURE 11.220   Design 69 home page design.

FIGURE 11.221   Design 69 second-level template for less content.

FIGURE 11.222   Design 69 second-level template for more content.

Photoshop source file name: Designs/1-80-xhtml-web/design_69/images/sources/design_69.psd

XHTML pages: index.htm, menu_item_2.htm, menu_item_3.htm

Photo credits: A5design

DESIGN 70

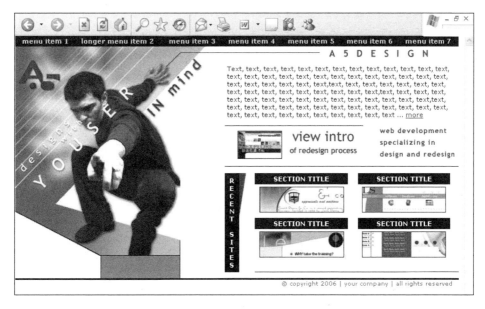

FIGURE 11.223   Design 70 home page design.

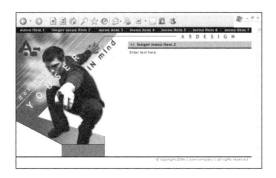

FIGURE 11.224   Design 70 second-level template for less content.

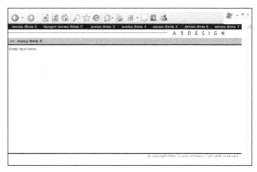

FIGURE 11.225   Design 70 second-level template for more content.

Photoshop source file name: `Designs/1-80-xhtml-web/design_70/images/sources/design_70.psd`

XHTML pages: `index.htm`, `menu_item_2.htm`, `menu_item_3.htm`

Photo credits: A5design

DESIGN 71

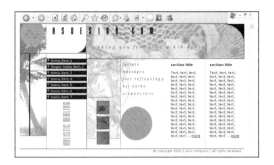

FIGURE 11.226 Design 71 home page design.

FIGURE 11.227 Design 71 second-level template for less content.

FIGURE 11.228 Design 71 second-level template for more content.

FIGURE 11.229 Design 71 second-level template for more content.

Photoshop source file name: Designs/1-80-xhtml-web/design_71/images/sources/design_71.psd

XHTML pages: index.htm, menu_item_2.htm, menu_item_3.htm, menu_item_4.htm

Photo credits: Joe Eccher

DESIGN 72

FIGURE 11.230   Design 72 home page design.

FIGURE 11.231   Design 72 second-level template for less content.

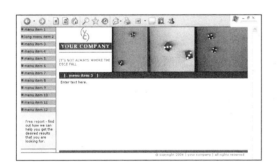

FIGURE 11.232   Design 72 second-level template for more content.

FIGURE 11.233   Design 72 second-level template for more content.

Photoshop source file name: Designs/1-80-xhtml-web/design_72/images/sources/design_72.psd

XHTML pages: index.htm, menu_item_2.htm, menu_item_3.htm, menu_item_4.htm

Photo credits: A5design

DESIGN 73

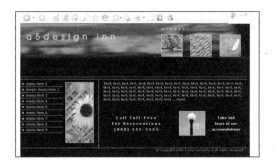

FIGURE 11.234 Design 73 home page design.

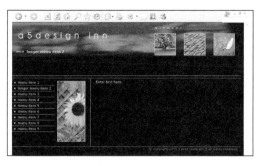

FIGURE 11.235 Design 73 second-level template for less content.

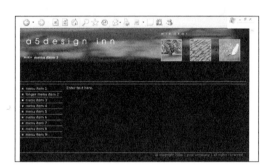

FIGURE 11.236 Design 73 second-level template for more content.

FIGURE 11.237 Design 73 second-level template for more content.

Photoshop source file name: Designs/1-80-xhtml-web/design_73/images/sources/design_73.psd

XHTML pages: index.htm, menu_item_2.htm, menu_item_3.htm, menu_item_4.htm

Photo credits: A5design

DESIGN 74

FIGURE 11.238   Design 74 home page design.

FIGURE 11.239   Design 74 second-level template for less content.

FIGURE 11.240   Design 74 second-level template for more content.

FIGURE 11.241   Design 74 second-level template for more content.

Photoshop source file name: Designs/1-80-xhtml-web/design_74/images/sources/ design_74.psd, bg_images.psd

XHTML pages: index.htm, menu_item_2.htm, menu_item_3.htm, menu_item_4.htm

Photo credits: A5design

DESIGN 75

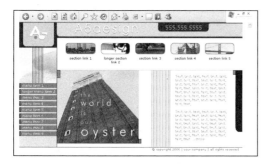

FIGURE 11.242   Design 75 home page design.

FIGURE 11.243   Design 75 second-level template for less content.

FIGURE 11.244   Design 75 second-level template for more content.

FIGURE 11.245   Design 75 second-level template for more content.

Photoshop source file name: Designs/1-80-xhtml-web/design_75/images/sources/ design_75.psd

XHTML pages: index.htm, menu_item_2.htm, menu_item_3.htm, menu_item_4.htm

Photo credits: Joe Eccher, A5design

DESIGN 76

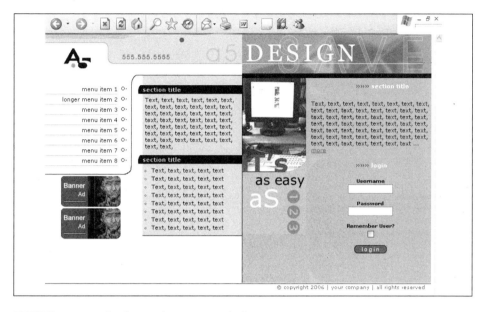

FIGURE 11.246   Design 76 home page design.

FIGURE 11.247   Design 76 second-level template for less content.

FIGURE 11.248   Design 76 second-level template for more content.

Photoshop source file name: Designs/1-80-xhtml-web/design_76/images/sources/design_76.psd

XHTML pages: index.htm, menu_item_2.htm, menu_item_3.htm

Photo credits: A5design

DESIGN 77

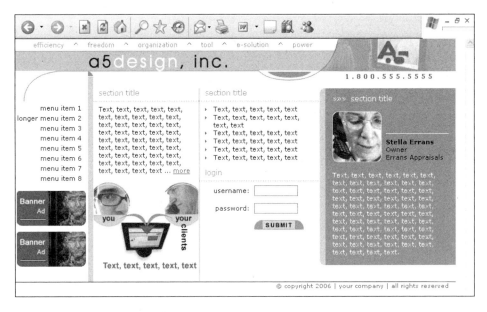

FIGURE 11.249 Design 77 home page design.

FIGURE 11.250 Design 77 second-level template for less content.

FIGURE 11.251 Design 77 second-level template for more content.

Photoshop source file name: Designs/1-80-xhtml-web/design_77/images/sources/design_77.psd

XHTML pages: index.htm, menu_item_2.htm, menu_item_3.htm

Photo credits: Joe Eccher, A5design

DESIGN 78

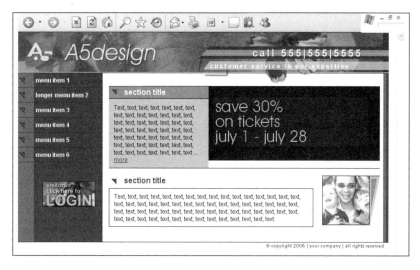

FIGURE 11.252   Design 78 home page design.

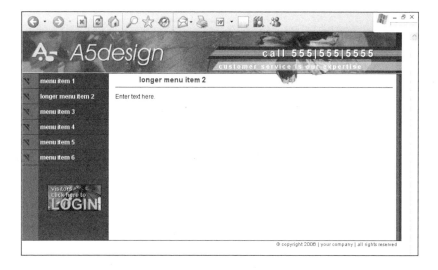

FIGURE 11.253   Design 78 second-level template for less content.

Photoshop source file name: Designs/1-80-xhtml-web/design_78/images/sources/
design_78.psd

XHTML pages: index.htm, menu_item_2.htm

Photo credits: Lori Discoe

DESIGN 79

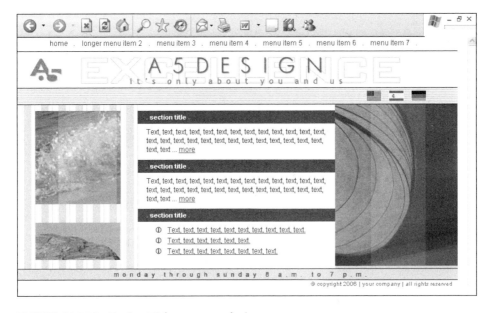

FIGURE 11.254   Design 79 home page design.

FIGURE 11.255   Design 79 second-level template for less content.

FIGURE 11.256   Design 79 second-level template for more content.

Photoshop source file name: `Designs/1-80-xhtml-web/design_79/images/sources/design_79.psd`

XHTML pages: `index.htm, menu_item_2.htm, menu_item_3.htm`

Photo credits: Joe Eccher

DESIGN 80

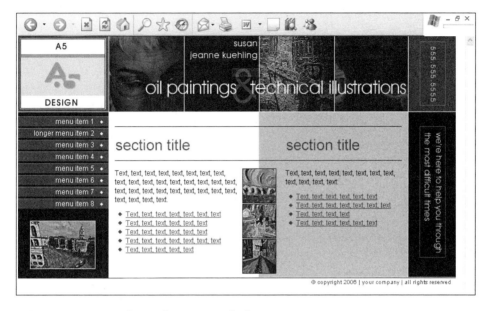

FIGURE 11.257   Design 80 home page design.

FIGURE 11.258   Design 80 second-level
template for less content.

FIGURE 11.259   Design 80 second-level
template for more content.

Photoshop source file name: `Designs/1-80-xhtml-web/design_80/images/sources/`
`design_80.psd`

XHTML pages: `index.htm`, `menu_item_2.htm`, `menu_item_3.htm`

Photo credits: A5design

DESIGN 81

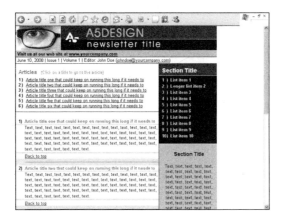

FIGURE 11.260 E-newsletter design.

Photoshop source file name: Designs/81-90-enewsletters/design_81/images/sources/design_81.psd

XHTML pages: index.htm

Photo credits: A5design

DESIGN 82

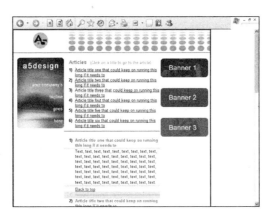

FIGURE 11.261 E-newsletter design.

Photoshop source file name: Designs/81-90-enewsletters/design_82/images/sources/design_82.psd

XHTML pages: index.htm

Photo credits: A5design

DESIGN 83

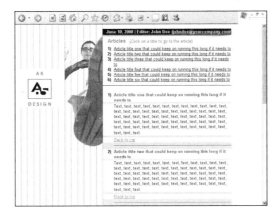

FIGURE 11.262 E-newsletter design.

Photoshop source file name: Designs/81-90-enewsletters/design_83/images/sources/design_83.psd

XHTML pages: index.htm

Photo credits: A5design

DESIGN 84

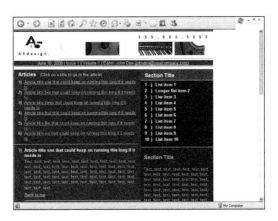

FIGURE 11.263 E-newsletter design.

Photoshop source file name: Designs/81-90-enewsletters/design_84/images/sources/design_84.psd

XHTML pages: index.htm

Photo credits: A5design

DESIGN 85

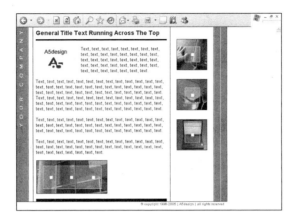

FIGURE 11.264 E-newsletter design.

Photoshop source file name: Designs/81-90-enewsletters/design_85/images/sources/design_85.psd

XHTML pages: index.htm

Photo credits: Lisa Murillo, A5design

DESIGN 86

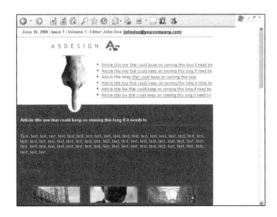

FIGURE 11.265 E-newsletter design.

Photoshop source file name: Designs/81-90-enewsletters/design_86/images/sources/design_86.psd

XHTML pages: index.htm

Photo credits: Lisa Murillo, A5design

DESIGN 87

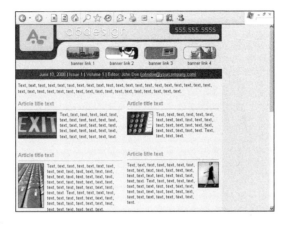

FIGURE 11.266 E-newsletter design.

Photoshop source file name: `Designs/81-90-enewsletters/design_87/images/sources/`
`design_87.psd`

XHTML pages: `index.htm`

Photo credits: Lisa Murillo, Joe Eccher, A5design

DESIGN 88

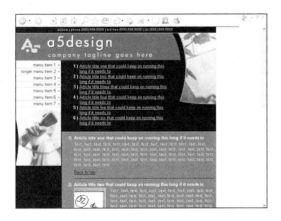

FIGURE 11.267 E-newsletter design.

Photoshop source file name: `Designs/81-90-enewsletters/design_88/images/sources/`
`design_88.psd`

XHTML pages: `index.htm`

Photo credits: Lisa Murillo

DESIGN 89

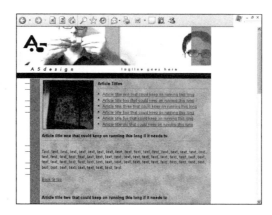

FIGURE 11.268 E-newsletter design.

Photoshop source file name: Designs/81-90-enewsletters/design_89/images/sources/design_89.psd

XHTML pages: index.htm

Photo credits: A5design

DESIGN 90

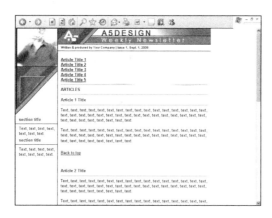

FIGURE 11.269 E-newsletter design.

Photoshop source file name: Designs/81-90-enewsletters/design_90/images/sources/design_90.psd

XHTML pages: index.htm

Photo credits: A5design

DESIGN 91

FIGURE 11.270   Signature design.

Photoshop source file name: Designs/91-100-signatures/design_91/images/sources/
design_91.psd
XHTML pages: index.htm
Photo credits: A5design

DESIGN 92

FIGURE 11.271   Signature design.

Photoshop source file name: Designs/91-100-signatures/design_92/images/sources/
design_92.psd
XHTML pages: index.htm
Photo credits: Lori Discoe

DESIGN 93

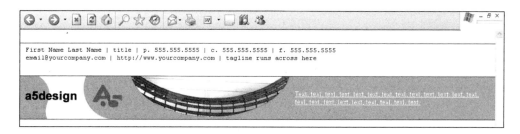

FIGURE 11.272   Signature design.

Photoshop source file name: Designs/91-100-signatures/design_93/images/sources/design_93.psd
XHTML pages: index.htm
Photo credits: Lisa Murillo

DESIGN 94

FIGURE 11.273   Signature design.

Photoshop source file name: Designs/91-100-signatures/design_94/images/sources/design_94.psd
XHTML pages: index.htm
Photo credits: A5design

DESIGN 95

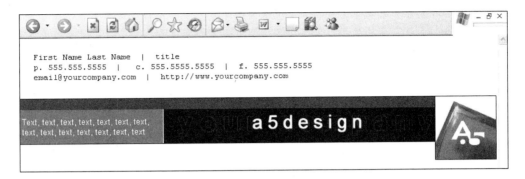

FIGURE 11.274   Signature design.

Photoshop source file name: Designs/91-100-signatures/design_95/images/sources/
design_95.psd

XHTML pages: index.htm

Photo credits: A5design

DESIGN 96

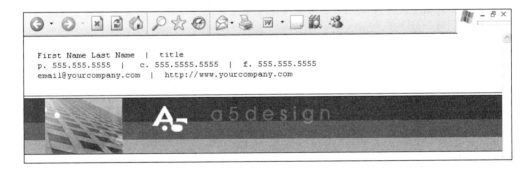

FIGURE 11.275   Signature design.

Photoshop source file name: Designs/91-100-signatures/design_96/images/sources/
design_96.psd

XHTML pages: index.htm

Photo credits: Lisa Murillo

DESIGN 97

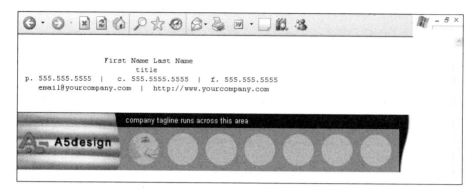

FIGURE 11.276 Signature design.

Photoshop source file name: Designs/91-100-signatures/design_97/images/sources/
design_97.psd

XHTML pages: index.htm

Photo credits: Lisa Murillo, A5design

DESIGN 98

FIGURE 11.277 Signature design.

Photoshop source file name: Designs/91-100-signatures/design_98/images/sources/
design_98.psd

XHTML pages: index.htm

Photo credits: Lisa Murillo

DESIGN 99

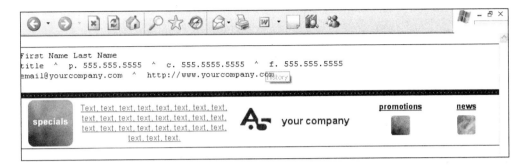

FIGURE 11.278   Signature design.

Photoshop source file name: Designs/91-100-signatures/design_99/images/sources/
design_99.psd
XHTML pages: index.htm
Photo credits: A5design

DESIGN 100

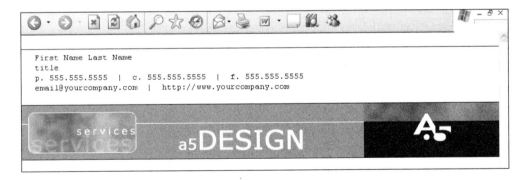

FIGURE 11.279   Signature design.

Photoshop source file name: Designs/91-100-signatures/design_100/images/sources/
design_100.psd
Photo credits: Joe Eccher

DESIGN 101

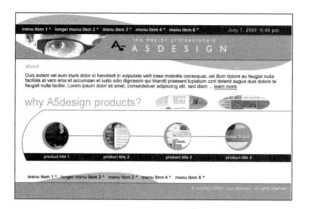

FIGURE 11.280   Home page design (Photoshop only).

Photoshop source file name: `Designs/101-120-photoshop-web/design_101/images/sources/design_101.psd`

Photo credits: A5design

DESIGN 102

FIGURE 11.281   Home page design (Photoshop only).

Photoshop source file name: `Designs/101-120-photoshop-web/design_102/images/sources/design_102.psd`

Photo credits: Joe Eccher, Justin Discoe

DESIGN 103

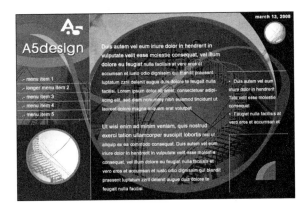

FIGURE 11.282 Home page design (Photoshop only).

Photoshop source file name: Designs/101-120-photoshop-web/design_103/images/sources/ design_103.psd

Photo credits: idlerphotography.com

DESIGN 104

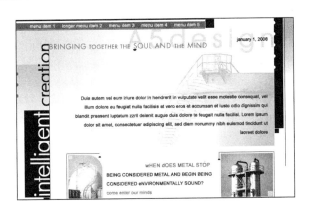

FIGURE 11.283 Home page design (Photoshop only).

Photoshop source file name: Designs/101-120-photoshop-web/design_104/images/sources/ design_104.psd

Photo credits: idlerphotography.com

DESIGN 105

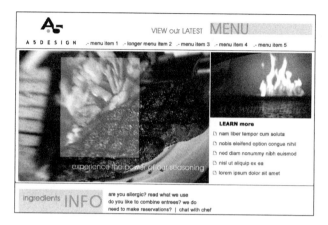

FIGURE 11.284   Home page design (Photoshop only).

Photoshop source file name: Designs/101-120-photoshop-web/design_105/images/sources/ design_105.psd

Photo credits: idlerphotography.com

DESIGN 106

FIGURE 11.285   Home page design (Photoshop only).

Photoshop source file name: Designs/101-120-photoshop-web/design_101/images/sources/ design_106.psd

Photo credits: A5design

DESIGN 107

FIGURE 11.286   Home page design (Photoshop only).

Photoshop source file name: Designs/101-120-photoshop-web/design_107/images/sources/design_107.psd

Photo credits: Lisa Murillo, Joe Eccher

DESIGN 108

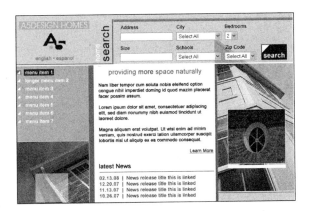

FIGURE 11.287   Home page design (Photoshop only).

Photoshop source file name: Designs/101-120-photoshop-web/design_108/images/sources/design_108.psd

Photo credits: idlerphotography.com

DESIGN 109

FIGURE 11.288   Home page design (Photoshop only).

Photoshop source file name: Designs/101-120-photoshop-web/design_109/images/sources/
design_109.psd

Photo credits: idlerphotography.com, Joe Eccher

DESIGN 110

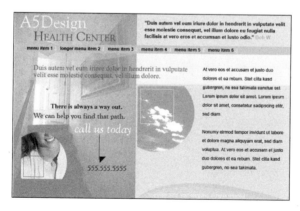

FIGURE 11.289   Home page design (Photoshop only).

Photoshop source file name: Designs/101-120-photoshop-web/design_110/images/sources/
design_110.psd

Photo credits: idlerphotography.com

DESIGN 111

FIGURE 11.290 Home page design (Photoshop only).

Photoshop source file name: `Designs/101-120-photoshop-web/design_111/images/sources/`
`design_111.psd`

Photo credits: idlerphotography.com

DESIGN 112

FIGURE 11.291 Home page design (Photoshop only).

Photoshop source file name: `Designs/101-120-photoshop-web/design_112/images/sources/`
`design_112.psd`

Photo credits: idlerphotography.com

DESIGN 113

FIGURE 11.292   Home page design (Photoshop only).

Photoshop source file name: Designs/101-120-photoshop-web/design_113/images/sources/
design_113.psd

Photo credits: Joe Eccher

DESIGN 114

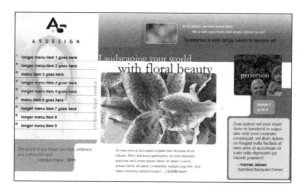

FIGURE 11.293   Home page design (Photoshop only).

Photoshop source file name: Designs/101-120-photoshop-web/design_114/images/sources/
design_114.psd

Photo credits: idlerphotography.com, Joe Eccher

DESIGN 115

FIGURE 11.294   Home page design (Photoshop only).

Photoshop source file name: `Designs/101-120-photoshop-web/design_115/images/sources/`
`design_115.psd`
Photo credits: Joe Eccher

DESIGN 116

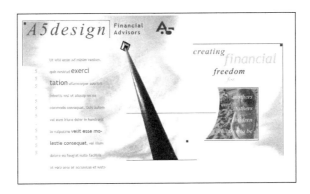

FIGURE 11.295 Home page design (Photoshop only).

Photoshop source file name: `Designs/101-120-photoshop-web/design_116/images/sources/`
`design_116.psd`
Photo credits: idlerphotography.com, Joe Eccher

DESIGN 117

FIGURE 11.296 Home page design (Photoshop only).

Photoshop source file name: Designs/101-120-photoshop-web/design_117/images/sources/design_117.psd

Photo credits: idlerphotography.com

DESIGN 118

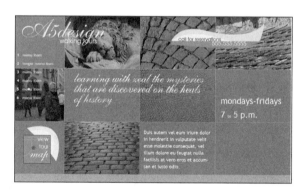

FIGURE 11.297 Home page design (Photoshop only).

Photoshop source file name: 1Designs/101-120-photoshop-web/design_118/images/sources/design_118.psd

Photo credits: Joe Eccher

DESIGN 119

FIGURE 11.298   Home page design (Photoshop only).

Photoshop source file name: `Designs/101-120-photoshop-web/design_119/images/sources/design_119.psd`

Photo credits: idlerphotography.com

DESIGN 120

FIGURE 11.299   Home page design (Photoshop only).

Photoshop source file name: `Designs/101-120-photoshop-web/design_120/images/sources/design_120.psd`

Photo credits: A5design

DESIGN 121

FIGURE 11.300   Design 121 home page design.

FIGURE 11.301   Design 121 second-level template for less content.

FIGURE 11.302   Design 121 second-level template for more content.

Photoshop source file names: Designs/121-140-css-web/design_101/images/sources/ design_121.psd, design_121_sl.psd, bg_body_figure.psd

XHTML pages: index.htm, menu_item_2.htm, menu_item_3.htm

Photo credits: idlerphotography.com

DESIGN 122

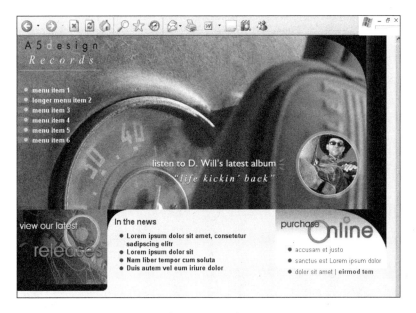

FIGURE 11.303   Design 122 home page design.

FIGURE 11.304   Design 122 second-level template for less content.

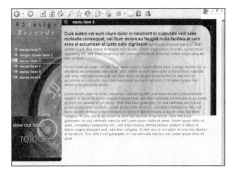

FIGURE 11.305   Design 122 second-level template for more content.

Photoshop source file names: Designs/121-140-css-web/design_122/images/sources/
design_122.psd, design_122_sl.psd

XHTML pages: index.htm, menu_item_2.htm, menu_item_3.htm

Photo credits: idlerphotography.com

DESIGN 123

FIGURE 11.306 Design 123 home page design.

FIGURE 11.307 Design 123 second-level template for less content.

FIGURE 11.308 Design 123 second-level template for more content.

Photoshop source file names: Designs/121-140-css-web/design_123/images/sources/ design_123.psd, bg-left-column.psd

XHTML pages: index.htm, menu_item_2.htm, menu_item_3.htm

Photo credits: idlerphotography.com

DESIGN 124

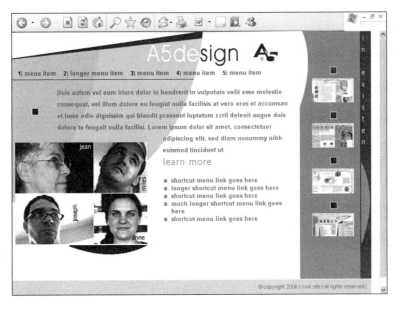

FIGURE 11.309   Design 124 home page design.

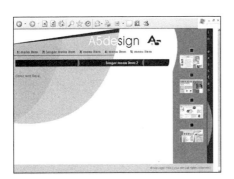

FIGURE 11.310   Design 124 second-level template for less content.

FIGURE 11.311   Design 124 second-level template for more content.

Photoshop source file names: Designs/121-140-css-web/design_124/images/sources/design_124.psd, bg_design_124.psd

XHTML pages: index.htm, menu_item_2.htm, menu_item_3.htm

Photo credits: Joe Eccher

DESIGN 125

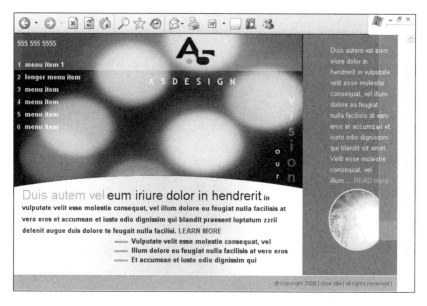

FIGURE 11.312   Design 125 home page design.

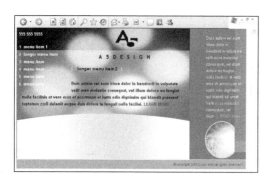

FIGURE 11.314   Design 125 second-level template for more content.

FIGURE 11.313   Design 125 second-level template for less content.

Photoshop source file name: Designs/121-140-css-web/design_125/images/sources/design_125.psd

XHTML pages: index.htm, menu_item_2.htm, menu_item_3.htm

Photo credits: A5design

DESIGN 126

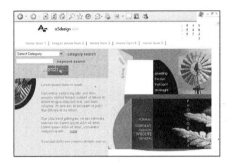

FIGURE 11.315   Design 126 home page design.

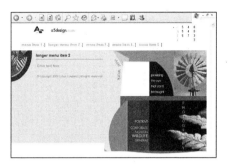

FIGURE 11.316   Design 126 second-level template for less content.

FIGURE 11.317   Design 126 second-level template for more content.

FIGURE 11. 318   Design 126 second-level template for more content.

Photoshop source file name: Designs/121-140-css-web/design_126/images/sources/
design_126.psd

XHTML pages: index.htm, menu_item_2.htm, menu_item_3.htm, menu_item_4.htm

Photo credits: idlerphotography.com

DESIGN 127

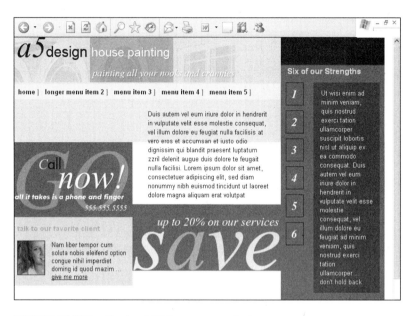

FIGURE 11.319   Design 127 home page design.

FIGURE 11.320   Design 127 second-level template for less content.

FIGURE 11.321   Design 127 second-level template for more content.

Photoshop source file names: `Designs/121-140-css-web/design_127/images/sources/design_127.psd, bg_design_127.psd`

XHTML pages: `index.htm, menu_item_2.htm, menu_item_3.htm`

Photo credits: idlerphotography.com

DESIGN 128

FIGURE 11.322   Design 128 home page design.

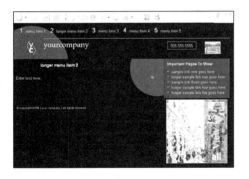

FIGURE 11.323   Design 128 second-level template for less content.

FIGURE 11.324   Design 128 second-level template for more content.

Photoshop source file name: Designs/121-140-css-web/design_128/images/sources/design_128.psd

XHTML pages: index.htm, menu_item_2.htm, menu_item_3.htm

Photo credits: A5design

DESIGN 129

FIGURE 11.325   Design 129 home page design.

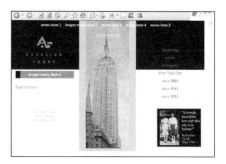

FIGURE 11.326   Design 129 second-level template for less content.

FIGURE 11.327   Design 129 second-level template for more content.

FIGURE 11.328   Design 129 second-level template for more content.

Photoshop source file names: Designs/121-140-css-web/design_129/images/sources/ design_129.psd, bg_design_129.psd

XHTML pages: index.htm, menu_item_2.htm, menu_item_3.htm, menu_item_4.htm

Photo credits: Justin Discoe, Lori Discoe

DESIGN 130

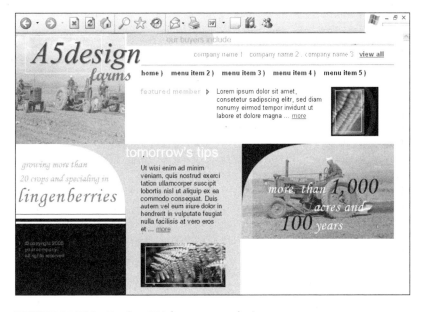

FIGURE 11.329   Design 130 home page design.

FIGURE 11.330   Design 130 second-level template for less content.

FIGURE 11.331   Design 130 second-level template for more content.

Photoshop source file name: `Designs/121-140-css-web/design_130/images/sources/design_130.psd`

XHTML pages: `index.htm`, `menu_item_2.htm`, `menu_item_3.htm`

Photo credits: idlerphotography.com, Joe Eccher

DESIGN 131

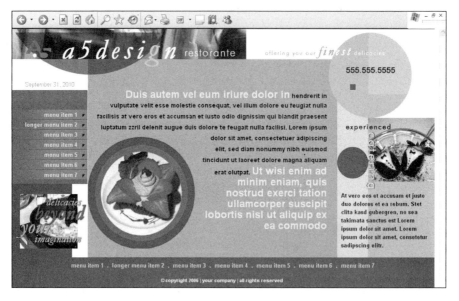

FIGURE 11.332   Design 131 home page design.

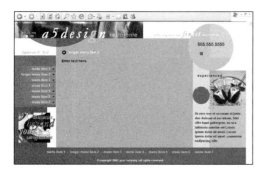

FIGURE 11.333   Design 131 second-level template for less content.

FIGURE 11.334   Design 131 second-level template for more content.

Photoshop source file name: `Designs/121-140-css-web/design_131/images/sources/design_131.psd`

XHTML pages: `index.htm, menu_item_2.htm, menu_item_3.htm`

Photo credits: idlerphotography.com

DESIGN 132

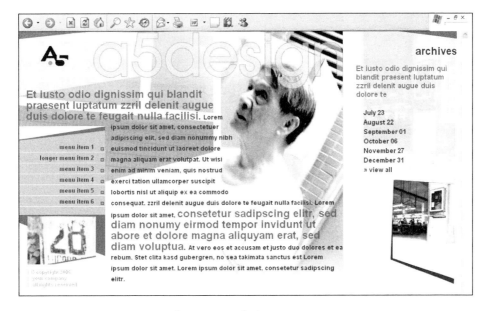

FIGURE 11.335   Design 132 home page design.

FIGURE 11.336   Design 132 second-level template for less content.

FIGURE 11.337   Design 132 second-level template for more content.

Photoshop source file names: Designs/121-140-css-web/design_132/images/sources/design_132.psd, bg_132.psd, bg_132_sl.psd

XHTML pages: index.htm, menu_item_2.htm, menu_item_3.htm

Photo credits: Justin Discoe

DESIGN 133

FIGURE 11.338 Design 133 home page design.

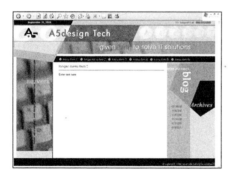

FIGURE 11.339 Design 133 second-level template for less content.

FIGURE 11.340 Design 133 second-level template for more content.

Photoshop source file name: Designs/121-140-css-web/design_133/images/sources/design_133.psd

XHTML pages: index.htm, menu_item_2.htm, menu_item_3.htm

Photo credits: idlerphotography.com

DESIGN 134

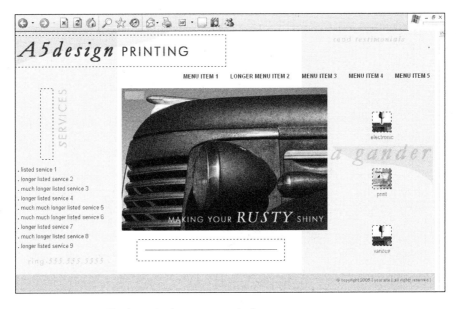

FIGURE 11.341   Design 134 home page design.

FIGURE 11.342   Design 134 second-level template for less content.

FIGURE 11.343   Design 134 second-level template for more content.

Photoshop source file name: Designs/121-140-css-web/design_134/images/sources/design_134.psd

XHTML pages: index.htm, menu_item_2.htm, menu_item_3.htm

Photo credits: idlerphotography.com

DESIGN 135

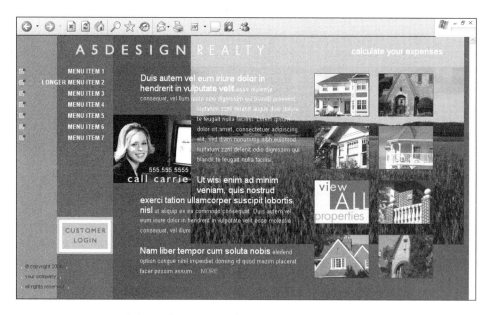

FIGURE 11.344 Design 135 home page design.

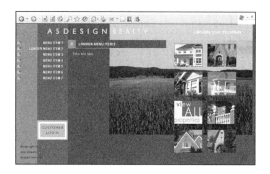

FIGURE 11.345 Design 135 second-level template for less content.

FIGURE 11.346 Design 135 second-level template for more content.

Photoshop source file names: Designs/121-140-css-web/design_135/images/sources/design_135.psd, bg_design_135.psd

XHTML pages: index.htm, menu_item_2.htm, menu_item_3.htm

Photo credits: idlerphotography.com

DESIGN 136

FIGURE 11.347   Design 136 home page design.

FIGURE 11.348   Design 136 second-level template for less content.

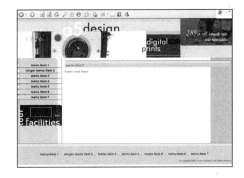

FIGURE 11.349   Design 136 second-level template for more content.

Photoshop source file name: `Designs/121-140-css-web/design_136/images/sources/design_136.psd`

XHTML pages: `index.htm, menu_item_2.htm, menu_item_3.htm`

Photo credits: idlerphotography.com

DESIGN 137

FIGURE 11.350 Design 137 home page design.

FIGURE 11.352 Design 137 second-level template for more content.

FIGURE 11.351 Design 137 second-level template for less content.

Photoshop source file name: `Designs/121-140-css-web/design_137/images/sources/design_137.psd`

XHTML pages: `index.htm, menu_item_2.htm, menu_item_3.htm`

Photo credits: idlerphotography.com

DESIGN 138

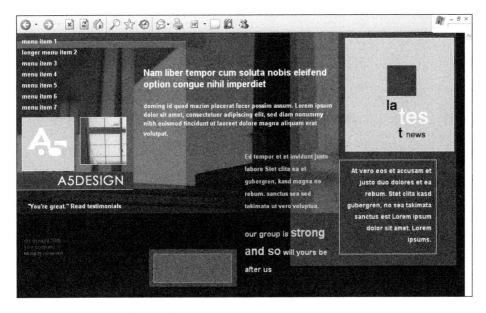

FIGURE 11.353 Design 138 home page design.

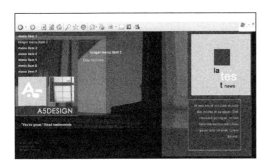

FIGURE 11.354 Design 138 second-level template for less content.

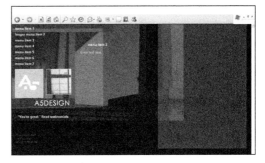

FIGURE 11.355 Design 138 second-level template for more content.

Photoshop source file names: Designs/121-140-css-web/design_138/images/sources/ design_138.psd, bg_design_138.psd

XHTML pages: index.htm, menu_item_2.htm, menu_item_3.htm

Photo credits: idlerphotography.com

DESIGN 139

FIGURE 11.356 Design 139 home page design.

FIGURE 11.357 Design 139 second-level template for less content.

FIGURE 11.359 Design 139 second-level template for more content.

FIGURE 11.358 Design 139 second-level template for more content.

Photoshop source file name: Designs/121-140-css-web/design_139/images/sources/design_139.psd

XHTML pages: index.htm, menu_item_2.htm, menu_item_3.htm, menu_item_4.htm

Photo credits: idlerphotography.com

DESIGN 140

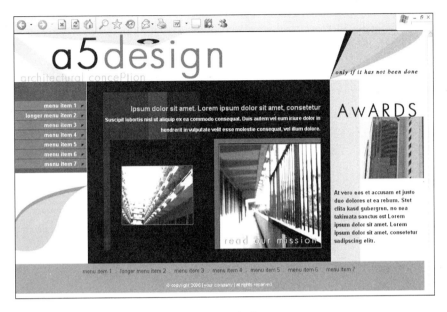

FIGURE 11.360 Design 140 home page design.

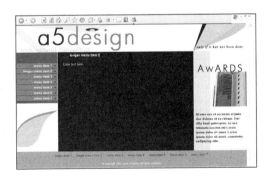

FIGURE 11.361 Design 140 second-level template for less content.

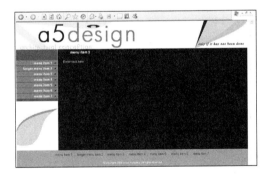

FIGURE 11.362 Design 140 second-level template for more content.

Photoshop source file name: Designs/121-140-css-web/design_140/images/sources/design_140.psd

XHTML pages: index.htm, menu_item_2.htm, menu_item_3.htm

Photo credits: Justin Discoe

SUMMARY

The designs included on the CD-ROM that comes with this book offer a variety of options for the reader. The types of designs include XHTML table-based coded Web sites, e-newsletters, signatures, Photoshop-only designs, and CSS-coded designs. They offer the reader not only a variety of designs that can be quickly customized and used but also a variety that can be used for inspiration as well.

Appendix | **About the CD-ROM**

This CD-ROM contains the 140 Free templates ready for your customization, along with the figure files, and software demos.

FOLDER CONTENTS

Chapters and Figures: This folder contains the electronic content for each chapter, which includes the text and images.

- Chapter 1 Figures
- Chapter 2 Figures
- Chapter 3 Figures
- Chapter 4 Figures
- Chapter 5 Figures
- Chapter 6 Figures
- Chapter 7 Figures
- Chapter 8 Figures
- Chapter 9 Figures
- Chapter 10 Figures
- Chapter 11 Figures

Designs: This folder contains the files for each of the 140 designs, including at least one Photoshop file and XHTML and CSS files.

- 1-80-xhtml-web
- 81-90-e-newsletters
- 91-100-signatures
- 101-120-photoshop-web
- 121-140-css-web

Software: This folder contains a trial version of the EZmenu 3.1 JavaScript menus mentioned in the book, along with a trial version of Photoshop CS2 for PCs and a link to download the software for Macs.

- EZmenu 3.1
- Photoshop CS2 (PC only)

OVERALL SYSTEM REQUIREMENTS

Hardware Requirements

Following are the hardware requirements, per the specifications for Adobe Photoshop CS, which is the most robust software required for this book.

Windows

- Intel Pentium III or 4 processor
- Microsoft Windows 2000 with Service Pack 3 or Windows XP
- 192 MB of RAM (256 MB recommended)
- 280 MB of available hard-disk space
- Color monitor with 16-bit color or greater video card
- 800 × 600 or greater monitor resolution
- CD-ROM drive

Mac

- PowerPC G3, G4, or G5 processor
- Mac OS X v.10.2.4, 10.2.5, 10.2.6, or 10.2.7
- 192 MB of RAM (256 MB recommended)
- 320 MB of available hard-disk space
- Color monitor with 16-bit color or greater video card
- 800 × 600 or greater monitor resolution
- CD-ROM drive

Software Requirements

Photoshop CS or higher: (Note: Because Adobe Photoshop alters the way it handles text in .psd files with seemingly each new version, some of the files included on the CD-ROM may require the reader to modify text layers when opening a file because some files were created with Photoshop 7.0.

Software Manufacturer: Adobe Systems Incorporated

Web Address: *http://www.adobe.com/*

Windows

- Intel Pentium III or 4 processor
- Microsoft Windows 2000 with Service Pack 3 or Windows XP
- 192 MB of RAM (256 MB recommended)
- 280 MB of available hard-disk space
- Color monitor with 16-bit color or greater video card
- 800 × 600 or greater monitor resolution
- CD-ROM drive

Mac

- PowerPC G3, G4, or G5 processor
- Mac OS X v.10.2.4, 10.2.5, 10.2.6, or 10.2.7
- 192 MB of RAM (256 MB recommended)
- 320 MB of available hard-disk space
- Color monitor with 16-bit color or greater video card
- 800 × 600 or greater monitor resolution
- CD-ROM drive

HTML Editor Software: Any HTML editing or text-editor software can be used for designs included with this book. Macromedia ColdFusion Studio was used for this book. Following are the hardware requirements for that software package.

Software Manufacturer: Macromedia (Prior to being acquired by Adobe Systems Incorporated)

Web Address: *http://www.macromedia.com*

Hardware Requirements

- Operating system Microsoft Windows 2000, Microsoft Windows NT 4.0
- Min hard drive space 350 MB
- Min processor type Intel Pentium
- Min RAM size 256 MB
- Peripheral / Interface devices CD-ROM, Mouse or compatible device

Browser: Internet Explorer 6.0

Software Manufacturer: Microsoft Corporation

Web Address: http://www.microsoft.com

Hardware Requirements

- 486 /66 MHz processor
- RAM and disk space requirements vary depending on operating system. Windows 98, for example, requires at least 16MB RAM and 25.8MB disk space

Index